# STROBE EDGE

Vol. 1

Story & Art by
Io Sakisaka

# STROBE EDGE

## Volume 1
## CONTENTS

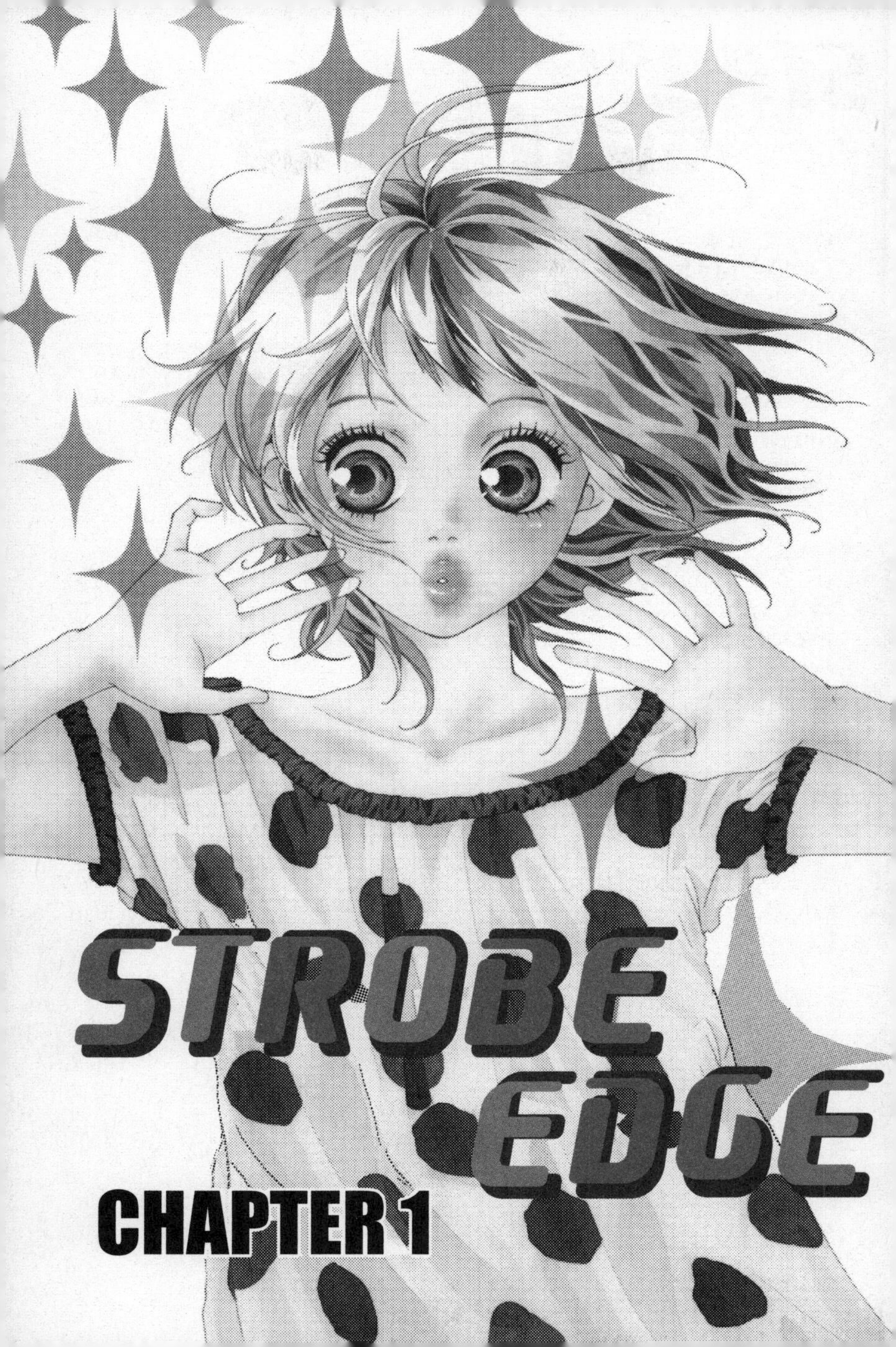
STROBE EDGE
CHAPTER 1

# GREETINGS

HELLO! THIS IS IO SAKISAKA. THANK YOU FOR CHECKING OUT THE FIRST VOLUME OF *STROBE EDGE*.

I WROTE *STROBE EDGE* BECAUSE I WANTED TO CRAFT A STORY THAT ILLUMINATED SOME SPECIFIC EMOTIONS THAT EVERYONE HAS HAD.

I WANTED TO DRAW THE SENSATION YOU FEEL IN THE WINDOW OF TIME BETWEEN ONE EVENT AND ANOTHER.

IN A SINGLE MOMENT, PEOPLE THINK ABOUT ALL SORTS OF THINGS. WE MAY NEVER PUT THEM INTO WORDS OR WRITE THEM DOWN, BUT WE FEEL THE SENSATION OF THEM FLYING THROUGH OUR MINDS.

I THOUGHT THAT PERHAPS BY EXAMINING THAT SENSATION AND TEASING IT OUT HERE, READERS WILL BE ABLE TO SYMPATHIZE WITH IT. I HOPE THAT WILL BE THE CASE!

I WONDER HOW WELL THINGS WILL WORK OUT FOR ME...

ANYWAY, *STROBE EDGE* STARTS HERE!

•THINGS YOU MIGHT WANT TO HAVE AROUND WHILE READING THIS MANGA:
  •YOUR FAVORITE DRINK
  •POTATO CHIPS (BUT BE CAREFUL WITH GREASY FINGERS!)
  •AN OPEN MIND

★ IO SAKISAKA ★

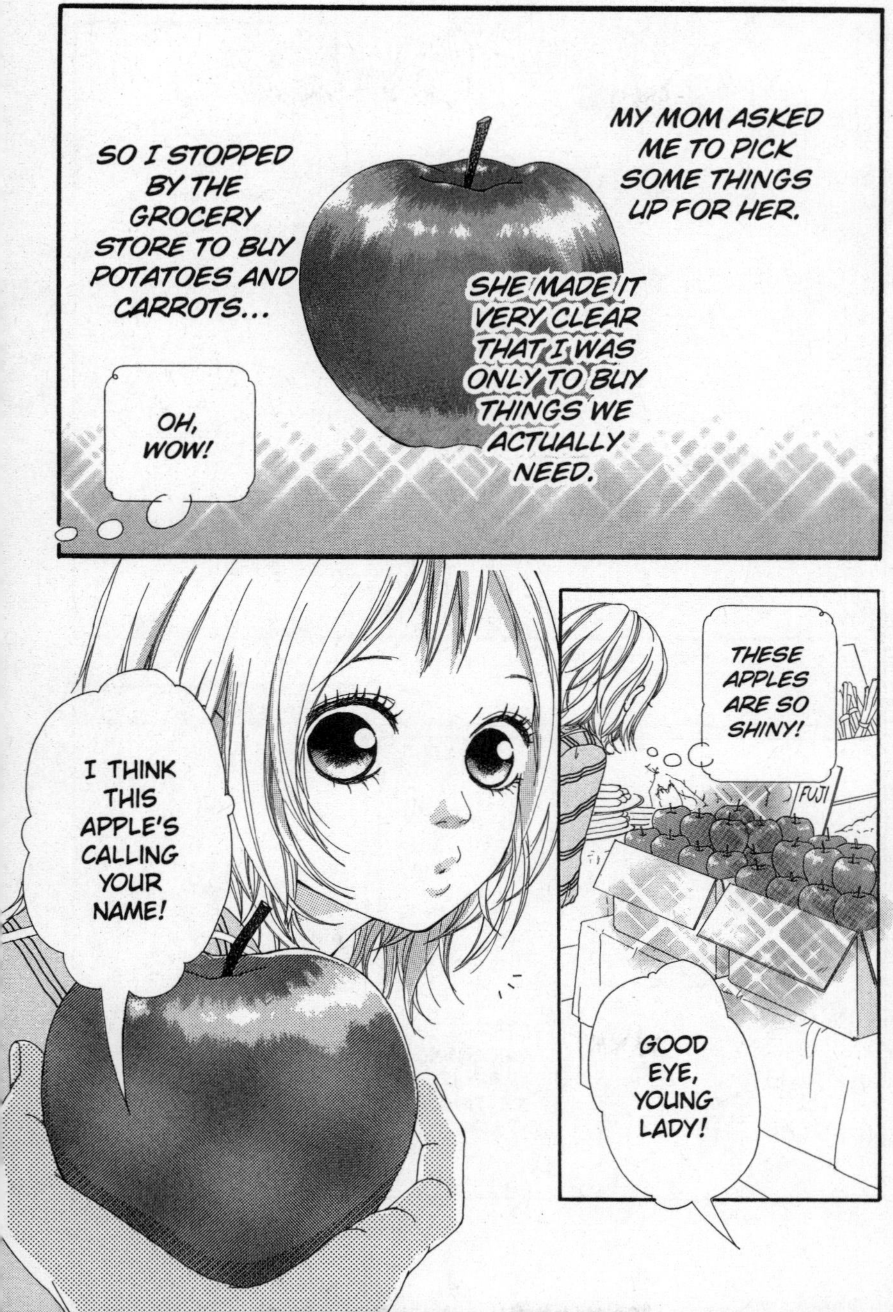
MY MOM ASKED ME TO PICK SOME THINGS UP FOR HER.
SHE MADE IT VERY CLEAR THAT I WAS ONLY TO BUY THINGS WE ACTUALLY NEED.
SO I STOPPED BY THE GROCERY STORE TO BUY POTATOES AND CARROTS...
OH, WOW!
THESE APPLES ARE SO SHINY!
FUJI
GOOD EYE, YOUNG LADY!
I THINK THIS APPLE'S CALLING YOUR NAME!

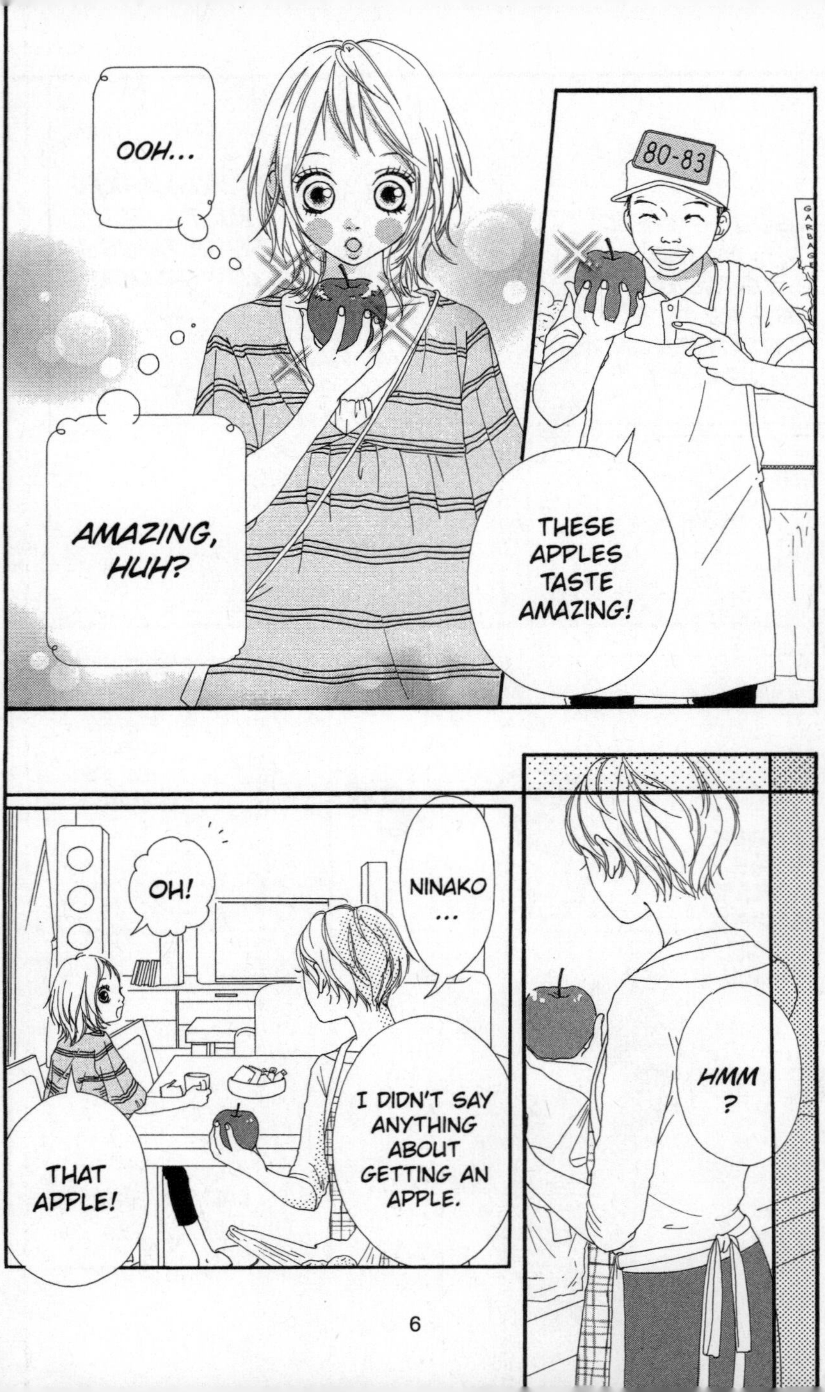
80-83
THESE APPLES TASTE AMAZING!
OOH...
AMAZING, HUH?
HMM?
NINAKO...
OH!
I DIDN'T SAY ANYTHING ABOUT GETTING AN APPLE.
THAT APPLE!

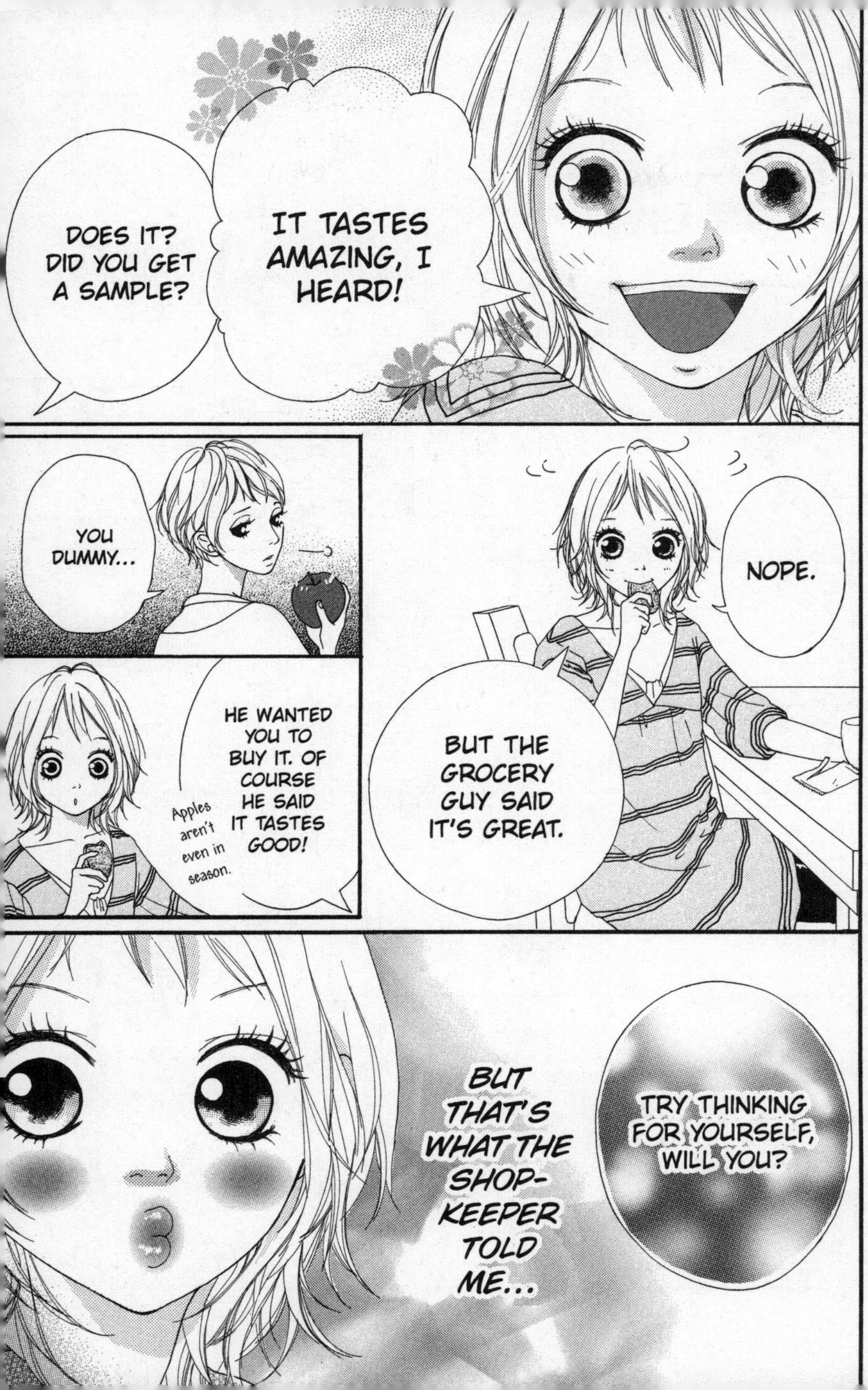
IT TASTES AMAZING, I HEARD!
DOES IT? DID YOU GET A SAMPLE?
NOPE.
BUT THE GROCERY GUY SAID IT'S GREAT.
YOU DUMMY...
HE WANTED YOU TO BUY IT. OF COURSE HE SAID IT TASTES GOOD!
Apples aren't even in season.
TRY THINKING FOR YOURSELF, WILL YOU?
BUT THAT'S WHAT THE SHOP-KEEPER TOLD ME...

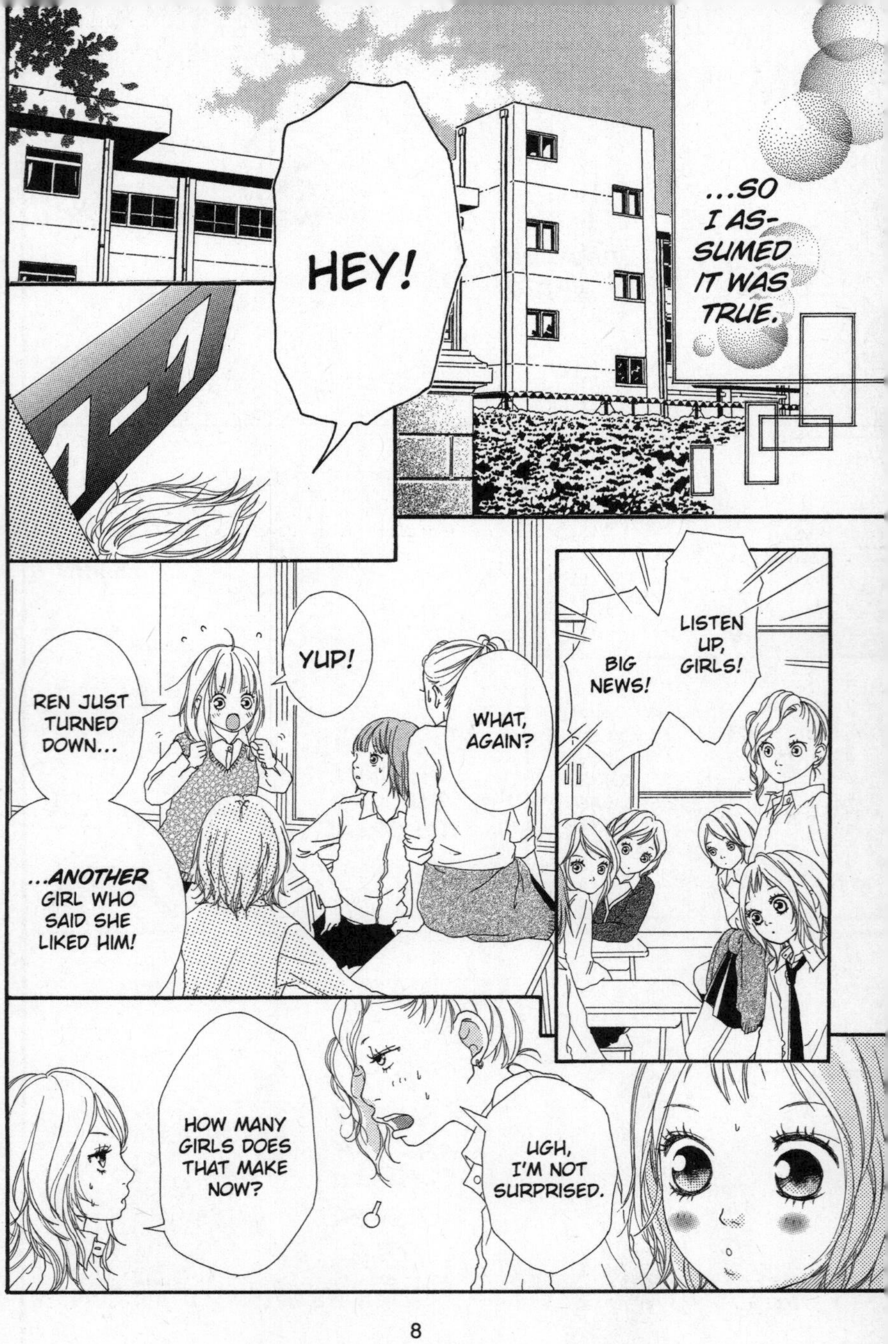
...SO I ASSUMED IT WAS TRUE.
HEY!
LISTEN UP, GIRLS!
BIG NEWS!
WHAT, AGAIN?
YUP!
REN JUST TURNED DOWN...
...*ANOTHER* GIRL WHO SAID SHE LIKED HIM!
UGH, I'M NOT SURPRISED.
HOW MANY GIRLS DOES THAT MAKE NOW?

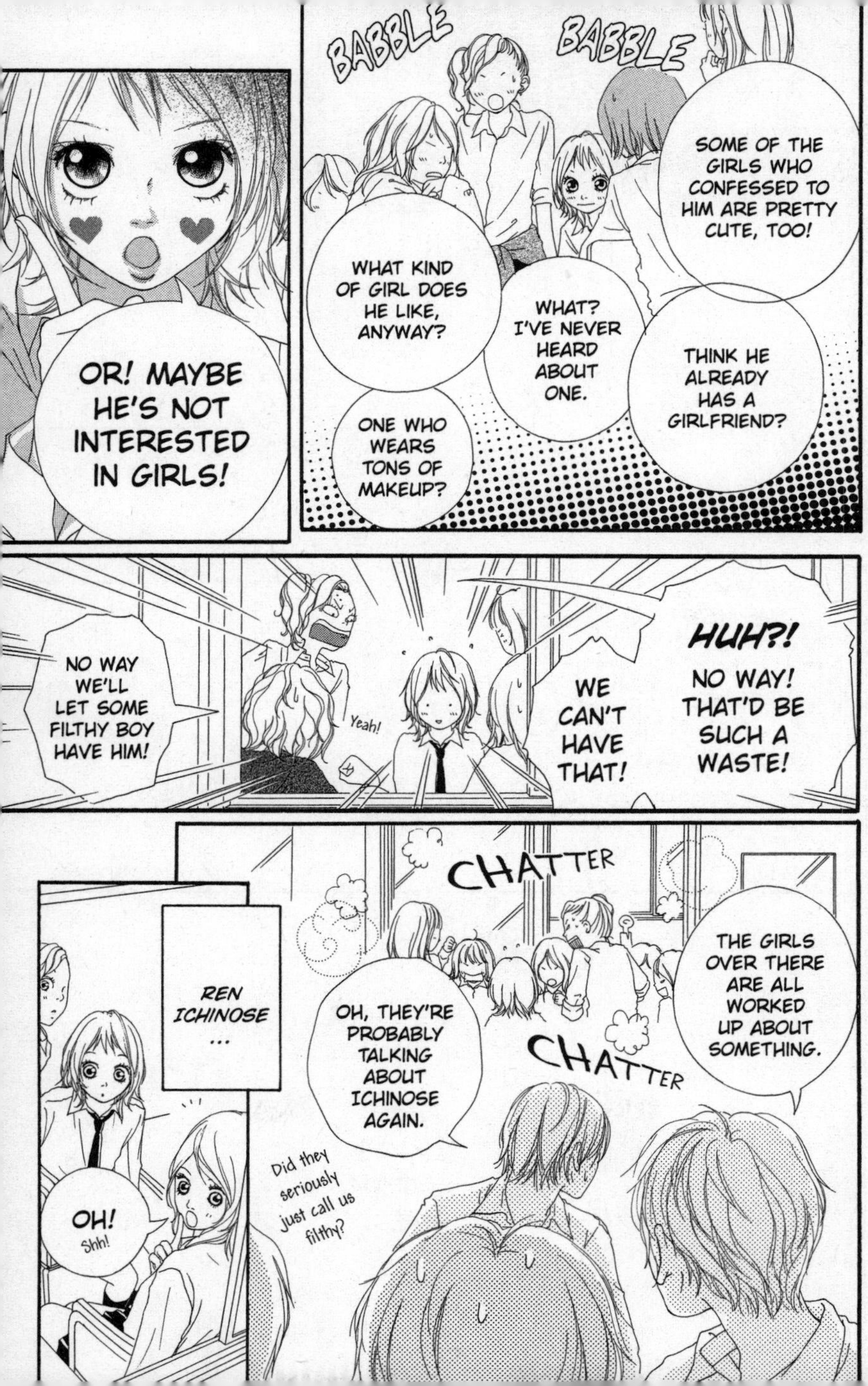
BABBLE
BABBLE
SOME OF THE GIRLS WHO CONFESSED TO HIM ARE PRETTY CUTE, TOO!
THINK HE ALREADY HAS A GIRLFRIEND?
WHAT? I'VE NEVER HEARD ABOUT ONE.
WHAT KIND OF GIRL DOES HE LIKE, ANYWAY?
ONE WHO WEARS TONS OF MAKEUP?
OR! MAYBE HE'S NOT INTERESTED IN GIRLS!
HUH?!
NO WAY! THAT'D BE SUCH A WASTE!
WE CAN'T HAVE THAT!
Yeah!
NO WAY WE'LL LET SOME FILTHY BOY HAVE HIM!
CHATTER
THE GIRLS OVER THERE ARE ALL WORKED UP ABOUT SOMETHING.
CHATTER
OH, THEY'RE PROBABLY TALKING ABOUT ICHINOSE AGAIN.
Did they seriously just call us filthy?
REN ICHINOSE ...
OH!
Shh!

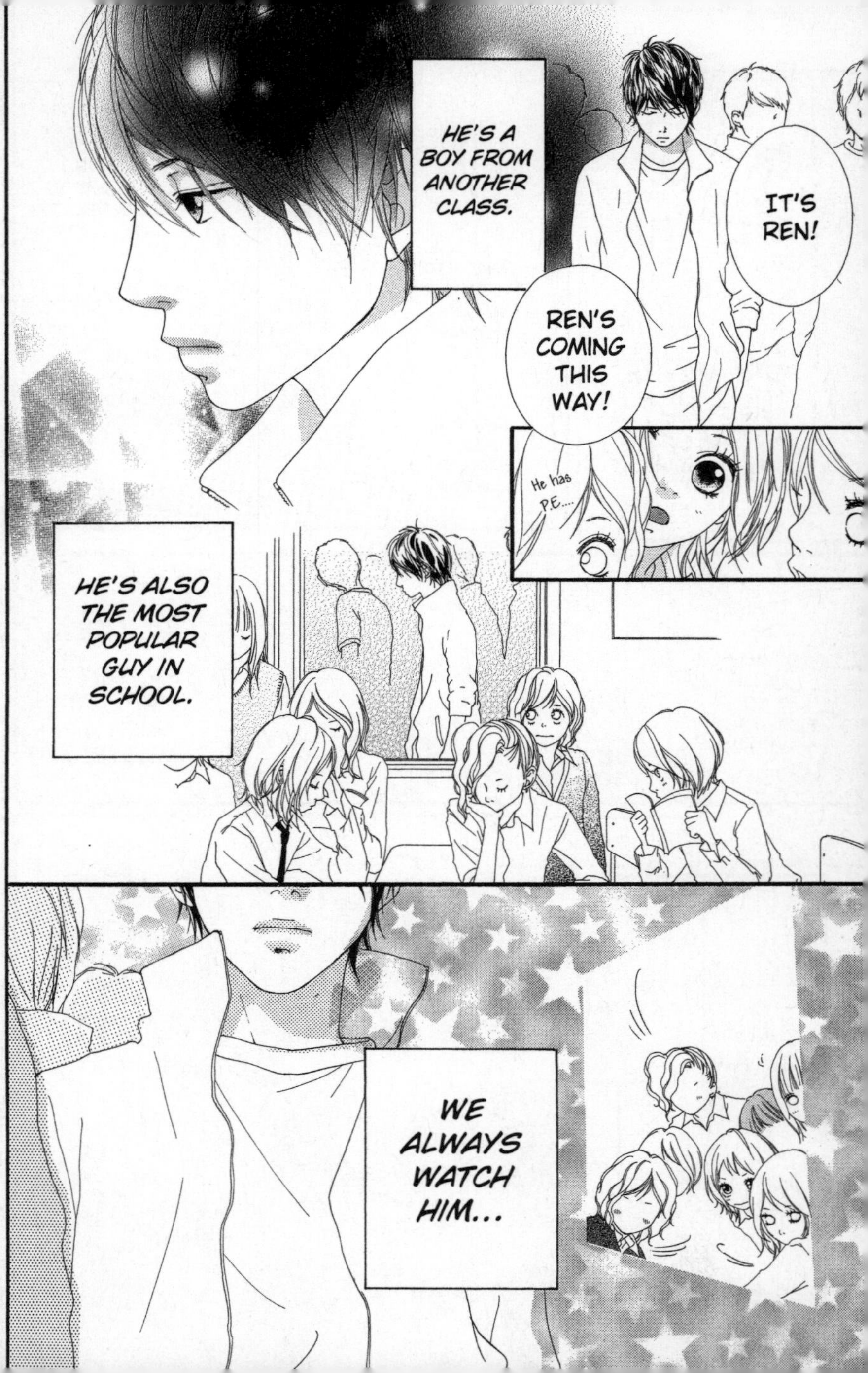
IT'S REN!
REN'S COMING THIS WAY!
HE'S A BOY FROM ANOTHER CLASS.
He has P.E....
HE'S ALSO THE MOST POPULAR GUY IN SCHOOL.
WE ALWAYS WATCH HIM...

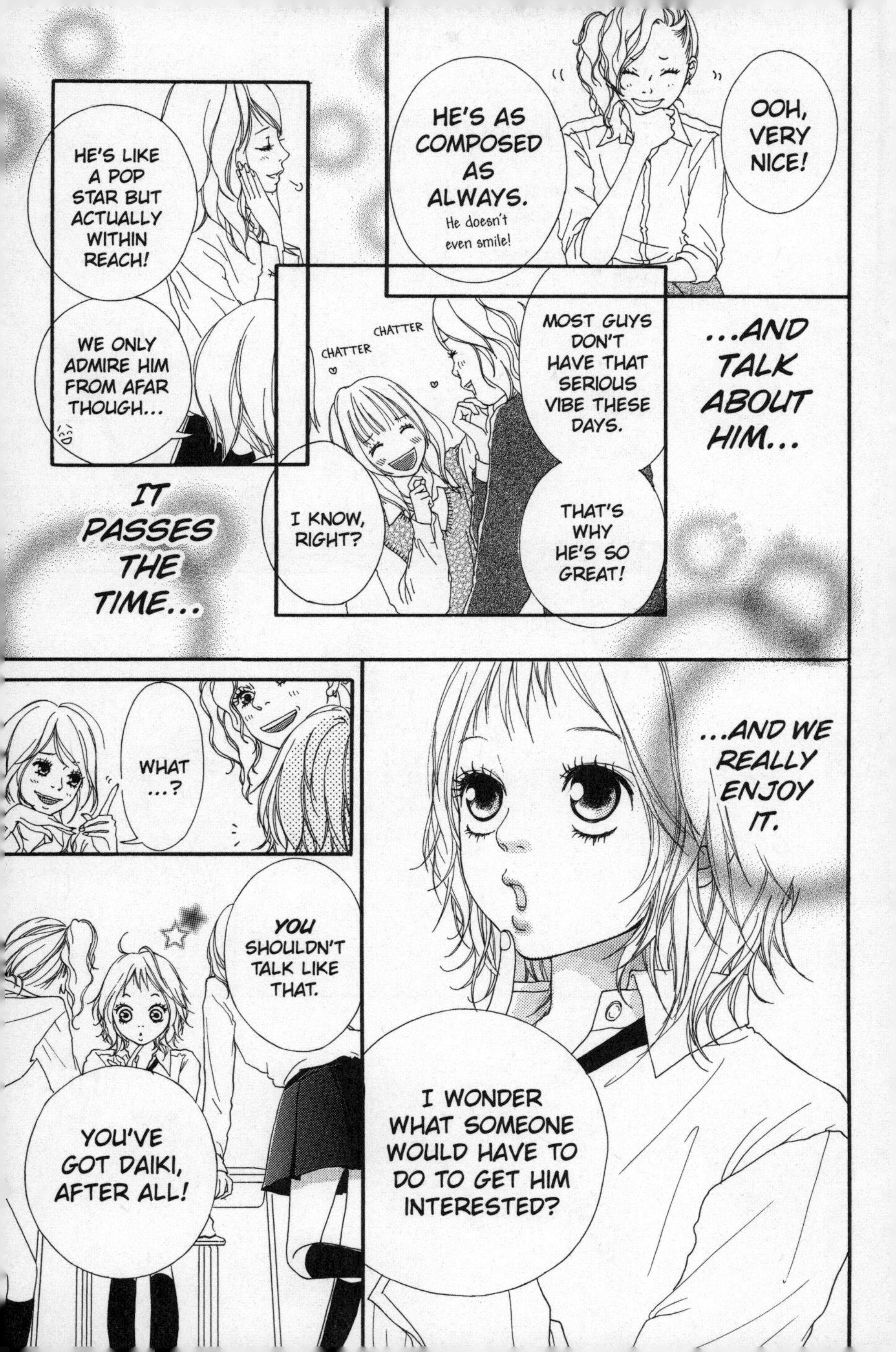

OOH, VERY NICE!
HE'S AS COMPOSED AS ALWAYS.
He doesn't even smile!
HE'S LIKE A POP STAR BUT ACTUALLY WITHIN REACH!
WE ONLY ADMIRE HIM FROM AFAR THOUGH...
...AND TALK ABOUT HIM...
MOST GUYS DON'T HAVE THAT SERIOUS VIBE THESE DAYS.
CHATTER
CHATTER
I KNOW, RIGHT?
THAT'S WHY HE'S SO GREAT!
IT PASSES THE TIME...
...AND WE REALLY ENJOY IT.
I WONDER WHAT SOMEONE WOULD HAVE TO DO TO GET HIM INTERESTED?
WHAT ...?
YOU SHOULDN'T TALK LIKE THAT.
YOU'VE GOT DAIKI, AFTER ALL!

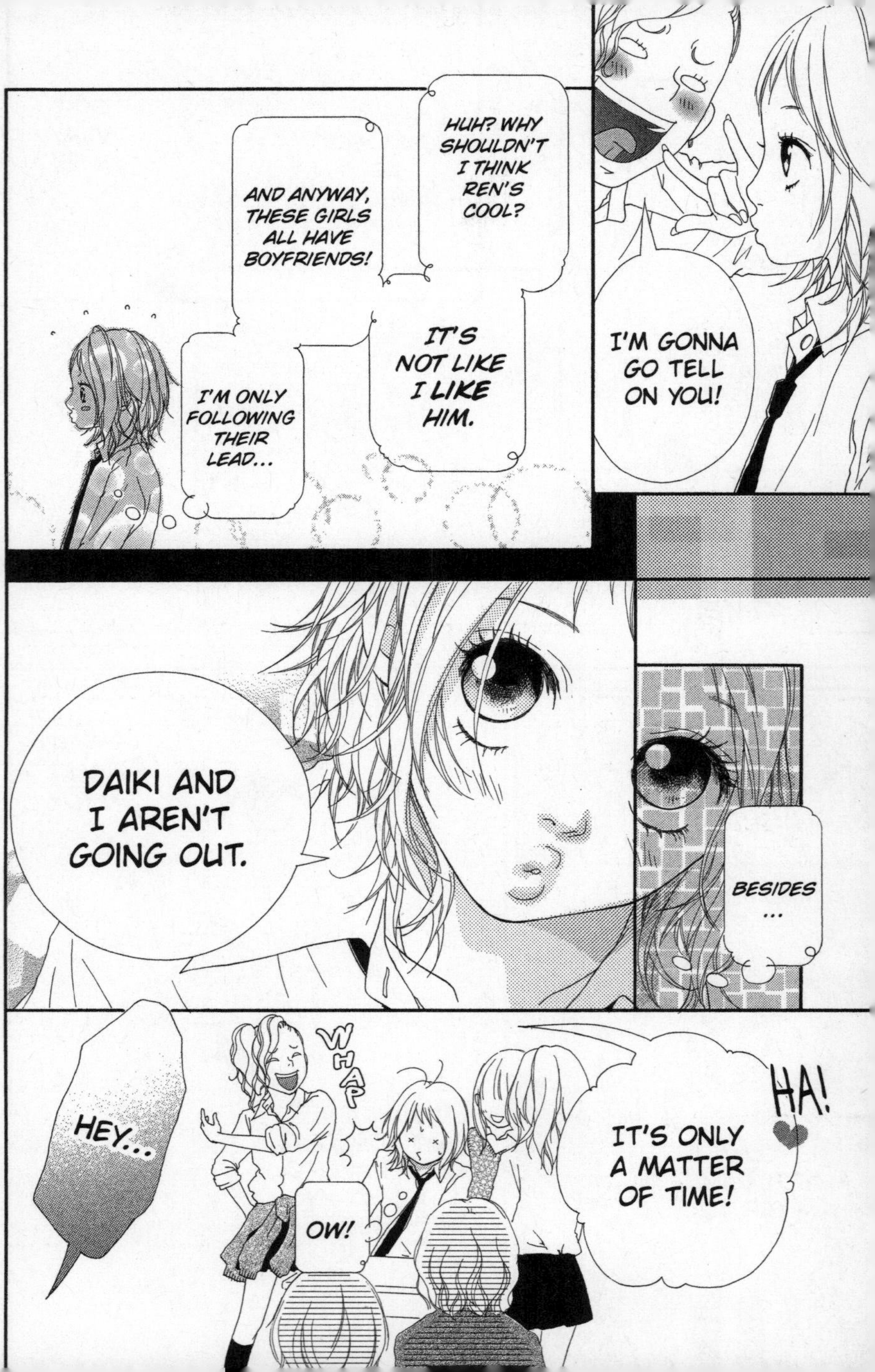
I'M GONNA GO TELL ON YOU!
HUH? WHY SHOULDN'T I THINK REN'S COOL?
AND ANYWAY, THESE GIRLS ALL HAVE BOYFRIENDS!
IT'S NOT LIKE I LIKE HIM.
I'M ONLY FOLLOWING THEIR LEAD...
DAIKI AND I AREN'T GOING OUT.
BESIDES...
HA!
IT'S ONLY A MATTER OF TIME!
WHAP
OW!
HEY...

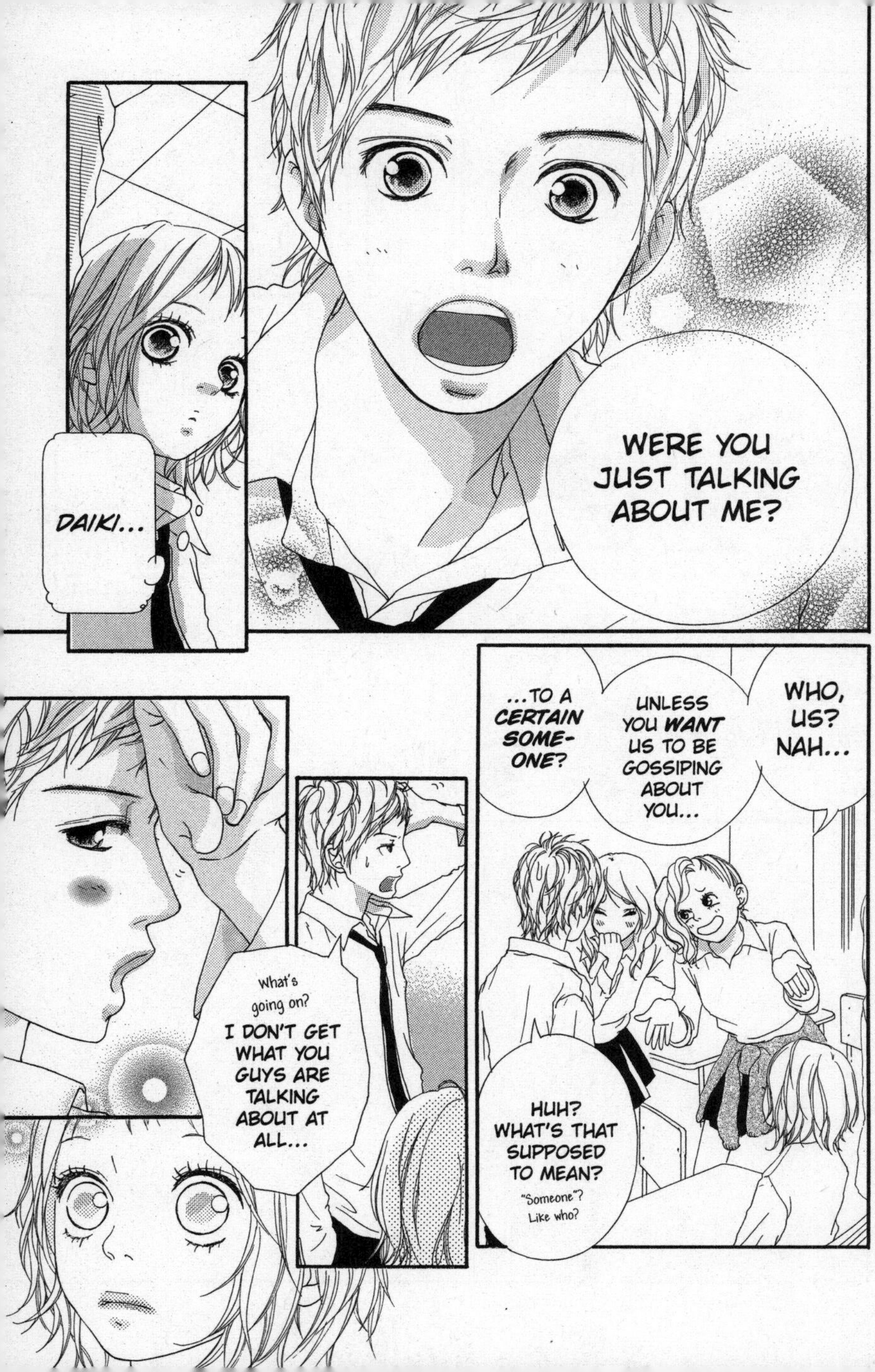
WERE YOU JUST TALKING ABOUT ME?
DAIKI...
WHO, US? NAH...
UNLESS YOU *WANT* US TO BE GOSSIPING ABOUT YOU...
...TO A *CERTAIN SOME-ONE*?
HUH? WHAT'S THAT SUPPOSED TO MEAN?
"Someone"? Like who?
What's going on?
I DON'T GET WHAT YOU GUYS ARE TALKING ABOUT AT ALL...

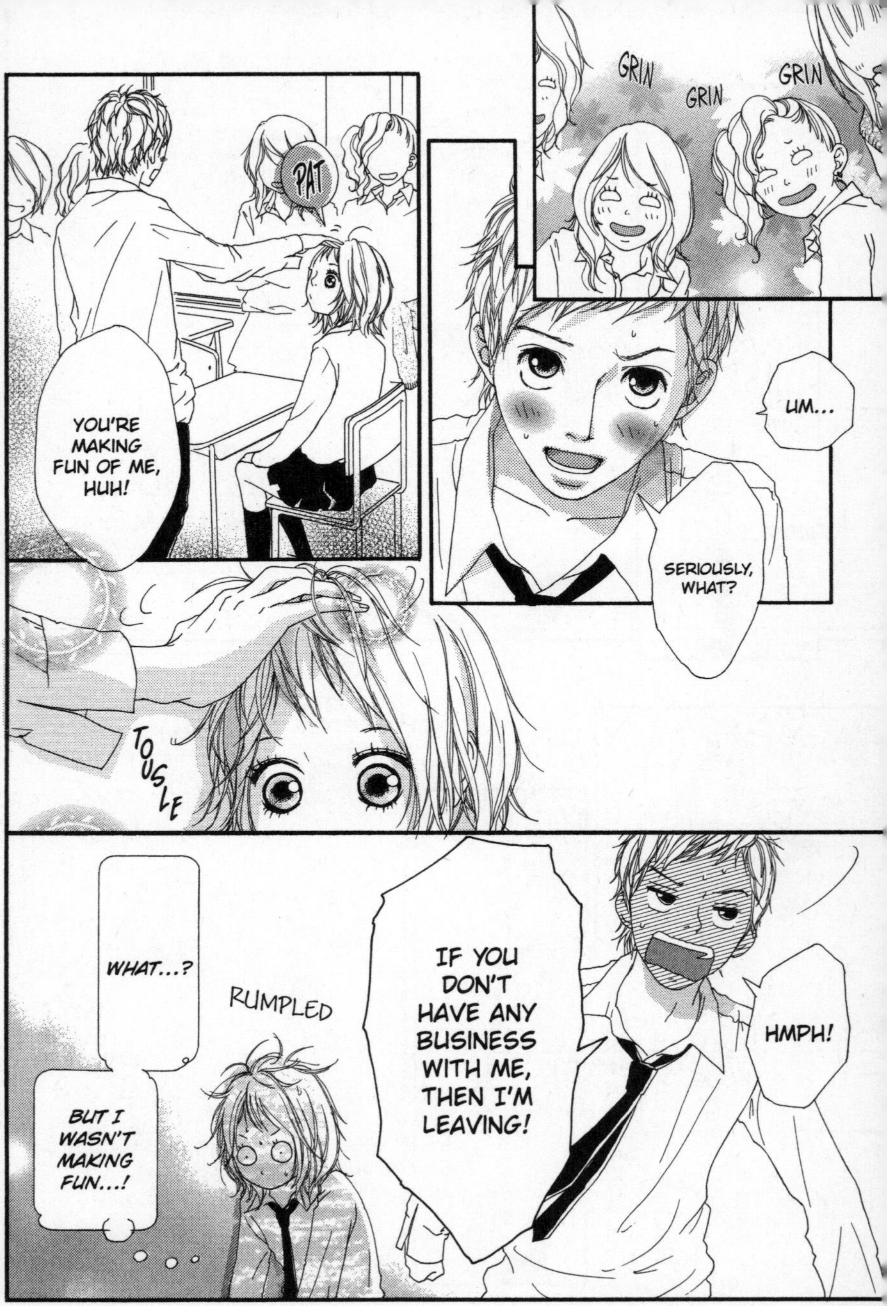
GRIN
GRIN
GRIN
UM...
SERIOUSLY, WHAT?
PAT
YOU'RE MAKING FUN OF ME, HUH!
TOUSLE
HMPH!
IF YOU DON'T HAVE ANY BUSINESS WITH ME, THEN I'M LEAVING!
RUMPLED
WHAT...?
BUT I WASN'T MAKING FUN...!

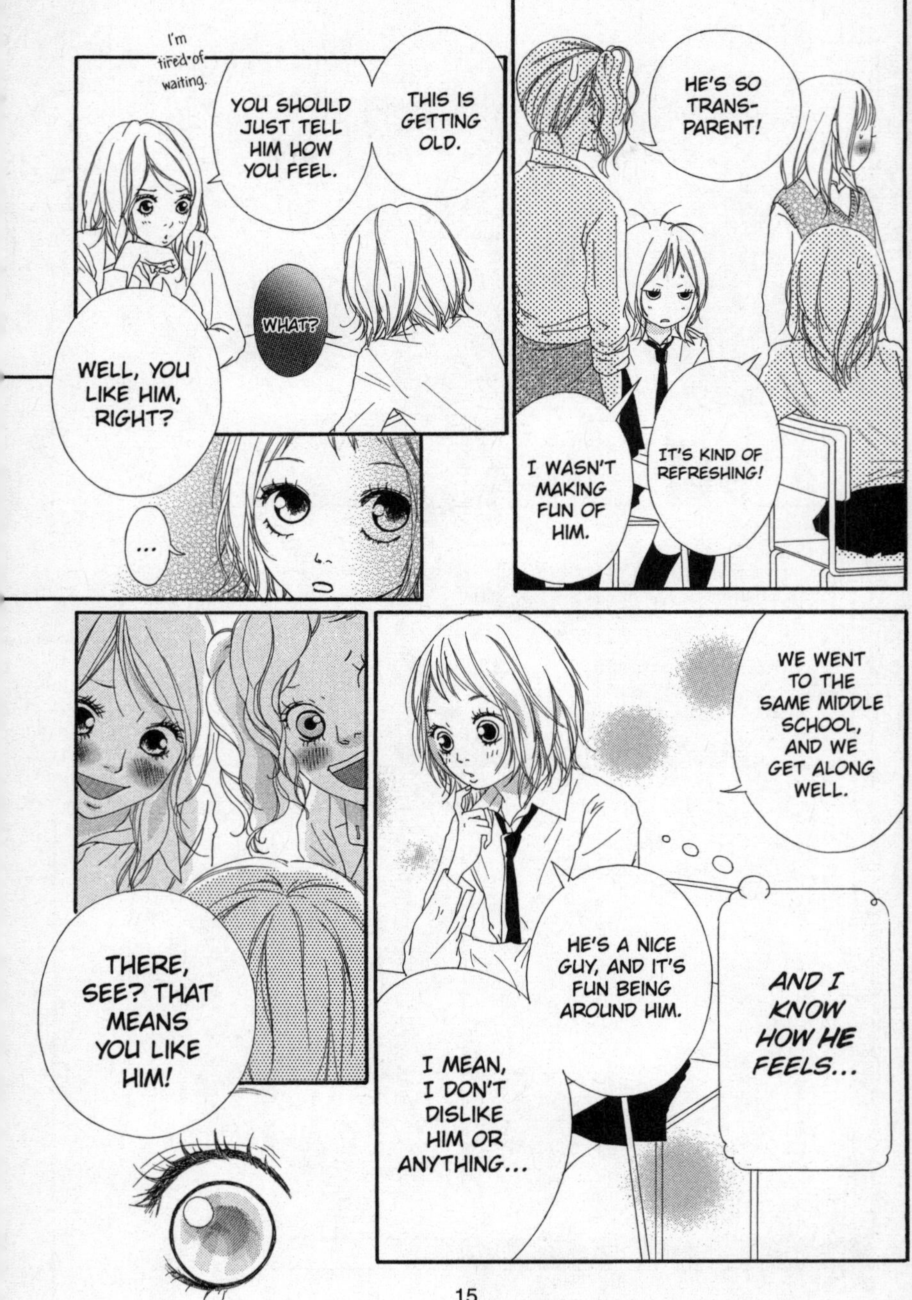
HE'S SO TRANS-PARENT!
IT'S KIND OF REFRESHING!
I WASN'T MAKING FUN OF HIM.
THIS IS GETTING OLD.
YOU SHOULD JUST TELL HIM HOW YOU FEEL.
I'm tired of waiting.
WHAT?
WELL, YOU LIKE HIM, RIGHT?
...
WE WENT TO THE SAME MIDDLE SCHOOL, AND WE GET ALONG WELL.
AND I KNOW HOW HE FEELS...
HE'S A NICE GUY, AND IT'S FUN BEING AROUND HIM.
I MEAN, I DON'T DISLIKE HIM OR ANYTHING...
THERE, SEE? THAT MEANS YOU LIKE HIM!

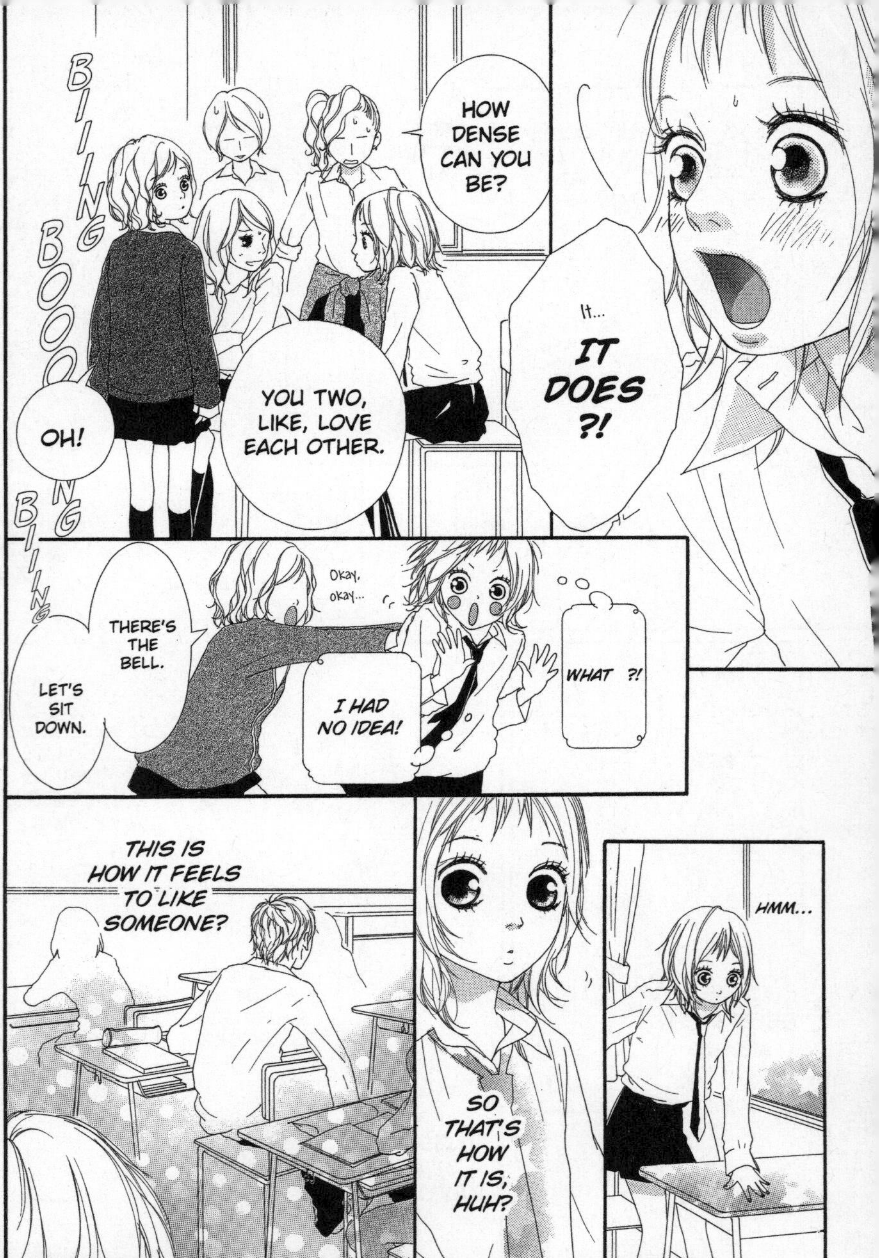
It...
IT DOES ?!
HOW DENSE CAN YOU BE?
YOU TWO, LIKE, LOVE EACH OTHER.
BIIING BOOONG
BIIING
OH!
WHAT ?!
Okay, okay...
I HAD NO IDEA!
THERE'S THE BELL.
LET'S SIT DOWN.
HMM...
SO THAT'S HOW IT IS, HUH?
THIS IS HOW IT FEELS TO LIKE SOMEONE?

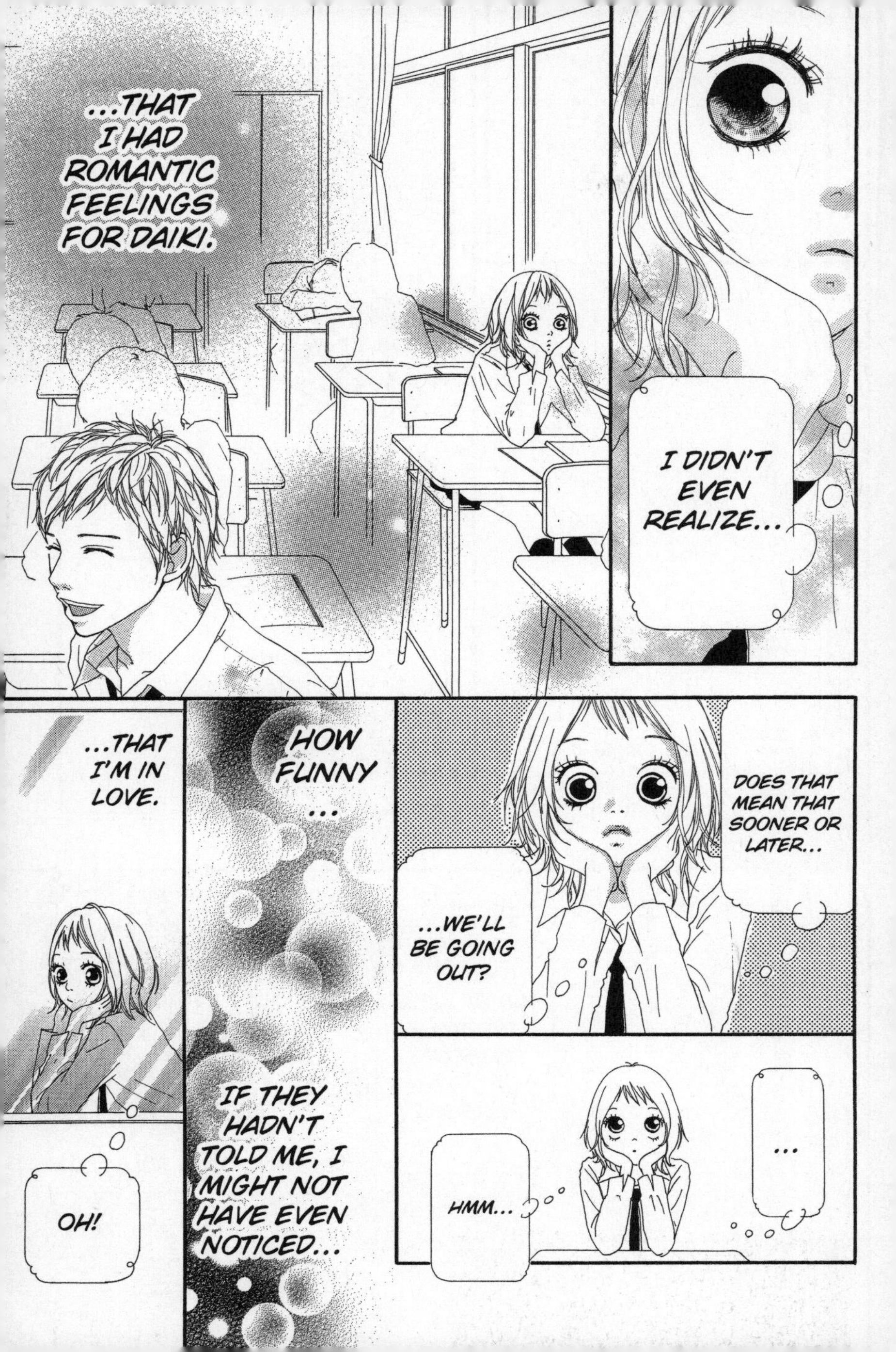
I DIDN'T EVEN REALIZE...
...THAT I HAD ROMANTIC FEELINGS FOR DAIKI.
DOES THAT MEAN THAT SOONER OR LATER...
...WE'LL BE GOING OUT?
...
HMM...
HOW FUNNY...
IF THEY HADN'T TOLD ME, I MIGHT NOT HAVE EVEN NOTICED...
...THAT I'M IN LOVE.
OH!

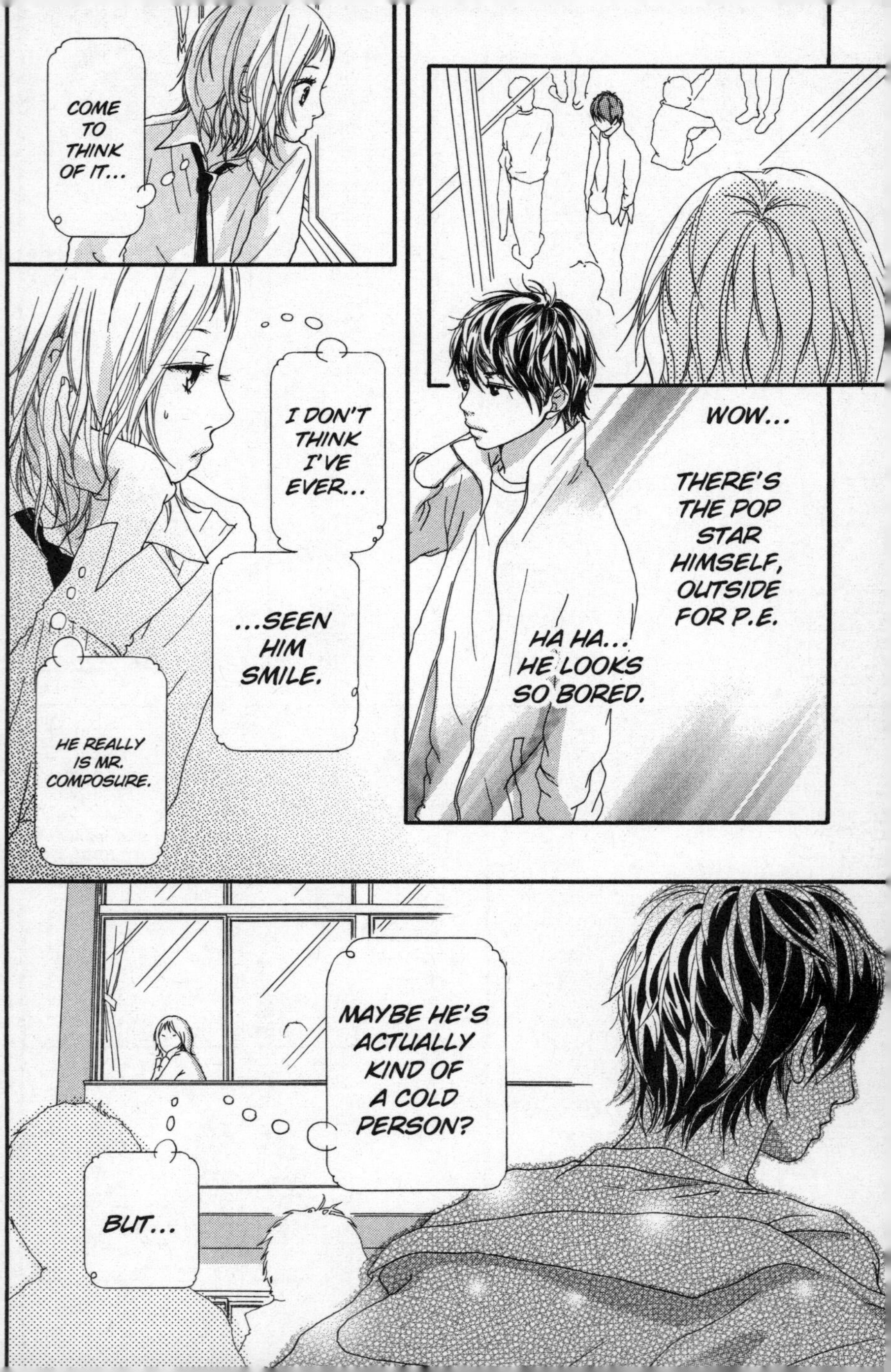
COME TO THINK OF IT...
WOW...
THERE'S THE POP STAR HIMSELF, OUTSIDE FOR P.E.
HA HA... HE LOOKS SO BORED.
I DON'T THINK I'VE EVER...
...SEEN HIM SMILE.
HE REALLY IS MR. COMPOSURE.
MAYBE HE'S ACTUALLY KIND OF A COLD PERSON?
BUT...

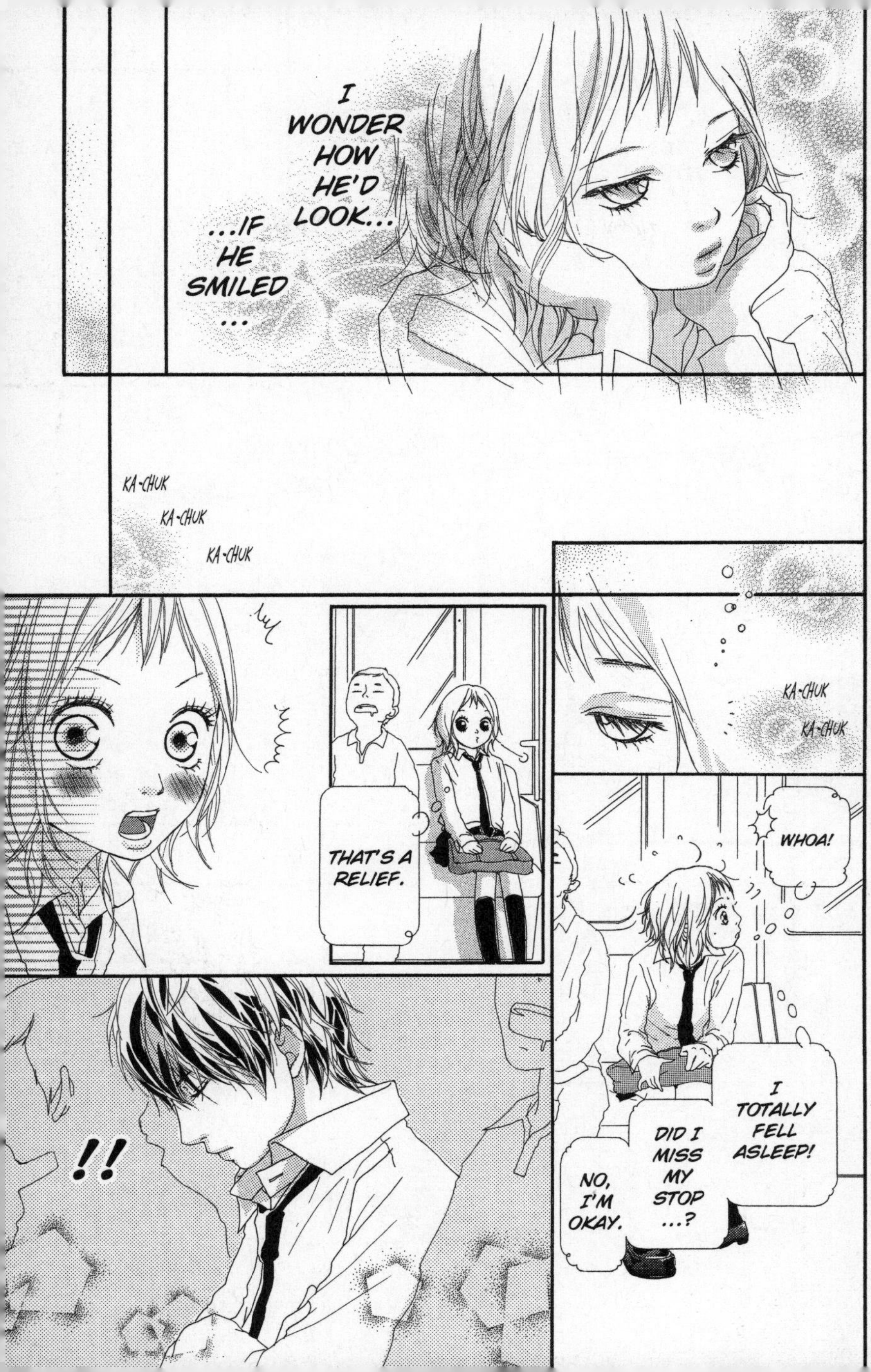
I WONDER HOW HE'D LOOK...
...IF HE SMILED ...
KA-CHUK
KA-CHUK
KA-CHUK
KA-CHUK
KA-CHUK
WHOA!
I TOTALLY FELL ASLEEP!
DID I MISS MY STOP ...?
NO, I'M OKAY.
THAT'S A RELIEF.
!!

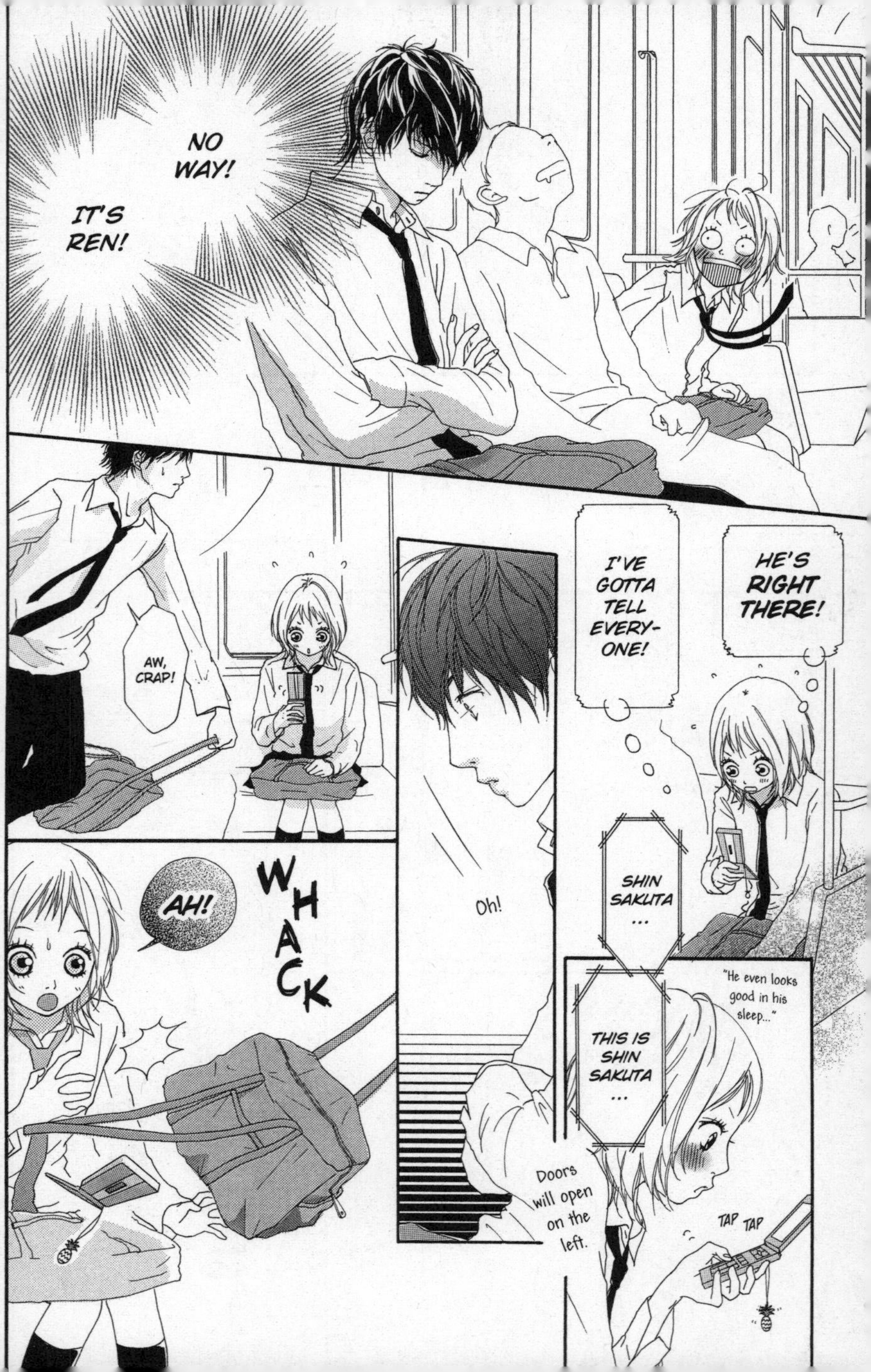

NO WAY!
IT'S REN!
HE'S RIGHT THERE!
I'VE GOTTA TELL EVERYONE!
SHIN SAKUTA ...
"He even looks good in his sleep..."
THIS IS SHIN SAKUTA ...
TAP TAP
Doors will open on the left.
Oh!
AW, CRAP!
WHACK
AH!

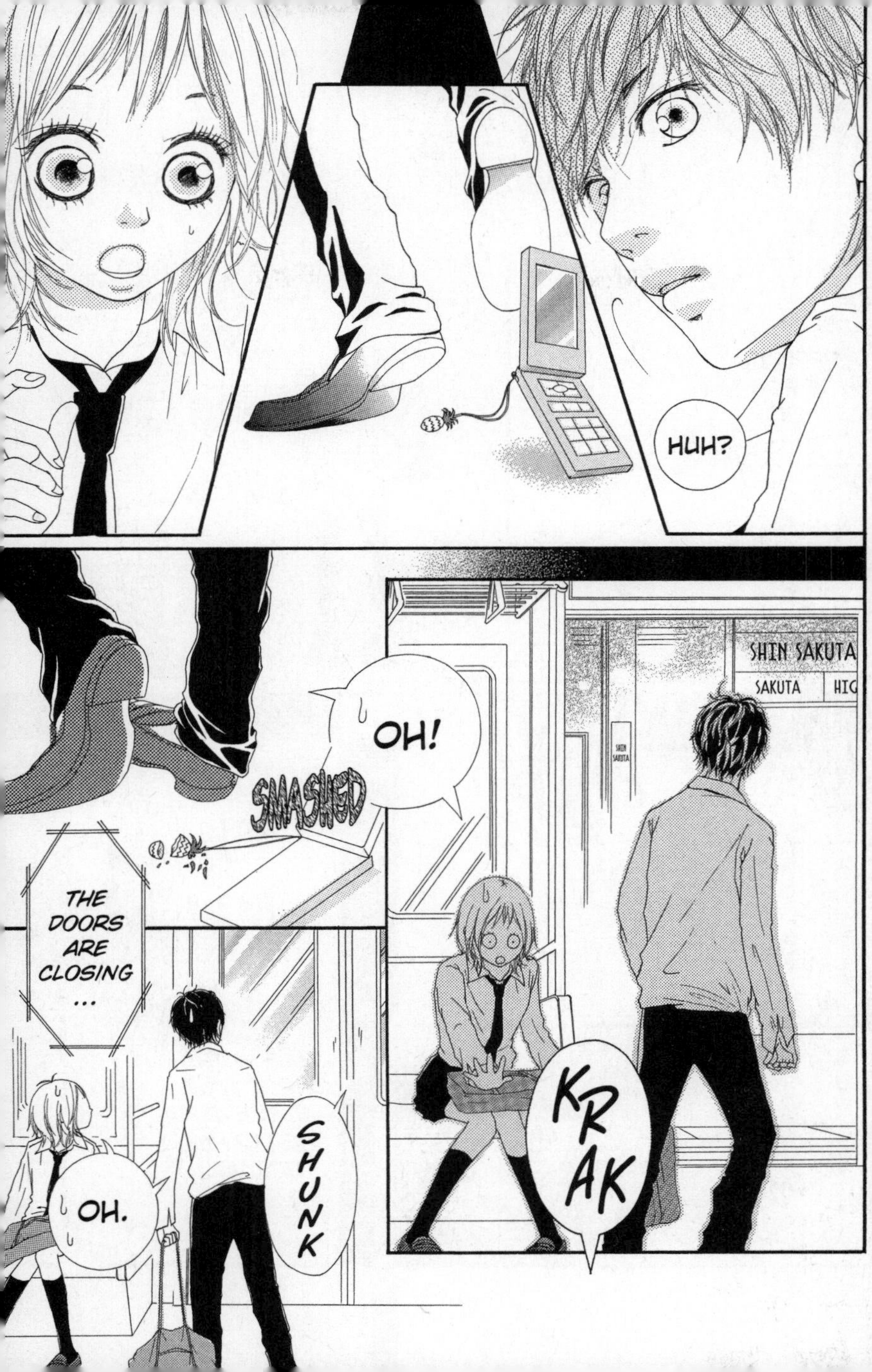
HUH?
SHIN SAKUTA
SAKUTA
HIG
SHIN SAKUTA
KRAK
OH!
SMASHED
THE DOORS ARE CLOSING ...
SHUNK
OH.

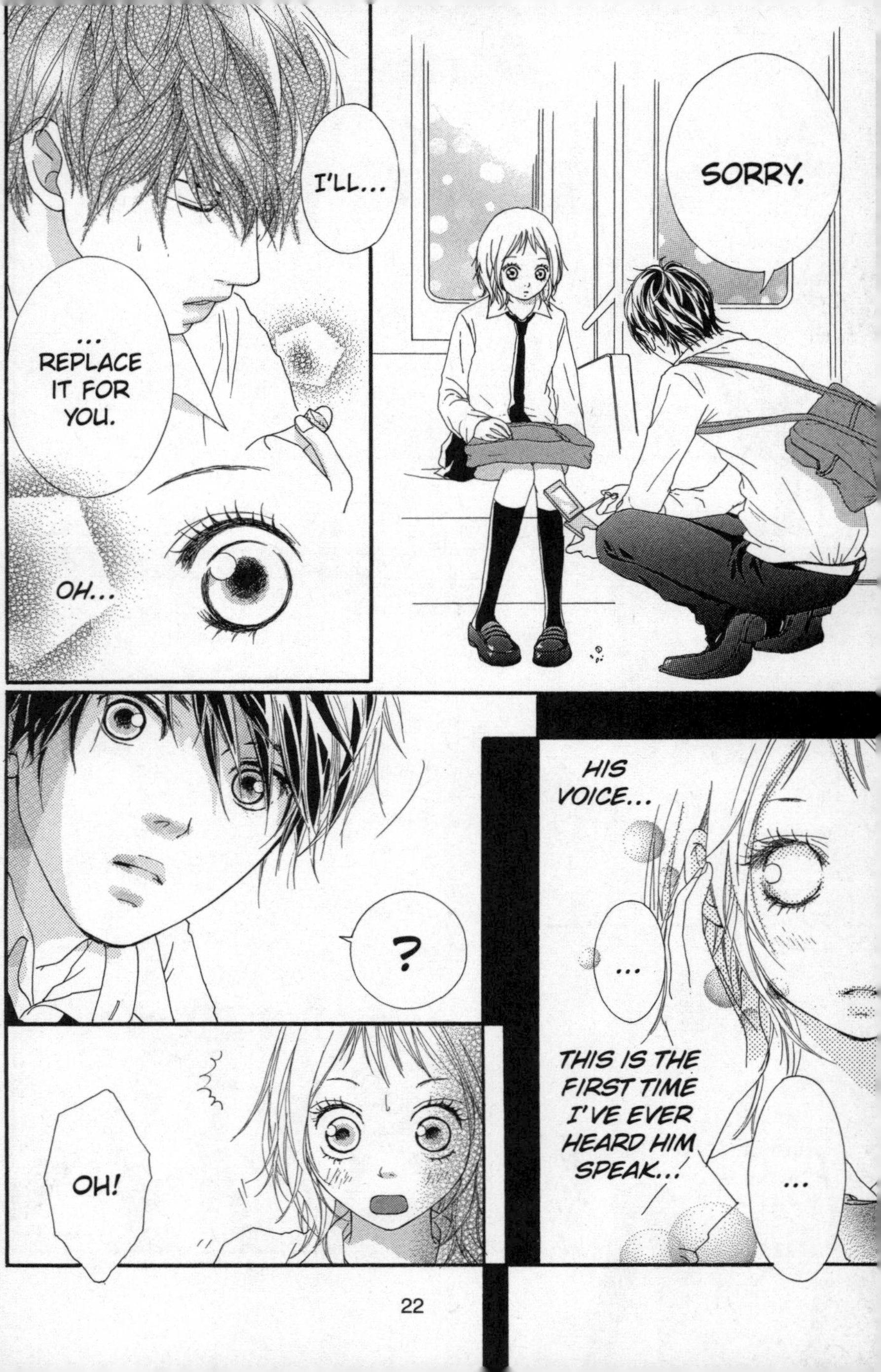
SORRY.
I'LL...
...REPLACE IT FOR YOU.
OH...
HIS VOICE...
...
THIS IS THE FIRST TIME I'VE EVER HEARD HIM SPEAK...
...
?
OH!

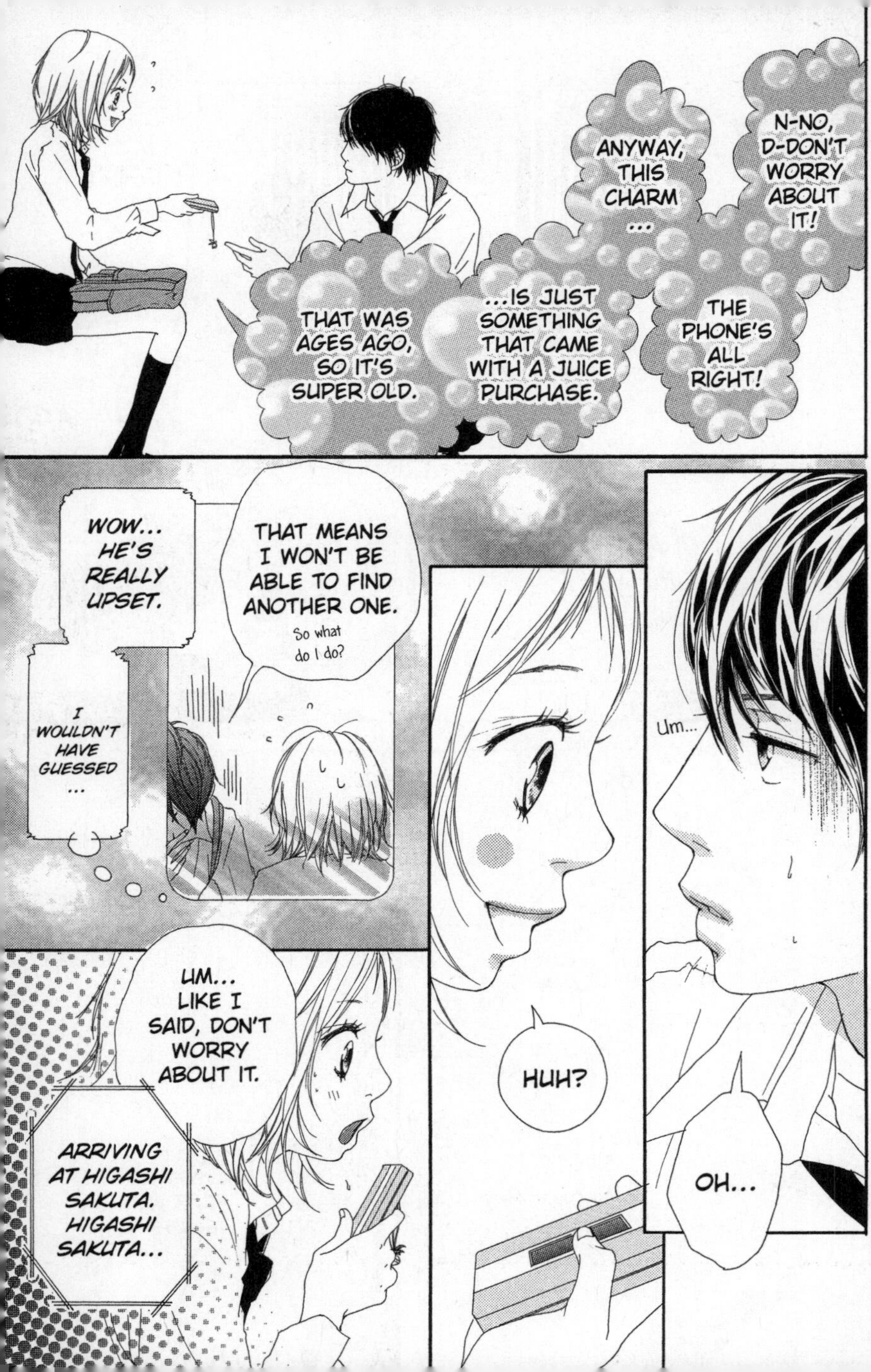
N-NO, D-DON'T WORRY ABOUT IT!
THE PHONE'S ALL RIGHT!
ANYWAY, THIS CHARM ...
...IS JUST SOMETHING THAT CAME WITH A JUICE PURCHASE.
THAT WAS AGES AGO, SO IT'S SUPER OLD.
THAT MEANS I WON'T BE ABLE TO FIND ANOTHER ONE.
So what do I do?
WOW... HE'S REALLY UPSET.
I WOULDN'T HAVE GUESSED ...
UM... LIKE I SAID, DON'T WORRY ABOUT IT.
ARRIVING AT HIGASHI SAKUTA. HIGASHI SAKUTA...
Um...
HUH?
OH...

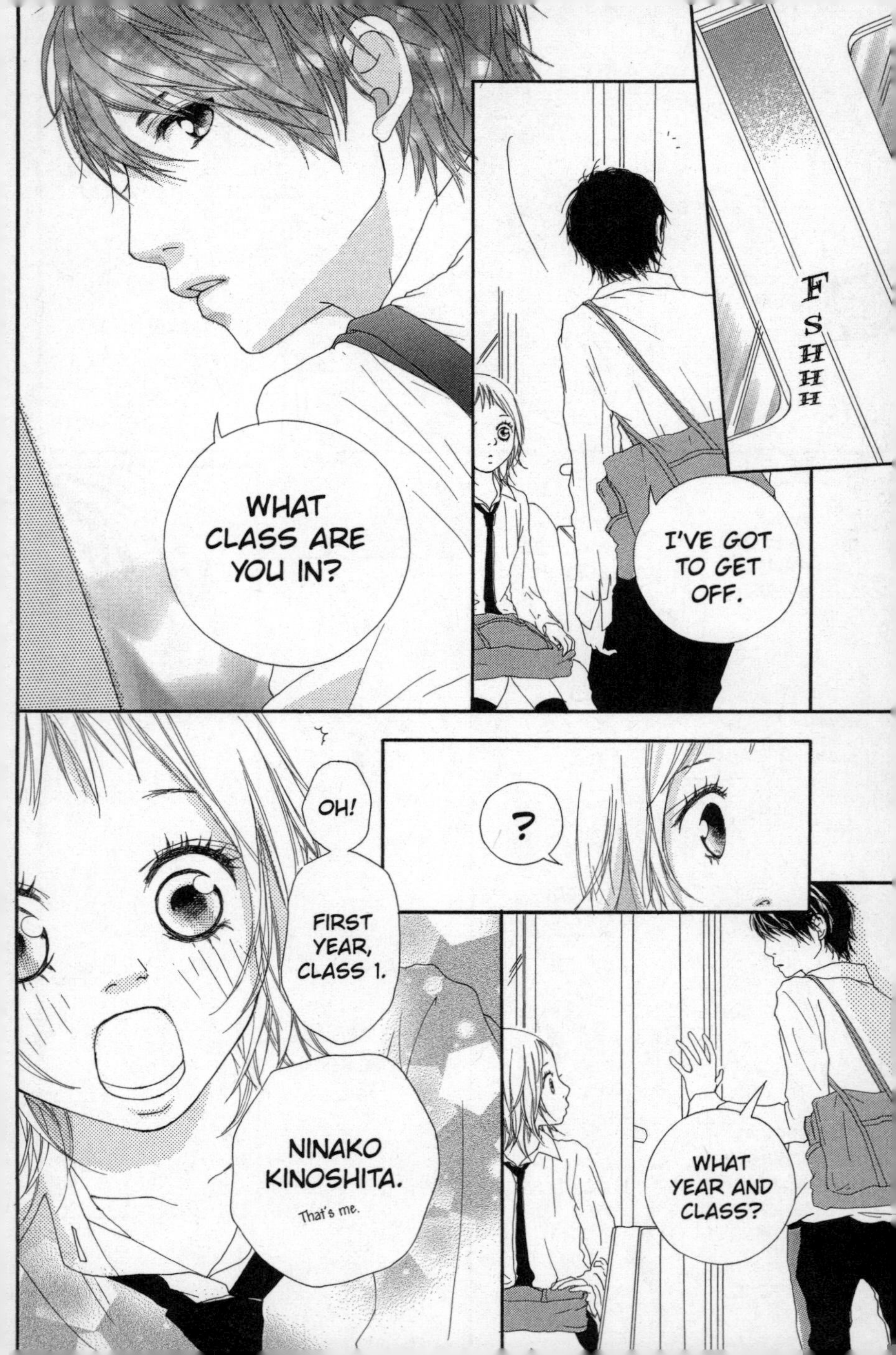
FSHHH
I'VE GOT TO GET OFF.
WHAT CLASS ARE YOU IN?
?
WHAT YEAR AND CLASS?
OH!
FIRST YEAR, CLASS 1.
NINAKO KINOSHITA.
That's me.

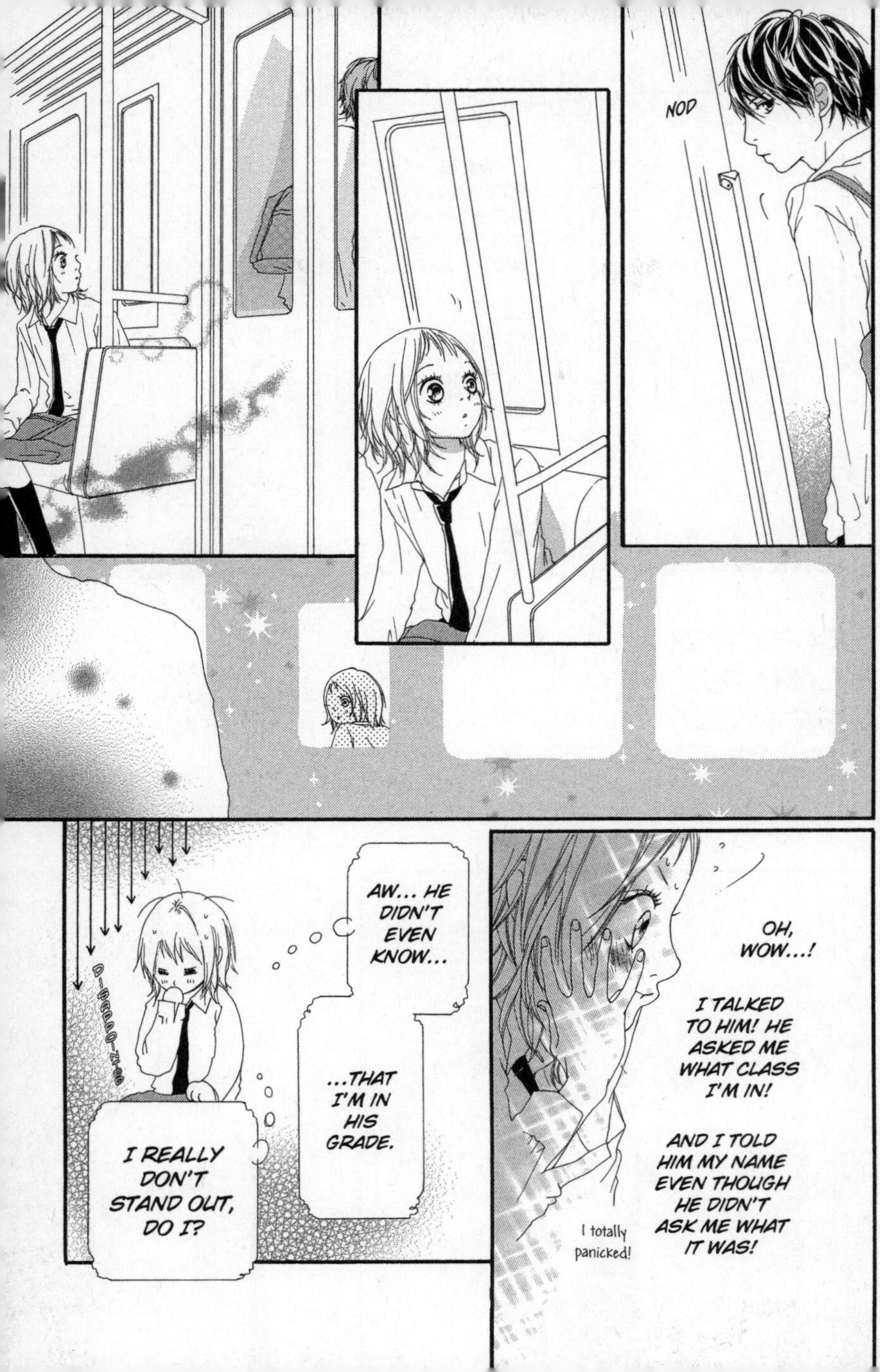
NOD
OH, WOW...!
I TALKED TO HIM! HE ASKED ME WHAT CLASS I'M IN!
AND I TOLD HIM MY NAME EVEN THOUGH HE DIDN'T ASK ME WHAT IT WAS!
I totally panicked!
AW... HE DIDN'T EVEN KNOW...
...THAT I'M IN HIS GRADE.
I REALLY DON'T STAND OUT, DO I?

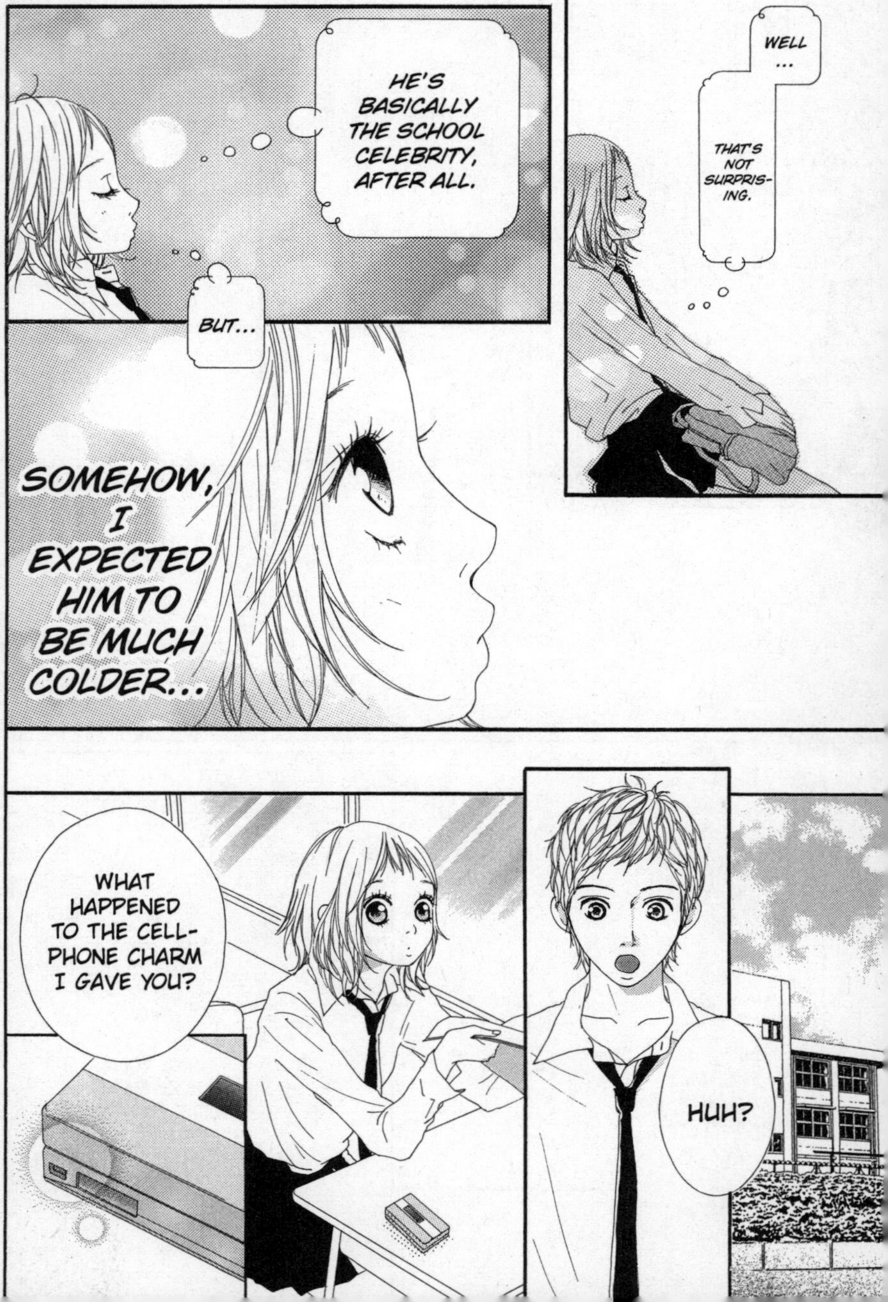
WELL...
THAT'S NOT SURPRISING.
HE'S BASICALLY THE SCHOOL CELEBRITY, AFTER ALL.
BUT...
SOMEHOW, I EXPECTED HIM TO BE MUCH COLDER...
WHAT HAPPENED TO THE CELL-PHONE CHARM I GAVE YOU?
HUH?

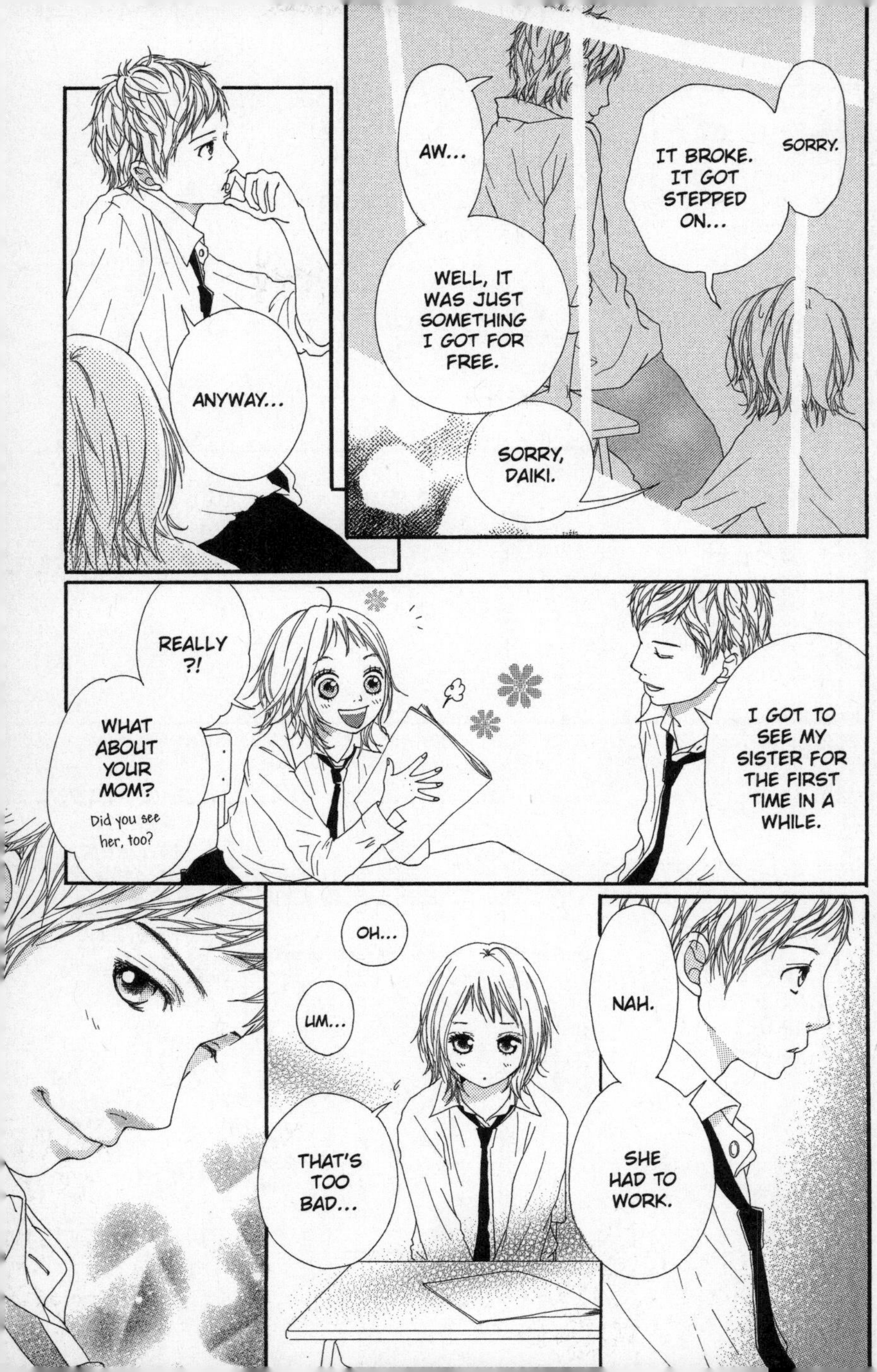
SORRY.
IT BROKE. IT GOT STEPPED ON...
AW...
WELL, IT WAS JUST SOMETHING I GOT FOR FREE.
SORRY, DAIKI.
ANYWAY...
I GOT TO SEE MY SISTER FOR THE FIRST TIME IN A WHILE.
REALLY ?!
WHAT ABOUT YOUR MOM? Did you see her, too?
NAH.
SHE HAD TO WORK.
OH...
UM...
THAT'S TOO BAD...

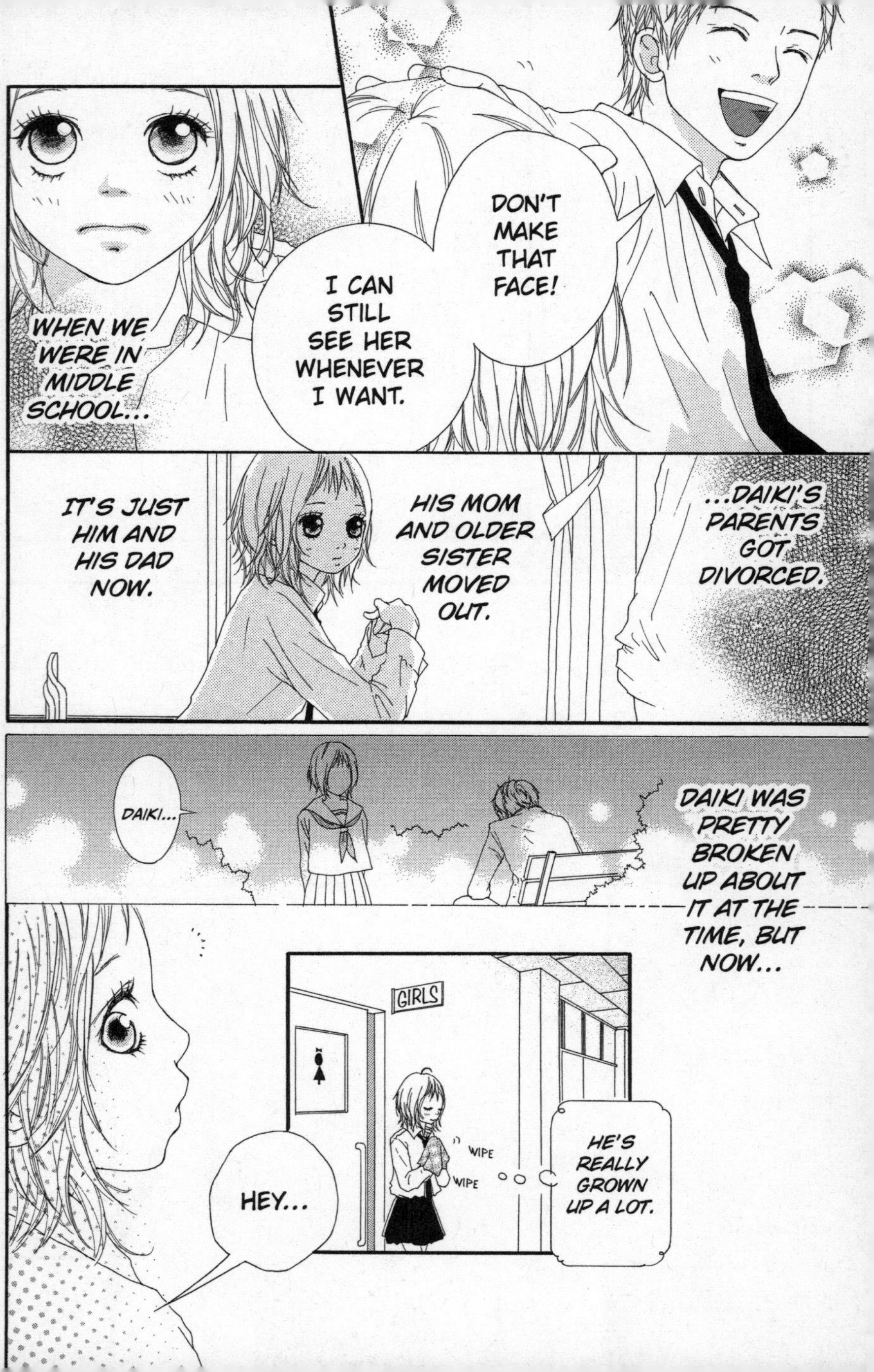
DON'T MAKE THAT FACE!
I CAN STILL SEE HER WHENEVER I WANT.
WHEN WE WERE IN MIDDLE SCHOOL...
...DAIKI'S PARENTS GOT DIVORCED.
HIS MOM AND OLDER SISTER MOVED OUT.
IT'S JUST HIM AND HIS DAD NOW.
DAIKI WAS PRETTY BROKEN UP ABOUT IT AT THE TIME, BUT NOW...
DAIKI...
HE'S REALLY GROWN UP A LOT.
WIPE
WIPE
GIRLS
HEY...

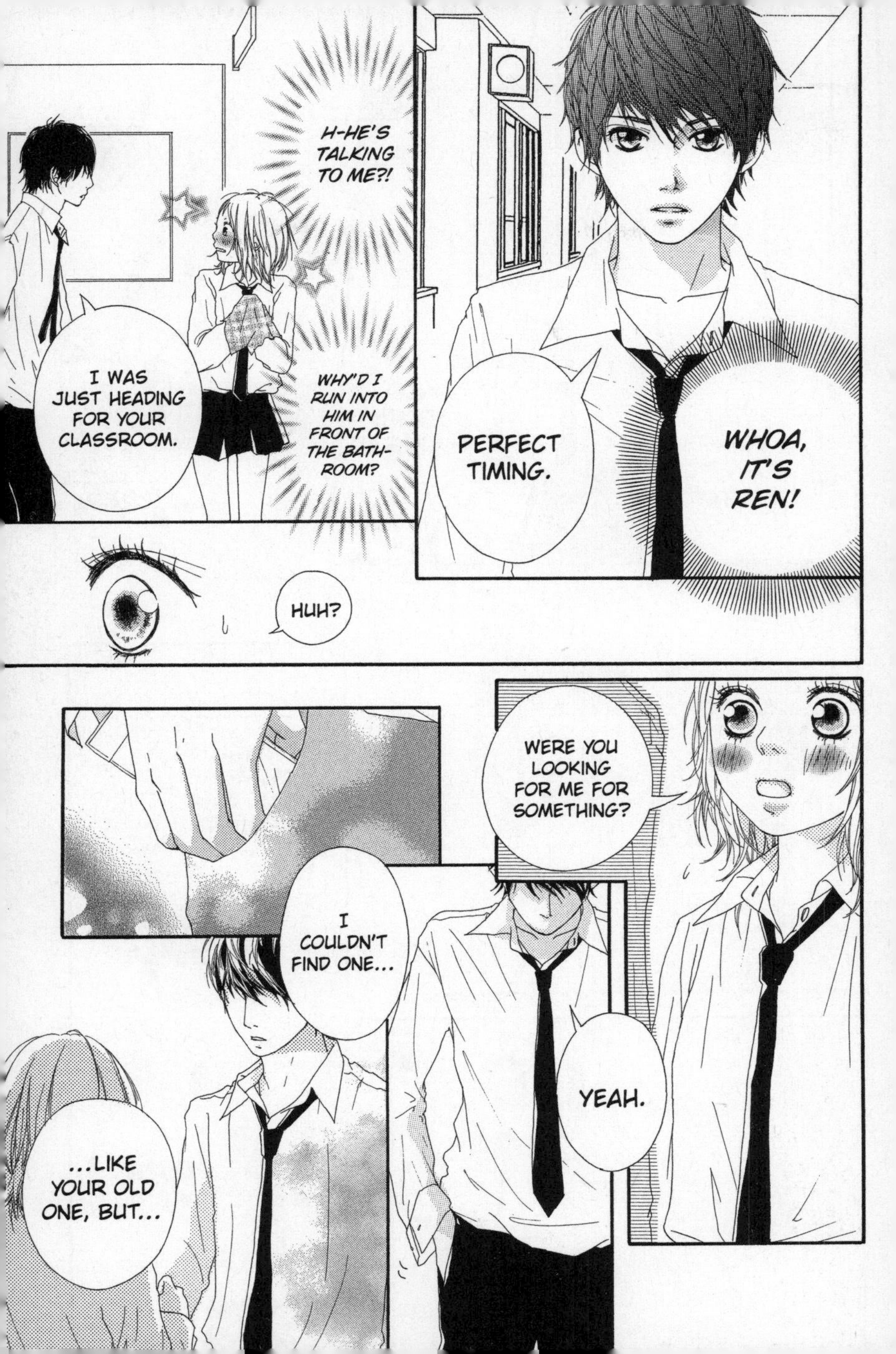
WHOA, IT'S REN!
PERFECT TIMING.
H-HE'S TALKING TO ME?!
WHY'D I RUN INTO HIM IN FRONT OF THE BATH-ROOM?
I WAS JUST HEADING FOR YOUR CLASSROOM.
HUH?
WERE YOU LOOKING FOR ME FOR SOMETHING?
YEAH.
I COULDN'T FIND ONE...
...LIKE YOUR OLD ONE, BUT...

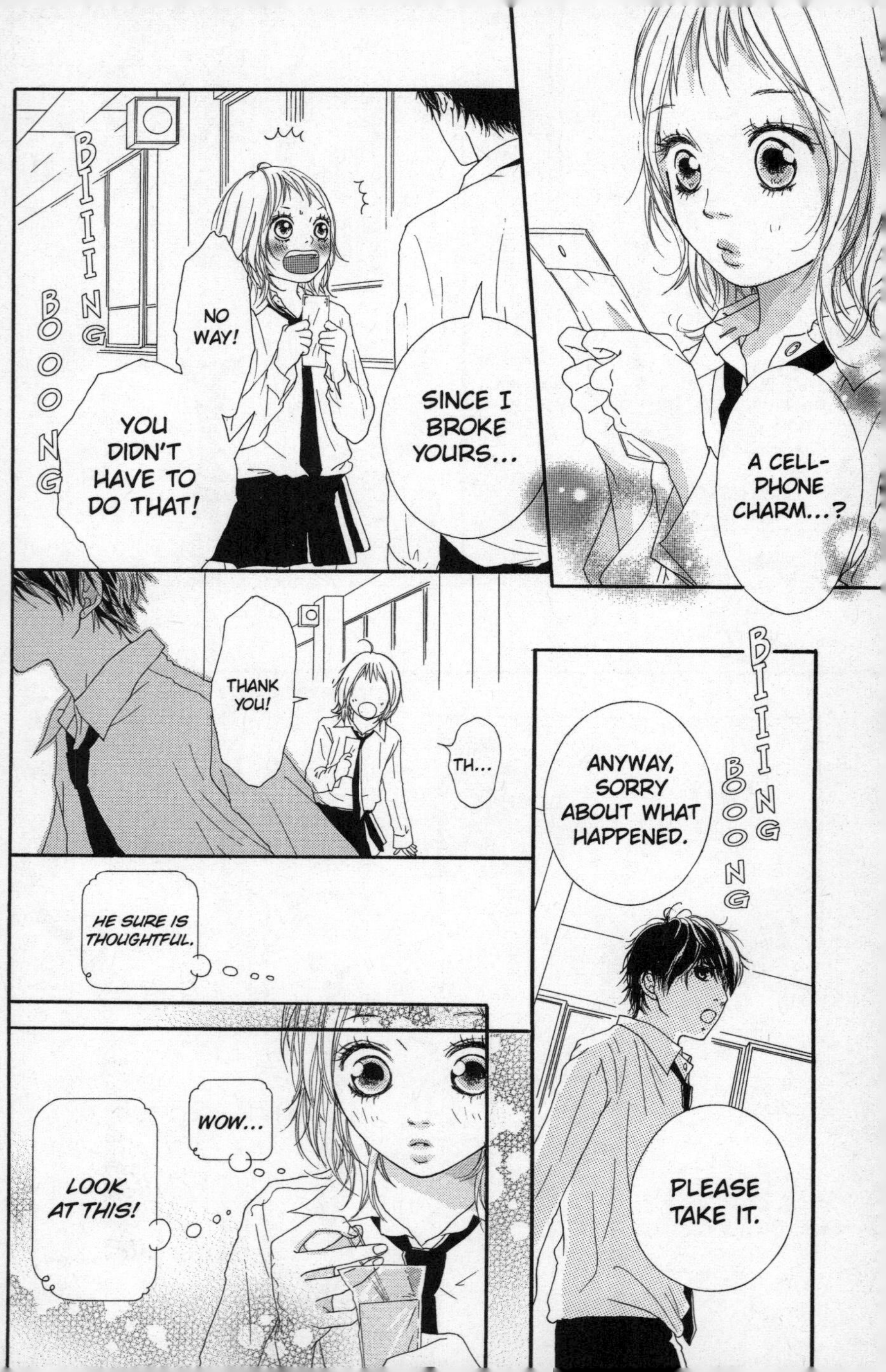
A CELL-PHONE CHARM...?
SINCE I BROKE YOURS...
NO WAY!
YOU DIDN'T HAVE TO DO THAT!
BIIING
BOOONG
BIIING
BOOONG
ANYWAY, SORRY ABOUT WHAT HAPPENED.
PLEASE TAKE IT.
TH...
THANK YOU!
HE SURE IS THOUGHTFUL.
WOW...
LOOK AT THIS!

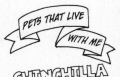

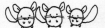

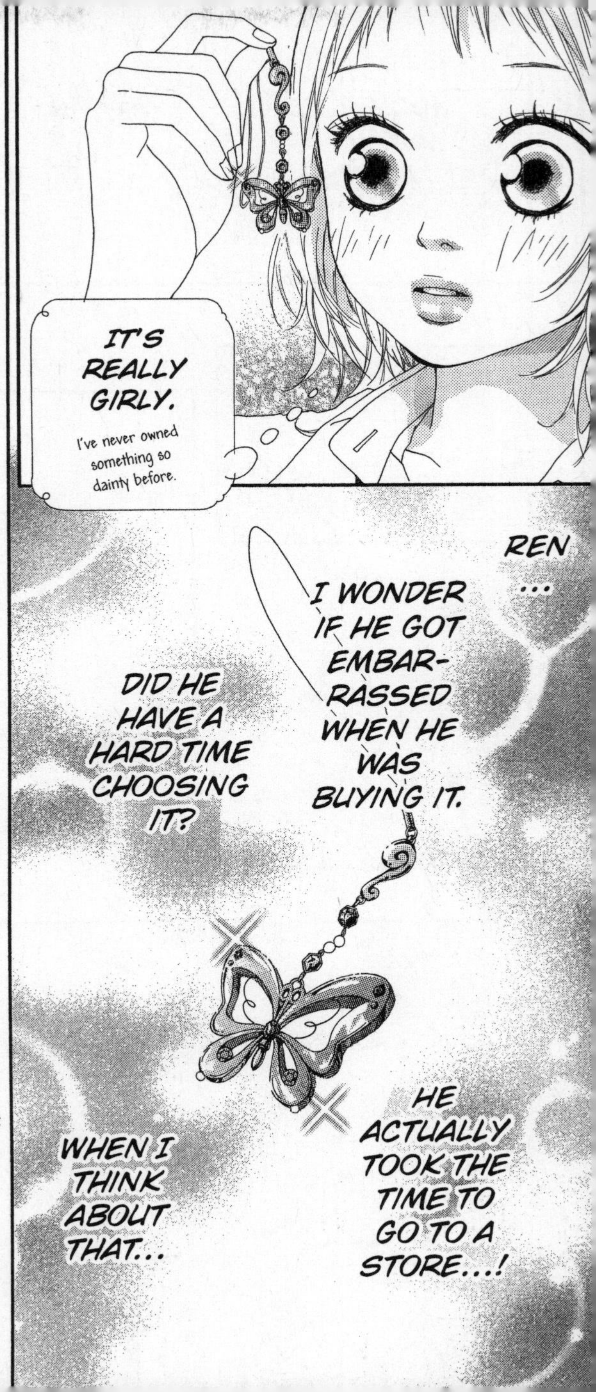
IT'S REALLY GIRLY.
I've never owned something so dainty before.
REN ...
I WONDER IF HE GOT EMBARRASSED WHEN HE WAS BUYING IT.
DID HE HAVE A HARD TIME CHOOSING IT?
HE ACTUALLY TOOK THE TIME TO GO TO A STORE...!
WHEN I THINK ABOUT THAT...

PETS THAT LIVE WITH ME

## CHINCHILLA

(RODENTIA: CHINCHILLIDAE)

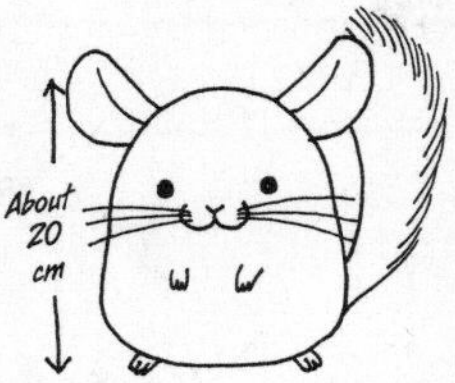
About 20 cm

Characteristics
- Stocky
- Short limbs
- Fuzzy little tail
- Doesn't like hot weather
- Loves dust baths
- Rather long life (over ten years!)
- Whenever people see one, they ask if it's a rabbit or a mouse.
- Often...

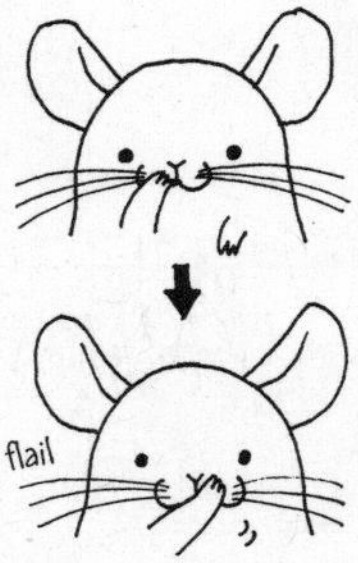
flail

"You idiot!"
...they make this kind of movement.

I have three of them.

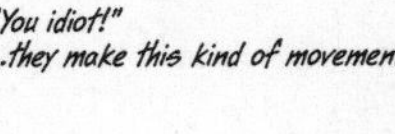

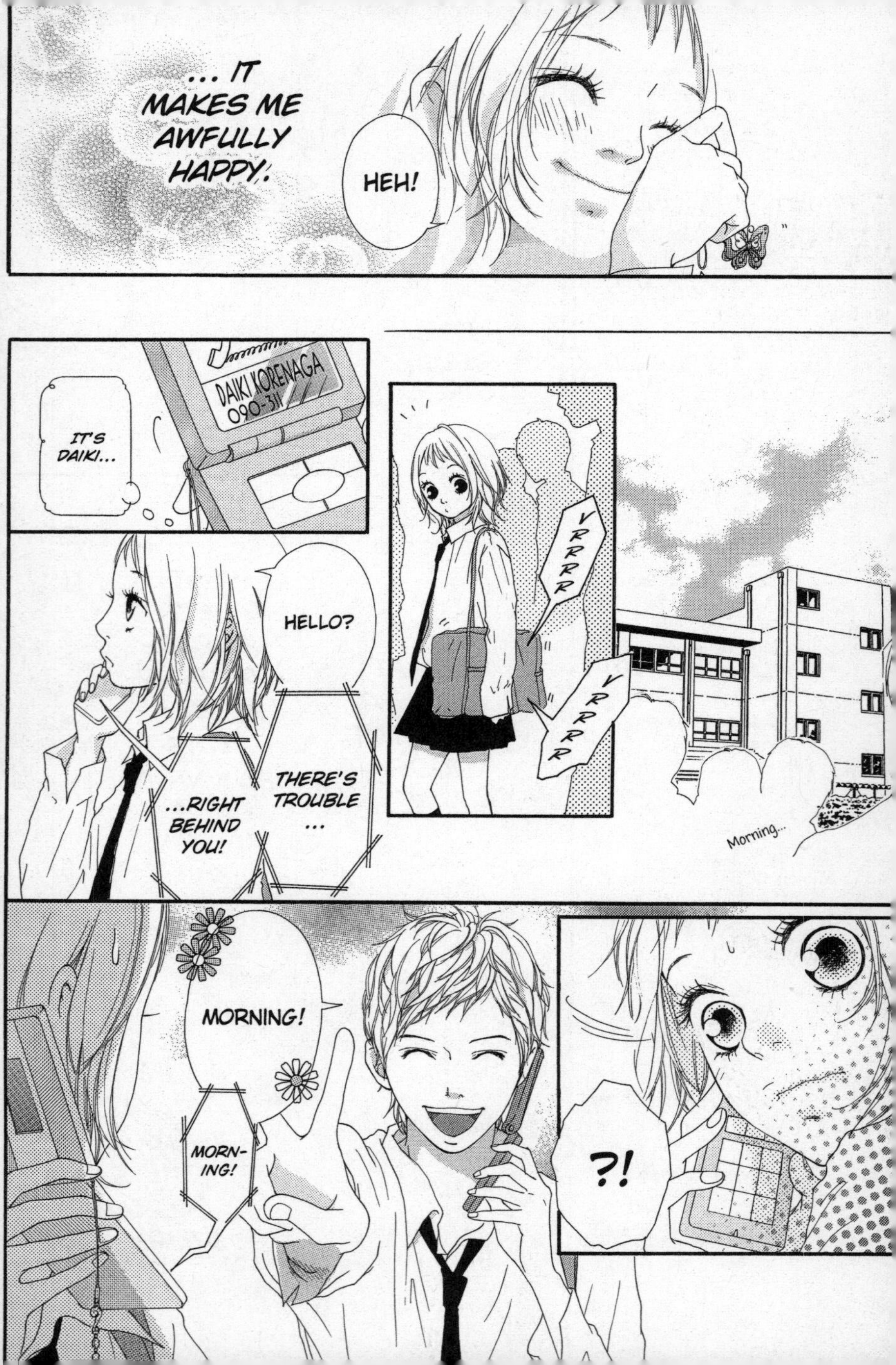

... IT MAKES ME AWFULLY HAPPY.
HEH!
Morning...
VRRRR
VRRRRR
DAIKI KORENAGA 090-311
IT'S DAIKI...
HELLO?
THERE'S TROUBLE ...
...RIGHT BEHIND YOU!
?!
MORNING!
MORN-ING!

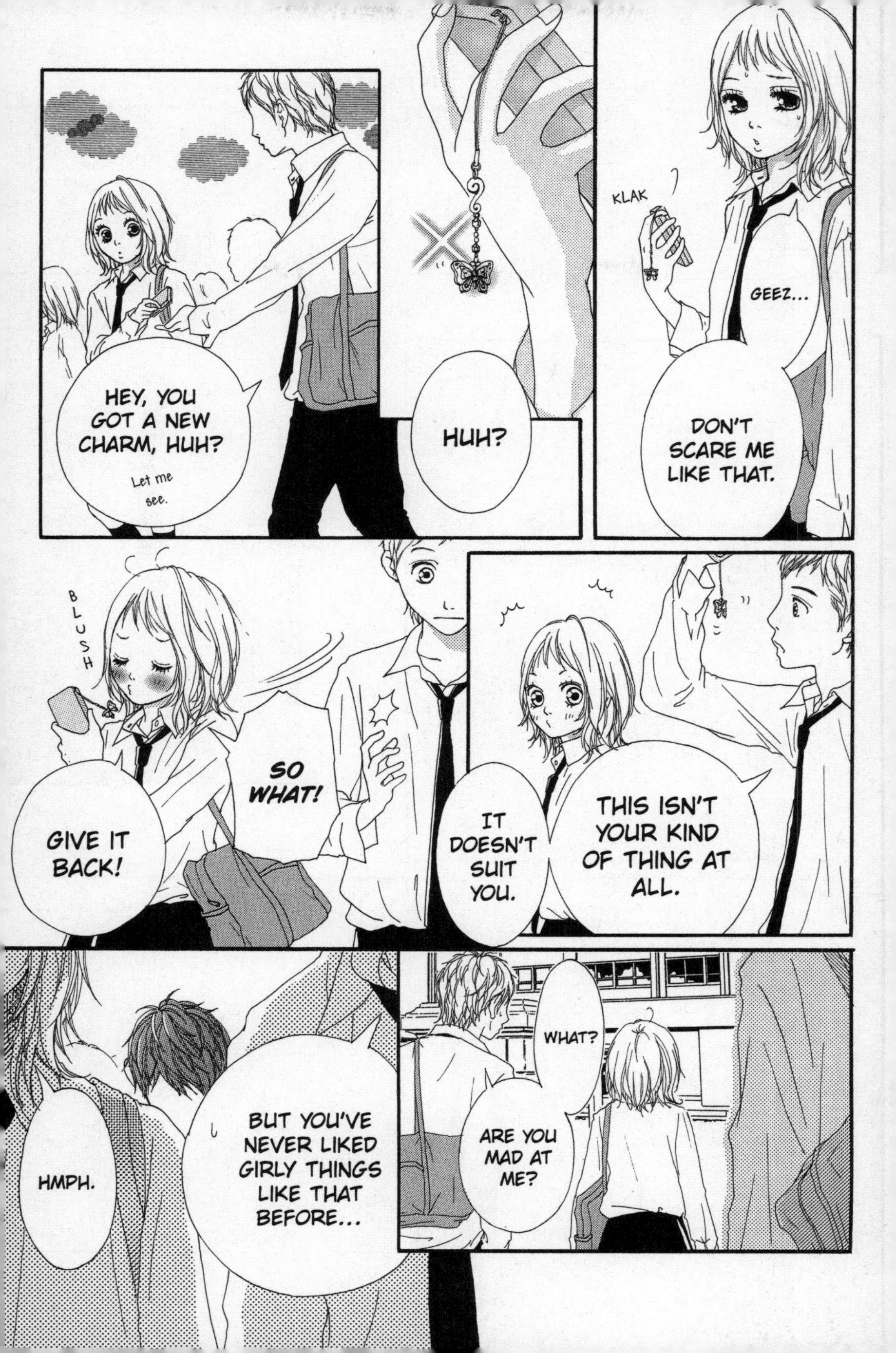
KLAK
GEEZ...
DON'T SCARE ME LIKE THAT.
HUH?
HEY, YOU GOT A NEW CHARM, HUH?
Let me see.
THIS ISN'T YOUR KIND OF THING AT ALL.
IT DOESN'T SUIT YOU.
BLUSH
SO WHAT!
GIVE IT BACK!
WHAT?
ARE YOU MAD AT ME?
BUT YOU'VE NEVER LIKED GIRLY THINGS LIKE THAT BEFORE...
HMPH.

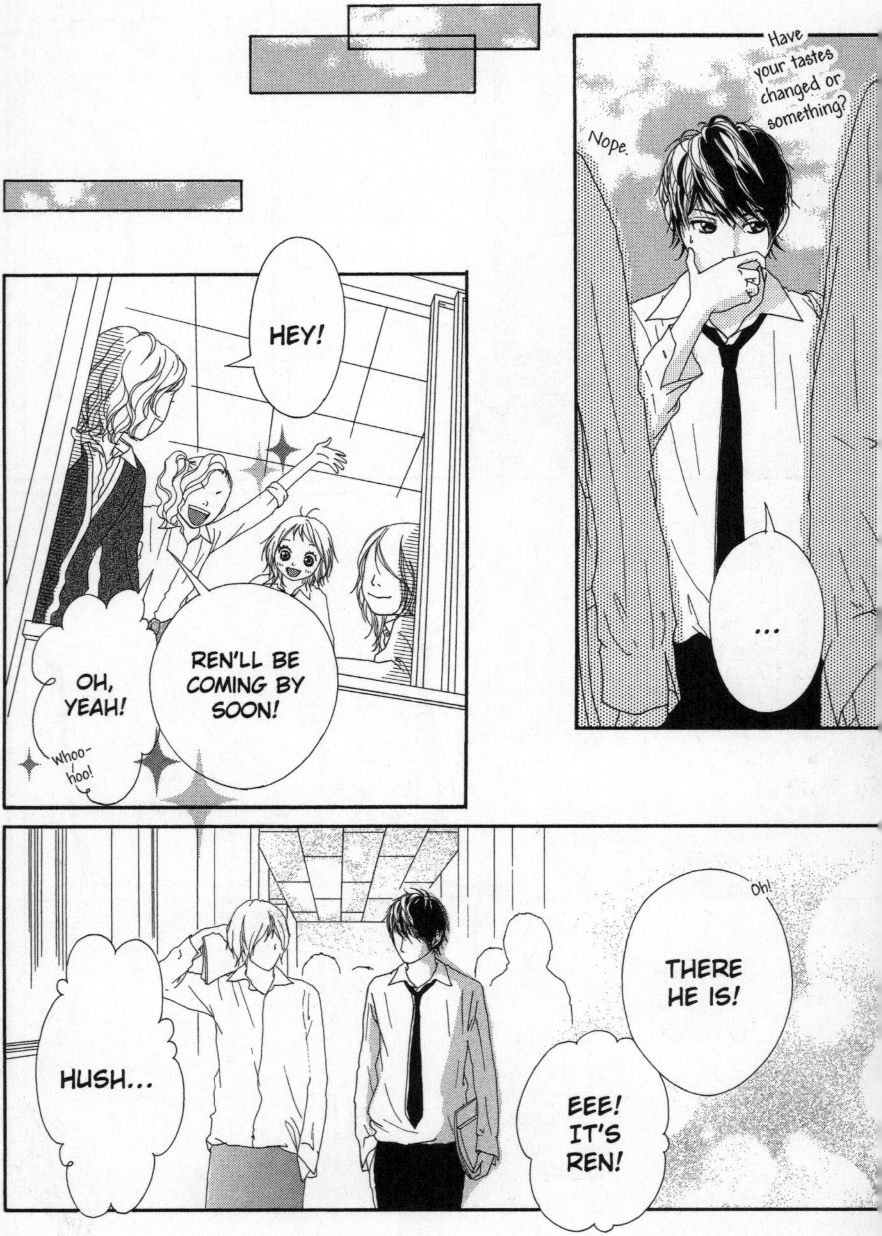
Have your tastes changed or something?
Nope.
...
HEY!
REN'LL BE COMING BY SOON!
OH, YEAH!
Whoo-hoo!
Oh!
THERE HE IS!
EEE! IT'S REN!
HUSH...

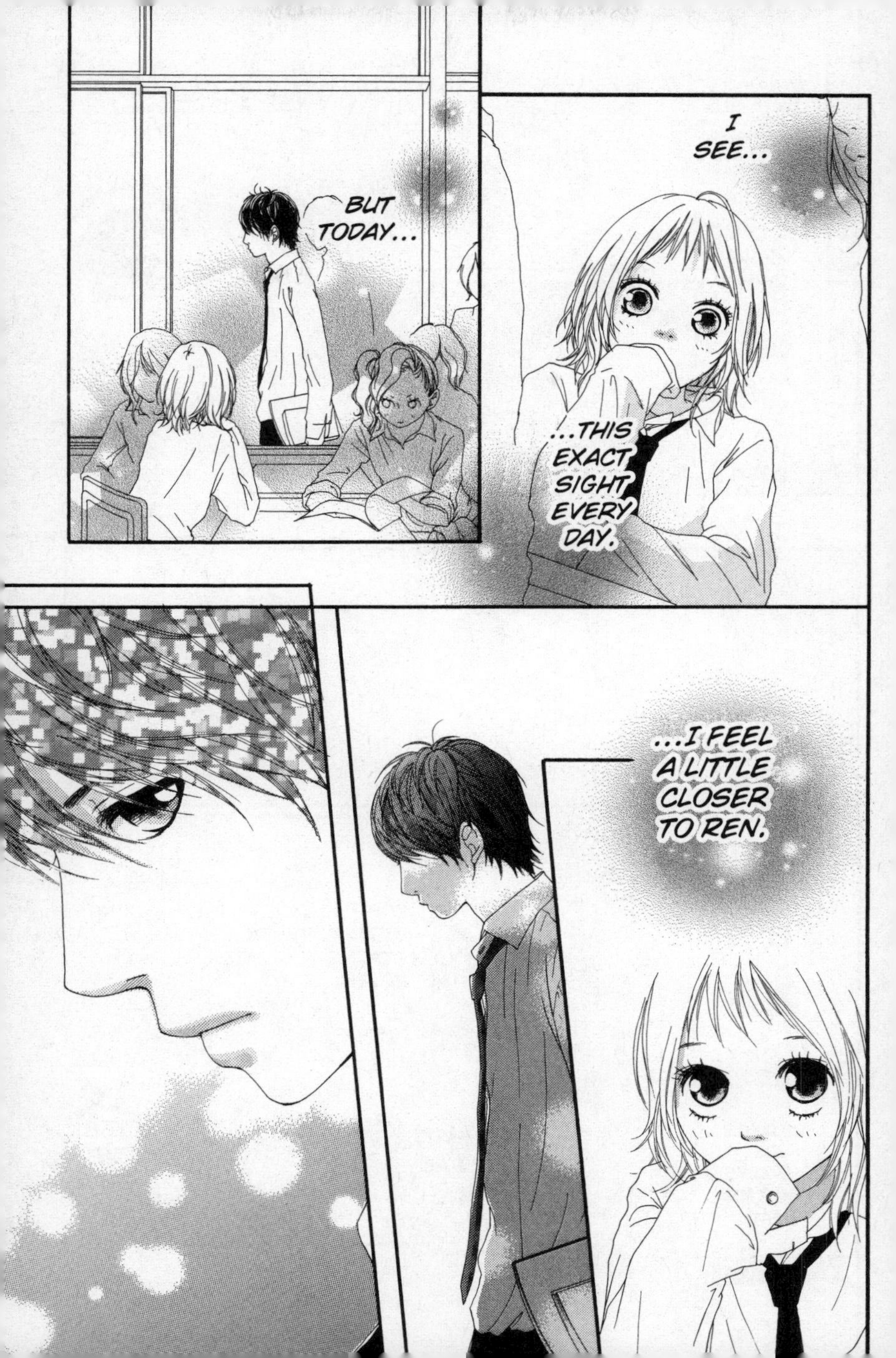
I SEE...
...THIS EXACT SIGHT EVERY DAY.
BUT TODAY...
...I FEEL A LITTLE CLOSER TO REN.

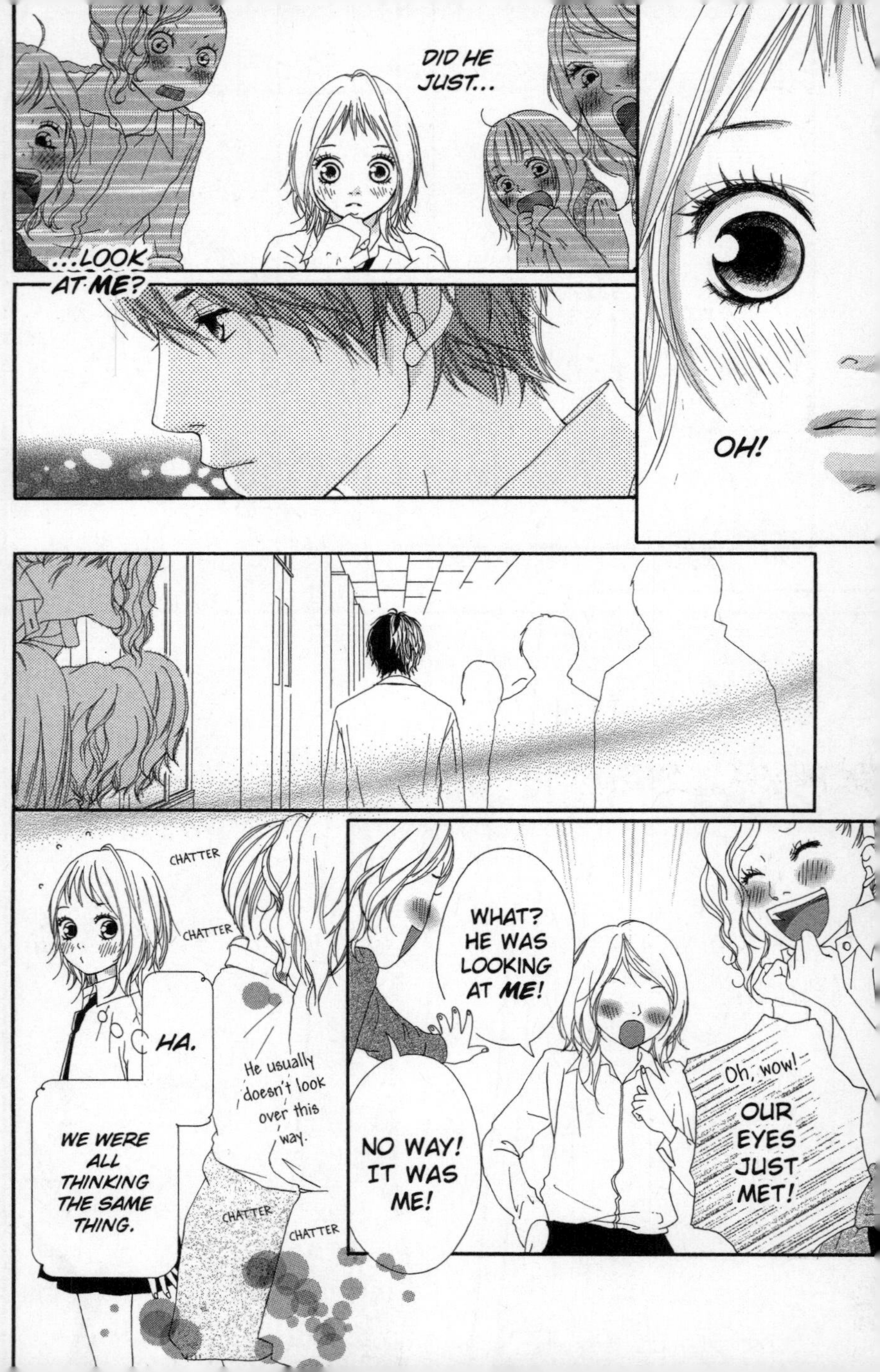
OH!
DID HE JUST...
...LOOK AT ME?
Oh, wow!
OUR EYES JUST MET!
WHAT? HE WAS LOOKING AT ME!
NO WAY! IT WAS ME!
CHATTER
CHATTER
He usually doesn't look over this way.
CHATTER
CHATTER
HA.
WE WERE ALL THINKING THE SAME THING.

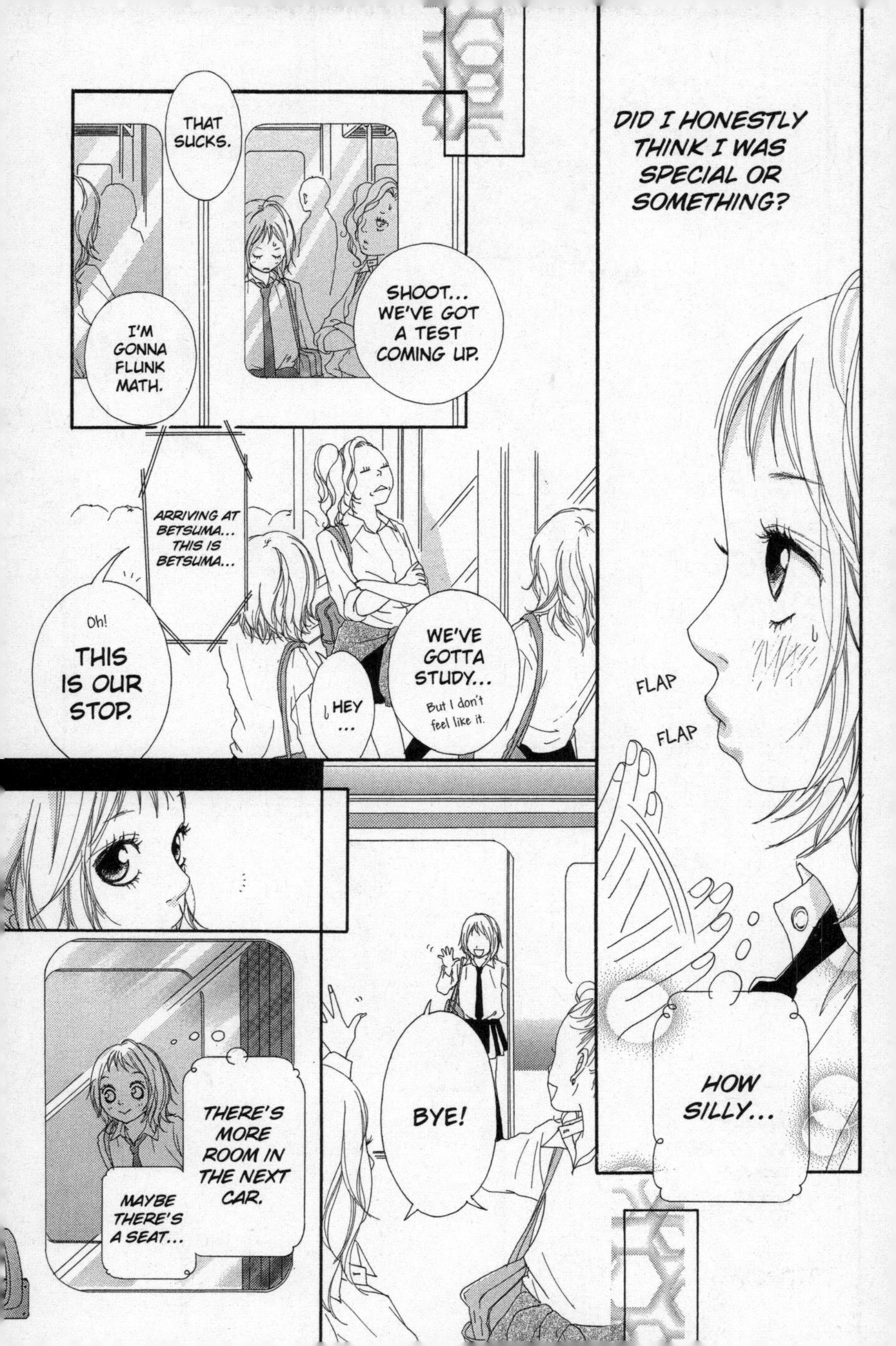
DID I HONESTLY THINK I WAS SPECIAL OR SOMETHING?
FLAP
FLAP
HOW SILLY...
SHOOT... WE'VE GOT A TEST COMING UP.
THAT SUCKS.
I'M GONNA FLUNK MATH.
WE'VE GOTTA STUDY... But I don't feel like it.
HEY ...
ARRIVING AT BETSUMA... THIS IS BETSUMA...
Oh! THIS IS OUR STOP.
BYE!
THERE'S MORE ROOM IN THE NEXT CAR.
MAYBE THERE'S A SEAT...

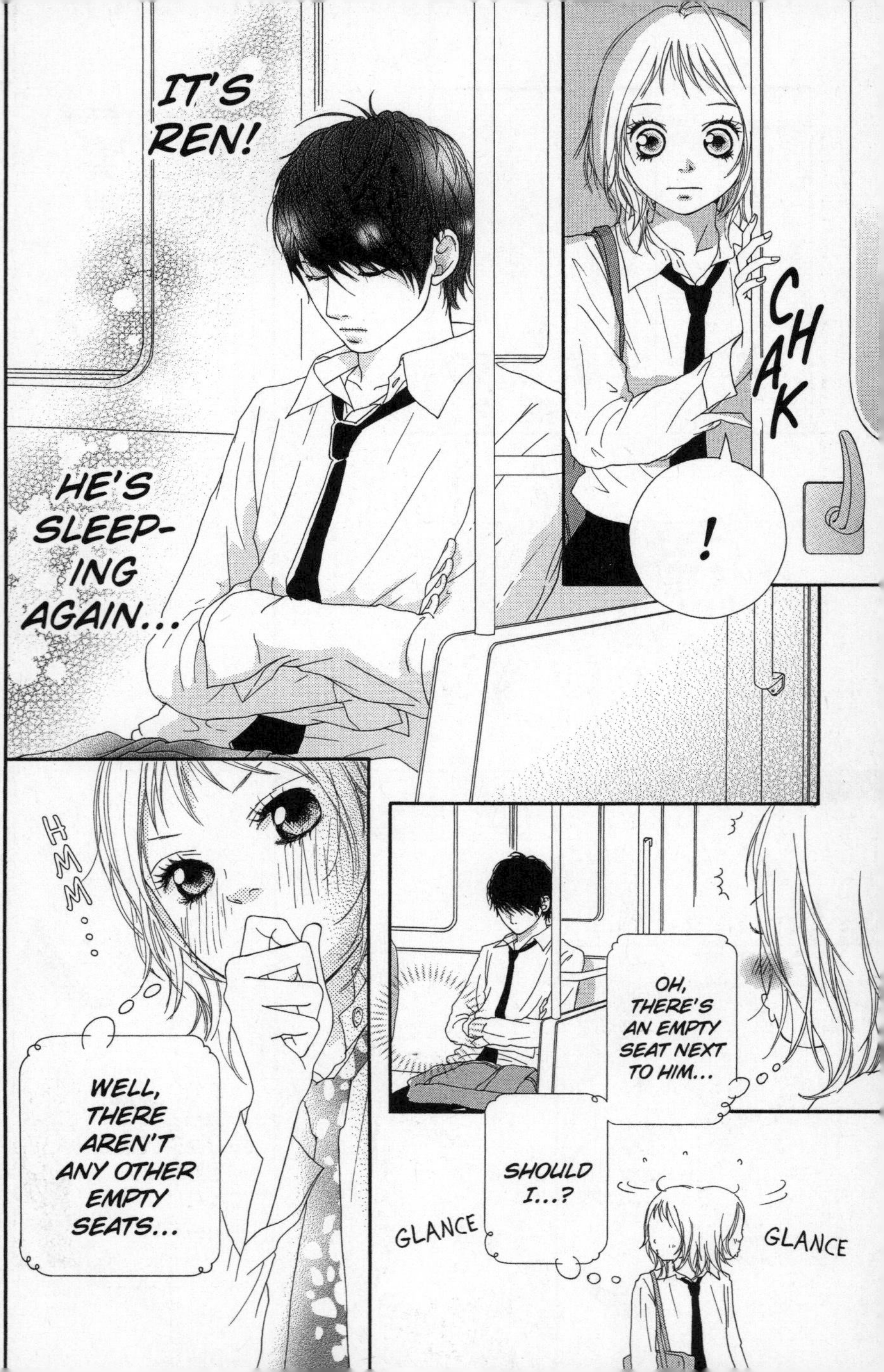
CHAK
!
IT'S REN!
HE'S SLEEPING AGAIN...
OH, THERE'S AN EMPTY SEAT NEXT TO HIM...
GLANCE
SHOULD I...?
GLANCE
HMM
WELL, THERE AREN'T ANY OTHER EMPTY SEATS...

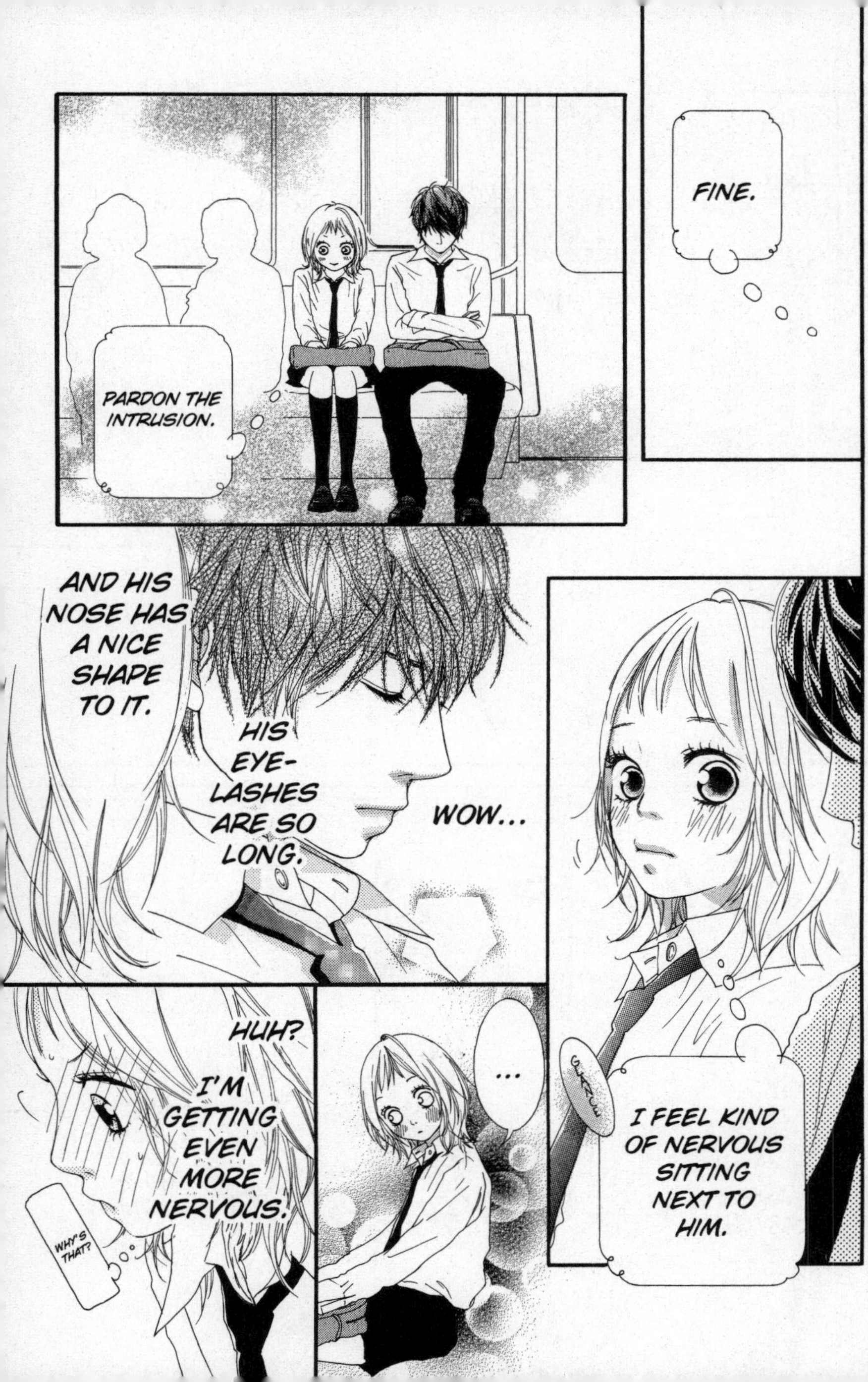
FINE.
PARDON THE INTRUSION.
GLANCE
I FEEL KIND OF NERVOUS SITTING NEXT TO HIM.
WOW...
HIS EYE-LASHES ARE SO LONG.
AND HIS NOSE HAS A NICE SHAPE TO IT.
...
HUH?
I'M GETTING EVEN MORE NERVOUS.
WHY'S THAT?

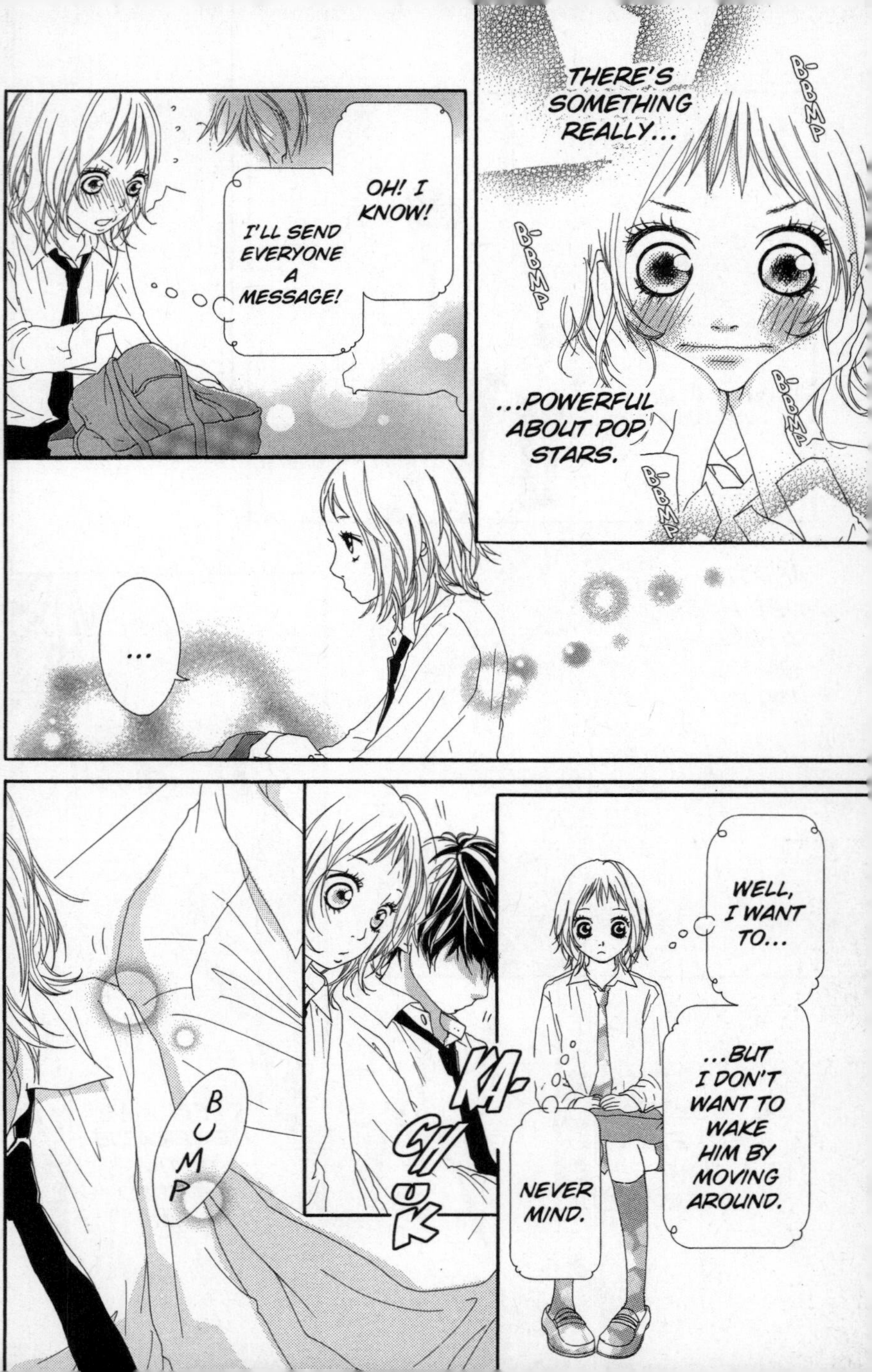
THERE'S SOMETHING REALLY...
B-BBMP
...POWERFUL ABOUT POP STARS.
B-BBMP
B-BBMP
B-BBMP
OH! I KNOW!
I'LL SEND EVERYONE A MESSAGE!
...
WELL, I WANT TO...
...BUT I DON'T WANT TO WAKE HIM BY MOVING AROUND.
NEVER MIND.
KA-CH-OK
BUMP

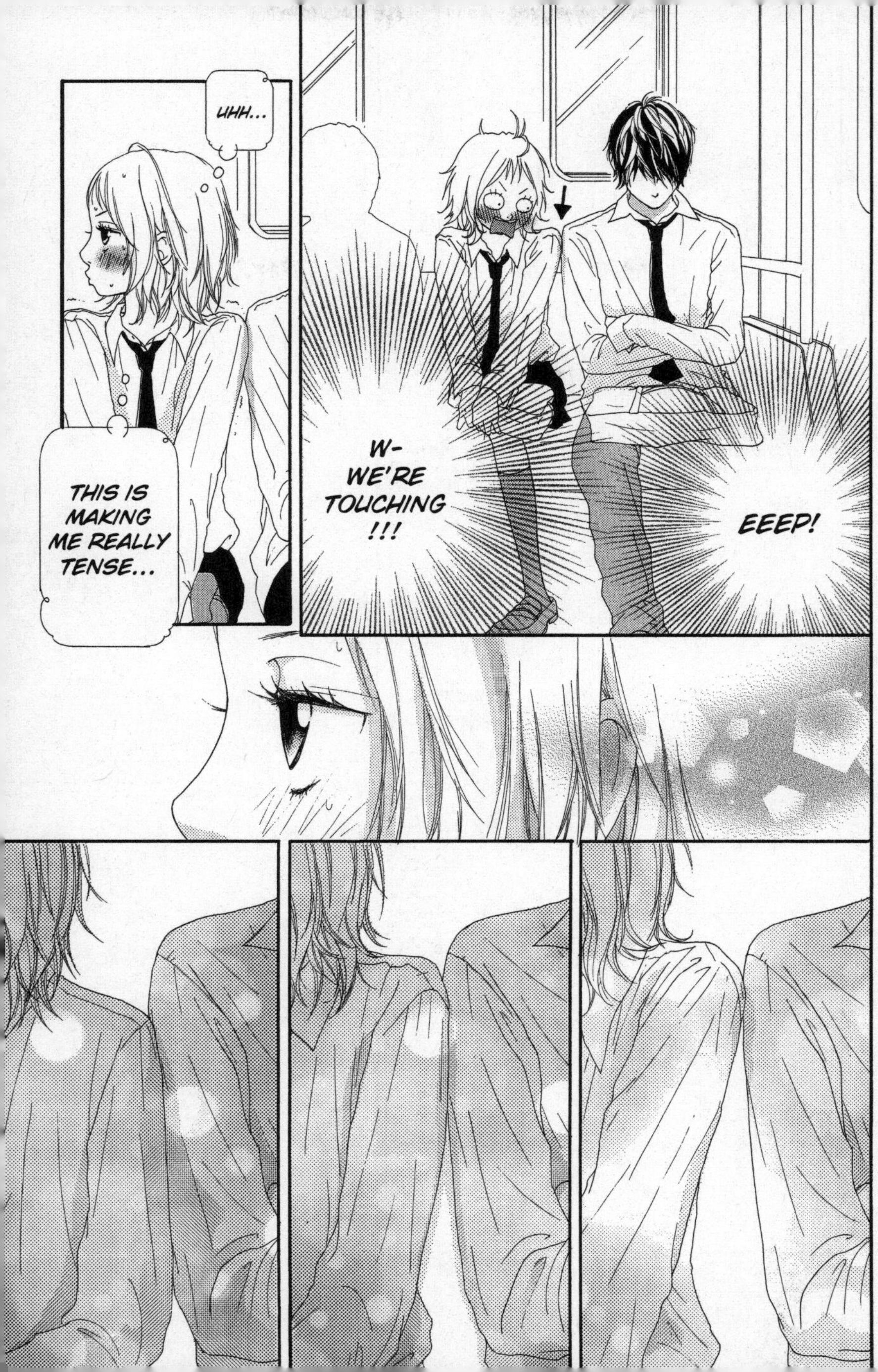
W- WE'RE TOUCHING !!!
EEEP!
UHH...
THIS IS MAKING ME REALLY TENSE...

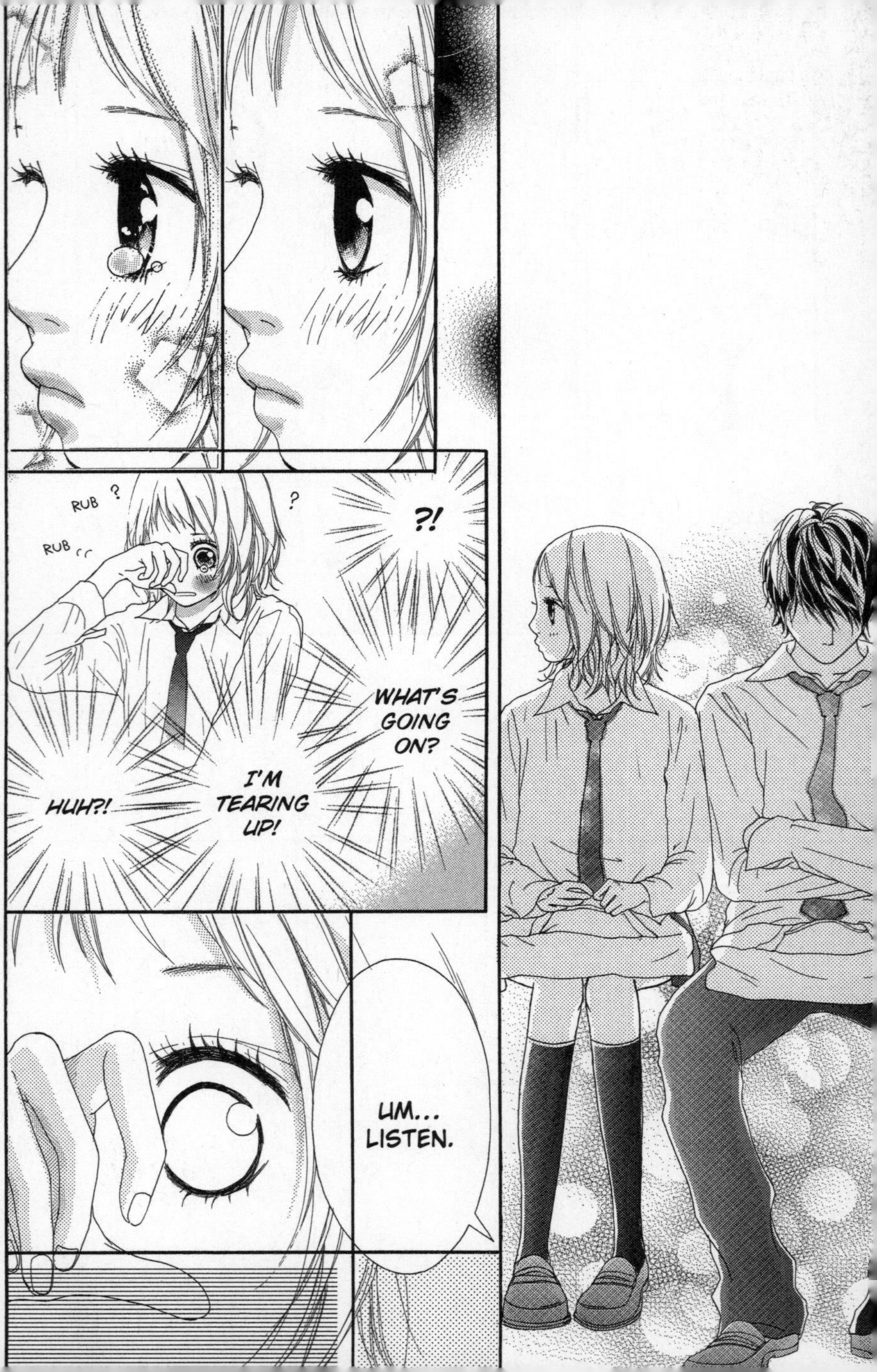
?!
?
RUB ?
RUB
WHAT'S GOING ON?
I'M TEARING UP!
HUH?!
UM... LISTEN.

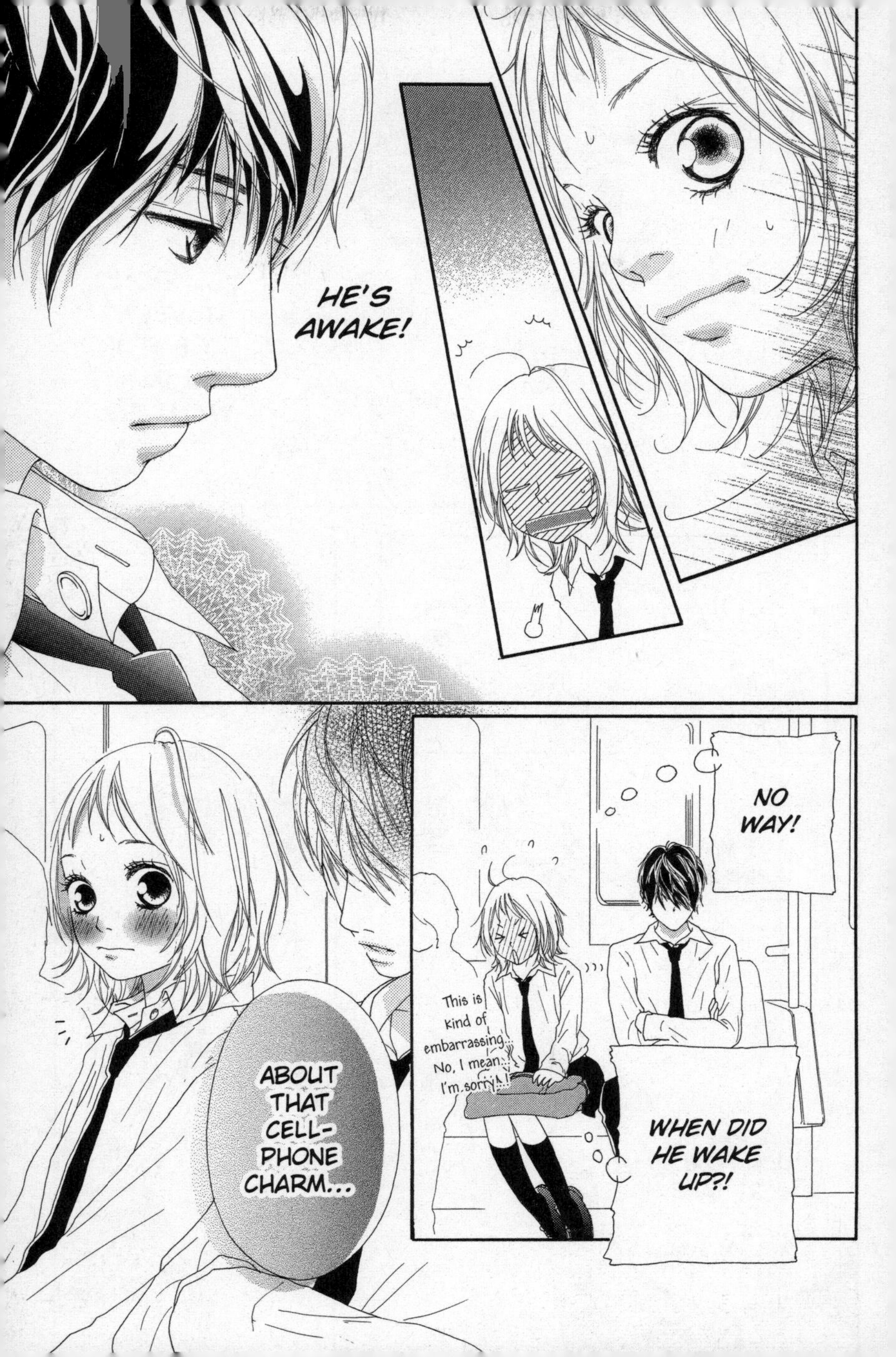
HE'S AWAKE!
NO WAY!
This is kind of embarrassing... No, I mean... I'm sorry...!
WHEN DID HE WAKE UP?!
ABOUT THAT CELL-PHONE CHARM...

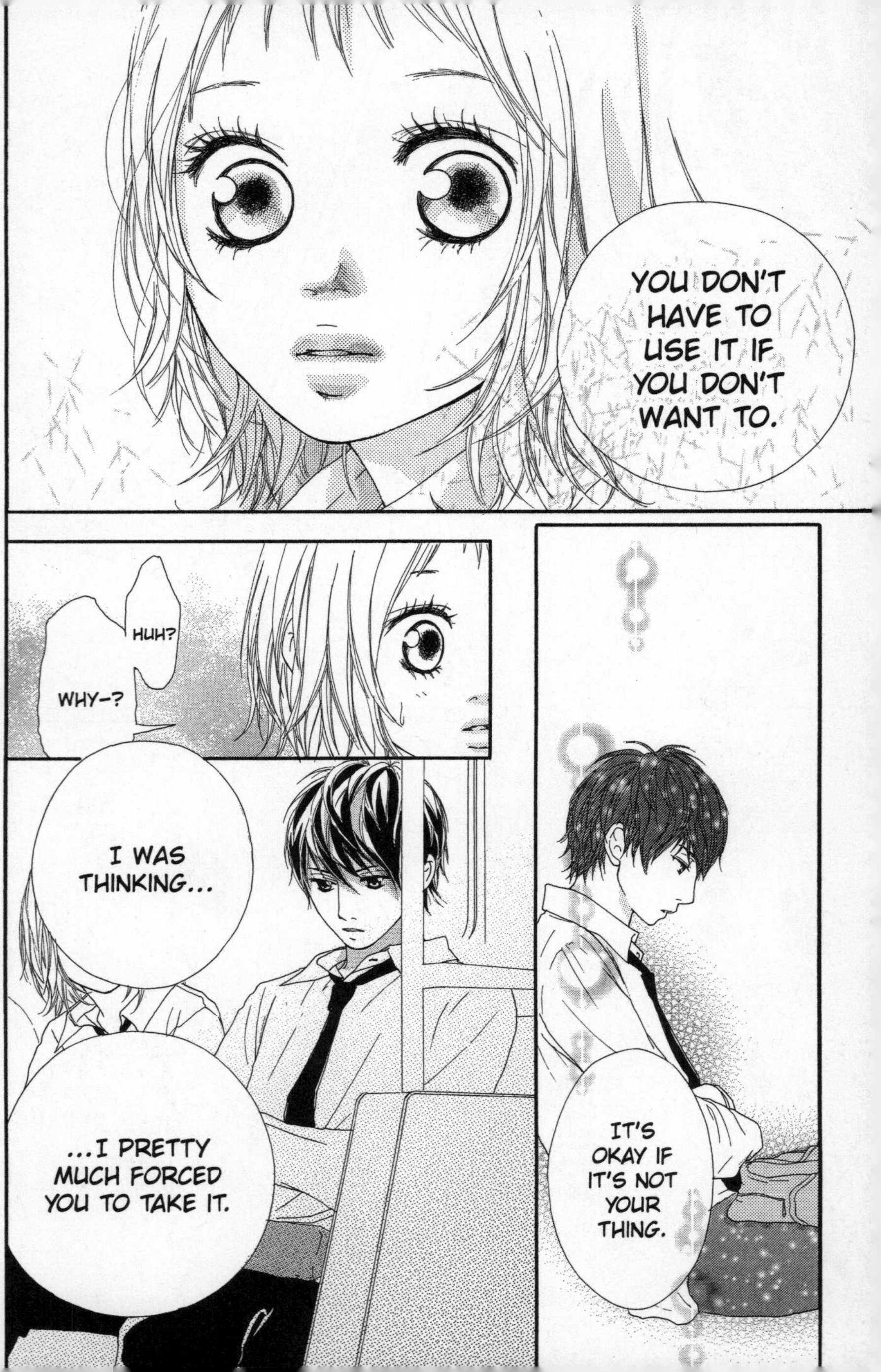
YOU DON'T HAVE TO USE IT IF YOU DON'T WANT TO.
IT'S OKAY IF IT'S NOT YOUR THING.
HUH? WHY-?
I WAS THINKING...
...I PRETTY MUCH FORCED YOU TO TAKE IT.

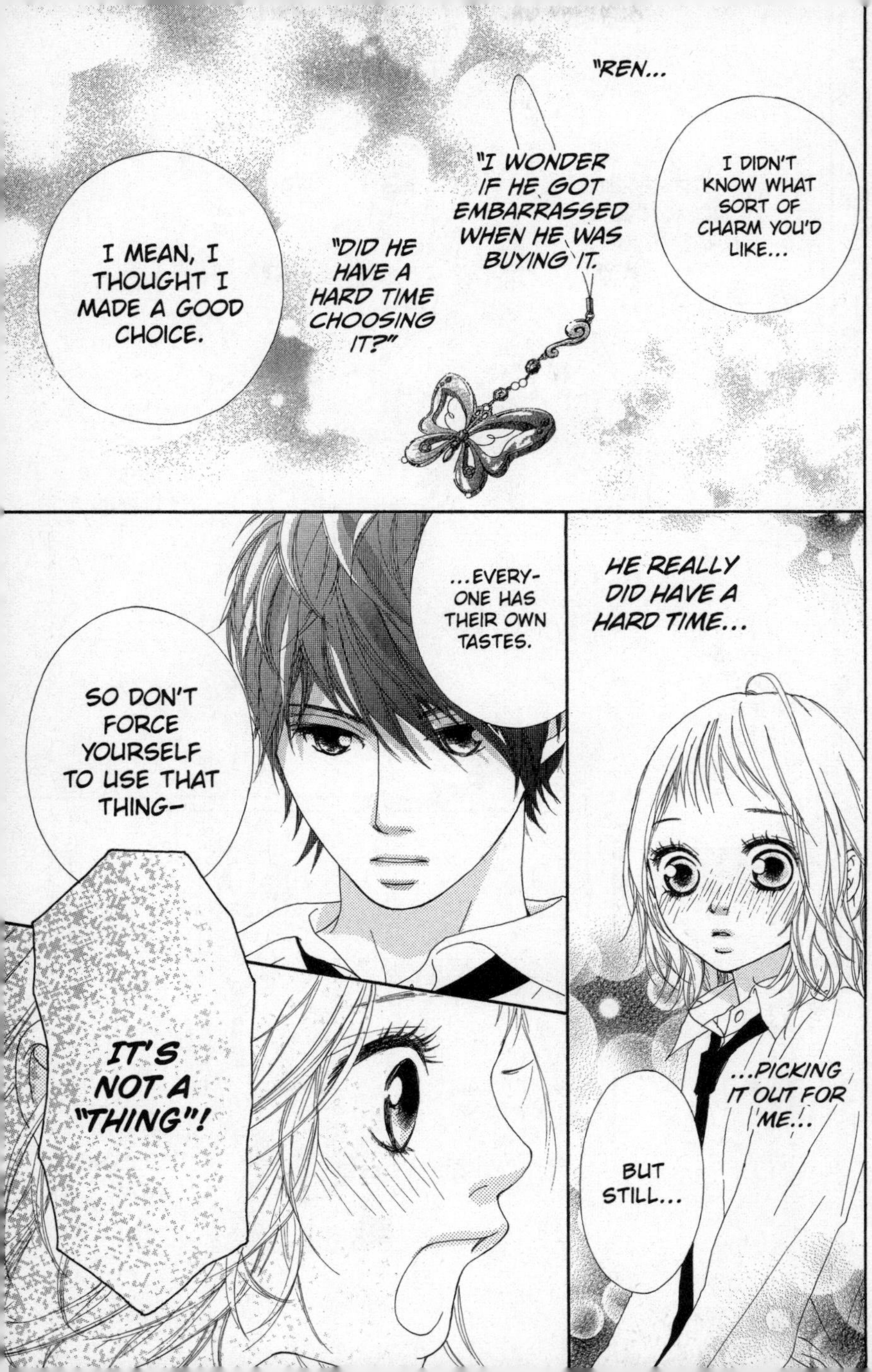
"REN...
I DIDN'T KNOW WHAT SORT OF CHARM YOU'D LIKE...
"I WONDER IF HE GOT EMBARRASSED WHEN HE WAS BUYING IT.
"DID HE HAVE A HARD TIME CHOOSING IT?"
I MEAN, I THOUGHT I MADE A GOOD CHOICE.
HE REALLY DID HAVE A HARD TIME...
...PICKING IT OUT FOR ME...
BUT STILL...
...EVERY-ONE HAS THEIR OWN TASTES.
SO DON'T FORCE YOURSELF TO USE THAT THING-
IT'S NOT A "THING"!

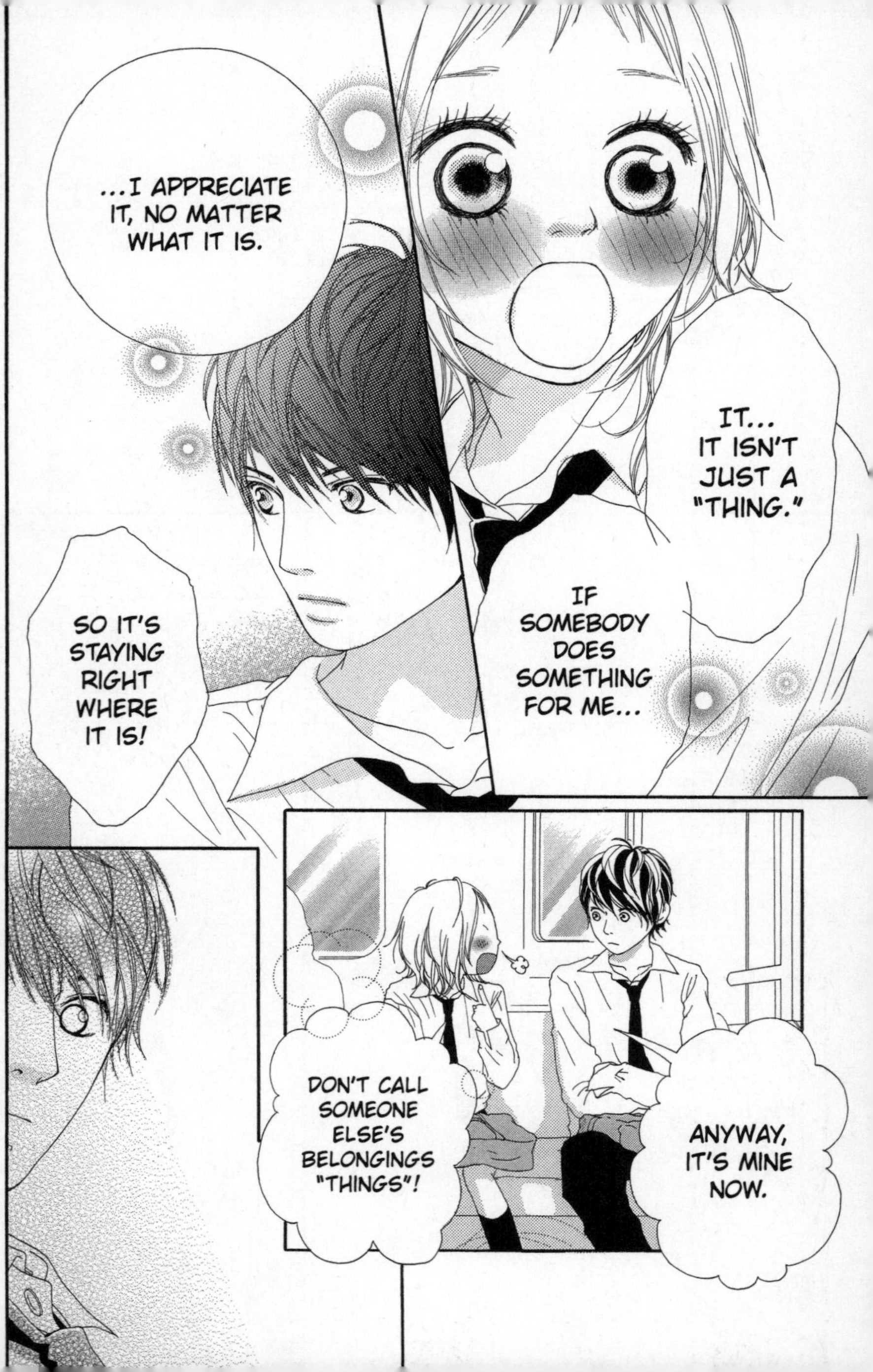
IT... IT ISN'T JUST A "THING."
IF SOMEBODY DOES SOMETHING FOR ME...
...I APPRECIATE IT, NO MATTER WHAT IT IS.
SO IT'S STAYING RIGHT WHERE IT IS!
ANYWAY, IT'S MINE NOW.
DON'T CALL SOMEONE ELSE'S BELONGINGS "THINGS"!

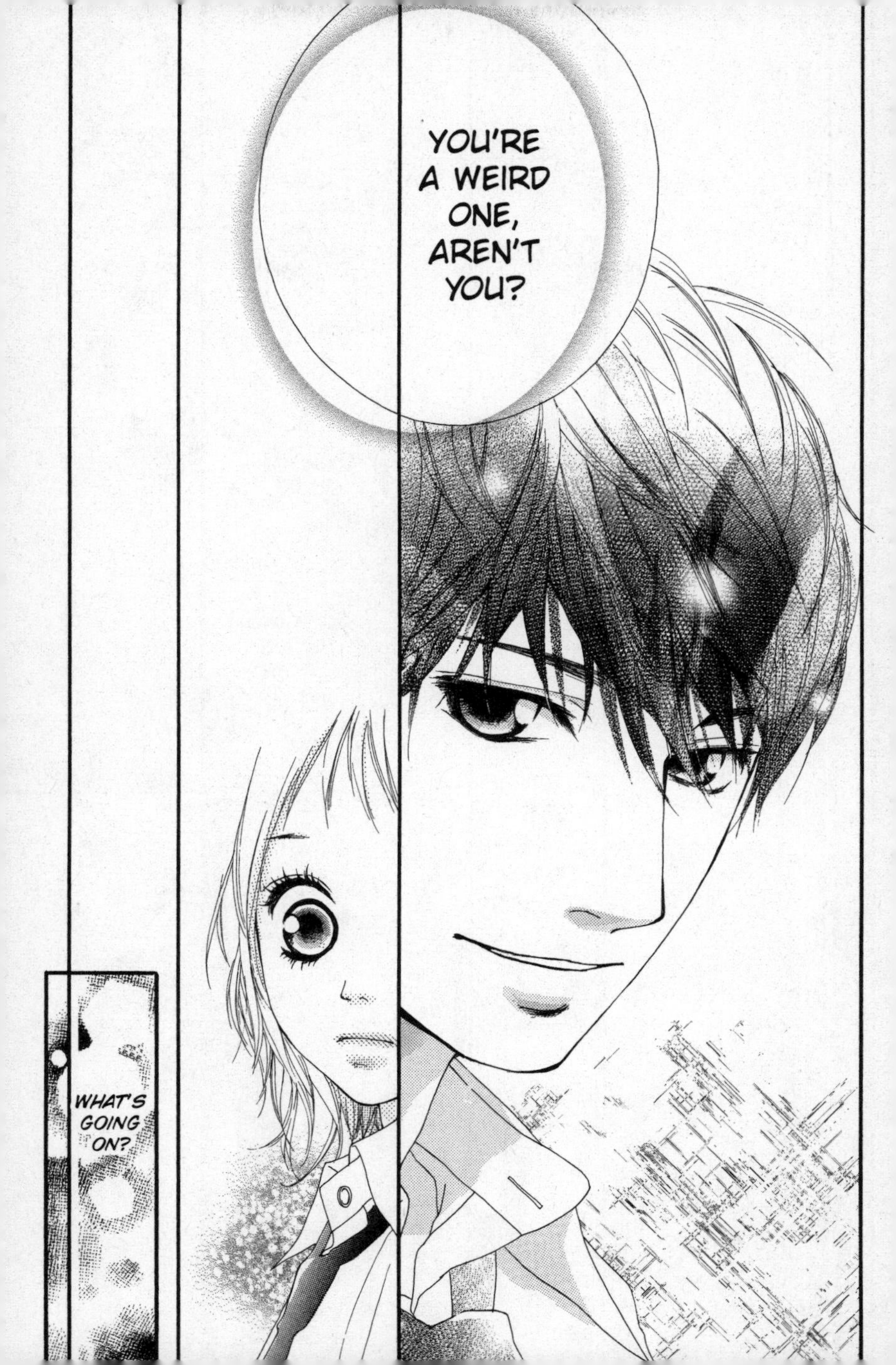
YOU'RE A WEIRD ONE, AREN'T YOU?
WHAT'S GOING ON?

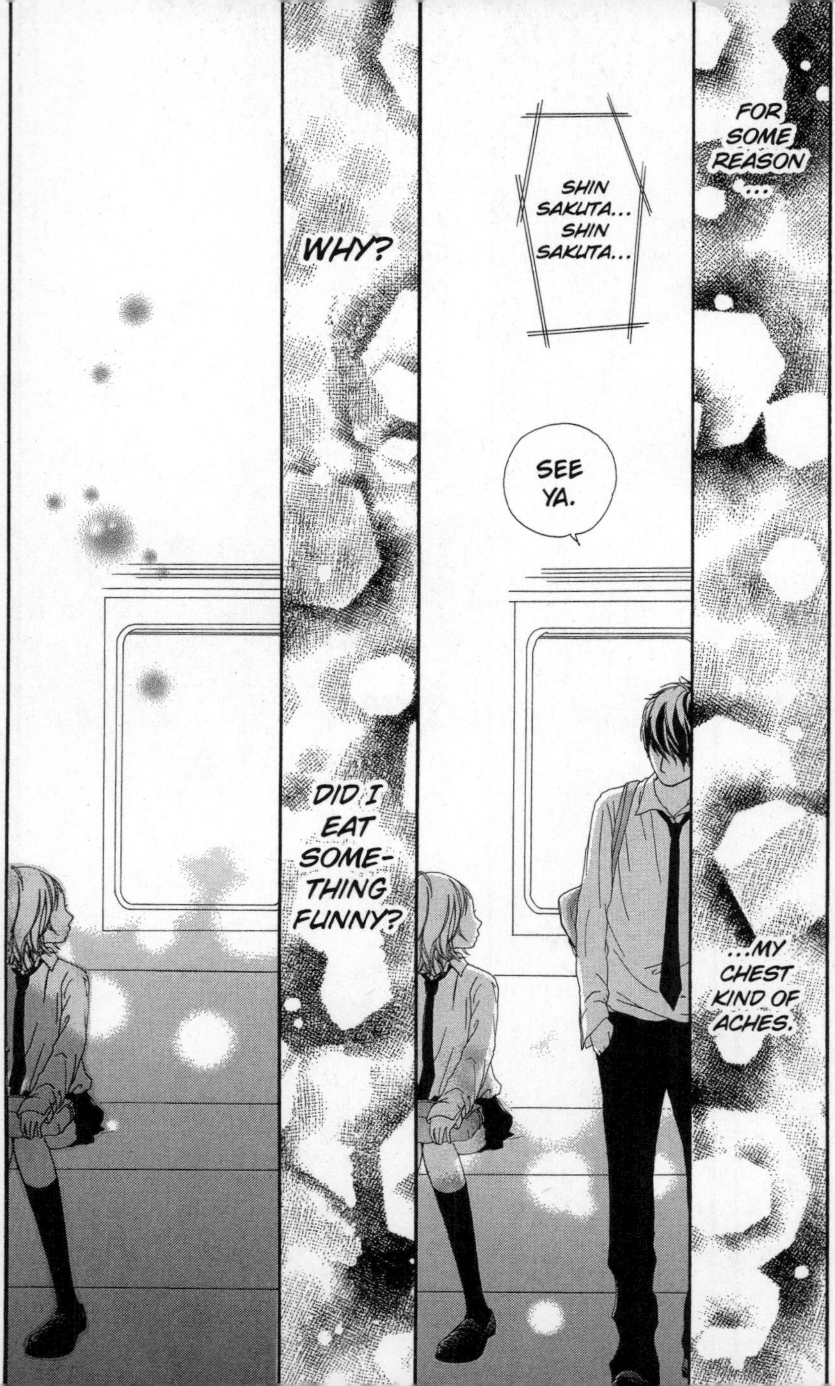
FOR SOME REASON...
...MY CHEST KIND OF ACHES.
SHIN SAKUTA... SHIN SAKUTA...
SEE YA.
WHY?
DID I EAT SOME-THING FUNNY?

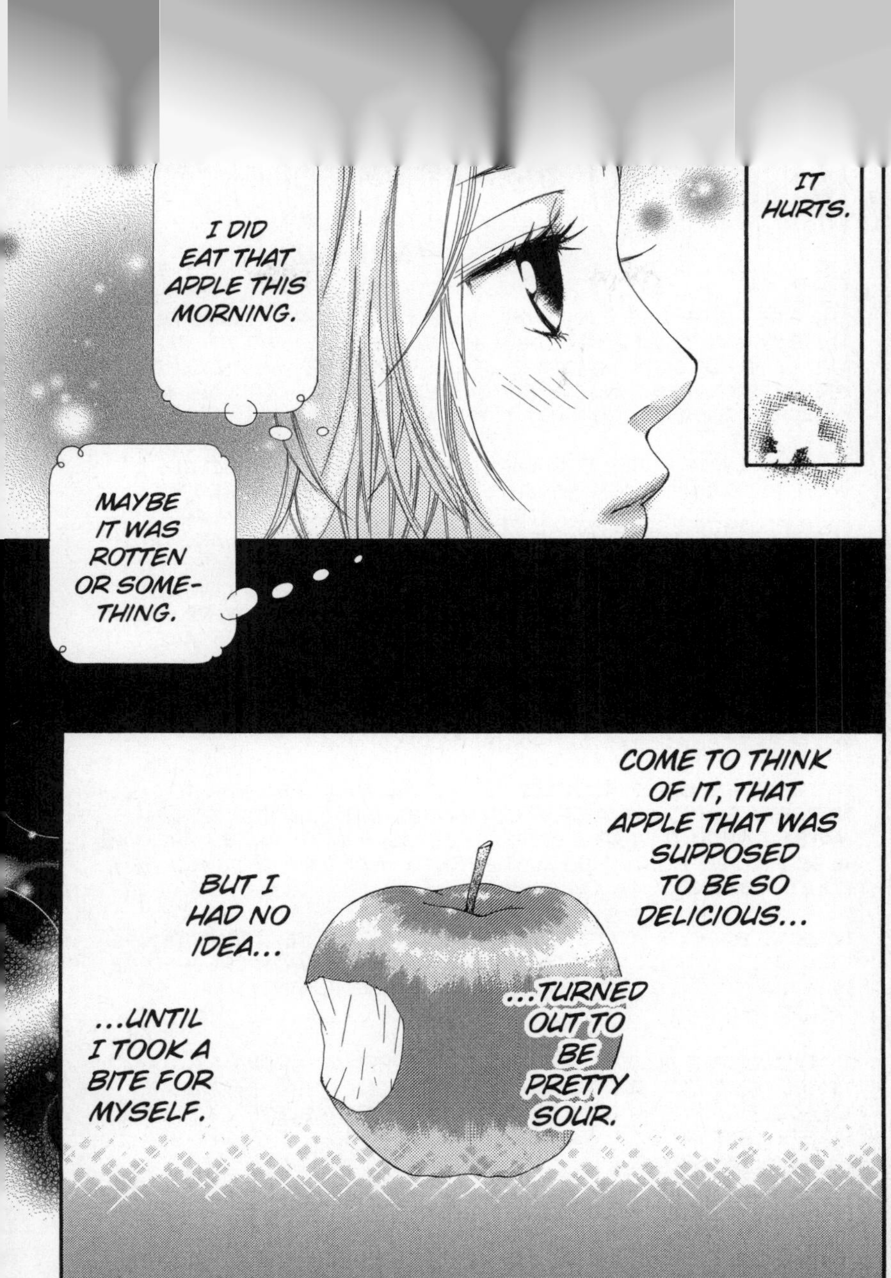
IT HURTS.
I DID EAT THAT APPLE THIS MORNING.
MAYBE IT WAS ROTTEN OR SOME-THING.
COME TO THINK OF IT, THAT APPLE THAT WAS SUPPOSED TO BE SO DELICIOUS...
...TURNED OUT TO BE PRETTY SOUR.
BUT I HAD NO IDEA...
...UNTIL I TOOK A BITE FOR MYSELF.

# TALKING ABOUT FIRST LOVE

## (NOT QUITE)

THE FIRST TIME I FELL IN LOVE, I WAS ABOUT THREE YEARS OLD.
THE BOY WAS CALLED MAA-CHAN. HE WAS MY AGE, AND WE WENT TO
THE SAME NURSERY SCHOOL. I LIKED HIM WHILE I WAS IN RABBIT
GROUP, AND WHEN I WAS IN BAMBI GROUP, AND WHEN I WAS IN
GIRAFFE GROUP. THAT'S WHAT I REMEMBER.

MAA-CHAN WAS SUPER POPULAR. MOST OF THE GIRLS IN CLASS
WERE IN LOVE WITH HIM, WHICH IS PRETTY IMPRESSIVE. HE WAS
A REALLY GENTLE KID, AND THERE WAS SOMETHING WARM AND...
"SPRING"-LIKE ABOUT HIM. (THAT'S HOW I REMEMBER IT, ANYWAY.)

MAA-CHAN'S BIRTHDAY WAS IN APRIL, SO HIS NAME WAS ALWAYS
CALLED FIRST (THE SCHOOL HAD A SYSTEM WHERE WE WERE CALLED
ON BY THE ORDER OF OUR BIRTH DATES), AND HE EVEN BECAME
A CLASS REP! HE WAS LIKE A BIG BROTHER, WHICH I THINK IS
PROBABLY WHY HE WAS SO POPULAR. I WAS BORN IN JUNE, WHICH
WASN'T THAT BIG A DIFFERENCE! I DIDN'T REALIZE THAT UNTIL
SEVERAL YEARS AFTER I GRADUATED, THOUGH.

EVERY MORNING I STRUGGLED TO CHOOSE WHAT I'D WEAR TO
NURSERY SCHOOL. MAA-CHAN LIKED QUIET GIRLS, SO I'D THINK
MAYBE I SHOULD WEAR A SKIRT TO BE MORE LADYLIKE. BUT HE WAS
ALSO FULL OF ENERGY, SO MAYBE PANTS WOULD BE GOOD—SO WE
COULD RUN AND PLAY TOGETHER!

LOOKING BACK ON IT, LITTLE KIDS THINK A LOT MORE ABOUT THINGS
THAN ADULTS THINK THEY DO. ON DAYS WHEN MY MOM DRESSED ME
IN FUNNY CLOTHES (THINGS I THOUGHT WERE FUNNY), I FELT SO
DISAPPOINTED.

I REMEMBERED ALL OF THIS AS I WAS FLIPPING THROUGH MY OLD
NURSERY SCHOOL CONTACT LIST. THEN I FOUND "SHE SAID THAT
SHE LOVED HIROSHI, TOO! ❤ AREN'T KIDS ADORABLE?!" (A TEACHER
WROTE THAT NOTE.) I WANTED TO PUNCH MYSELF. I WASN'T SO
FAITHFUL, AFTER ALL.

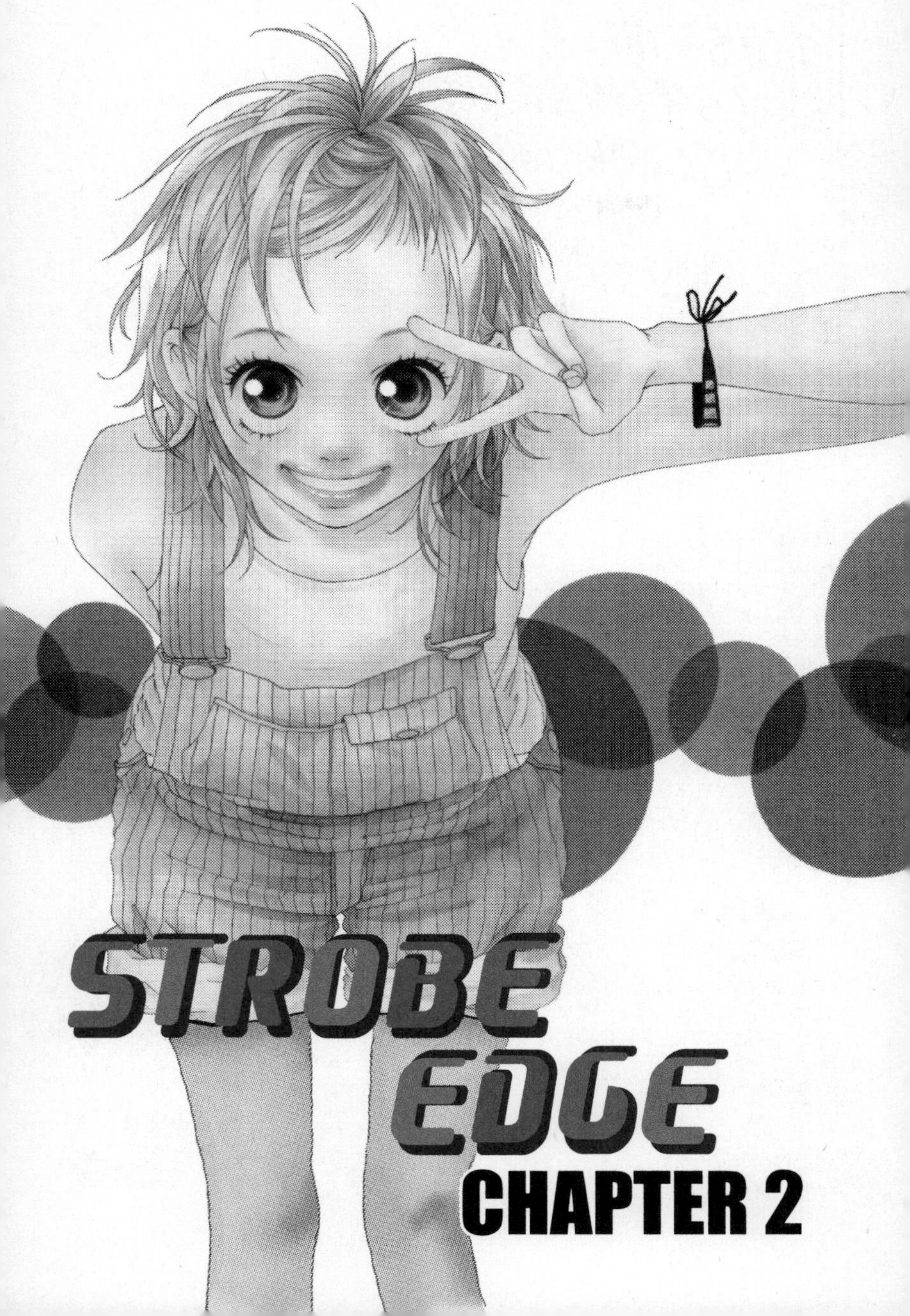
STROBE EDGE
CHAPTER 2

# THINGS THAT ALWAYS CROSS MY MIND WHEN I'M WORKING

I wish there were 30 hours in a day.

I wish I didn't have to sleep.

I wish my right hand could move three times faster.

I wish there were two or three more of me to help draw.

Why are there interesting TV specials at a time like this?!

I wish I had a ballpoint pen that didn't dry up.

Ah... I'm hungry...

I wish there was world peace.

Jeez, I'm tired! I'm going to fall asleep right now! Just kidding. I'm going to try to get some more done!

I want to take a trip by myself.

I wish I didn't have deadlines MUMBLE

Ebi sure is cute.

Oh, never mind. I'm going to sleep

★Saki★

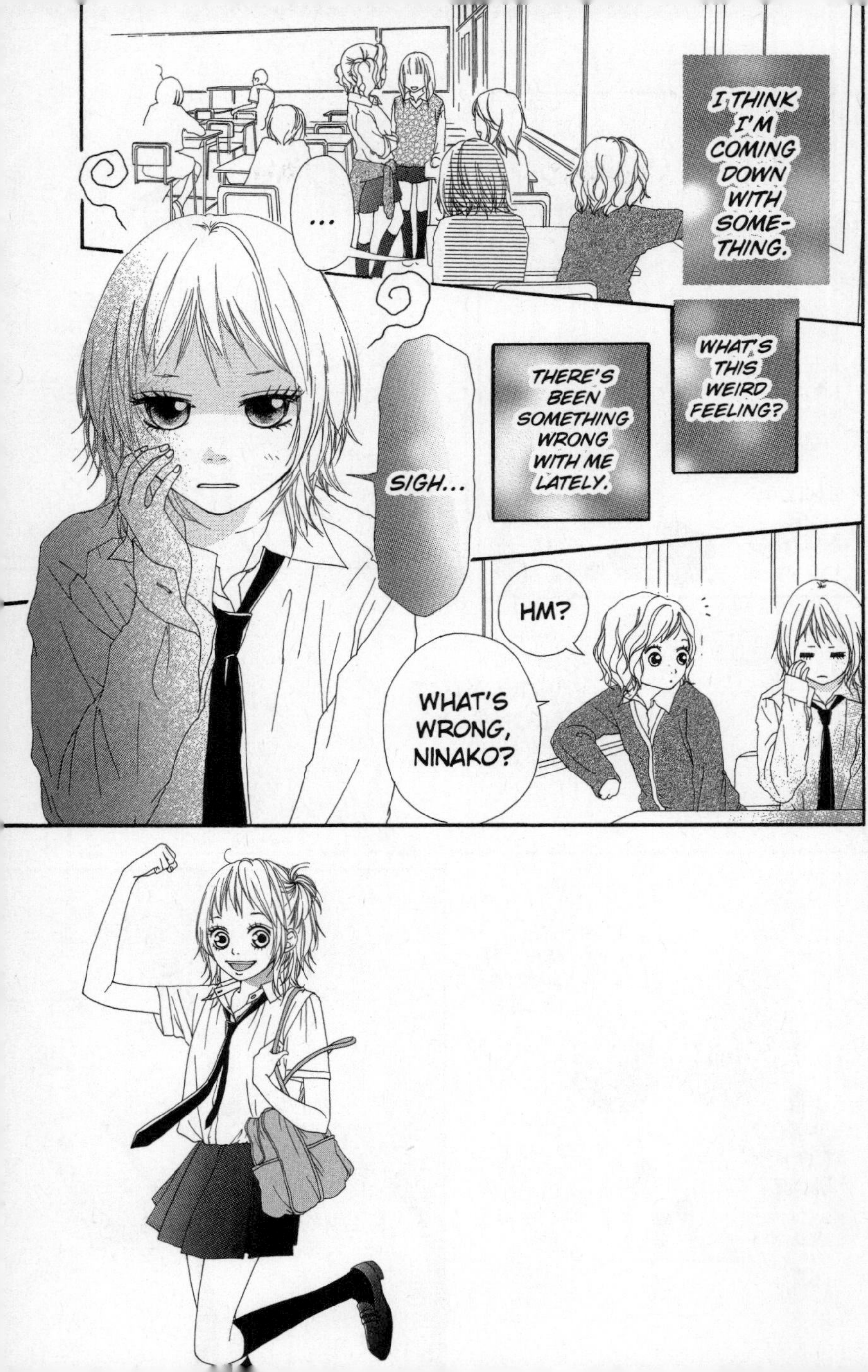
I THINK I'M COMING DOWN WITH SOME-THING.
...
WHAT'S THIS WEIRD FEELING?
THERE'S BEEN SOMETHING WRONG WITH ME LATELY.
SIGH...
HM?
WHAT'S WRONG, NINAKO?

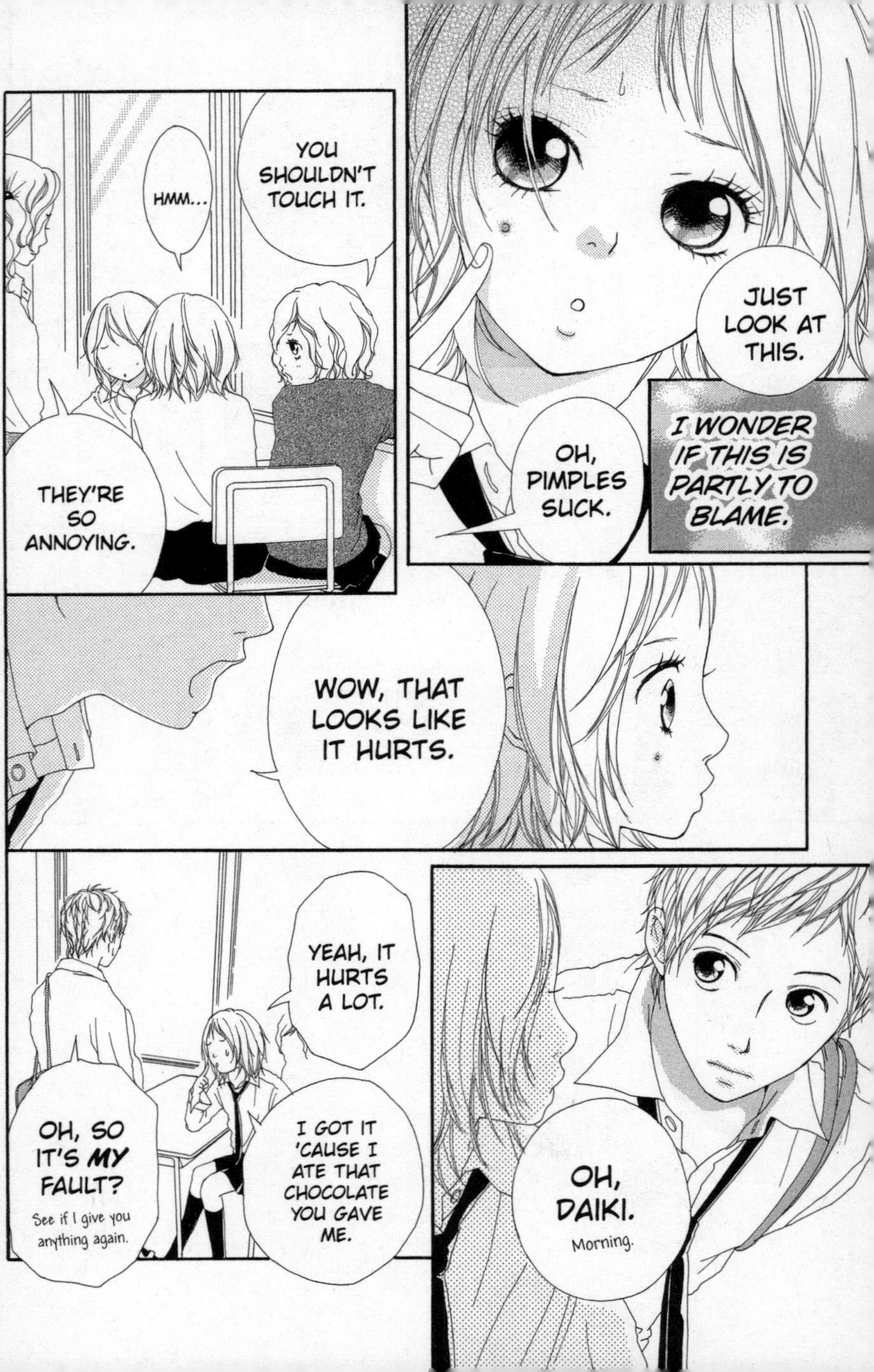
JUST LOOK AT THIS.
OH, PIMPLES SUCK.
I WONDER IF THIS IS PARTLY TO BLAME.
YOU SHOULDN'T TOUCH IT.
HMM...
THEY'RE SO ANNOYING.
WOW, THAT LOOKS LIKE IT HURTS.
OH, DAIKI.
Morning.
YEAH, IT HURTS A LOT.
I GOT IT 'CAUSE I ATE THAT CHOCOLATE YOU GAVE ME.
OH, SO IT'S *MY* FAULT?
See if I give you anything again.

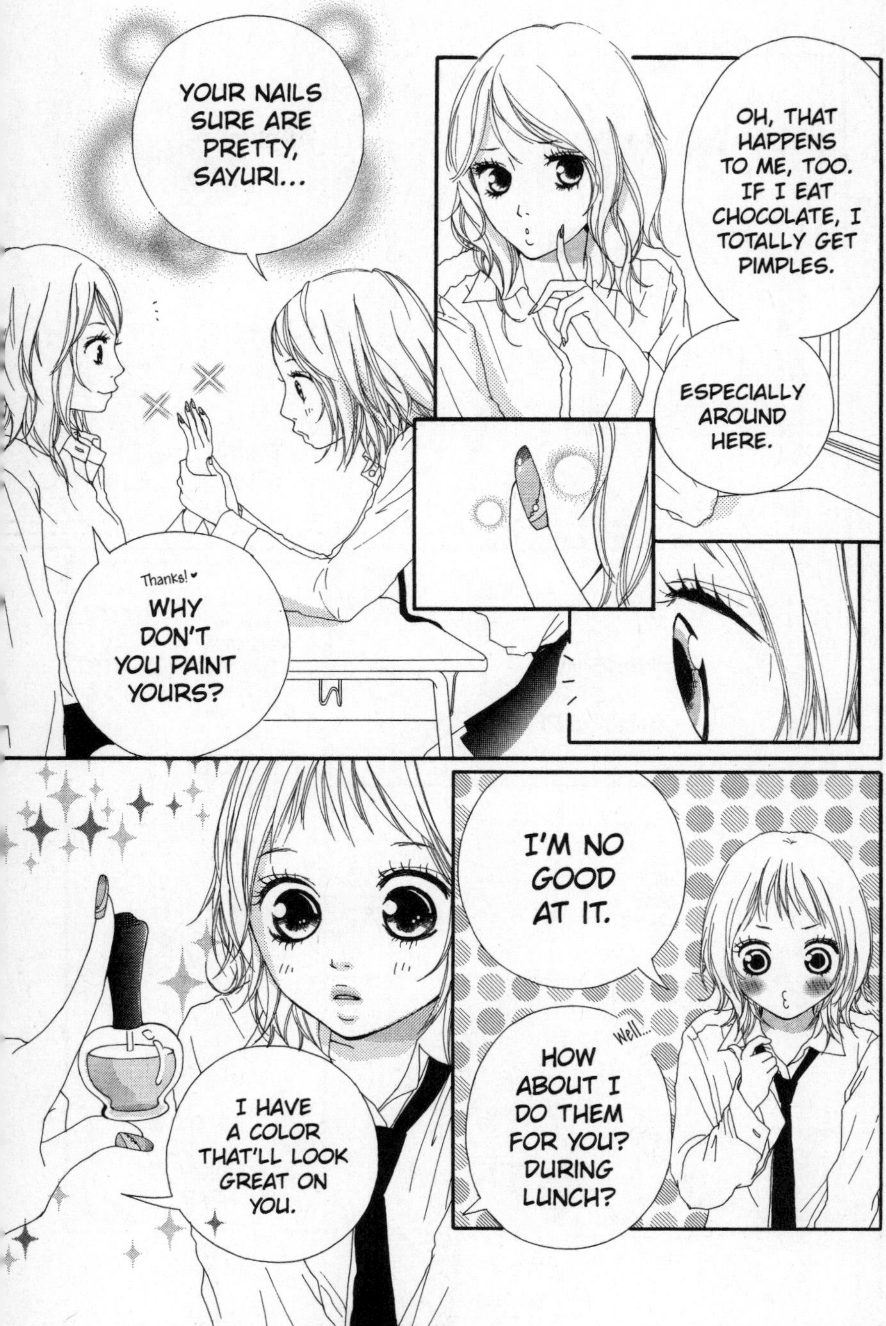
OH, THAT HAPPENS TO ME, TOO. IF I EAT CHOCOLATE, I TOTALLY GET PIMPLES.
ESPECIALLY AROUND HERE.
YOUR NAILS SURE ARE PRETTY, SAYURI...
Thanks! WHY DON'T YOU PAINT YOURS?
I'M NO GOOD AT IT.
Well...
HOW ABOUT I DO THEM FOR YOU? DURING LUNCH?
I HAVE A COLOR THAT'LL LOOK GREAT ON YOU.

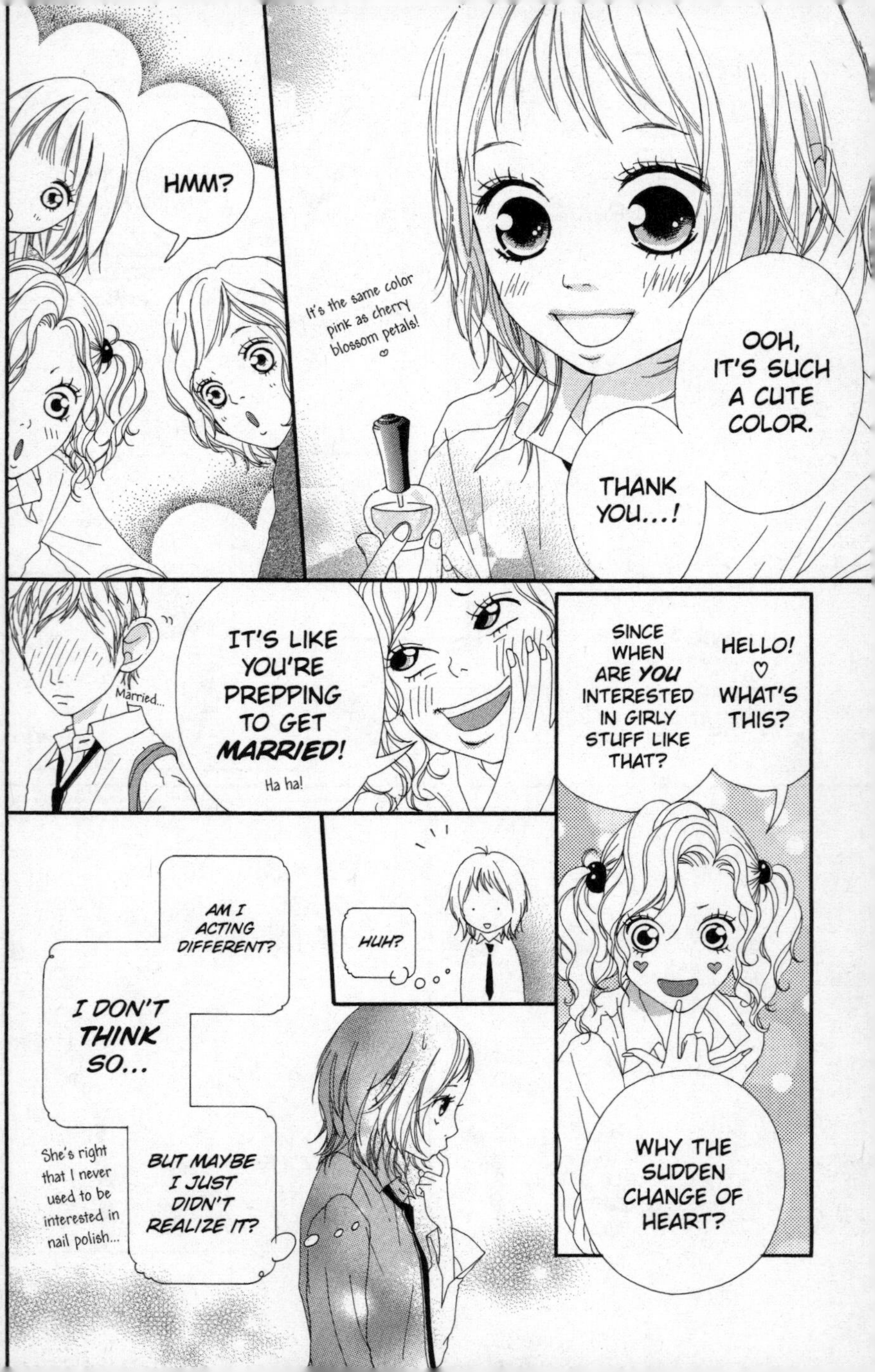

OOH, IT'S SUCH A CUTE COLOR.
THANK YOU...!
It's the same color pink as cherry blossom petals! ♡
HMM?
HELLO! ♡ WHAT'S THIS?
SINCE WHEN ARE *YOU* INTERESTED IN GIRLY STUFF LIKE THAT?
WHY THE SUDDEN CHANGE OF HEART?
IT'S LIKE YOU'RE PREPPING TO GET *MARRIED*!
Ha ha!
Married...
HUH?
AM I ACTING DIFFERENT?
I DON'T **THINK** SO...
BUT MAYBE I JUST DIDN'T REALIZE IT?
She's right that I never used to be interested in nail polish...

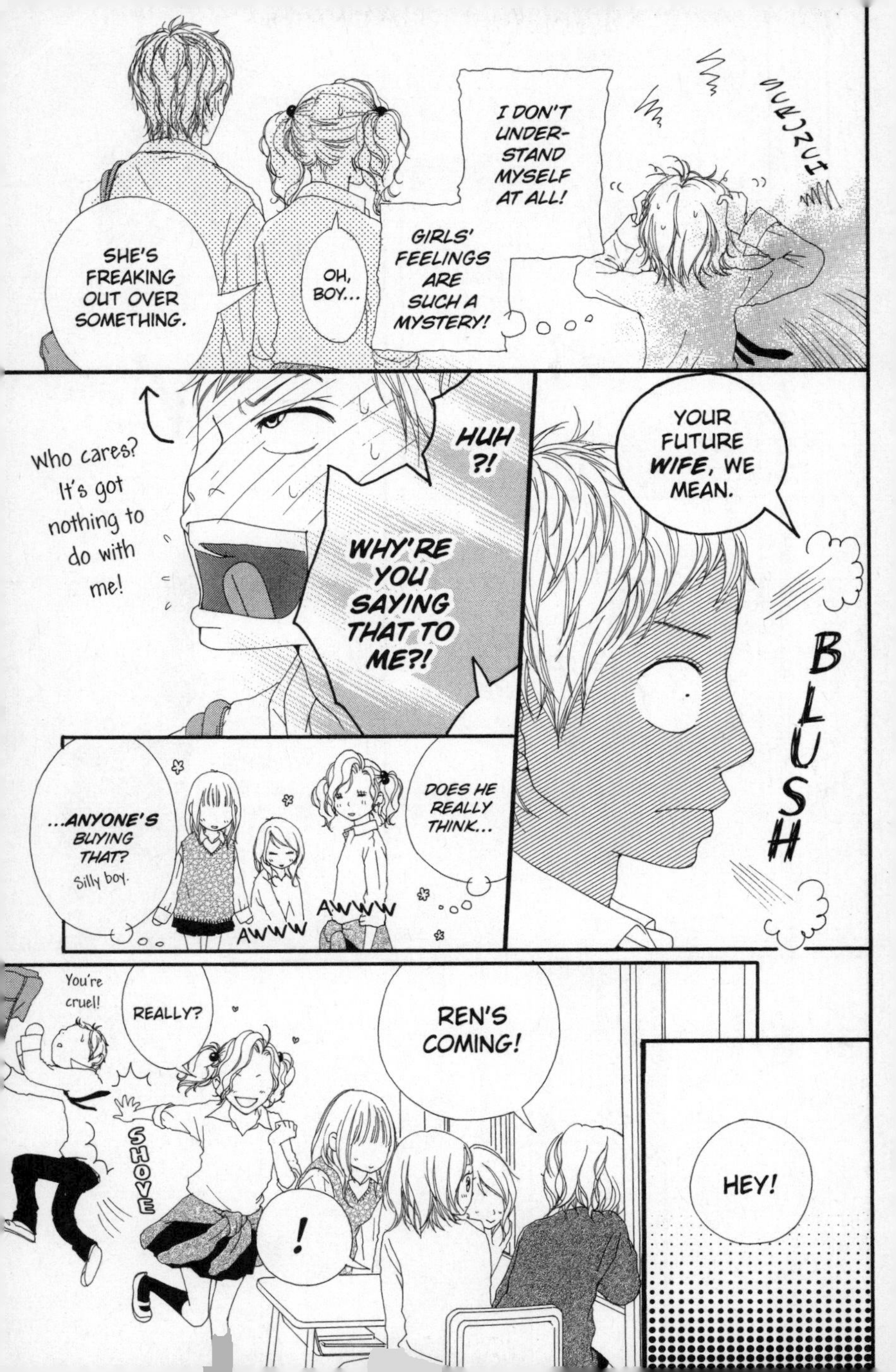
I DON'T UNDERSTAND MYSELF AT ALL!
GIRLS' FEELINGS ARE SUCH A MYSTERY!
OH, BOY...
SHE'S FREAKING OUT OVER SOMETHING.
YOUR FUTURE WIFE, WE MEAN.
BLUSH
HUH?!
WHY'RE YOU SAYING THAT TO ME?!
Who cares? It's got nothing to do with me!
DOES HE REALLY THINK...
AWWW
AWWW
...ANYONE'S BUYING THAT? Silly boy.
HEY!
REN'S COMING!
!
REALLY?
You're cruel!
SHOVE

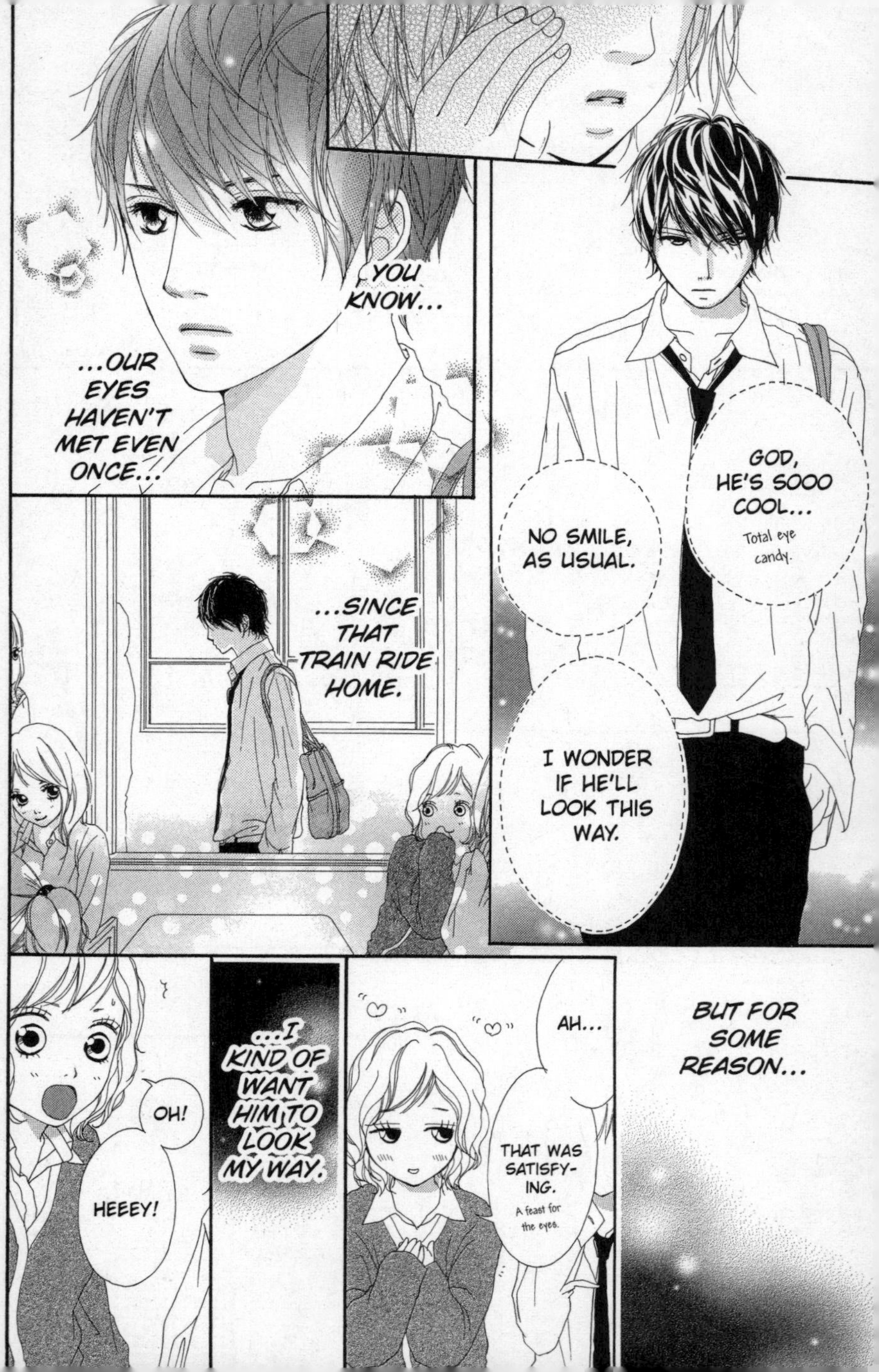
YOU KNOW...
...OUR EYES HAVEN'T MET EVEN ONCE...
GOD, HE'S SOOO COOL...
Total eye candy.
NO SMILE, AS USUAL.
I WONDER IF HE'LL LOOK THIS WAY.
...SINCE THAT TRAIN RIDE HOME.
BUT FOR SOME REASON...
AH...
THAT WAS SATISFY-ING.
A feast for the eyes.
...I KIND OF WANT HIM TO LOOK MY WAY.
OH!
HEEEY!

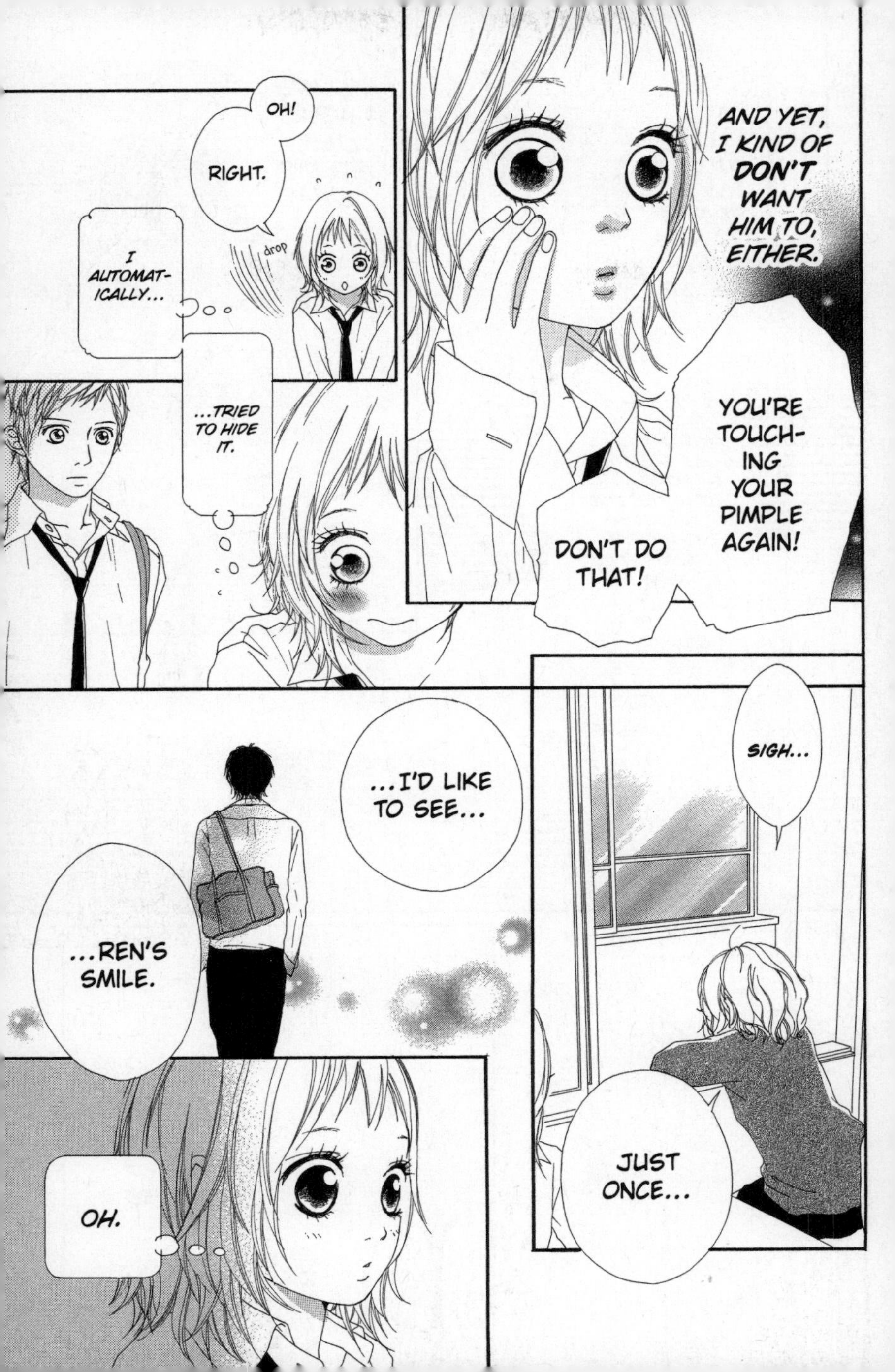
AND YET, I KIND OF DON'T WANT HIM TO, EITHER.
YOU'RE TOUCHING YOUR PIMPLE AGAIN!
DON'T DO THAT!
OH!
RIGHT.
drop
I AUTOMATICALLY...
...TRIED TO HIDE IT.
SIGH...
JUST ONCE...
...I'D LIKE TO SEE...
...REN'S SMILE.
OH.

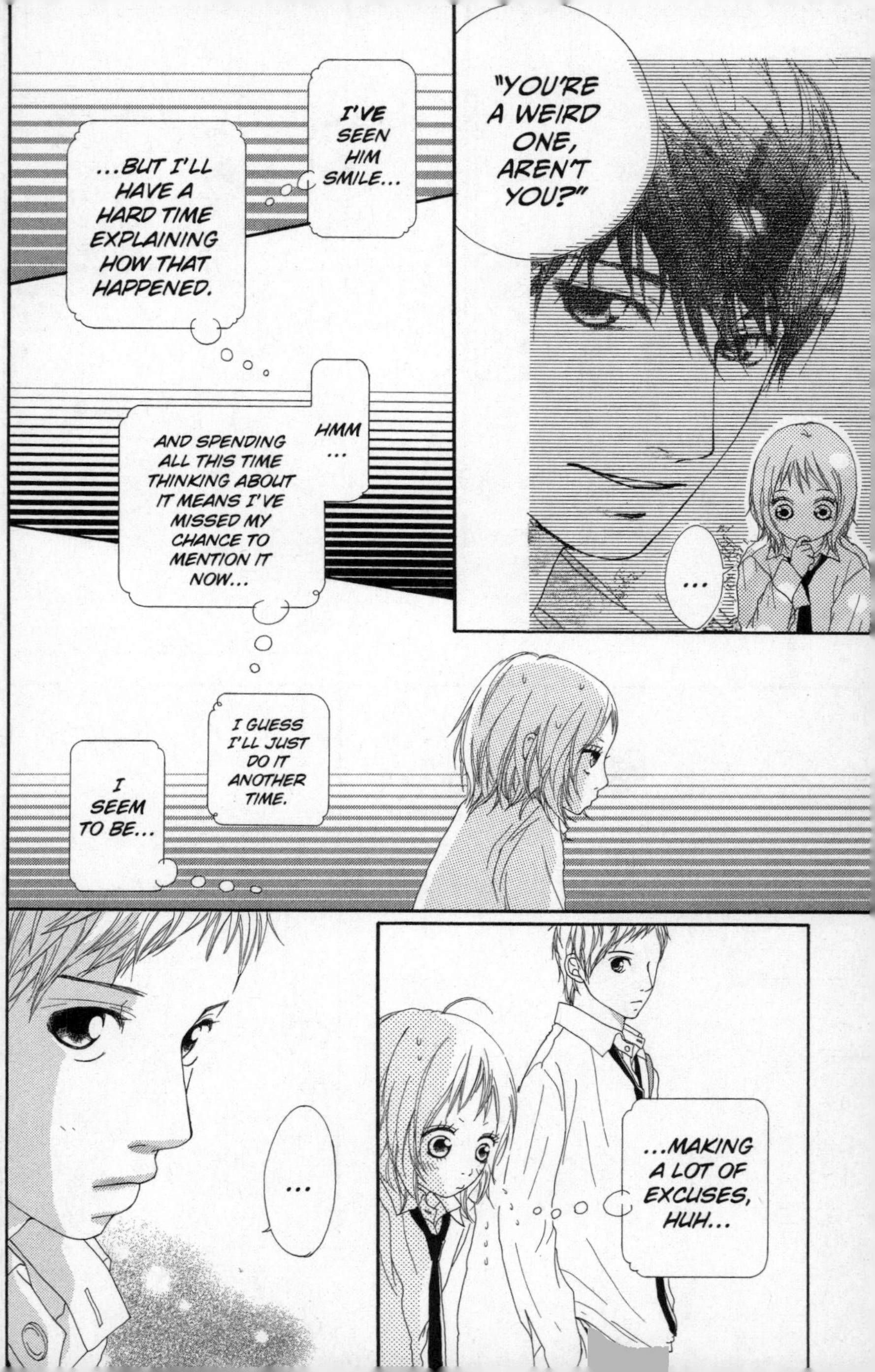
"YOU'RE A WEIRD ONE, AREN'T YOU?"
...
I'VE SEEN HIM SMILE...
...BUT I'LL HAVE A HARD TIME EXPLAINING HOW THAT HAPPENED.
HMM...
AND SPENDING ALL THIS TIME THINKING ABOUT IT MEANS I'VE MISSED MY CHANCE TO MENTION IT NOW...
I GUESS I'LL JUST DO IT ANOTHER TIME.
I SEEM TO BE...
...MAKING A LOT OF EXCUSES, HUH...
...

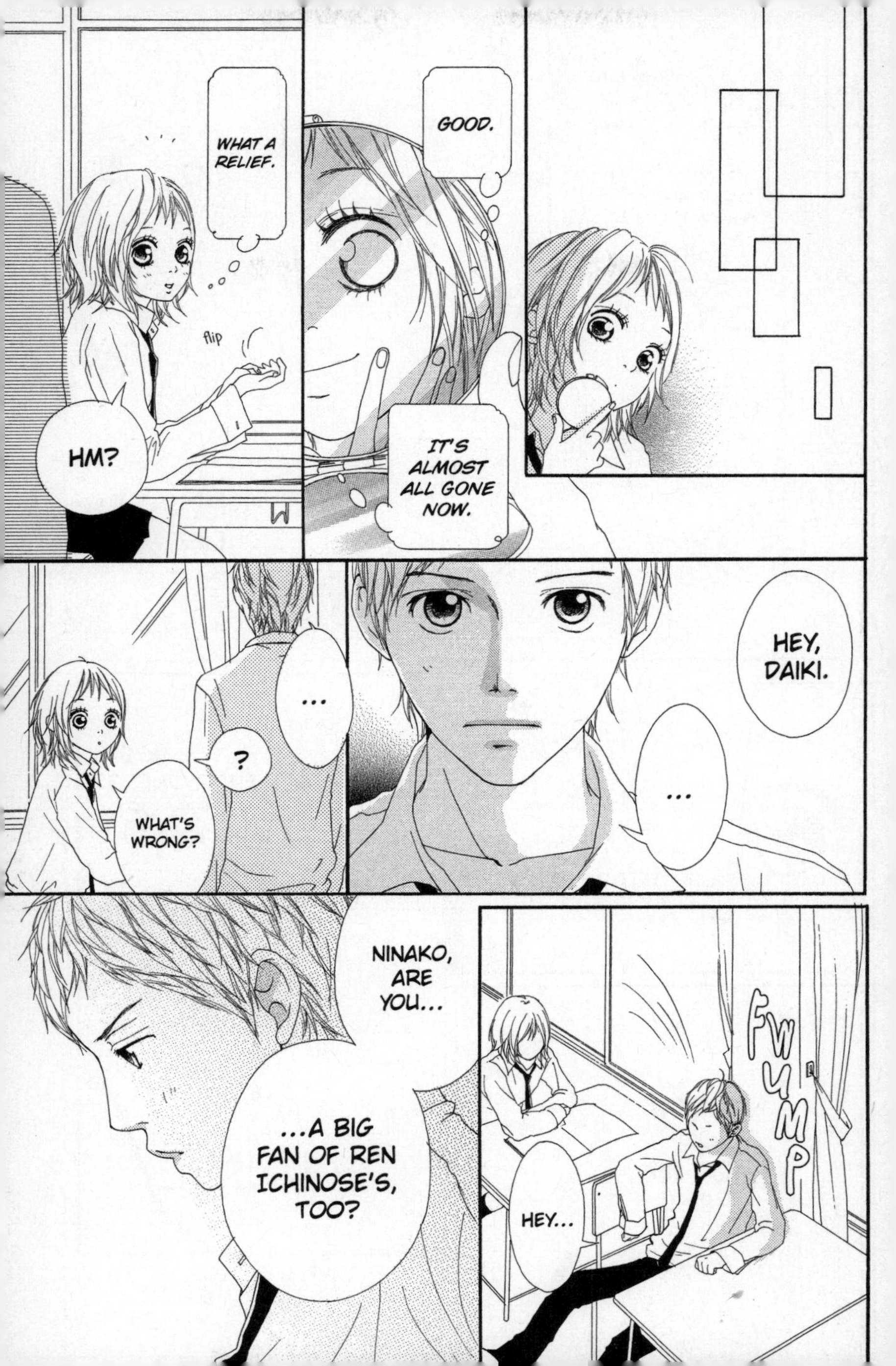
GOOD.
IT'S ALMOST ALL GONE NOW.
WHAT A RELIEF.
flip
HM?
HEY, DAIKI.
...
...
?
WHAT'S WRONG?
FWUMP
HEY...
NINAKO, ARE YOU...
...A BIG FAN OF REN ICHINOSE'S, TOO?

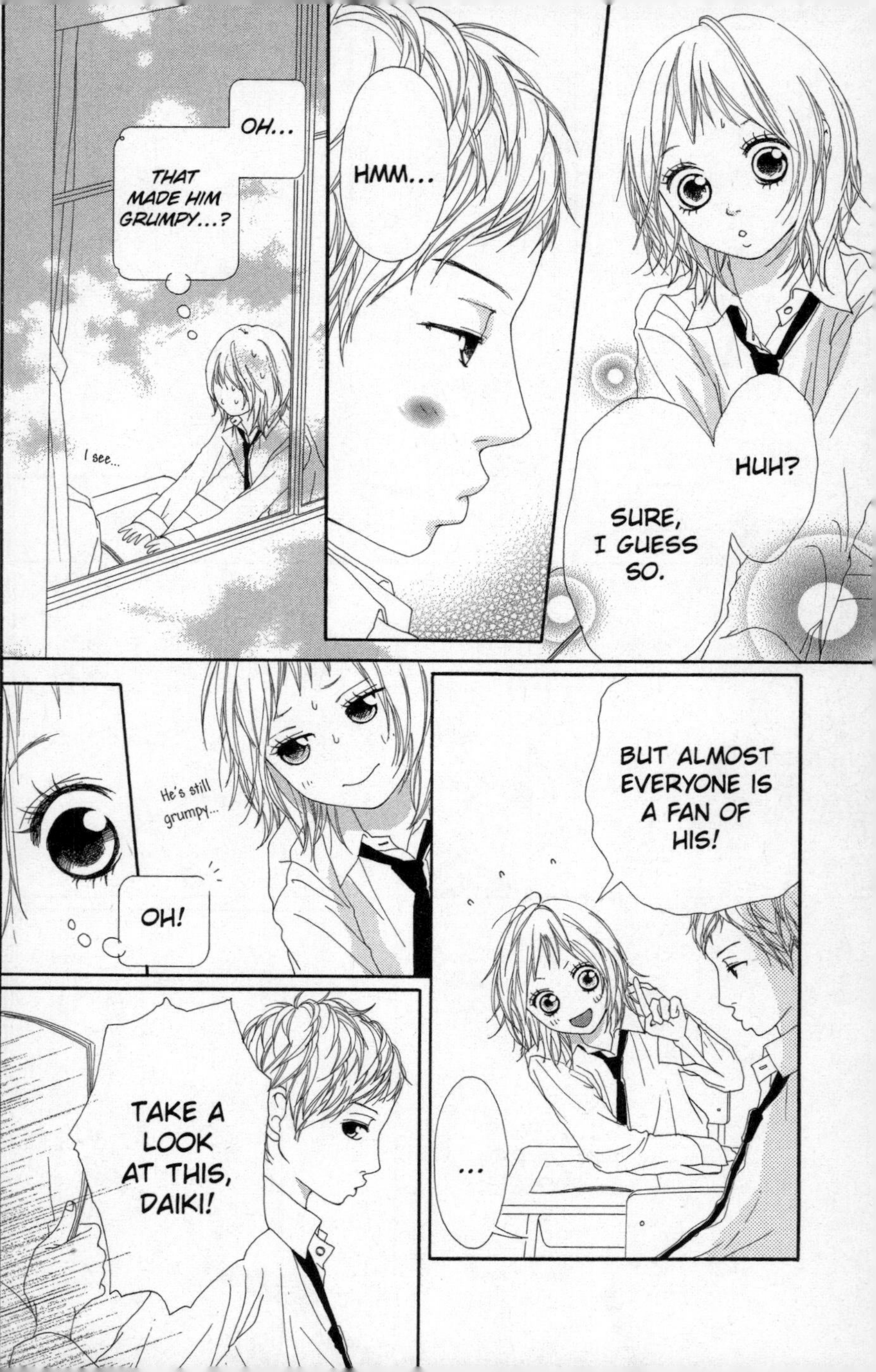
HUH?
SURE, I GUESS SO.
HMM...
OH...
THAT MADE HIM GRUMPY...?
I see...
BUT ALMOST EVERYONE IS A FAN OF HIS!
...
He's still grumpy...
OH!
TAKE A LOOK AT THIS, DAIKI!

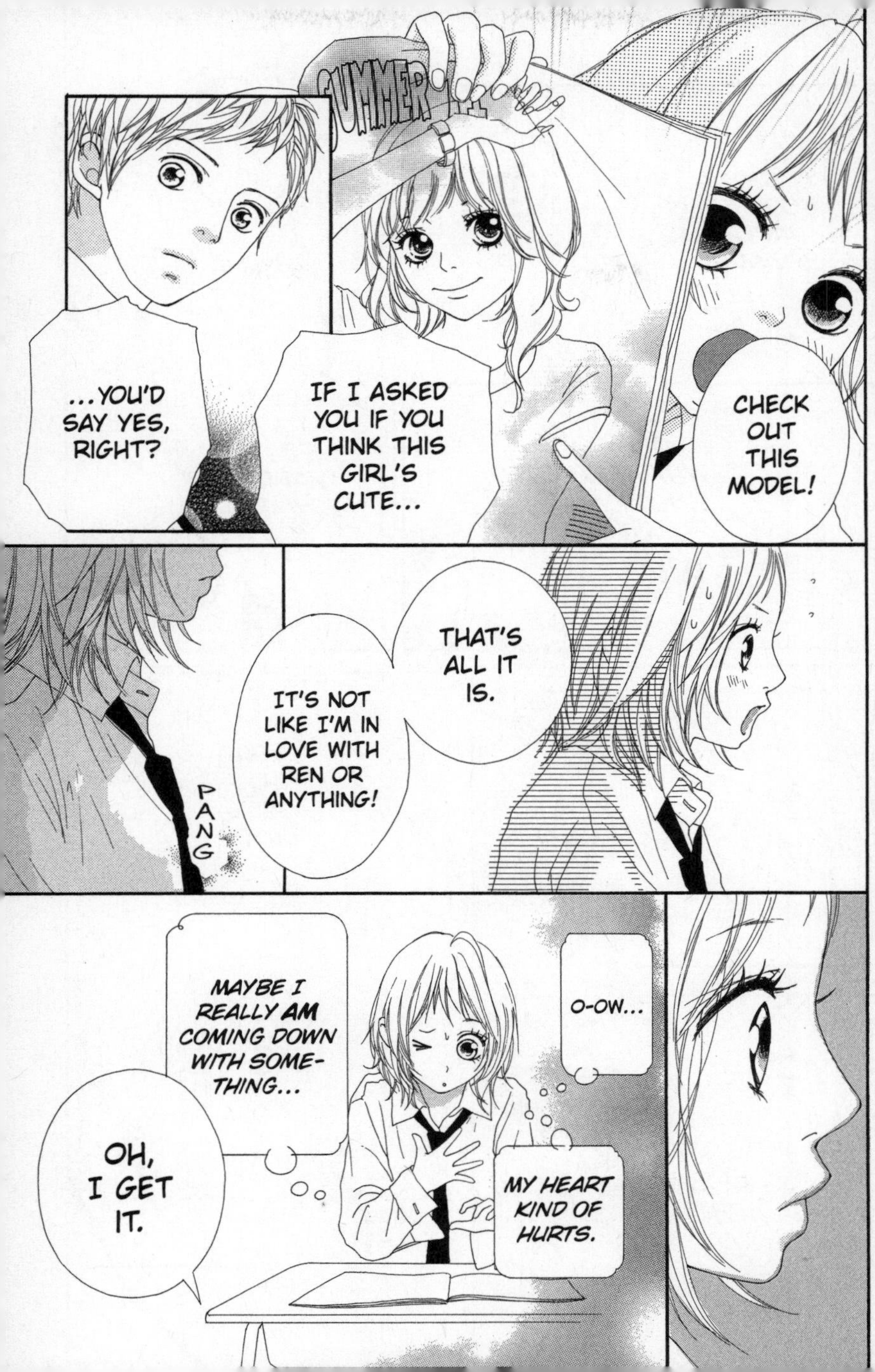
CHECK OUT THIS MODEL!
SUMMER
IF I ASKED YOU IF YOU THINK THIS GIRL'S CUTE...
...YOU'D SAY YES, RIGHT?
THAT'S ALL IT IS.
IT'S NOT LIKE I'M IN LOVE WITH REN OR ANYTHING!
PANG
O-OW...
MY HEART KIND OF HURTS.
MAYBE I REALLY AM COMING DOWN WITH SOME-THING...
OH, I GET IT.

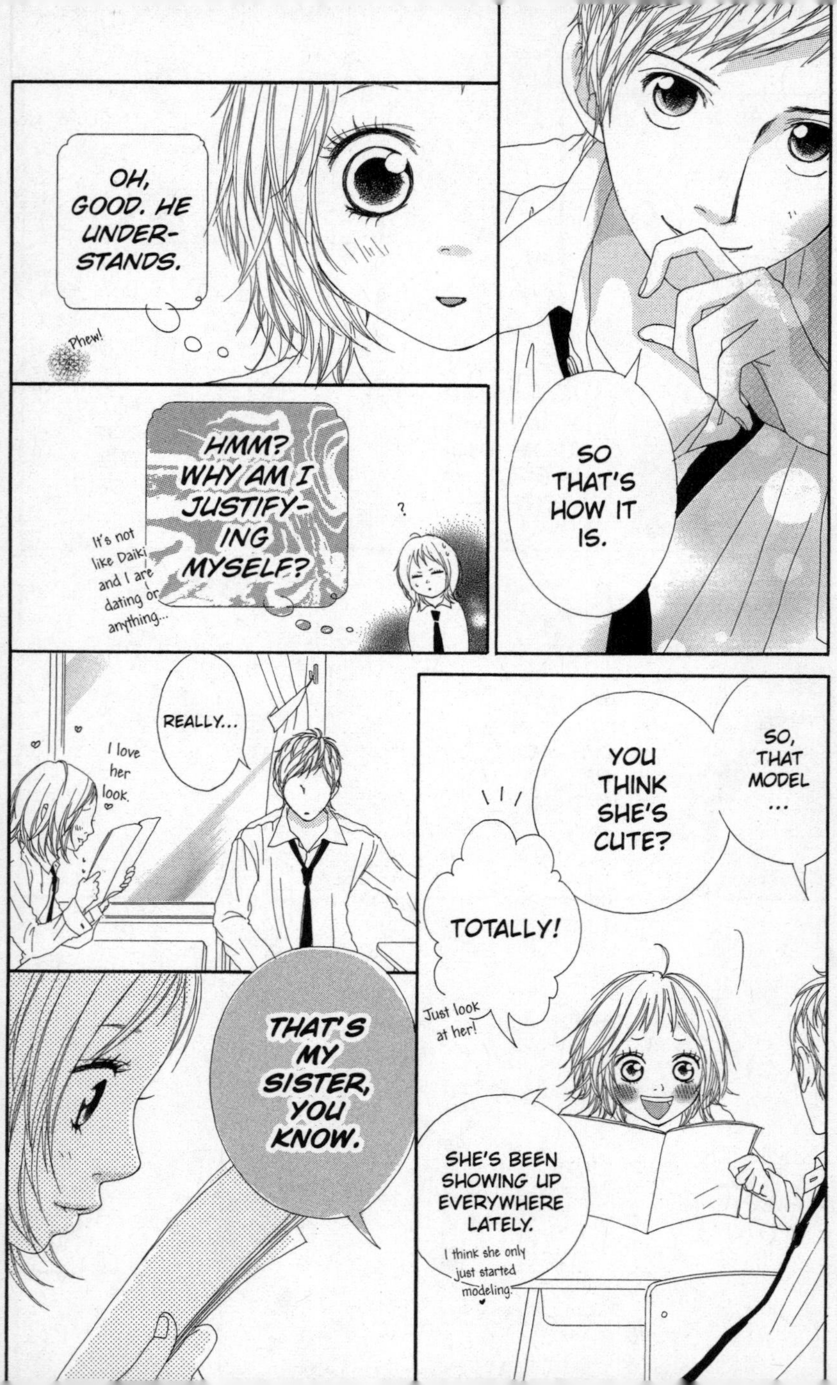
SO THAT'S HOW IT IS.
OH, GOOD. HE UNDER-STANDS.
Phew!
HMM? WHY AM I JUSTIFY-ING MYSELF?
It's not like Daiki and I are dating or anything...
?
SO, THAT MODEL ...
YOU THINK SHE'S CUTE?
TOTALLY!
Just look at her!
SHE'S BEEN SHOWING UP EVERYWHERE LATELY.
I think she only just started modeling.
REALLY...
I love her look.
THAT'S MY SISTER, YOU KNOW.

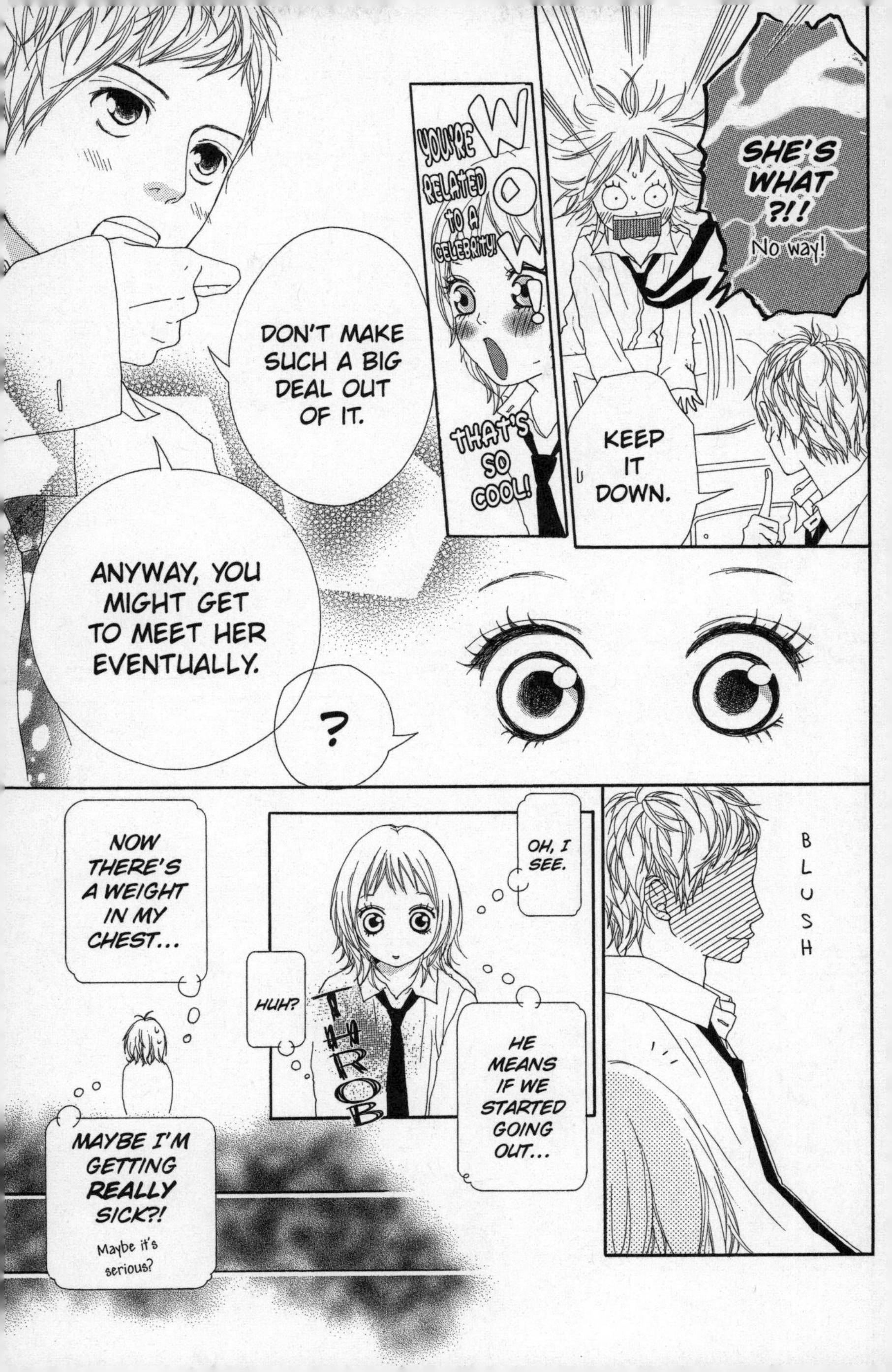
SHE'S WHAT ?!!
No way!
KEEP IT DOWN.
YOU'RE RELATED TO A CELEBRITY!
WOW
THAT'S SO COOL!
?
DON'T MAKE SUCH A BIG DEAL OUT OF IT.
ANYWAY, YOU MIGHT GET TO MEET HER EVENTUALLY.
BLUSH
OH, I SEE.
HE MEANS IF WE STARTED GOING OUT...
HUH?
THROB
NOW THERE'S A WEIGHT IN MY CHEST...
MAYBE I'M GETTING REALLY SICK?!
Maybe it's serious?

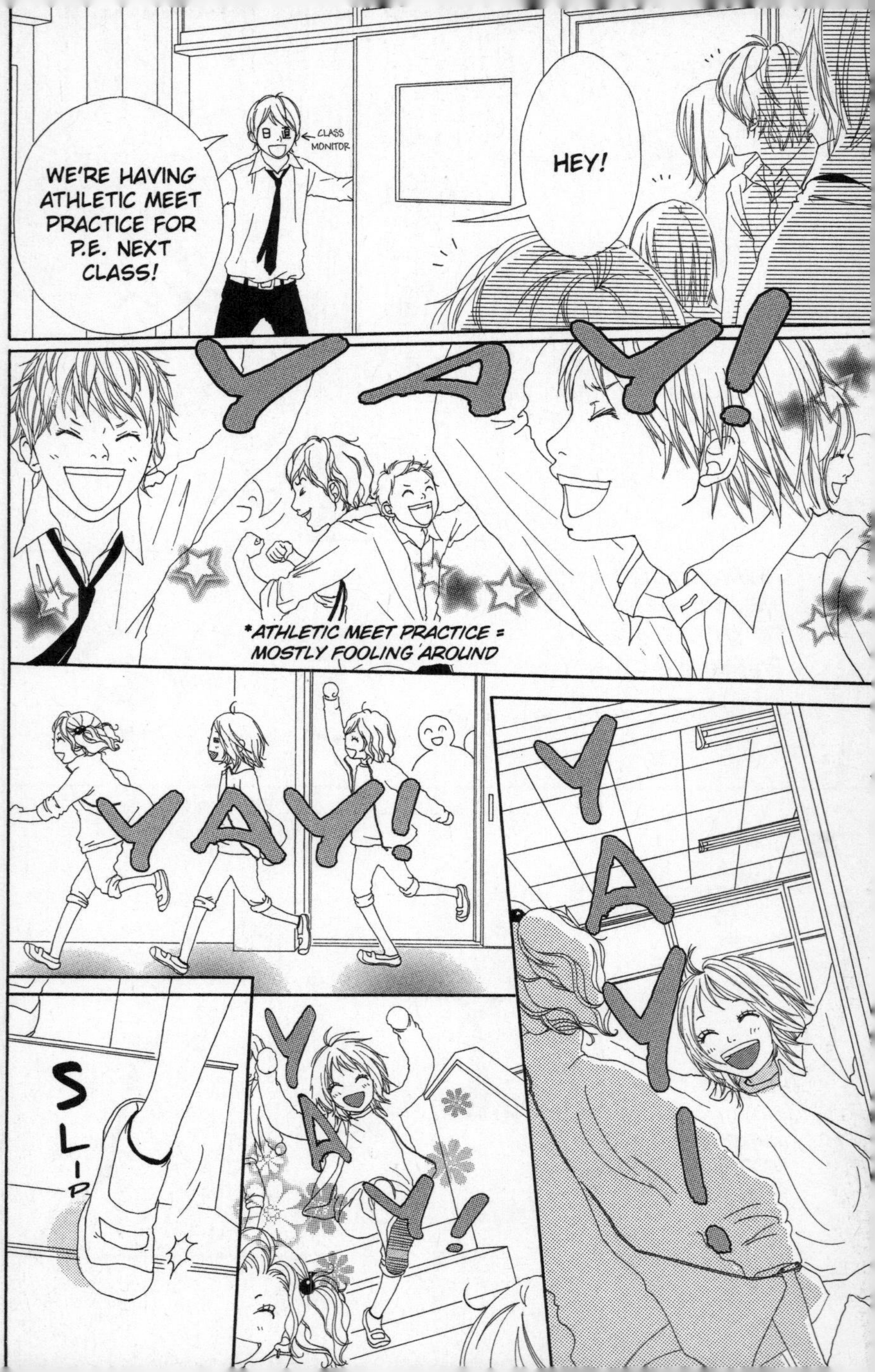
HEY!
CLASS MONITOR
WE'RE HAVING ATHLETIC MEET PRACTICE FOR P.E. NEXT CLASS!
YAY!
*ATHLETIC MEET PRACTICE = MOSTLY FOOLING AROUND
YAY!
YAY!
YAY!
SLIP

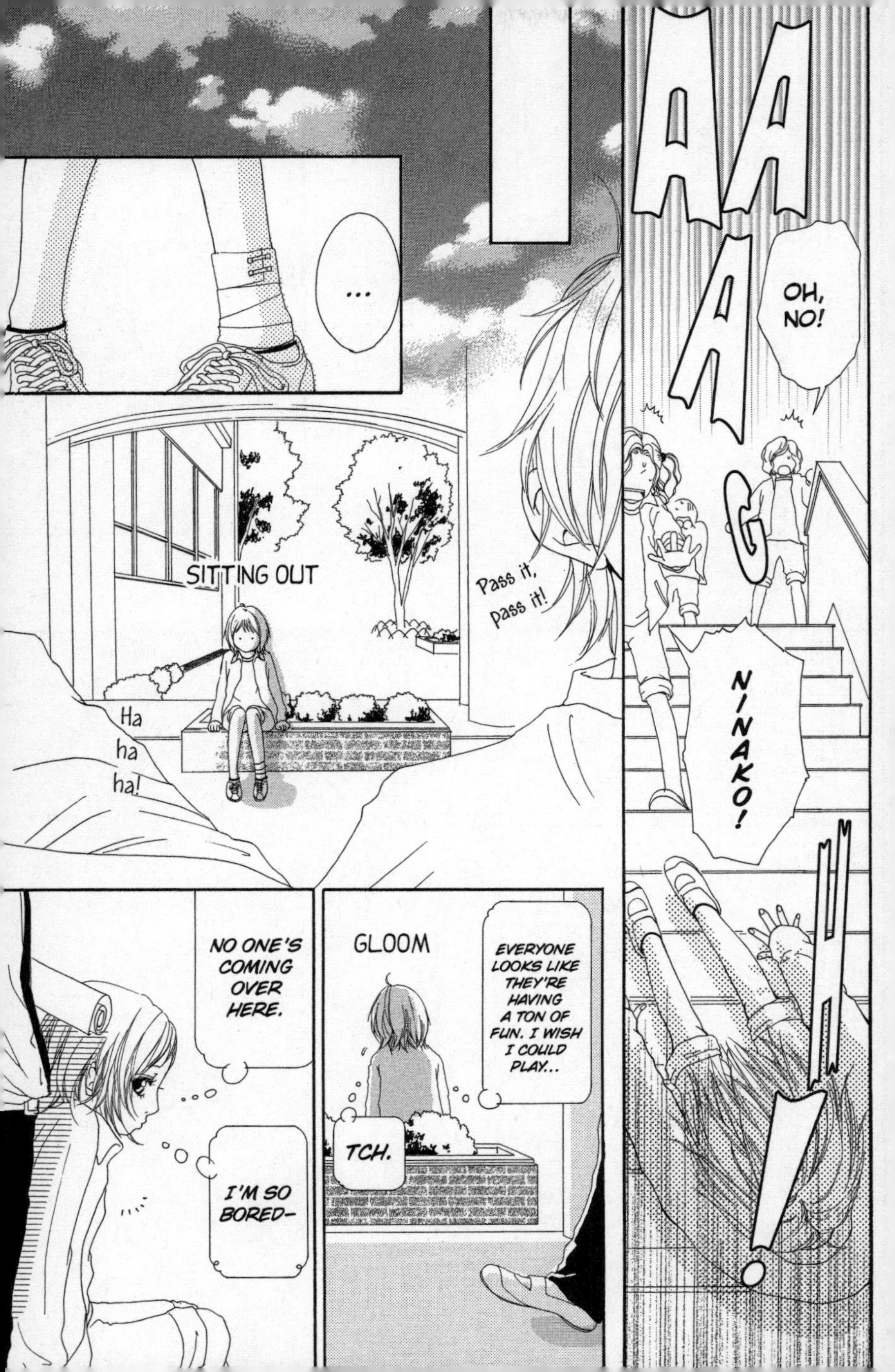
AAAAGH!
OH, NO!
NINAKO!
...
Pass it, pass it!
SITTING OUT
Ha ha ha!
EVERYONE LOOKS LIKE THEY'RE HAVING A TON OF FUN. I WISH I COULD PLAY...
GLOOM
TCH.
NO ONE'S COMING OVER HERE.
I'M SO BORED-

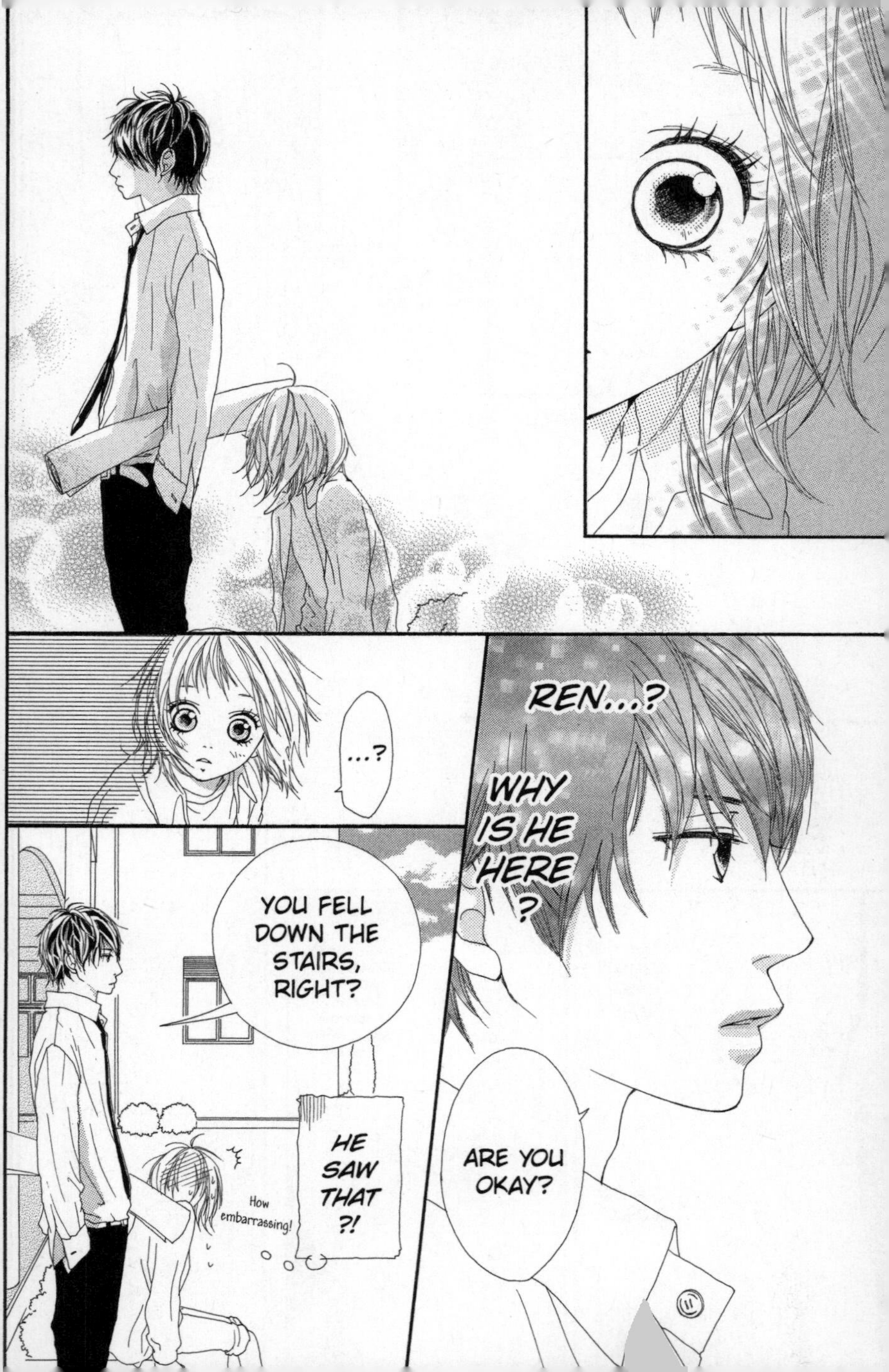
REN...?
WHY IS HE HERE?
ARE YOU OKAY?
...?
YOU FELL DOWN THE STAIRS, RIGHT?
HE SAW THAT?!
How embarrassing!

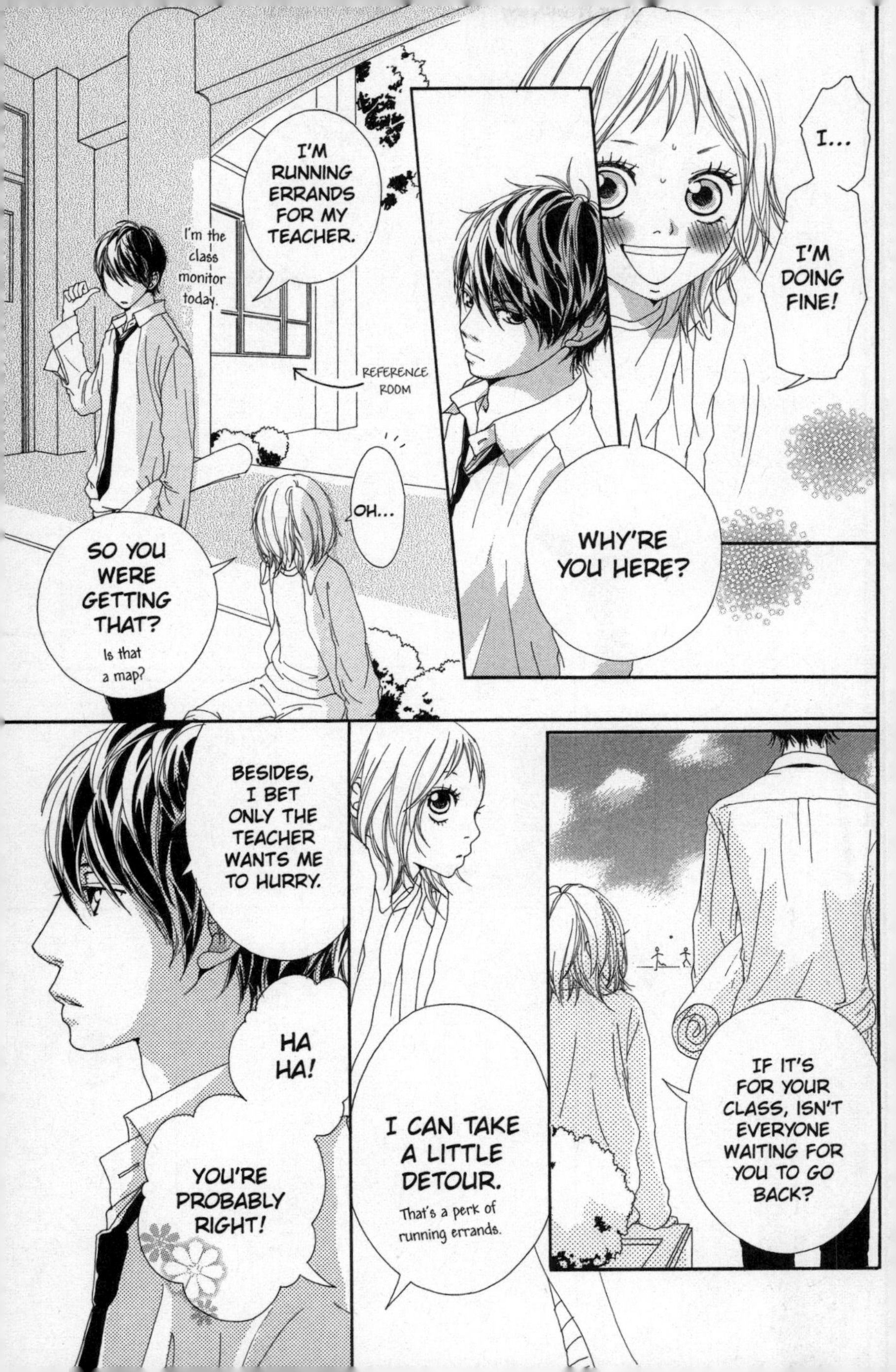
I...
I'M DOING FINE!
WHY'RE YOU HERE?
I'M RUNNING ERRANDS FOR MY TEACHER.
I'm the class monitor today.
REFERENCE ROOM
OH...
SO YOU WERE GETTING THAT?
Is that a map?
IF IT'S FOR YOUR CLASS, ISN'T EVERYONE WAITING FOR YOU TO GO BACK?
I CAN TAKE A LITTLE DETOUR.
That's a perk of running errands.
BESIDES, I BET ONLY THE TEACHER WANTS ME TO HURRY.
HA HA!
YOU'RE PROBABLY RIGHT!

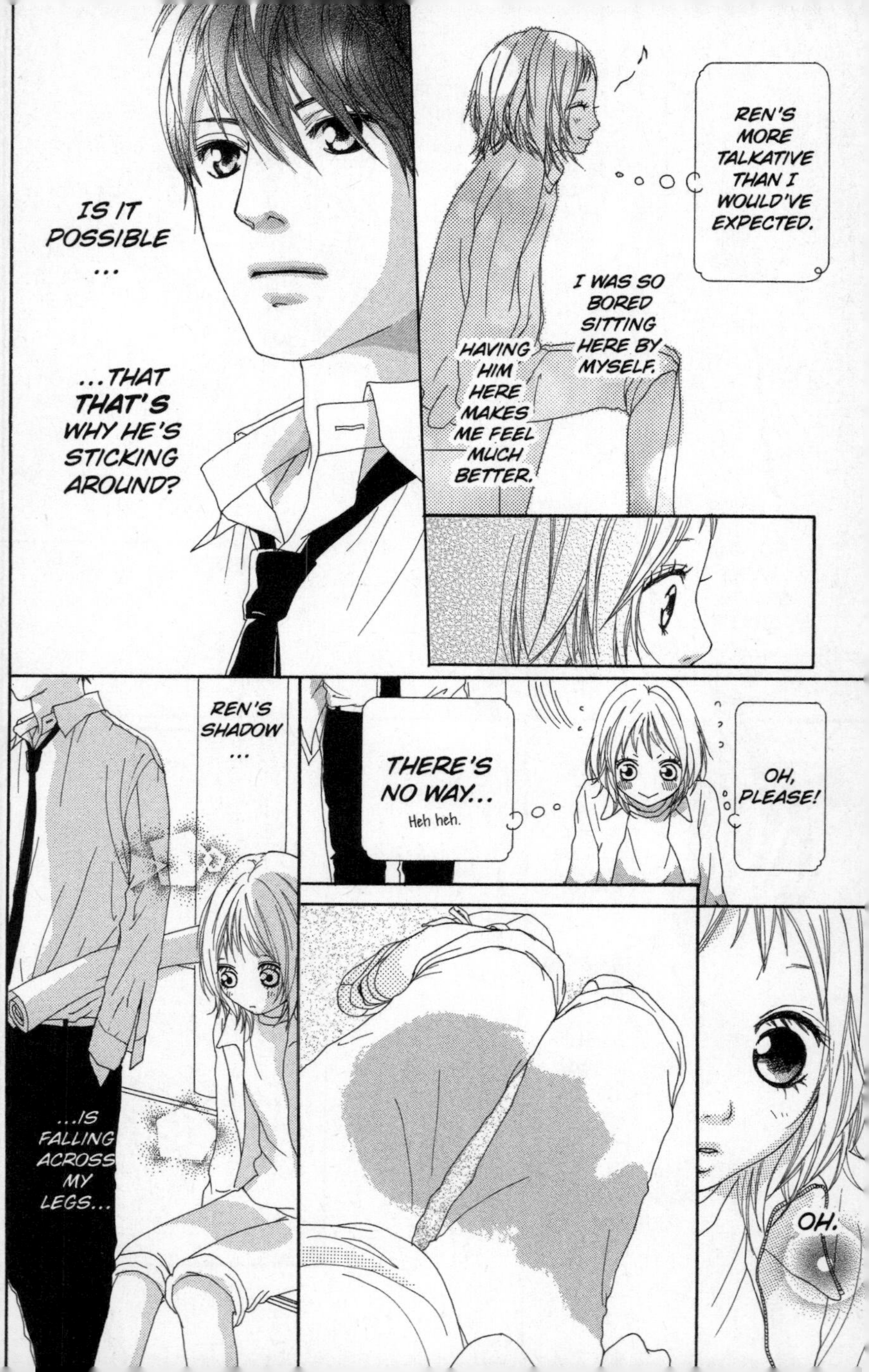
REN'S MORE TALKATIVE THAN I WOULD'VE EXPECTED.
I WAS SO BORED SITTING HERE BY MYSELF.
HAVING HIM HERE MAKES ME FEEL MUCH BETTER.
IS IT POSSIBLE...
...THAT THAT'S WHY HE'S STICKING AROUND?
OH, PLEASE!
THERE'S NO WAY...
Heh heh.
OH.
REN'S SHADOW...
...IS FALLING ACROSS MY LEGS...

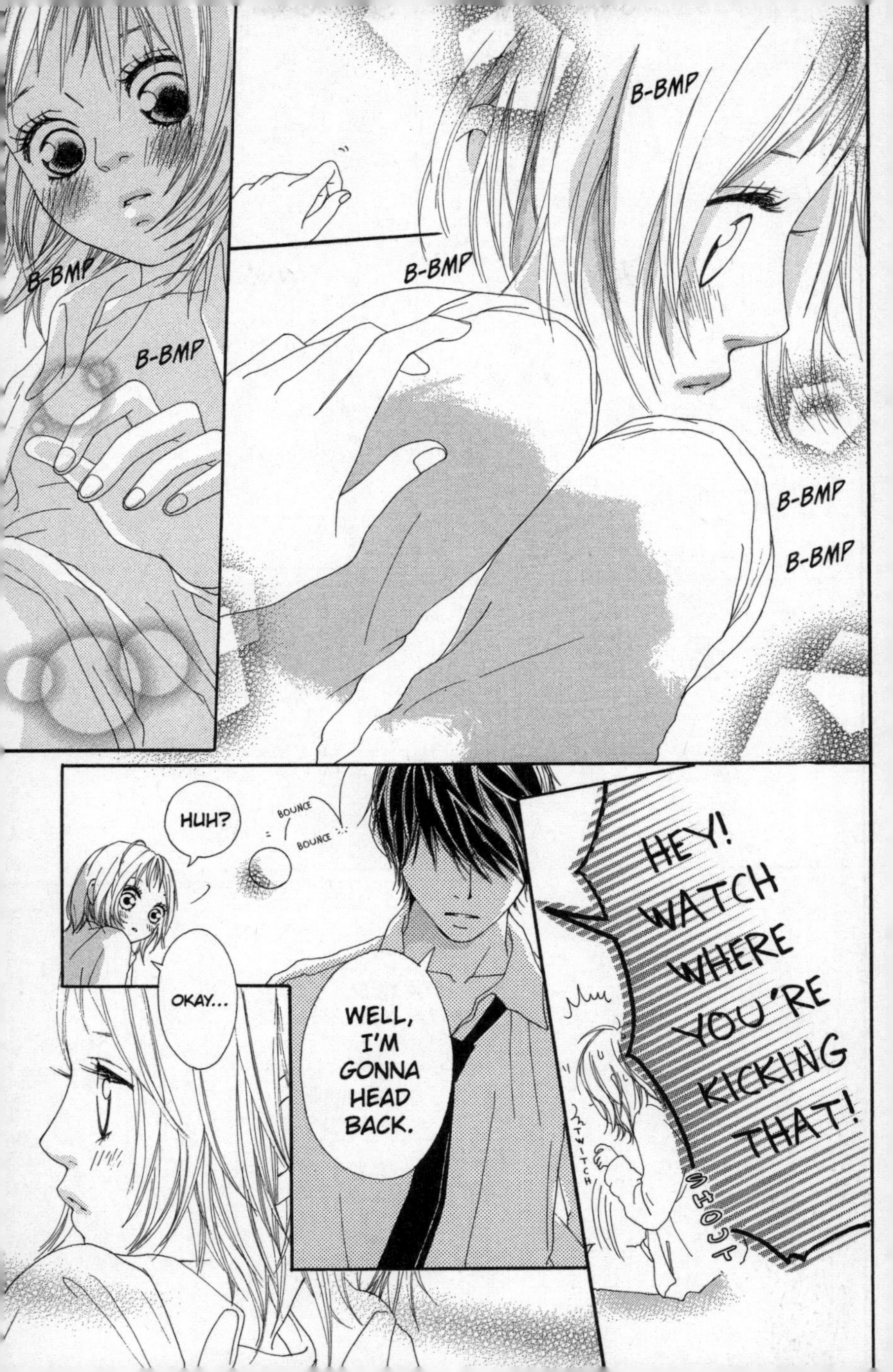
B-BMP
B-BMP
B-BMP
B-BMP
B-BMP
B-BMP
HEY! WATCH WHERE YOU'RE KICKING THAT!
SHOUT
TWITCH
WELL, I'M GONNA HEAD BACK.
HUH?
BOUNCE
BOUNCE
OKAY...

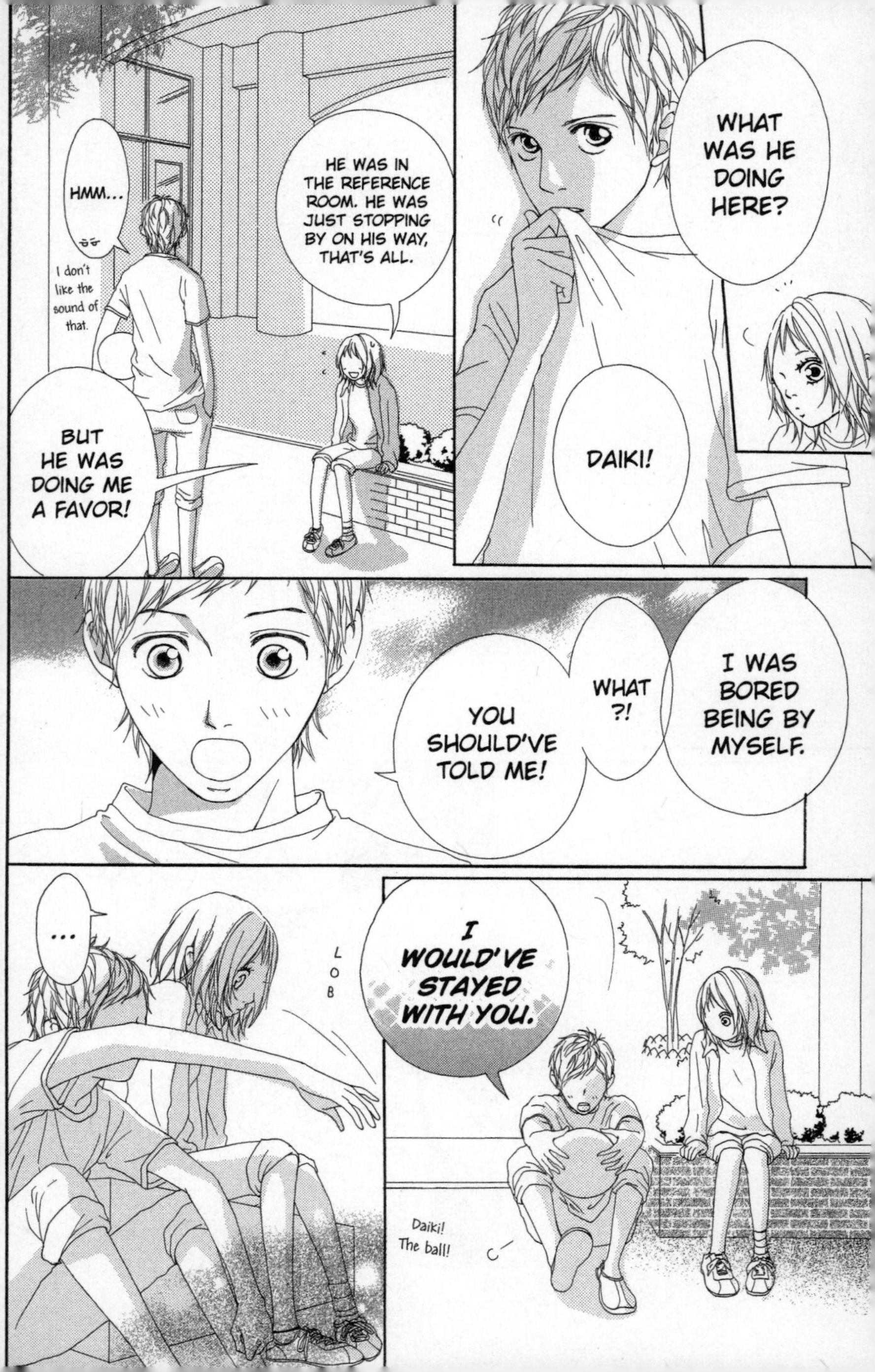
WHAT WAS HE DOING HERE?
DAIKI!
HE WAS IN THE REFERENCE ROOM. HE WAS JUST STOPPING BY ON HIS WAY, THAT'S ALL.
HMM...
I don't like the sound of that.
BUT HE WAS DOING ME A FAVOR!
I WAS BORED BEING BY MYSELF.
WHAT?!
YOU SHOULD'VE TOLD ME!
I WOULD'VE STAYED WITH YOU.
Daiki! The ball!
LOB
...

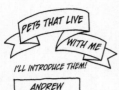

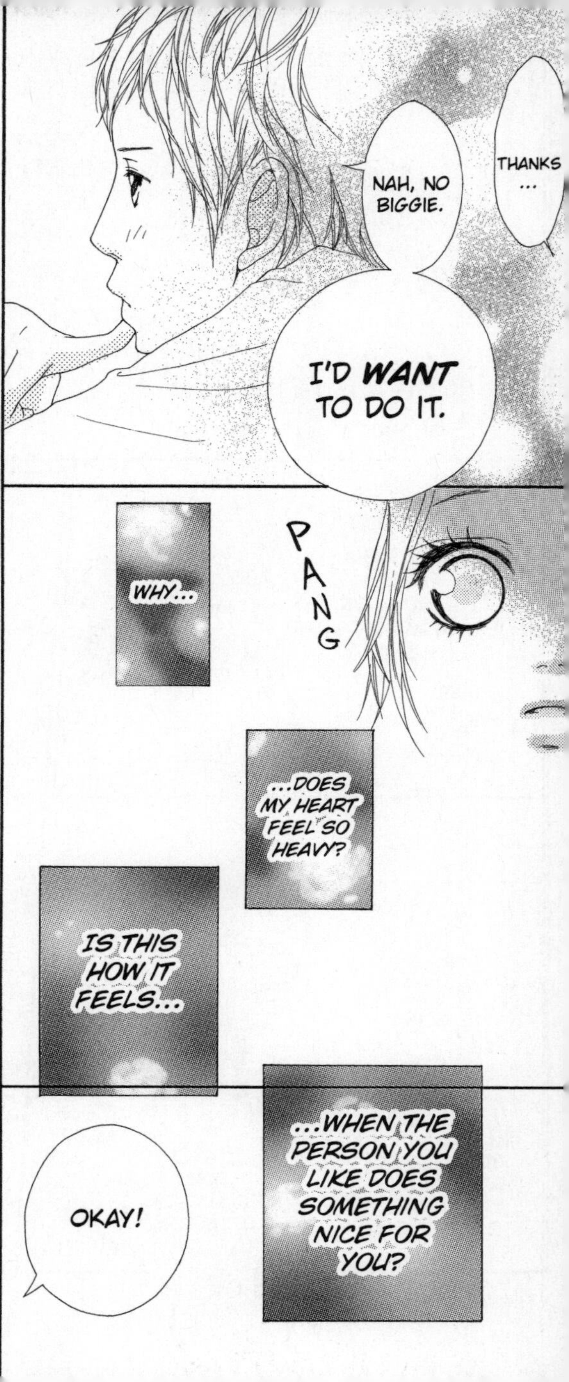
THANKS...
NAH, NO BIGGIE.
I'D **WANT** TO DO IT.
PANG
WHY...
...DOES MY HEART FEEL SO HEAVY?
IS THIS HOW IT FEELS...
...WHEN THE PERSON YOU LIKE DOES SOMETHING NICE FOR YOU?
OKAY!

## PETS THAT LIVE WITH ME

I'LL INTRODUCE THEM!

### ANDREW

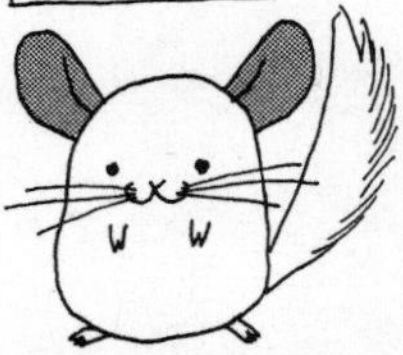

*I've had him the longest. He's white colored and very cautious—so cautious that he won't let people carry him. From behind he looks like a kagami mochi.**

### CINNAMON

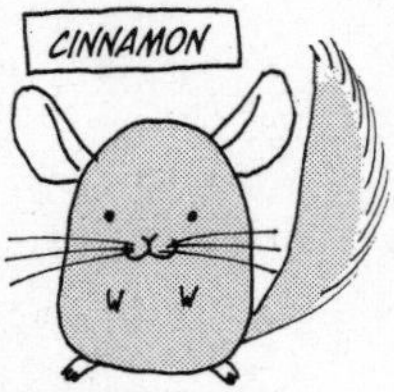

*I got him because I wanted to get Andrew a friend. His coat is cinnamon colored. That's why he's named Cinnamon. Uninspired, huh? He's incredibly jittery. He moves slowly, but he doesn't like being carried.*

### KOMUGI

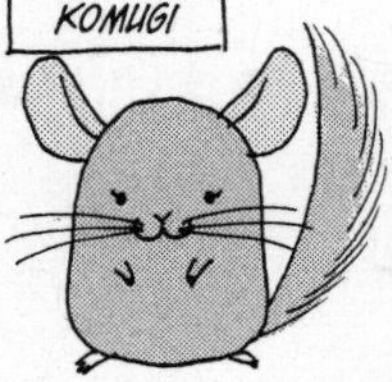

*I raised her from a baby. I wanted her to marry one of the other two. She and Andrew hit it off and exchanged vows! She's the only one who comes over to me and lets me pet her, but she doesn't like being carried.*

**To sum it up, none of my pets let me carry them.*

*A large rice cake offered to the gods during New Year's

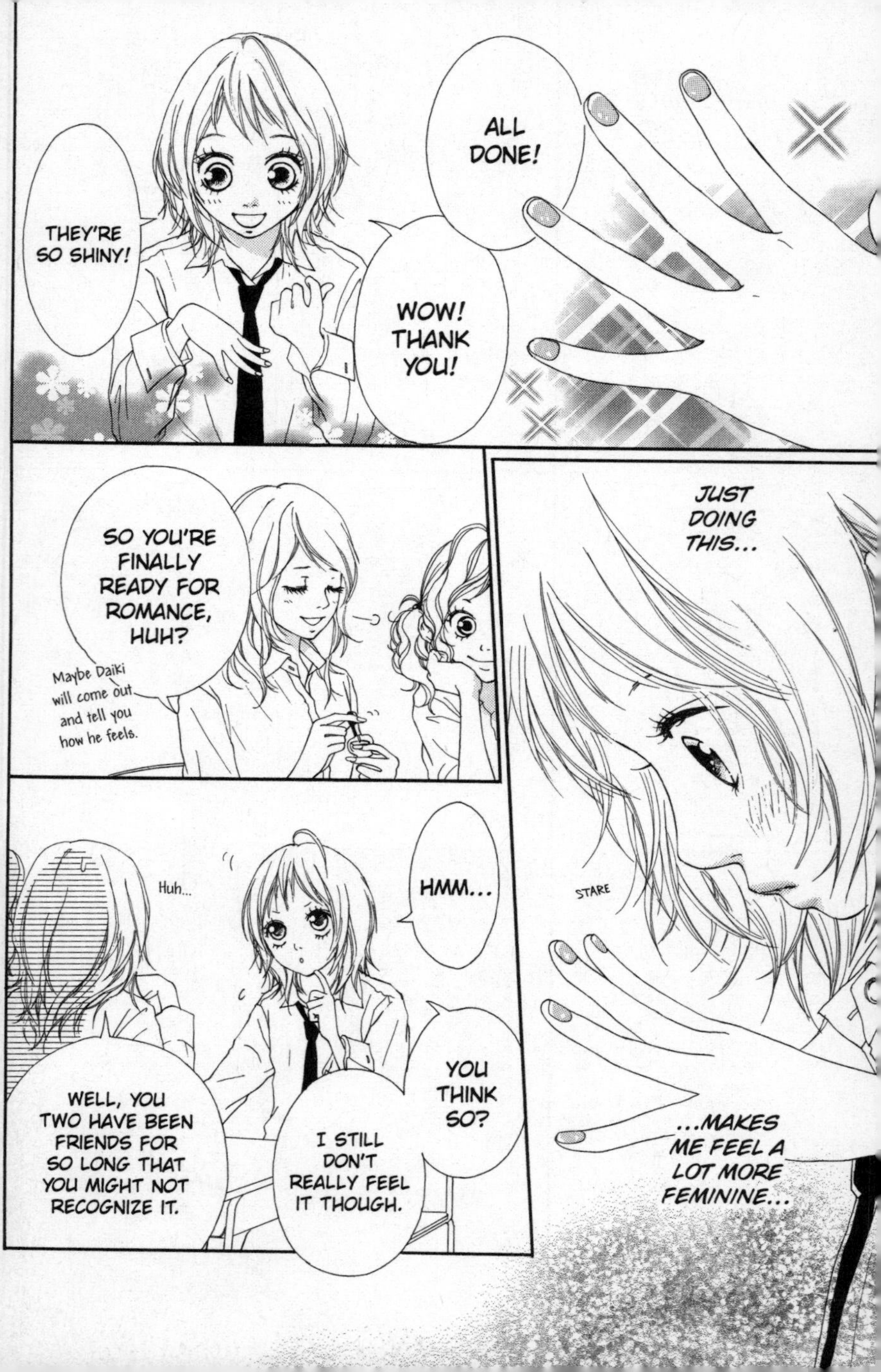
ALL DONE!
WOW! THANK YOU!
THEY'RE SO SHINY!
JUST DOING THIS...
STARE
...MAKES ME FEEL A LOT MORE FEMININE...
SO YOU'RE FINALLY READY FOR ROMANCE, HUH?
Maybe Daiki will come out and tell you how he feels.
HMM...
Huh...
YOU THINK SO?
I STILL DON'T REALLY FEEL IT THOUGH.
WELL, YOU TWO HAVE BEEN FRIENDS FOR SO LONG THAT YOU MIGHT NOT RECOGNIZE IT.

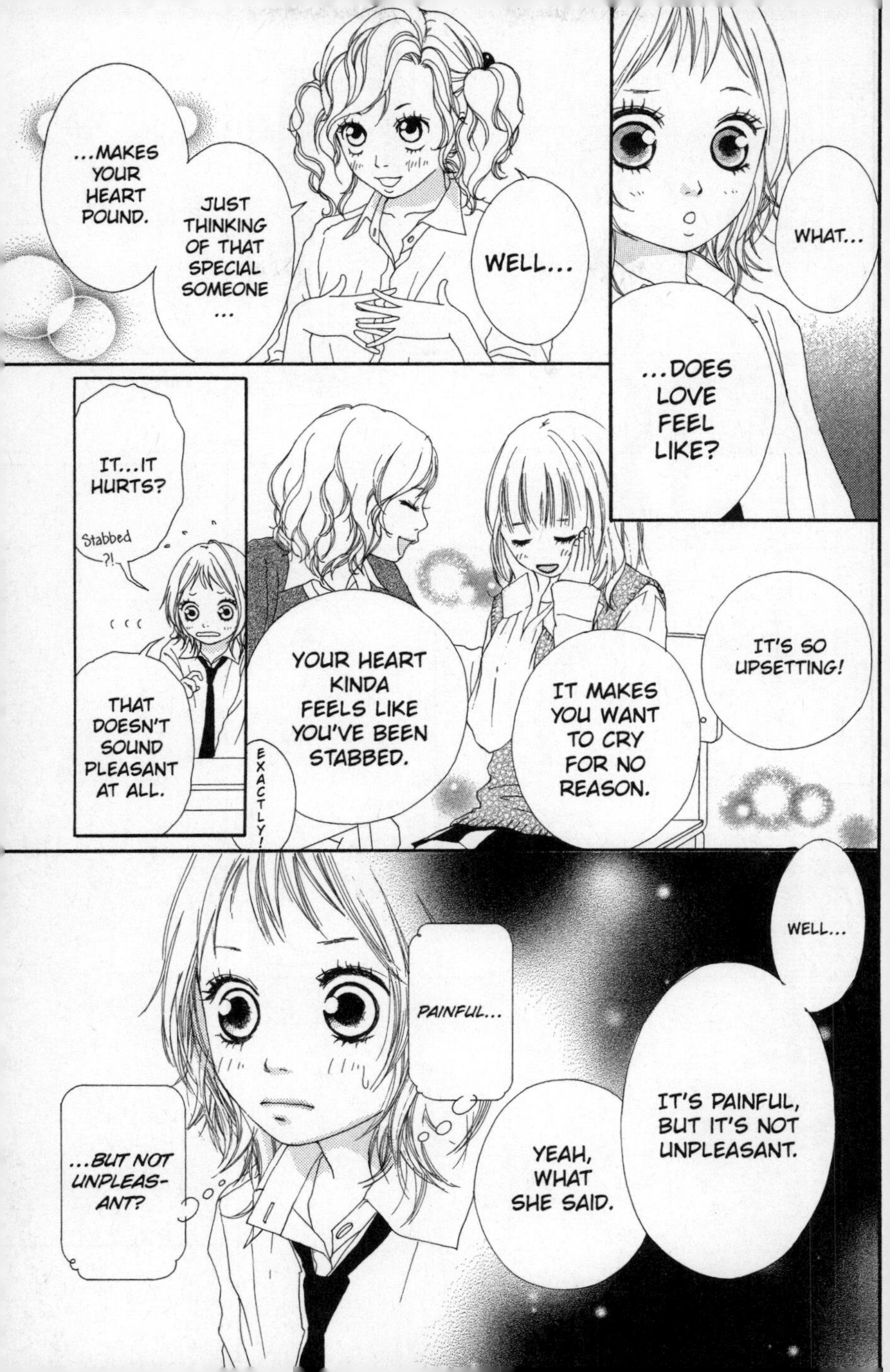
WHAT...
...DOES LOVE FEEL LIKE?
WELL...
JUST THINKING OF THAT SPECIAL SOMEONE...
...MAKES YOUR HEART POUND.
IT'S SO UPSETTING!
IT MAKES YOU WANT TO CRY FOR NO REASON.
YOUR HEART KINDA FEELS LIKE YOU'VE BEEN STABBED.
EXACTLY!
IT...IT HURTS?
Stabbed?!
THAT DOESN'T SOUND PLEASANT AT ALL.
WELL...
IT'S PAINFUL, BUT IT'S NOT UNPLEASANT.
YEAH, WHAT SHE SAID.
PAINFUL...
...BUT NOT UNPLEASANT?

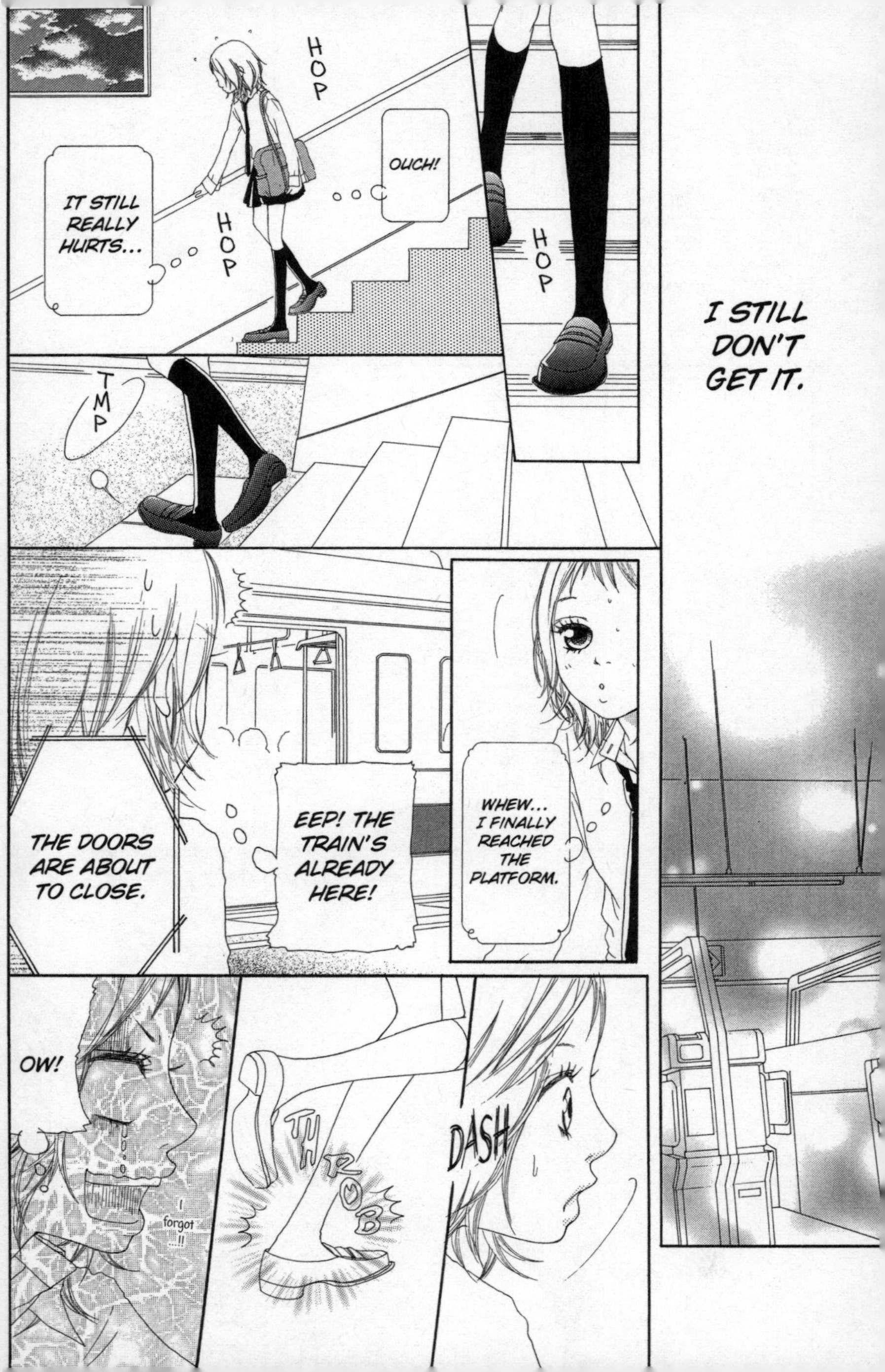
I STILL DON'T GET IT.
HOP
HOP
OUCH!
IT STILL REALLY HURTS...
HOP
TMP
WHEW... I FINALLY REACHED THE PLATFORM.
EEP! THE TRAIN'S ALREADY HERE!
THE DOORS ARE ABOUT TO CLOSE.
DASH
THROB
OW!
I forgot!!

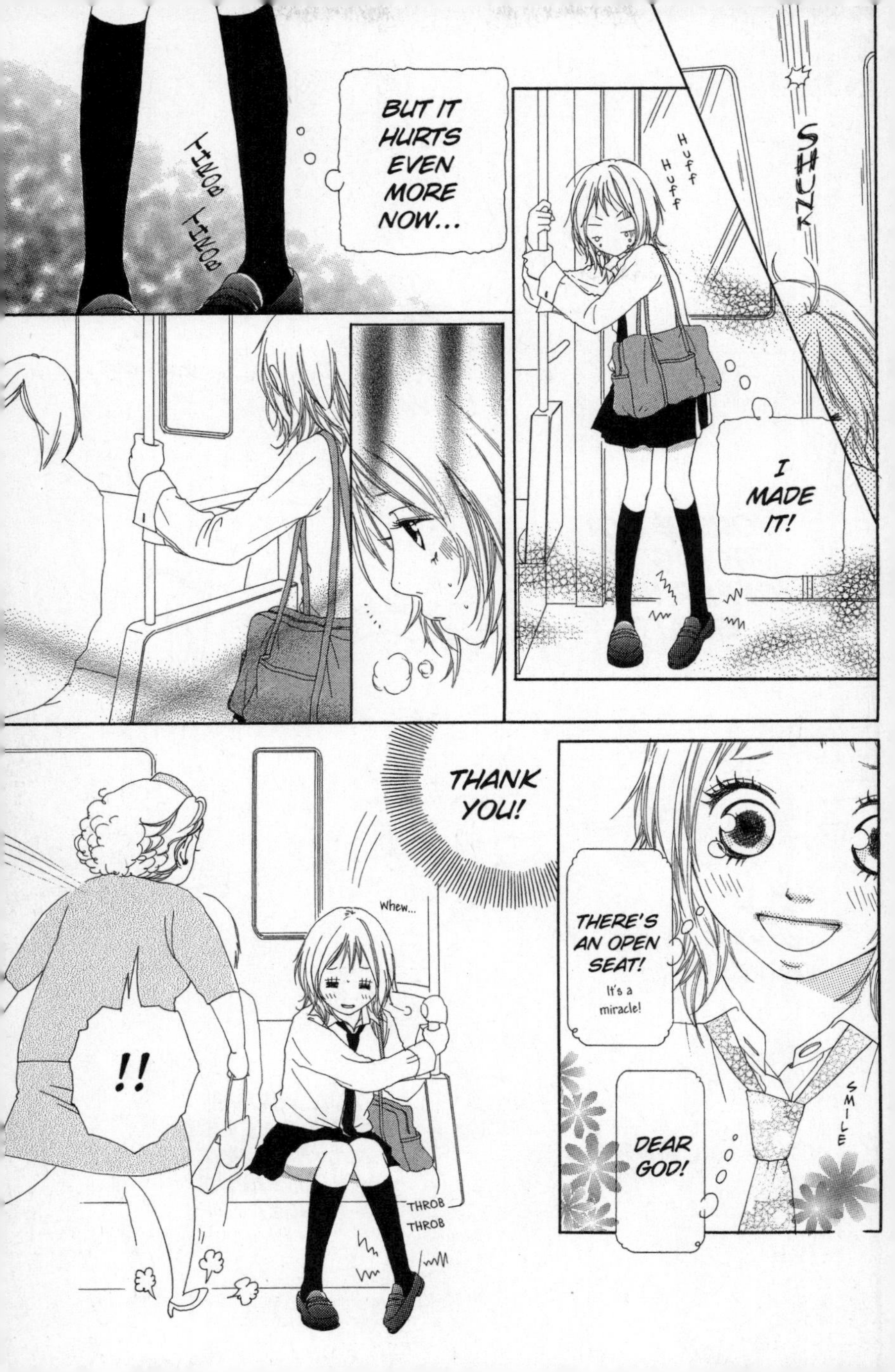
SHUNK
Huff Huff
I MADE IT!
BUT IT HURTS EVEN MORE NOW...
THERE'S AN OPEN SEAT!
It's a miracle!
DEAR GOD!
SMILE
THANK YOU!
Whew...
!!
THROB THROB

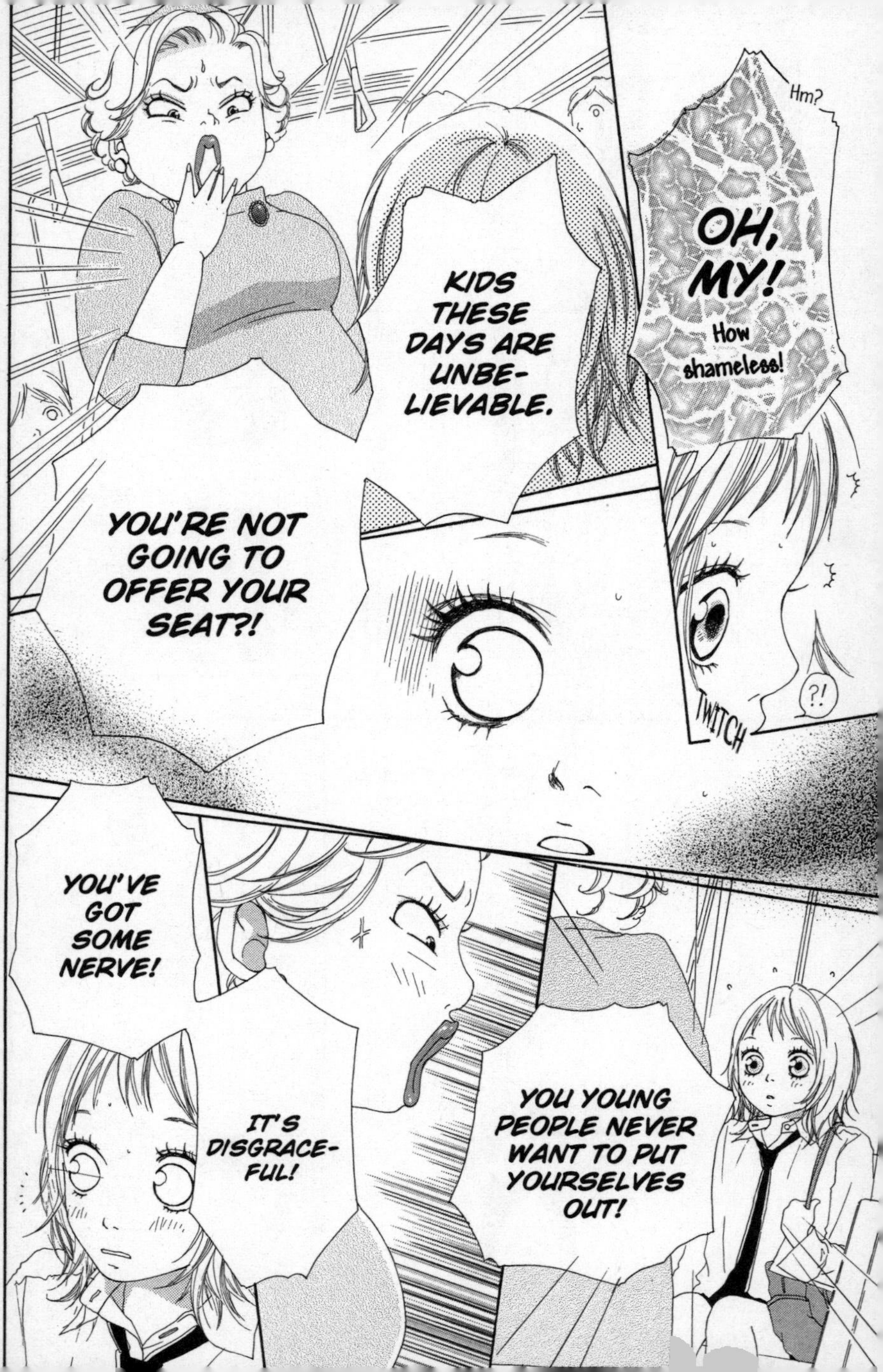
Hm?
OH, MY! How shameless!
KIDS THESE DAYS ARE UNBE-LIEVABLE.
YOU'RE NOT GOING TO OFFER YOUR SEAT?!
TWITCH
?!
YOU YOUNG PEOPLE NEVER WANT TO PUT YOURSELVES OUT!
IT'S DISGRACE-FUL!
YOU'VE GOT SOME NERVE!

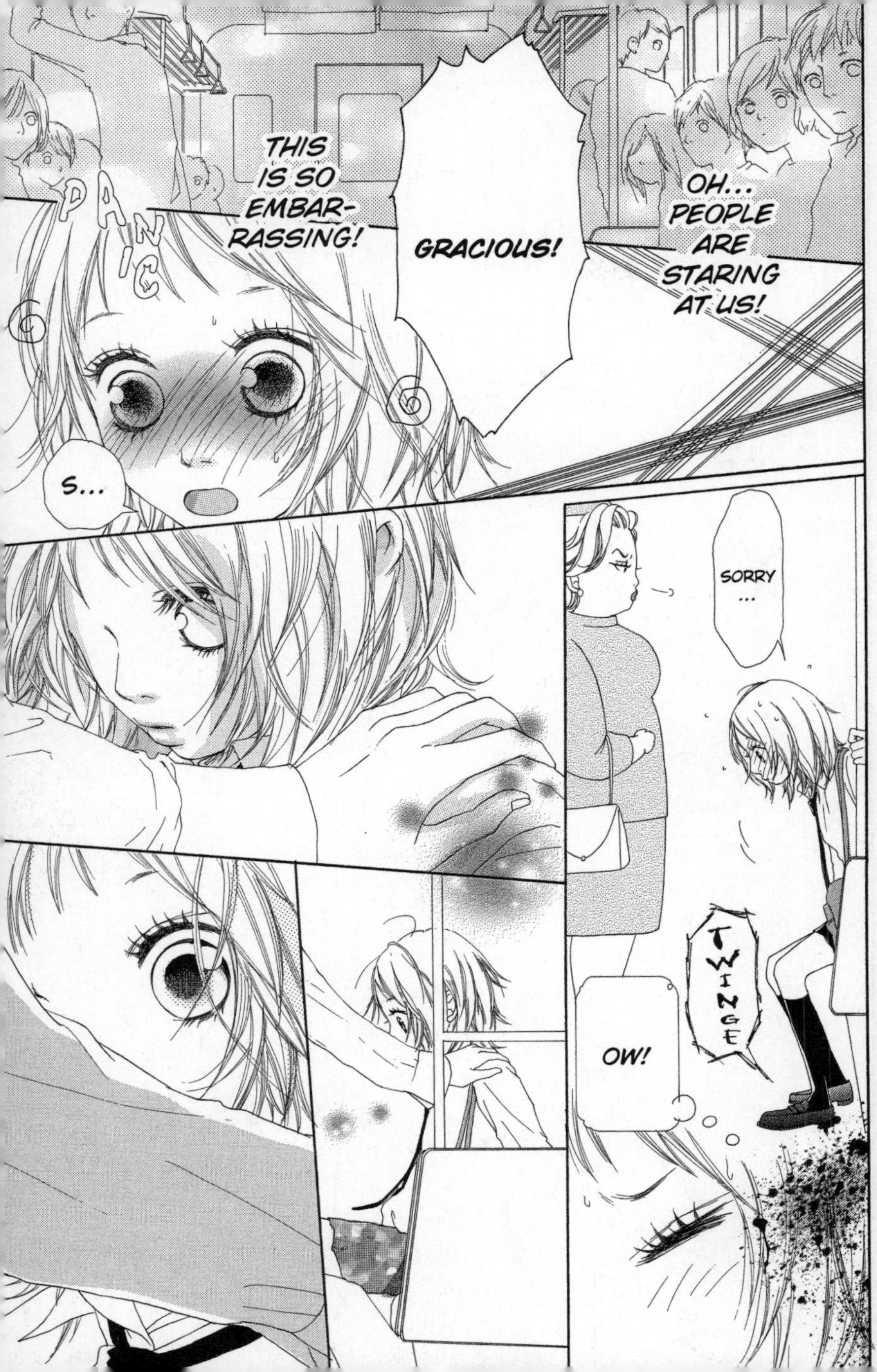

OH... PEOPLE ARE STARING AT US!
GRACIOUS!
THIS IS SO EMBARRASSING!
PANIC
S...
SORRY...
TWINGE
OW!

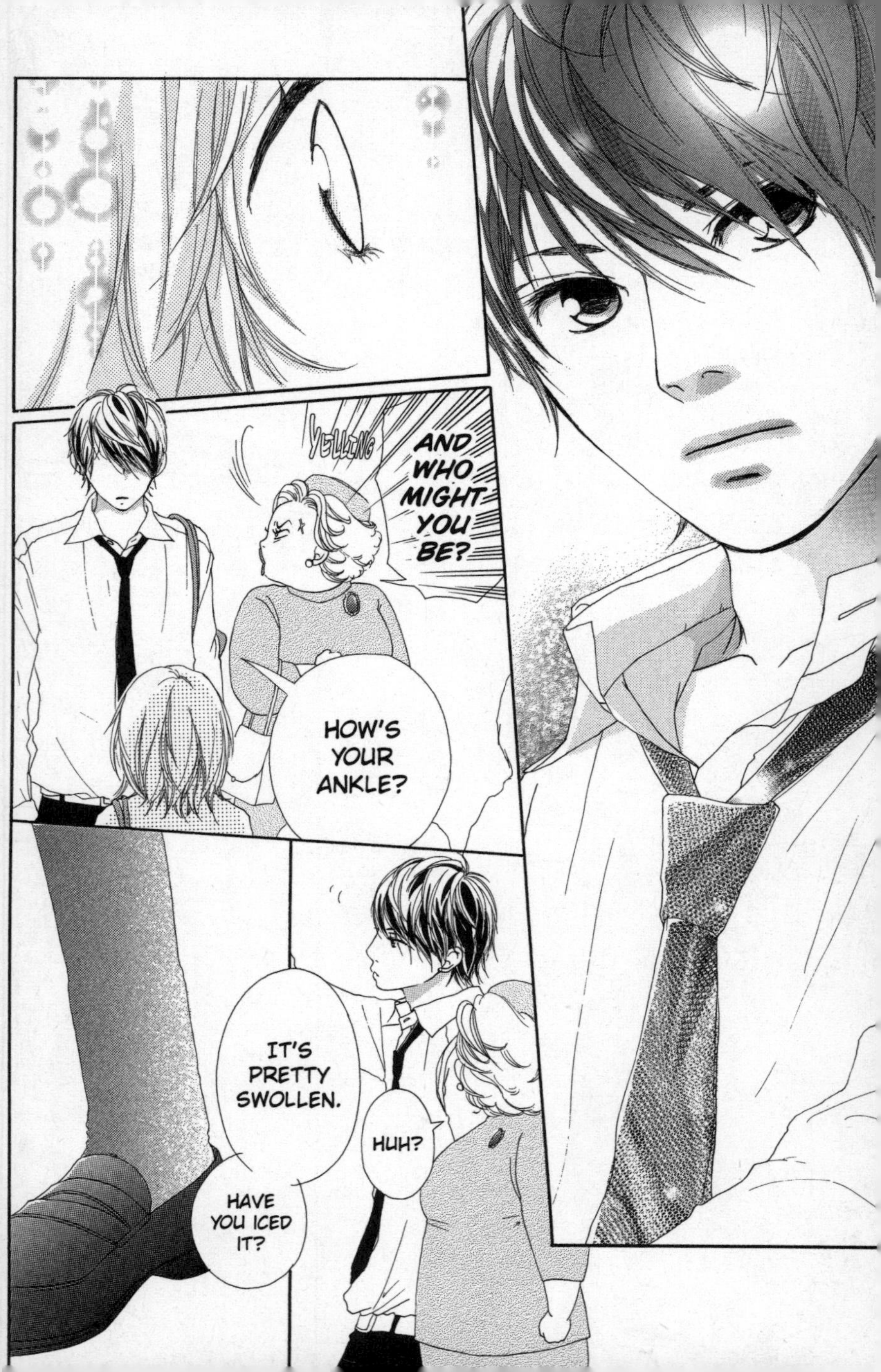
YELLING
AND WHO MIGHT YOU BE?
HOW'S YOUR ANKLE?
IT'S PRETTY SWOLLEN.
HUH?
HAVE YOU ICED IT?

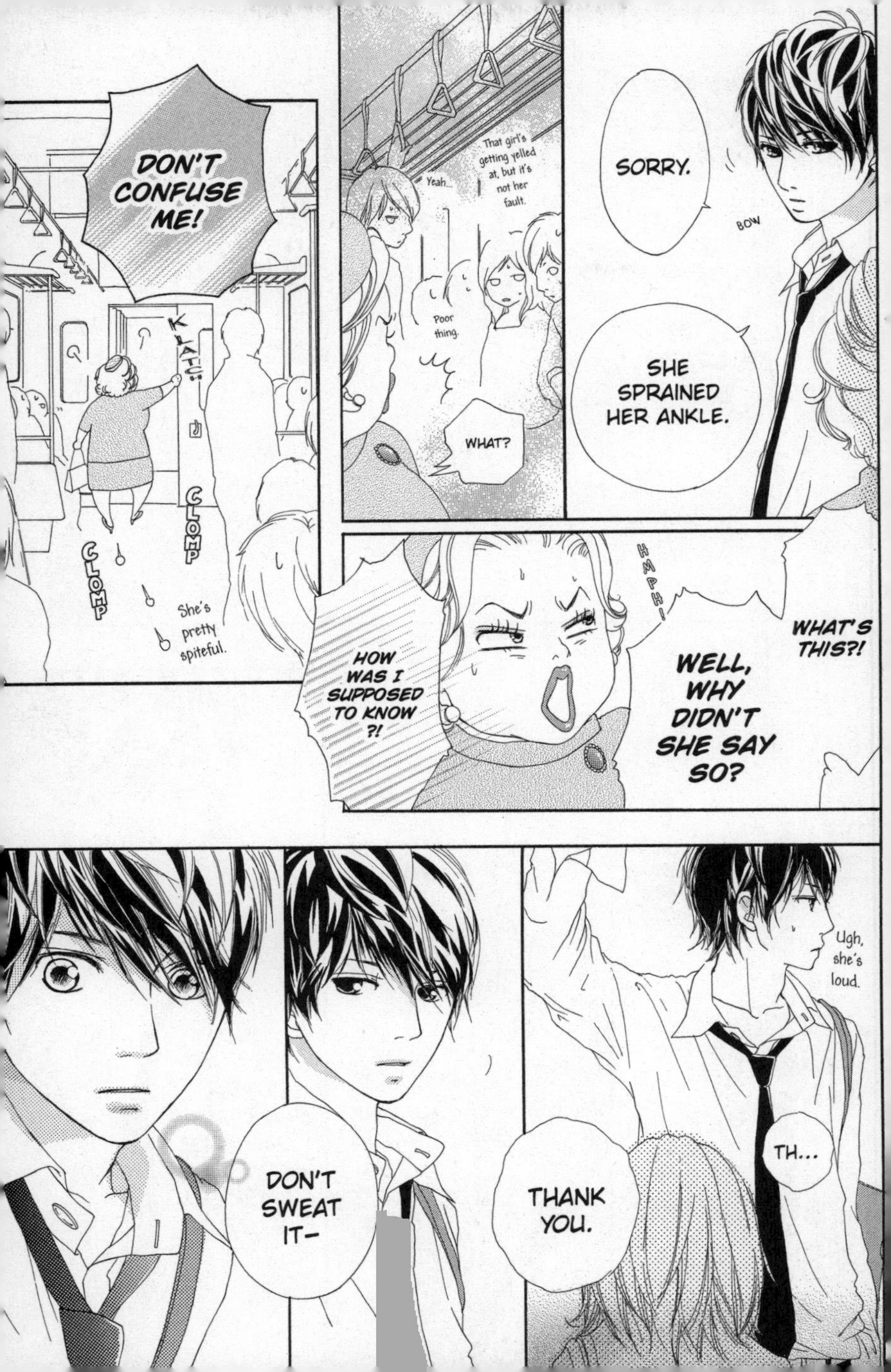
SORRY.
BOW
SHE SPRAINED HER ANKLE.
That girl's getting yelled at, but it's not her fault.
Yeah...
Poor thing.
WHAT?
WHAT'S THIS?!
WELL, WHY DIDN'T SHE SAY SO?
HMPH!
HOW WAS I SUPPOSED TO KNOW?!
DON'T CONFUSE ME!
KLATCH
CLOMP
CLOMP
She's pretty spiteful.
Ugh, she's loud.
TH...
THANK YOU.
DON'T SWEAT IT–

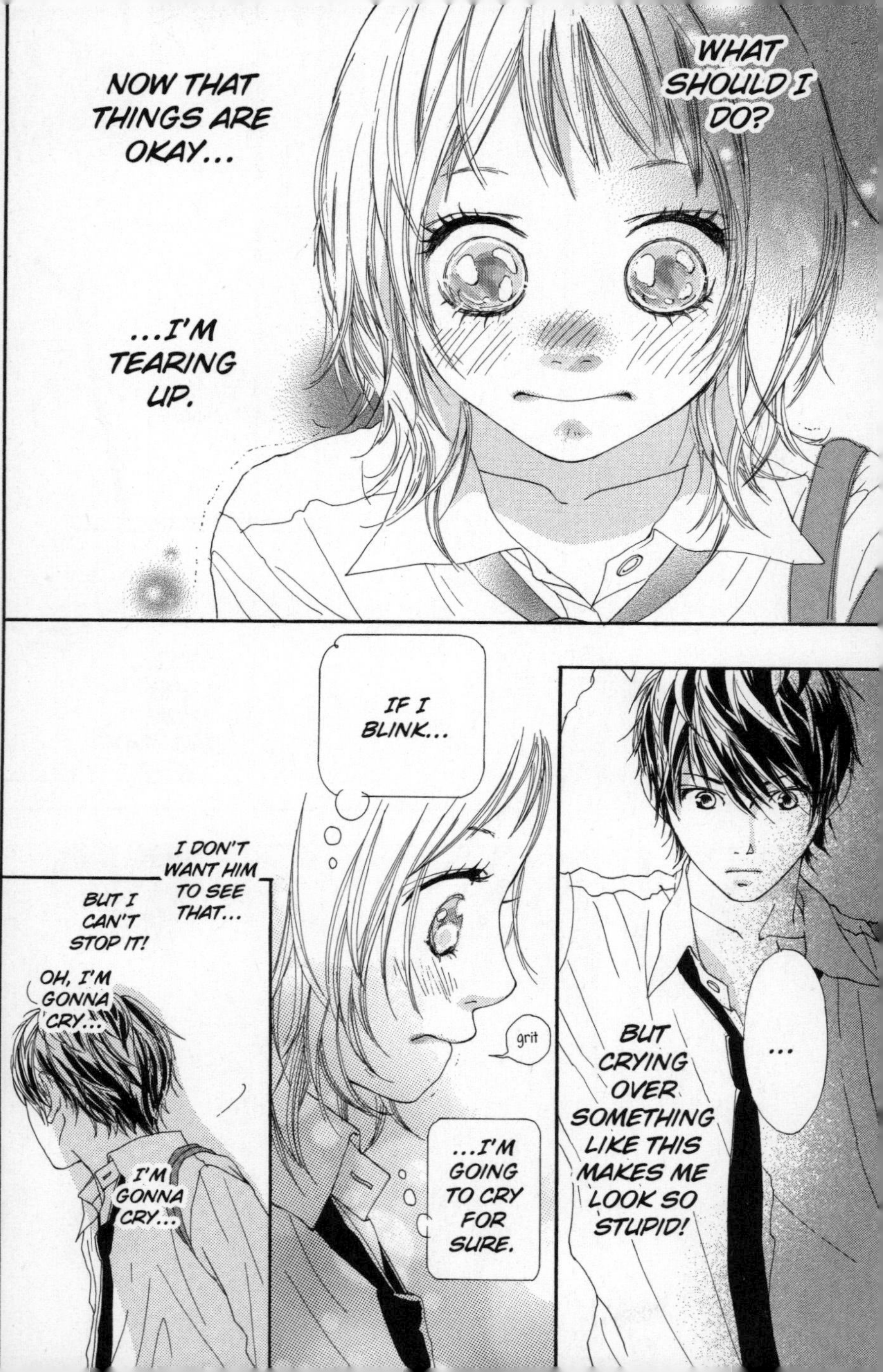
WHAT SHOULD I DO?
NOW THAT THINGS ARE OKAY...
...I'M TEARING UP.
...
BUT CRYING OVER SOMETHING LIKE THIS MAKES ME LOOK SO STUPID!
IF I BLINK...
grit
...I'M GOING TO CRY FOR SURE.
I DON'T WANT HIM TO SEE THAT...
BUT I CAN'T STOP IT!
OH, I'M GONNA CRY...
I'M GONNA CRY...

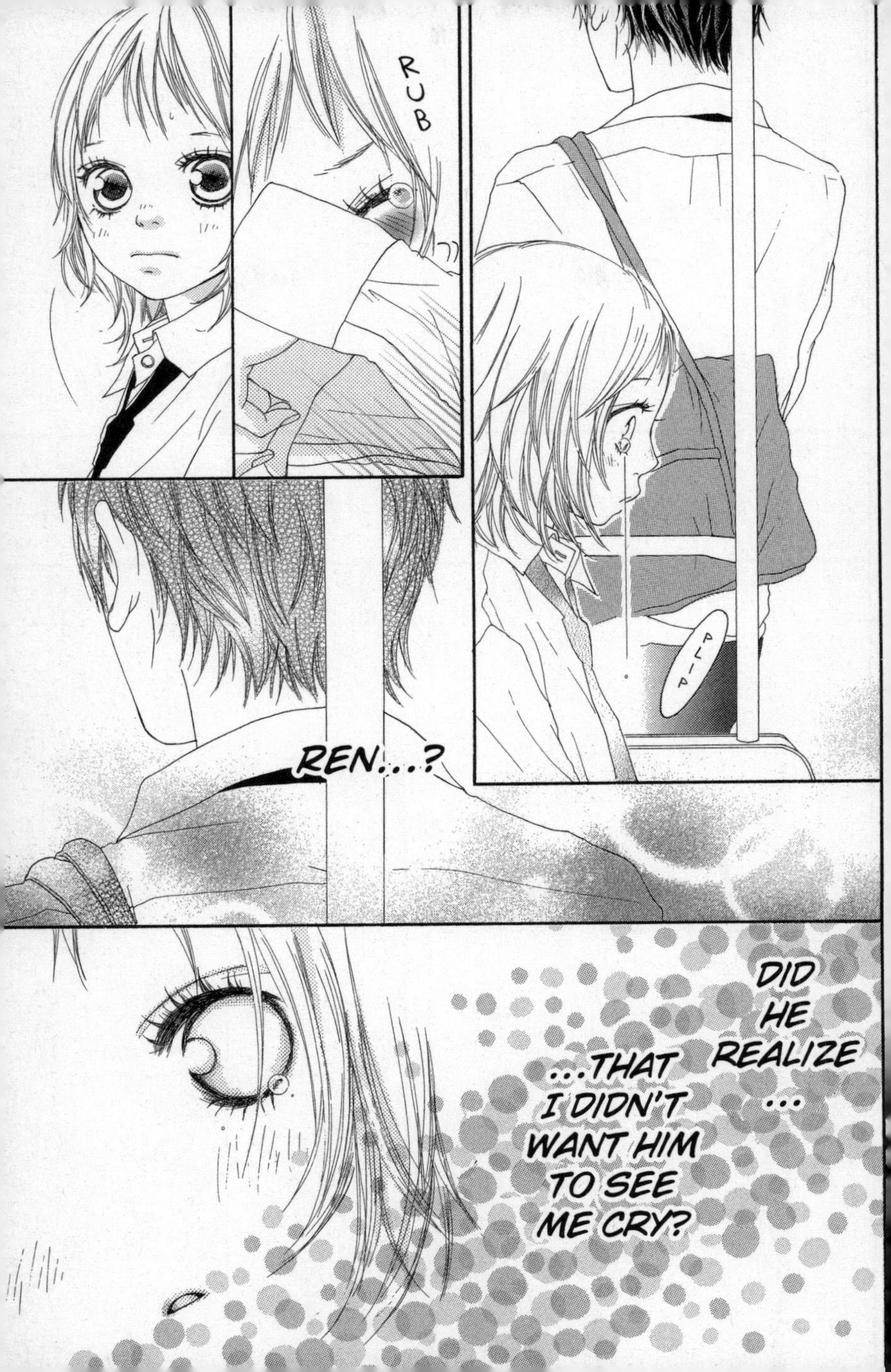
PLIP
RUB
REN...?
DID HE REALIZE ...
...THAT I DIDN'T WANT HIM TO SEE ME CRY?

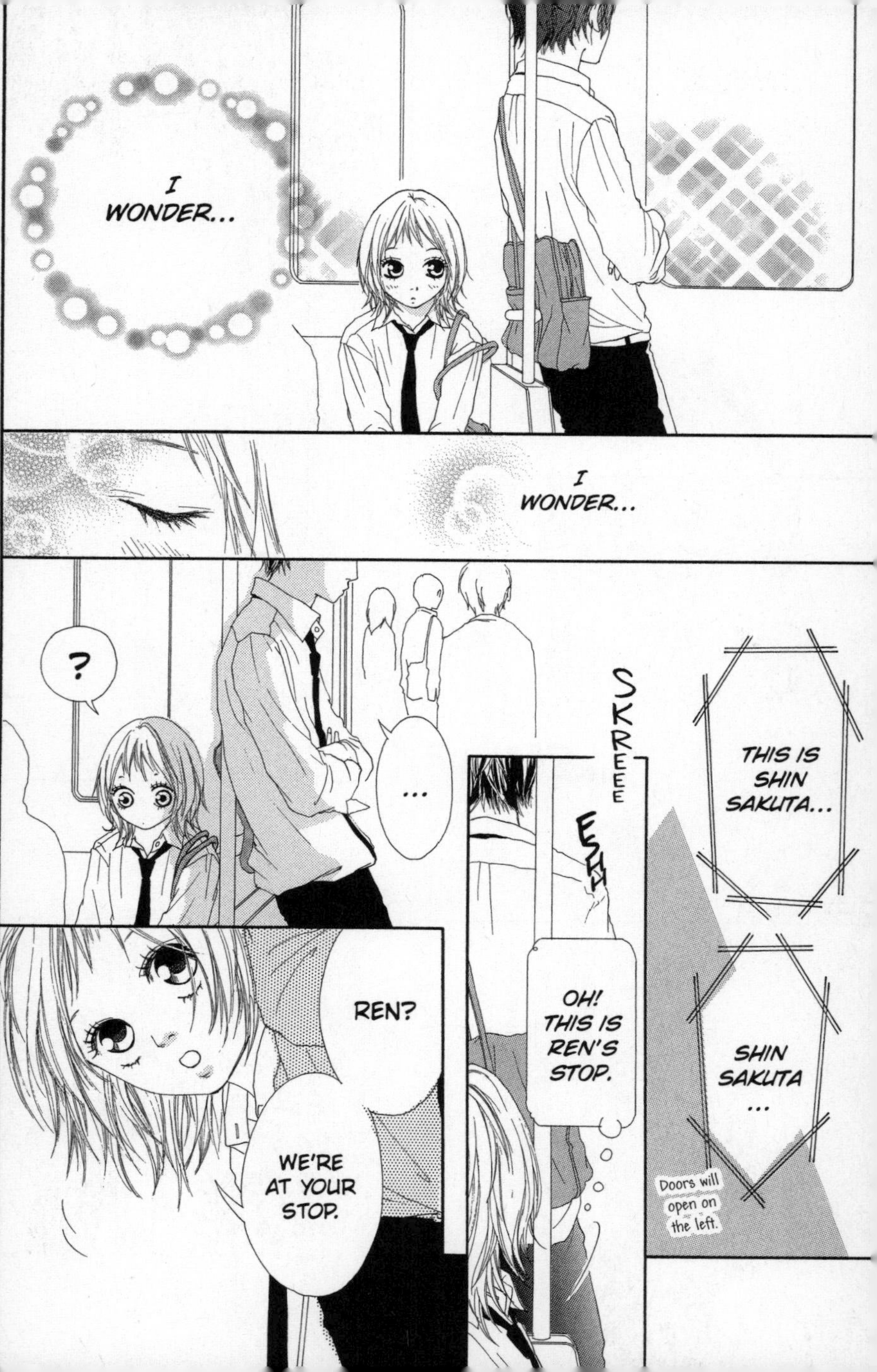
I WONDER...
I WONDER...
THIS IS SHIN SAKUTA...
SHIN SAKUTA ...
Doors will open on the left.
SKREEESHH
OH! THIS IS REN'S STOP.
?
...
REN?
WE'RE AT YOUR STOP.

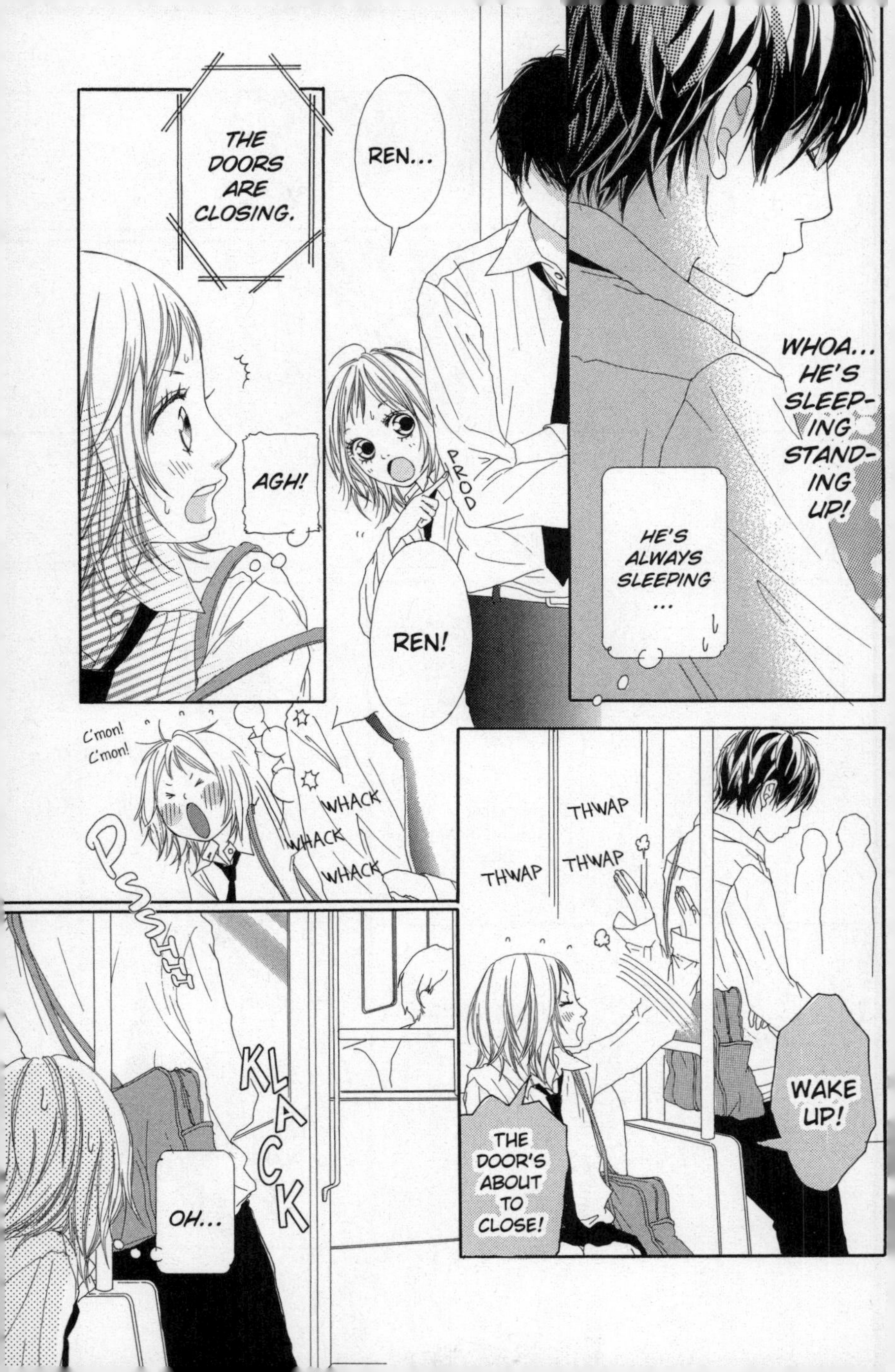
WHOA... HE'S SLEEPING STANDING UP!
HE'S ALWAYS SLEEPING...
REN...
PROD
REN!
THE DOORS ARE CLOSING.
AGH!
THWAP
THWAP
THWAP
WAKE UP!
THE DOOR'S ABOUT TO CLOSE!
C'mon! C'mon!
WHACK
WHACK
WHACK
PSHHH
KLACK
OH...

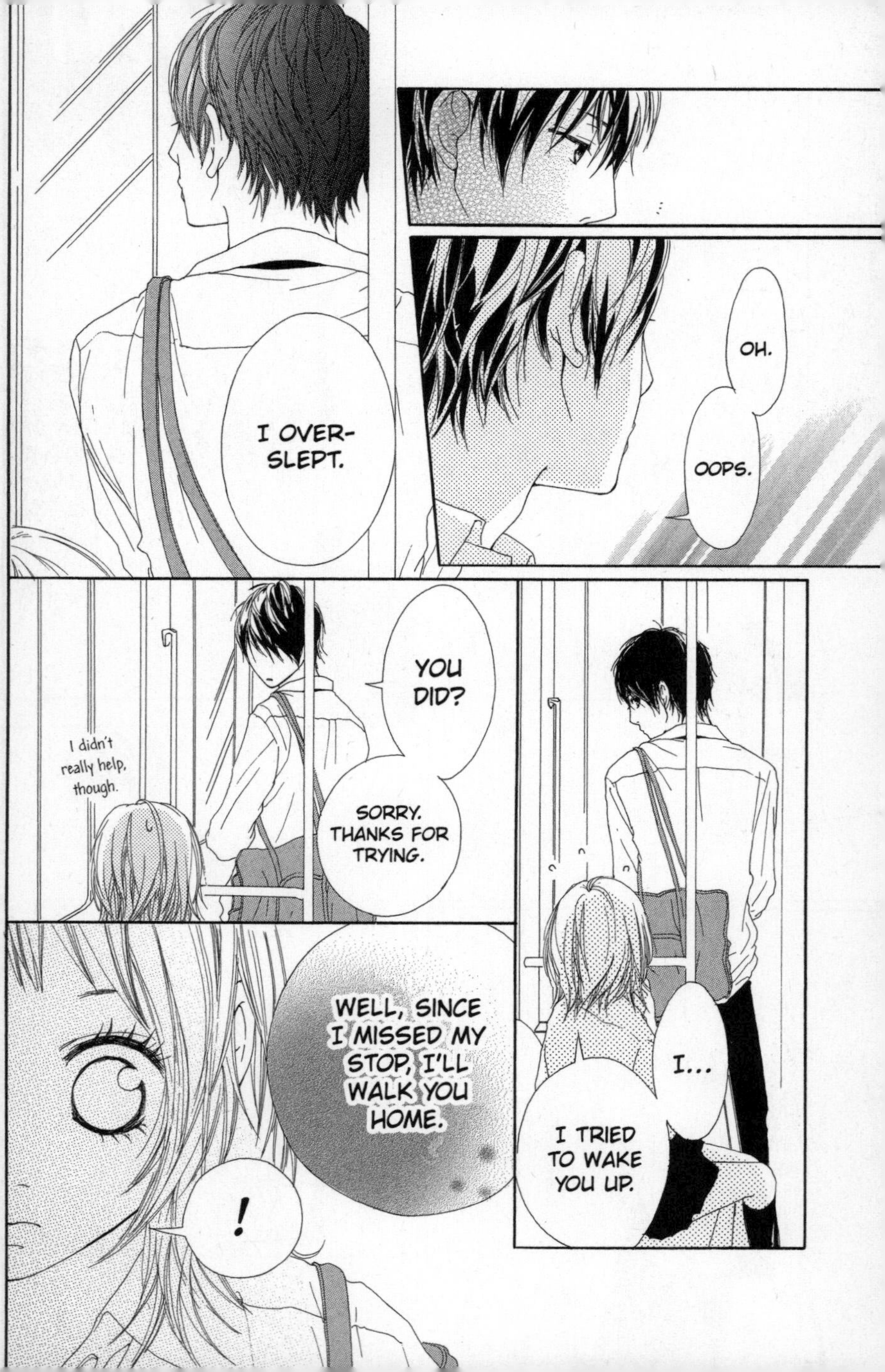
OH.
OOPS.
I OVER-SLEPT.
I...
I TRIED TO WAKE YOU UP.
YOU DID?
SORRY. THANKS FOR TRYING.
I didn't really help, though.
WELL, SINCE I MISSED MY STOP, I'LL WALK YOU HOME.
!

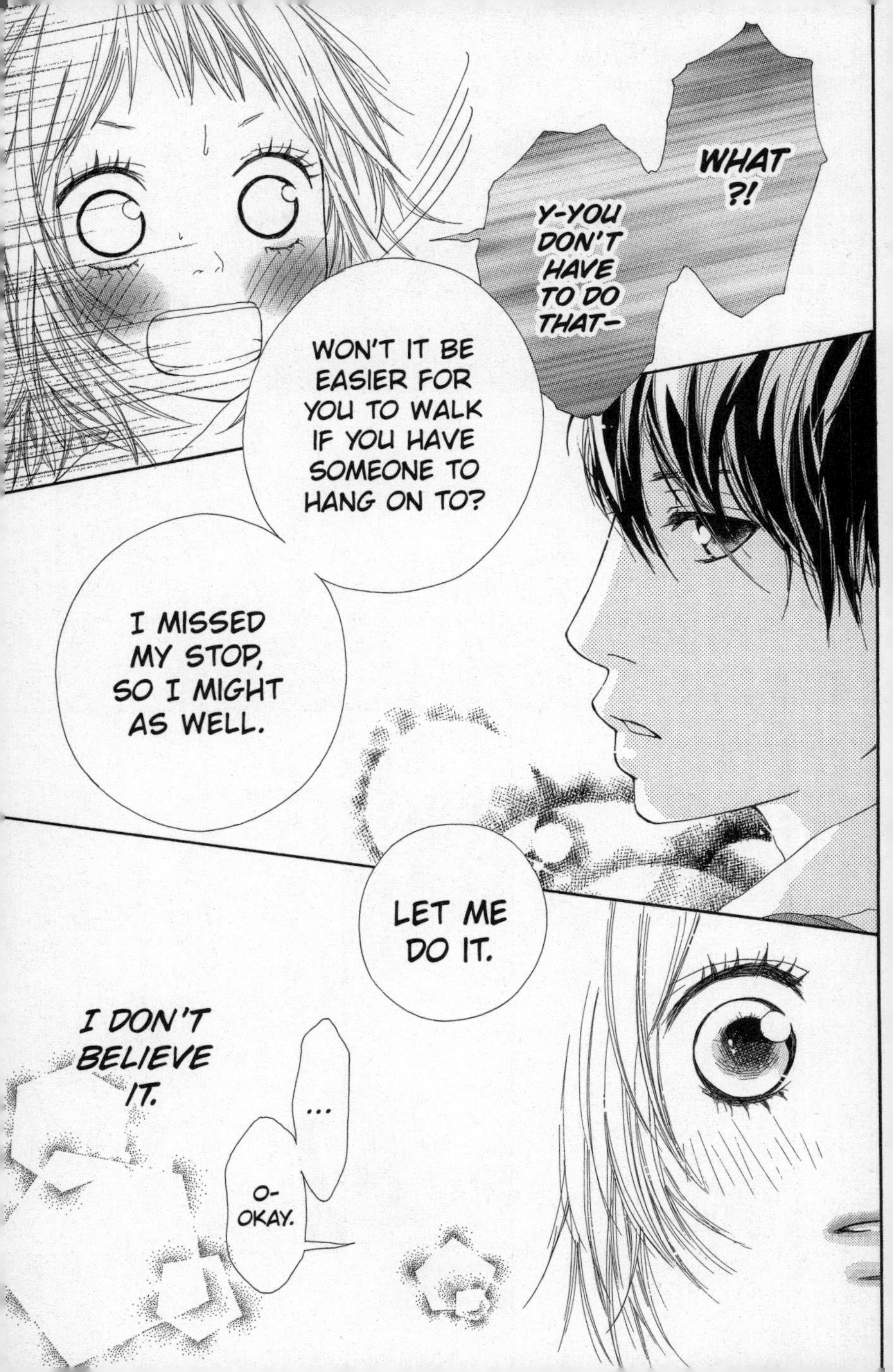
WHAT?!
Y-YOU DON'T HAVE TO DO THAT—
WON'T IT BE EASIER FOR YOU TO WALK IF YOU HAVE SOMEONE TO HANG ON TO?
I MISSED MY STOP, SO I MIGHT AS WELL.
LET ME DO IT.
...
O-OKAY.
I DON'T BELIEVE IT.

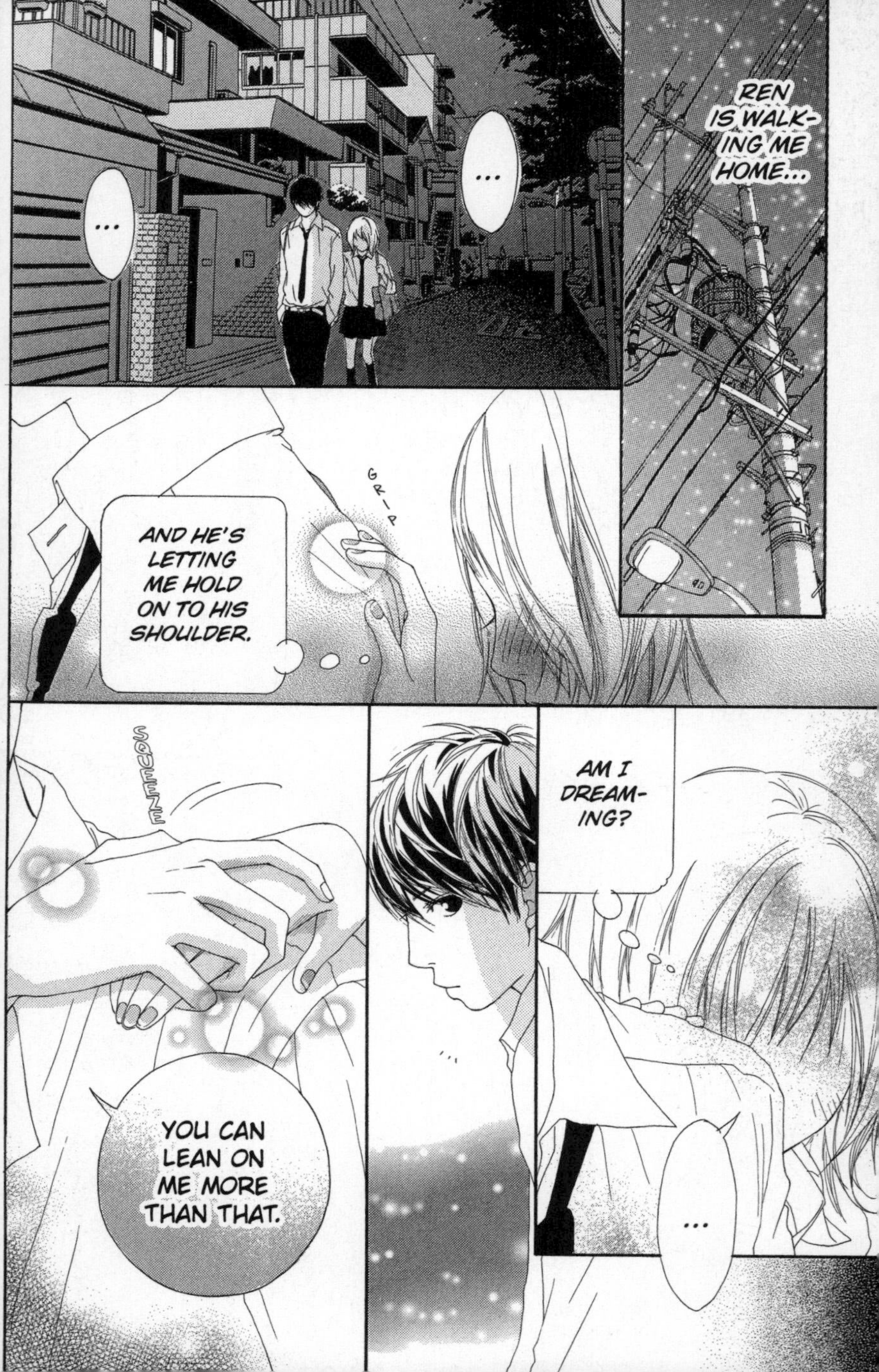
REN IS WALKING-ING ME HOME...
...
...
GRIP
AND HE'S LETTING ME HOLD ON TO HIS SHOULDER.
AM I DREAMING?
...
YOU CAN LEAN ON ME MORE THAN THAT.
SQUEEZE

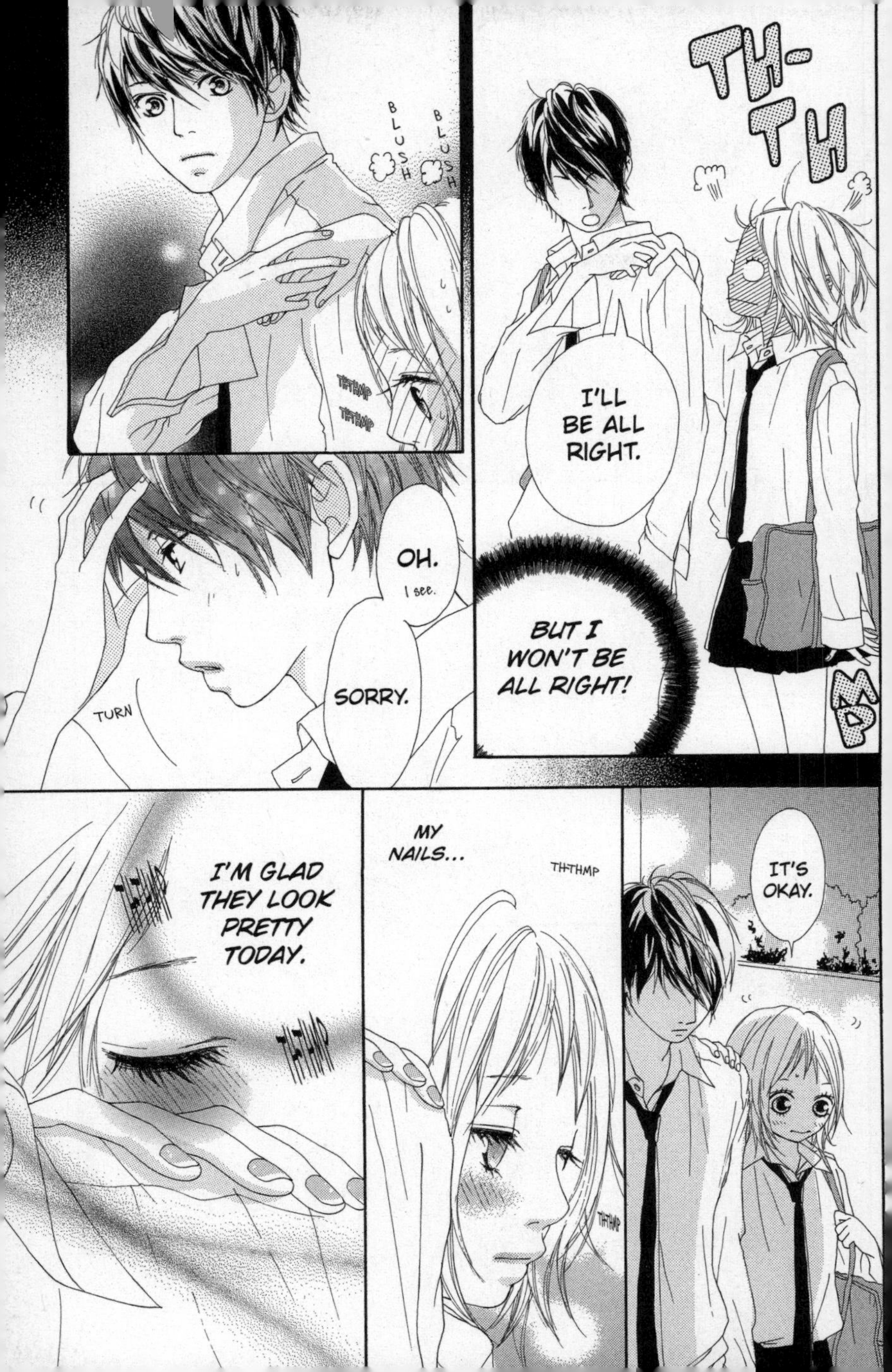
TH-TH
I'LL BE ALL RIGHT.
BUT I WON'T BE ALL RIGHT!
MMP
BLUSH
BLUSH
TH-THMP
TH-THMP
OH.
I see.
SORRY.
TURN
IT'S OKAY.
MY NAILS...
TH-THMP
THMP
I'M GLAD THEY LOOK PRETTY TODAY.

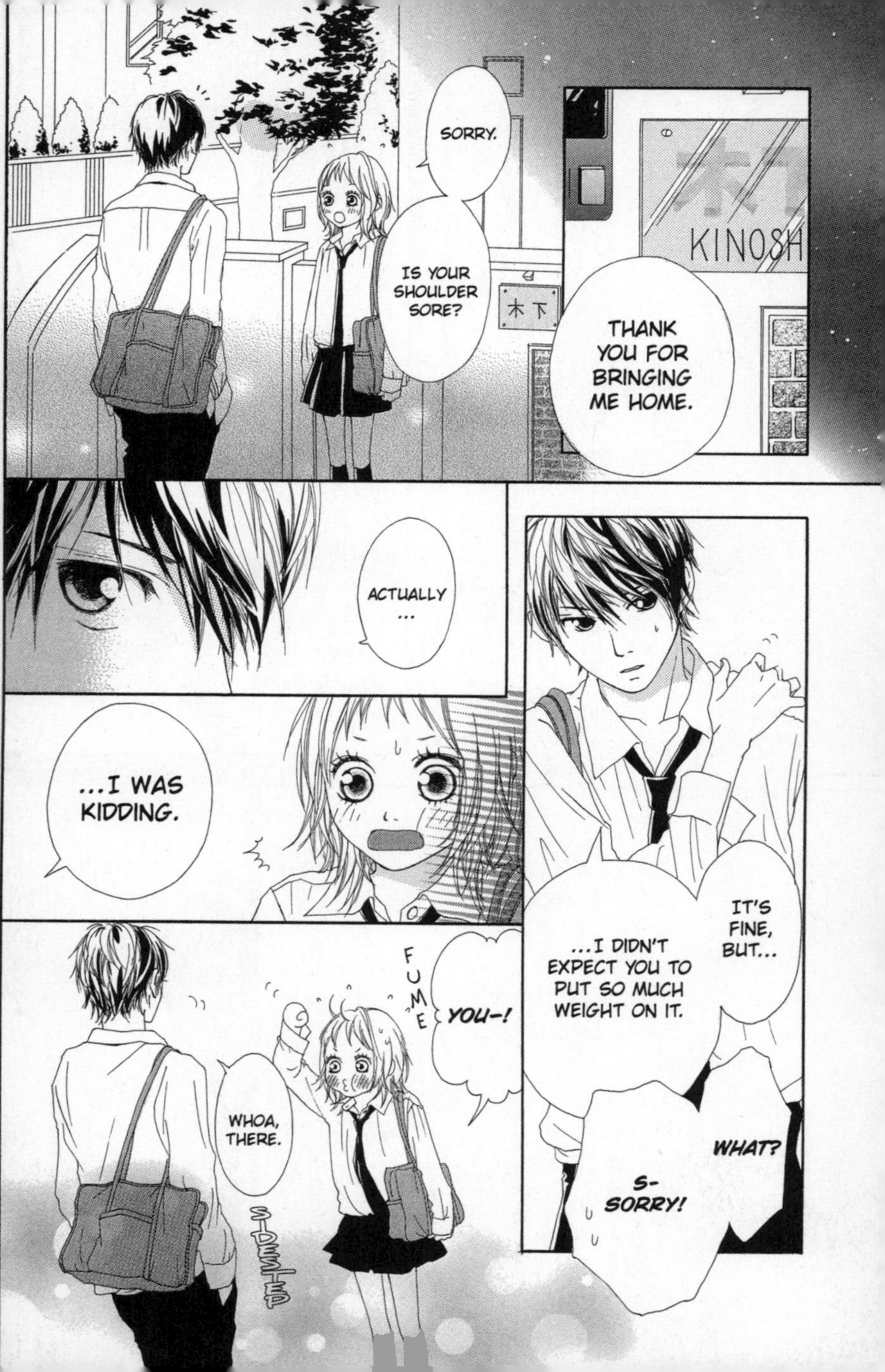
KINOSH
THANK YOU FOR BRINGING ME HOME.
SORRY.
IS YOUR SHOULDER SORE?
木下
IT'S FINE, BUT...
...I DIDN'T EXPECT YOU TO PUT SO MUCH WEIGHT ON IT.
WHAT?
S-SORRY!
ACTUALLY...
...I WAS KIDDING.
YOU-!
FUME
WHOA, THERE.
SIDESTEP

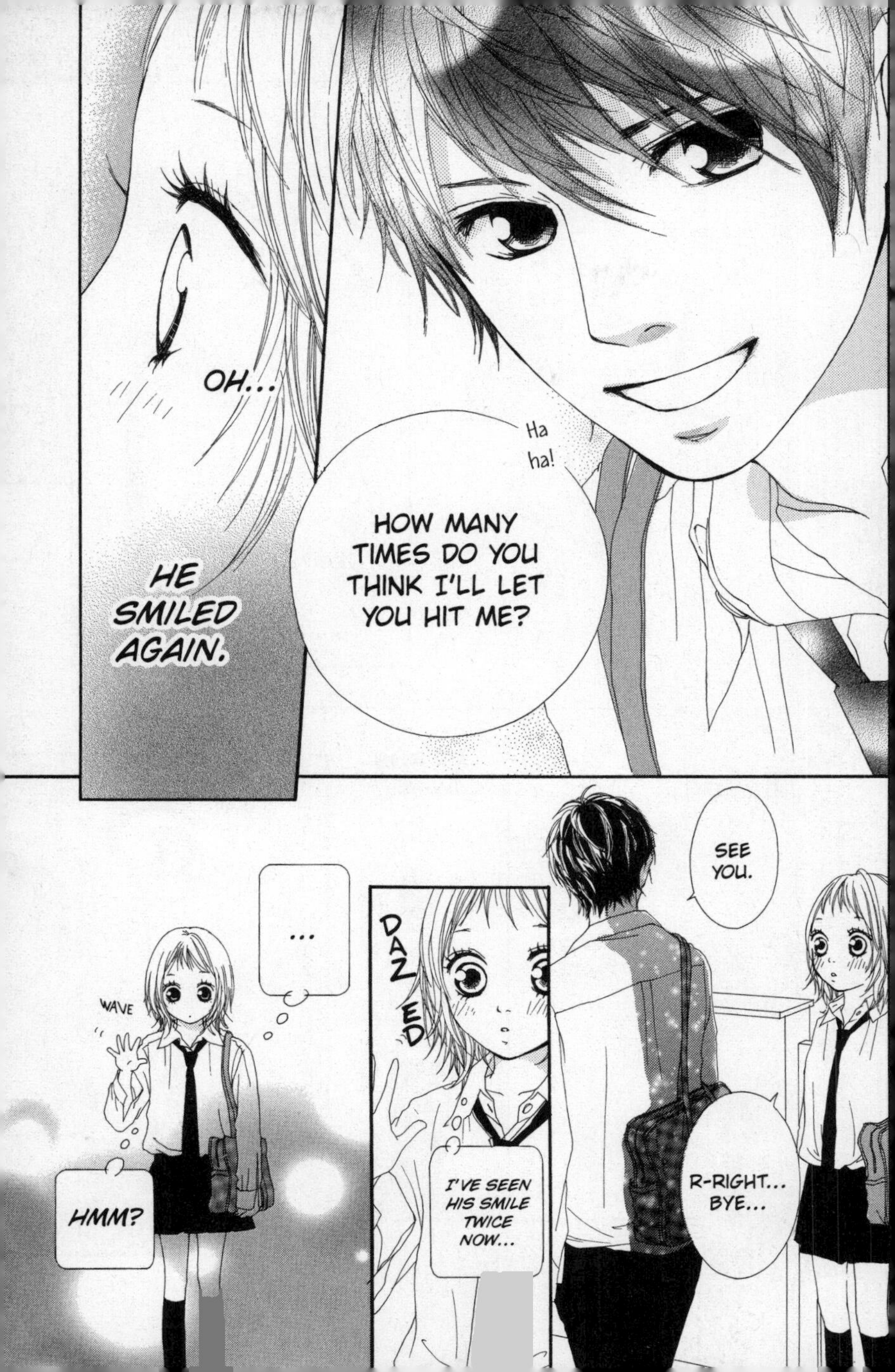
Ha ha!
HOW MANY TIMES DO YOU THINK I'LL LET YOU HIT ME?
OH...
HE SMILED AGAIN.
SEE YOU.
R-RIGHT... BYE...
DAZED
I'VE SEEN HIS SMILE TWICE NOW...
...
WAVE
HMM?

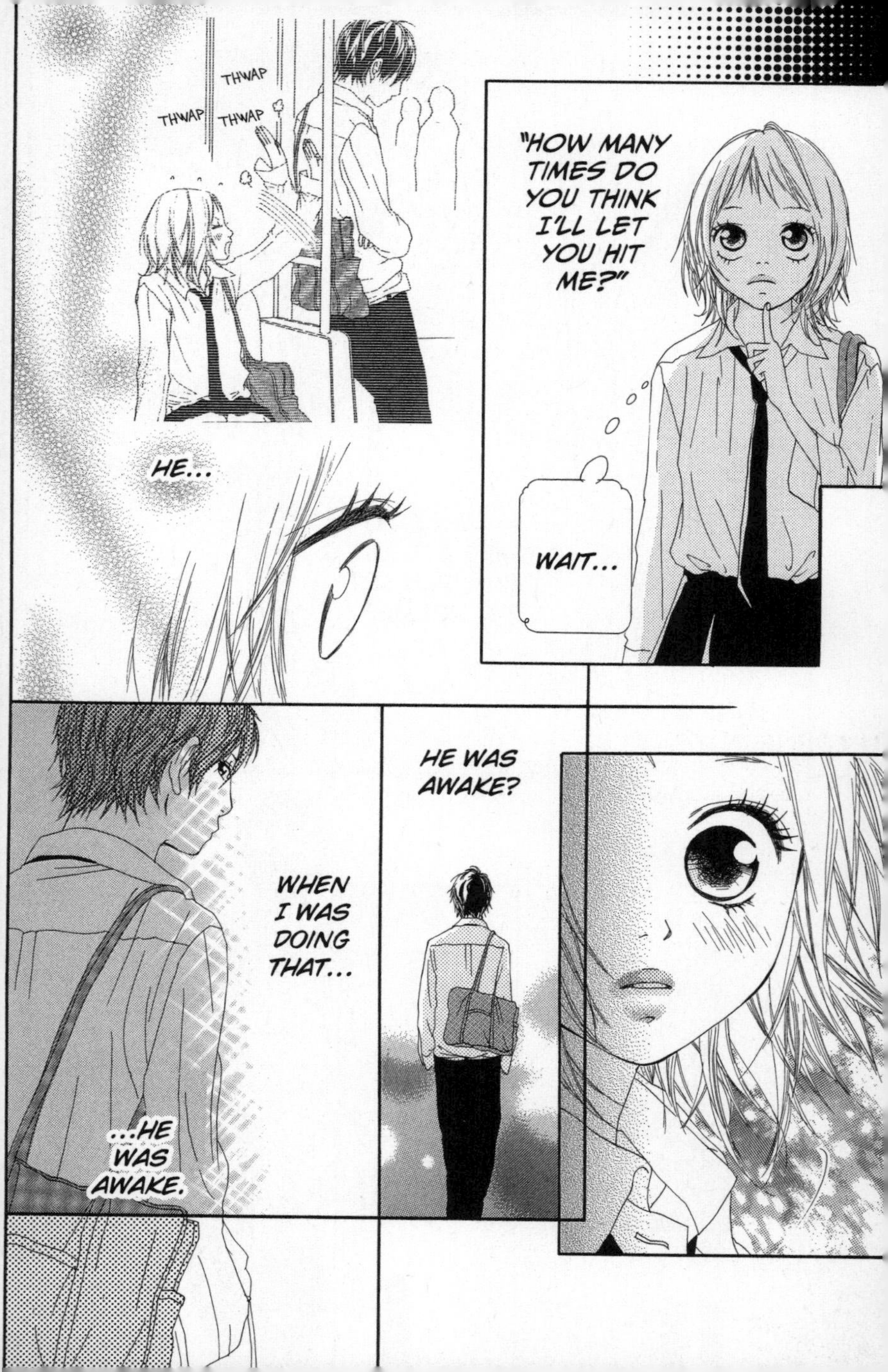

"HOW MANY TIMES DO YOU THINK I'LL LET YOU HIT ME?"
WAIT...
THWAP
THWAP
THWAP
HE...
HE WAS AWAKE?
WHEN I WAS DOING THAT...
...HE WAS AWAKE.

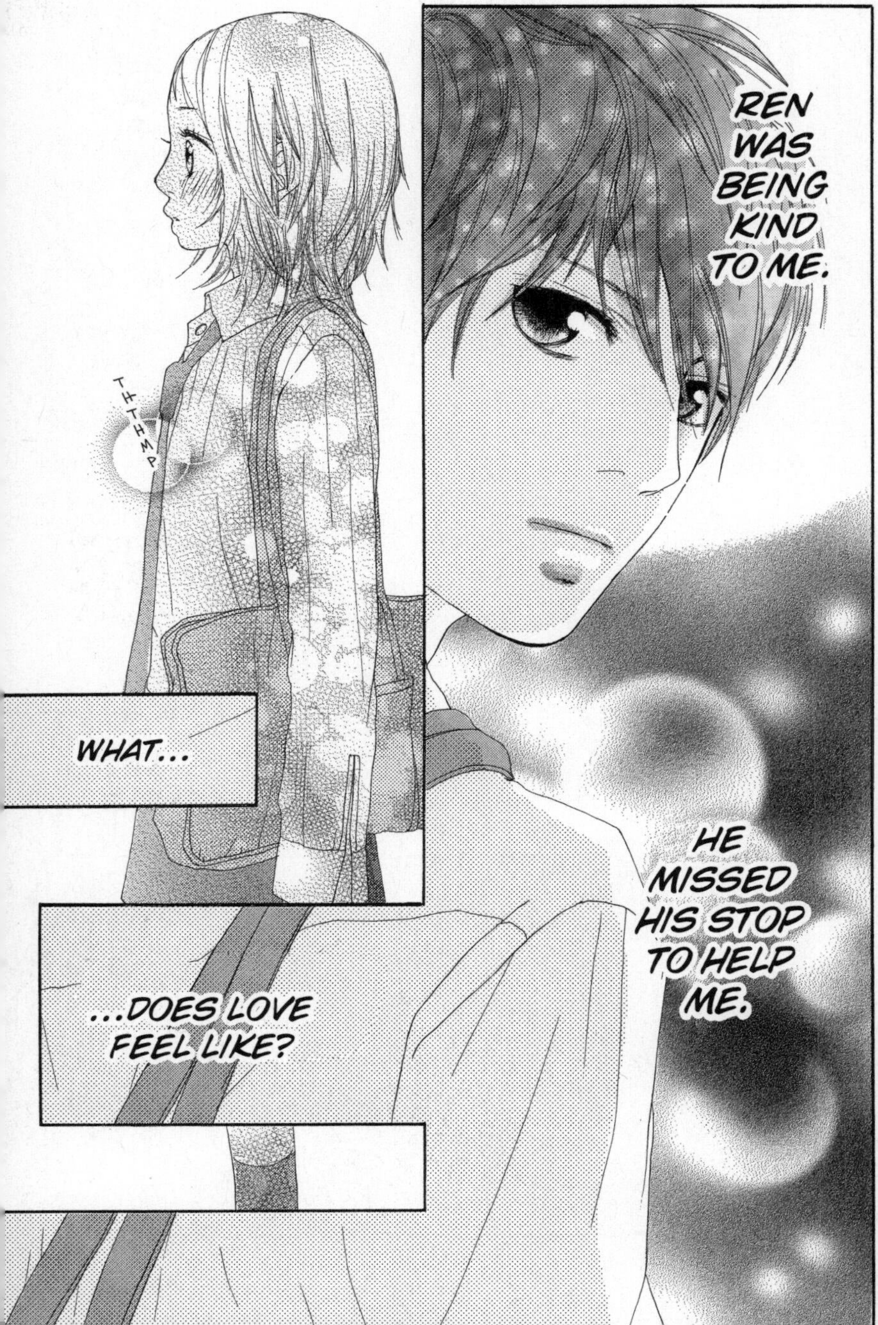
REN WAS BEING KIND TO ME.
HE MISSED HIS STOP TO HELP ME.
THTHMP
WHAT...
...DOES LOVE FEEL LIKE?

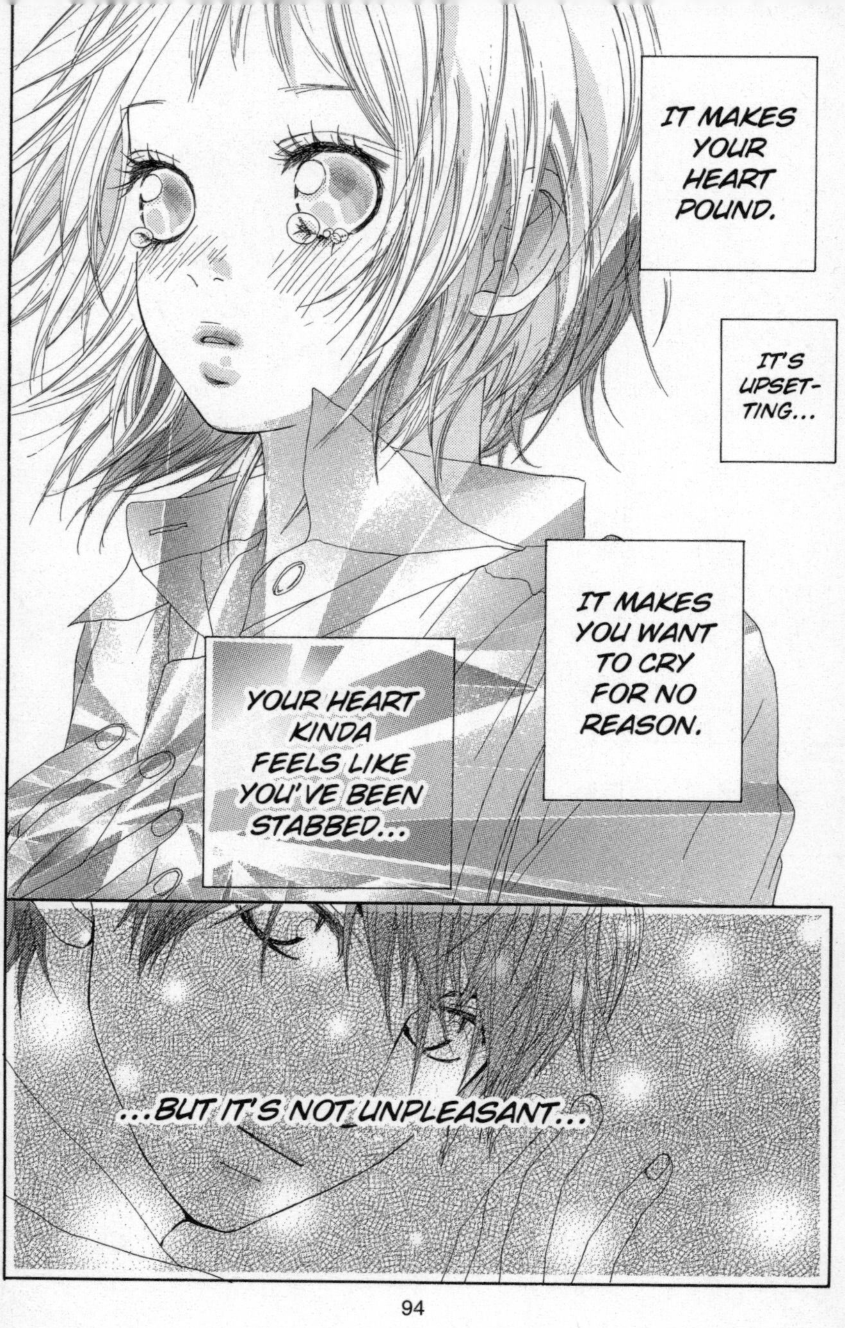
IT MAKES YOUR HEART POUND.
IT'S UPSET-TING...
IT MAKES YOU WANT TO CRY FOR NO REASON.
YOUR HEART KINDA FEELS LIKE YOU'VE BEEN STABBED...
...BUT IT'S NOT UNPLEASANT...

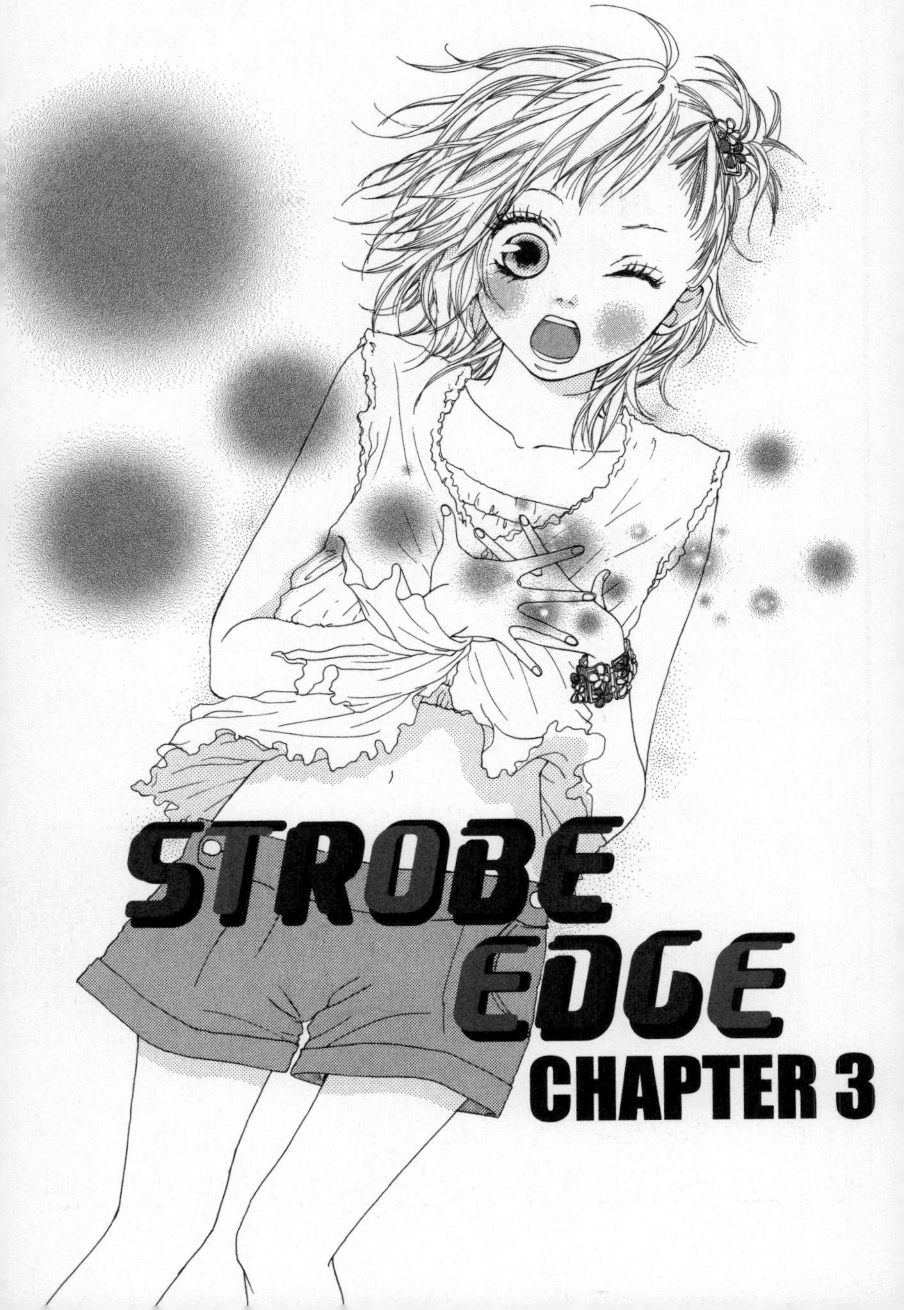
STROBE EDGE
CHAPTER 3

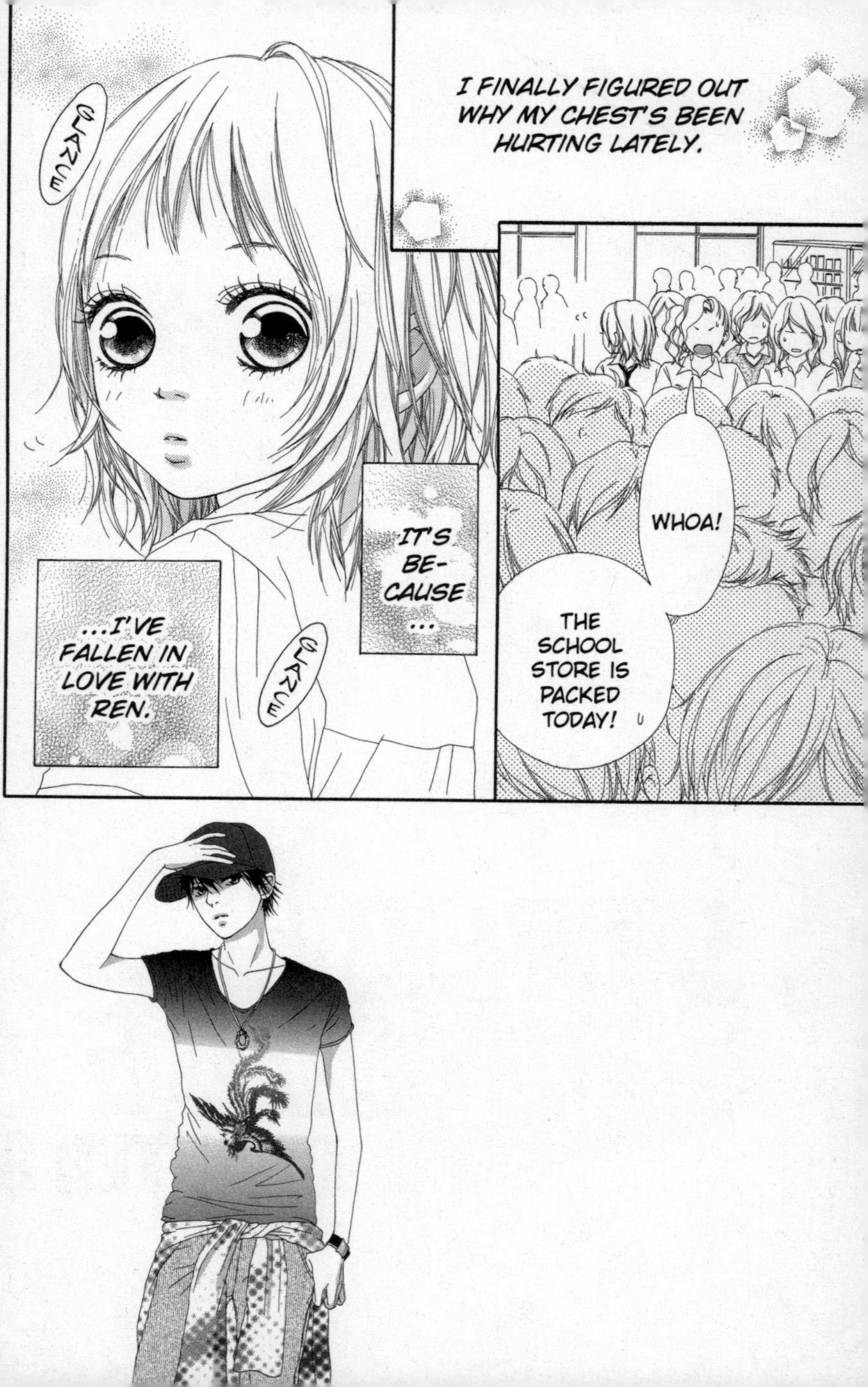
I FINALLY FIGURED OUT WHY MY CHEST'S BEEN HURTING LATELY.
WHOA!
THE SCHOOL STORE IS PACKED TODAY!
GLANCE
IT'S BE- CAUSE ...
GLANCE
...I'VE FALLEN IN LOVE WITH REN.

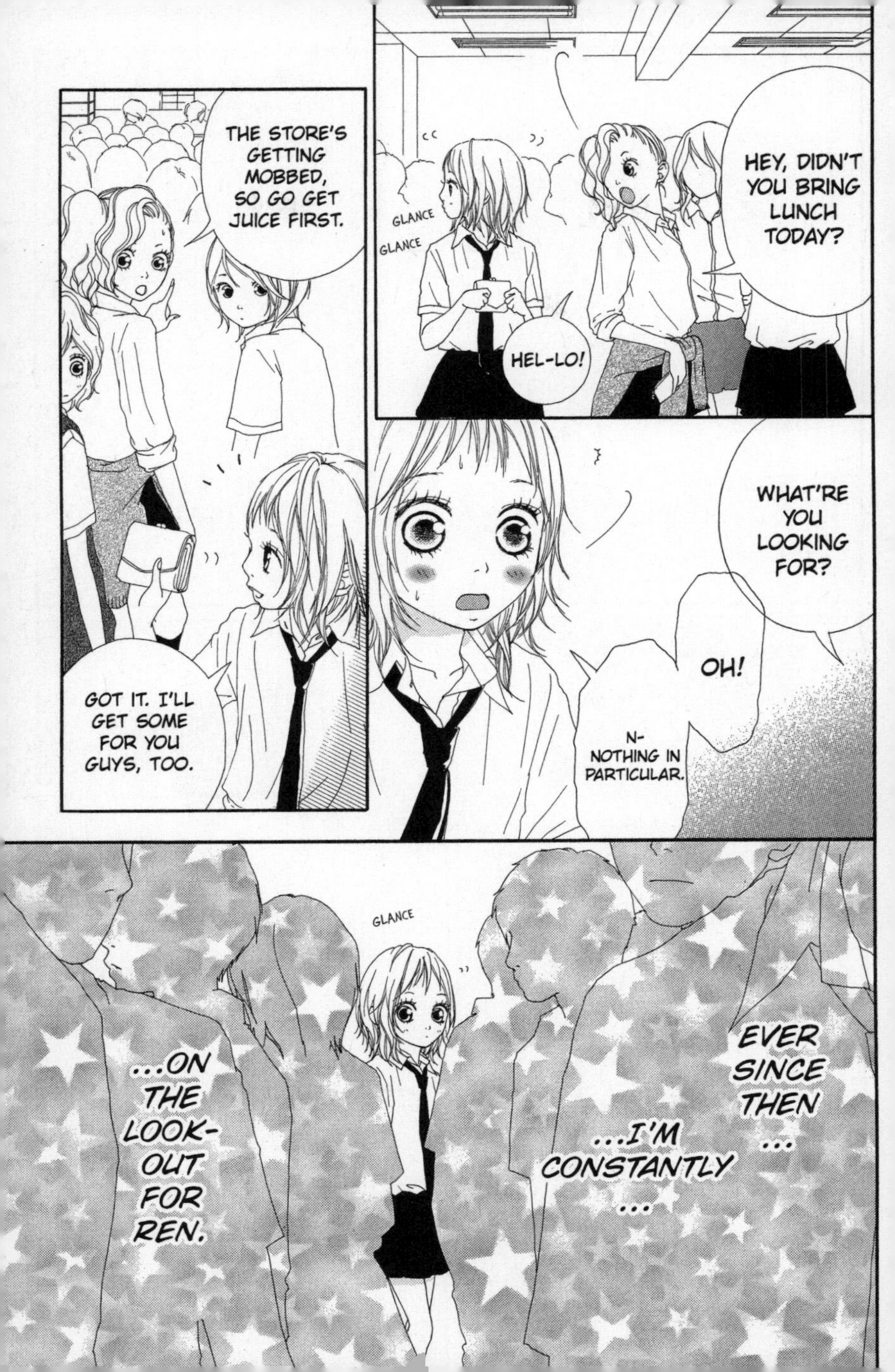
HEY, DIDN'T YOU BRING LUNCH TODAY?
GLANCE
GLANCE
HEL-LO!
WHAT'RE YOU LOOKING FOR?
OH!
N- NOTHING IN PARTICULAR.
THE STORE'S GETTING MOBBED, SO GO GET JUICE FIRST.
GOT IT. I'LL GET SOME FOR YOU GUYS, TOO.
GLANCE
EVER SINCE THEN ...
...I'M CONSTANTLY ...
...ON THE LOOK-OUT FOR REN.

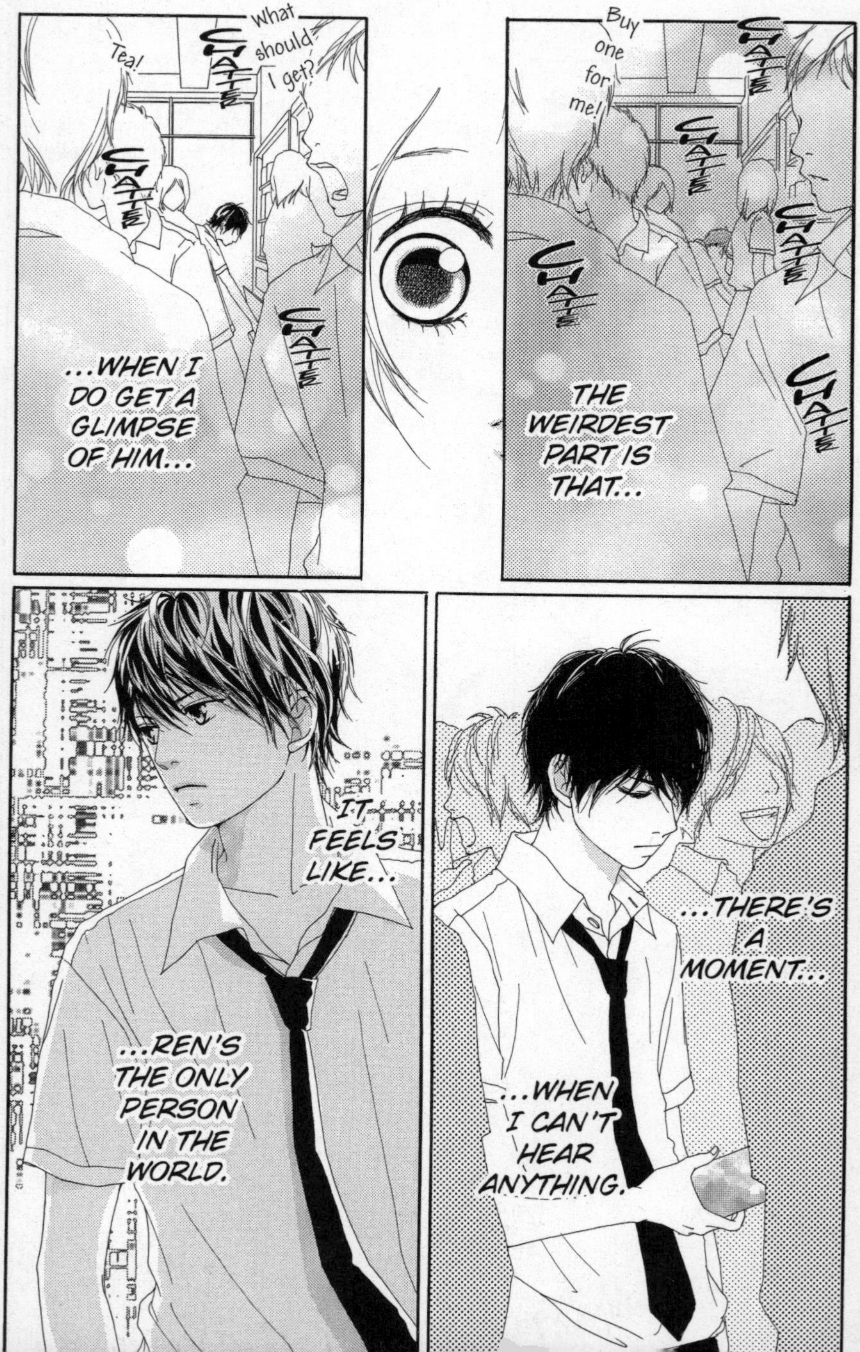
Buy one for me!
CHATTER
CHATTER
CHATTER
CHATTER
CHATTE
THE WEIRDEST PART IS THAT...
What should I get?
Tea!
CHATTER
CHATTER
CHATTER
...WHEN I DO GET A GLIMPSE OF HIM...
...THERE'S A MOMENT...
...WHEN I CAN'T HEAR ANYTHING.
IT FEELS LIKE...
...REN'S THE ONLY PERSON IN THE WORLD.

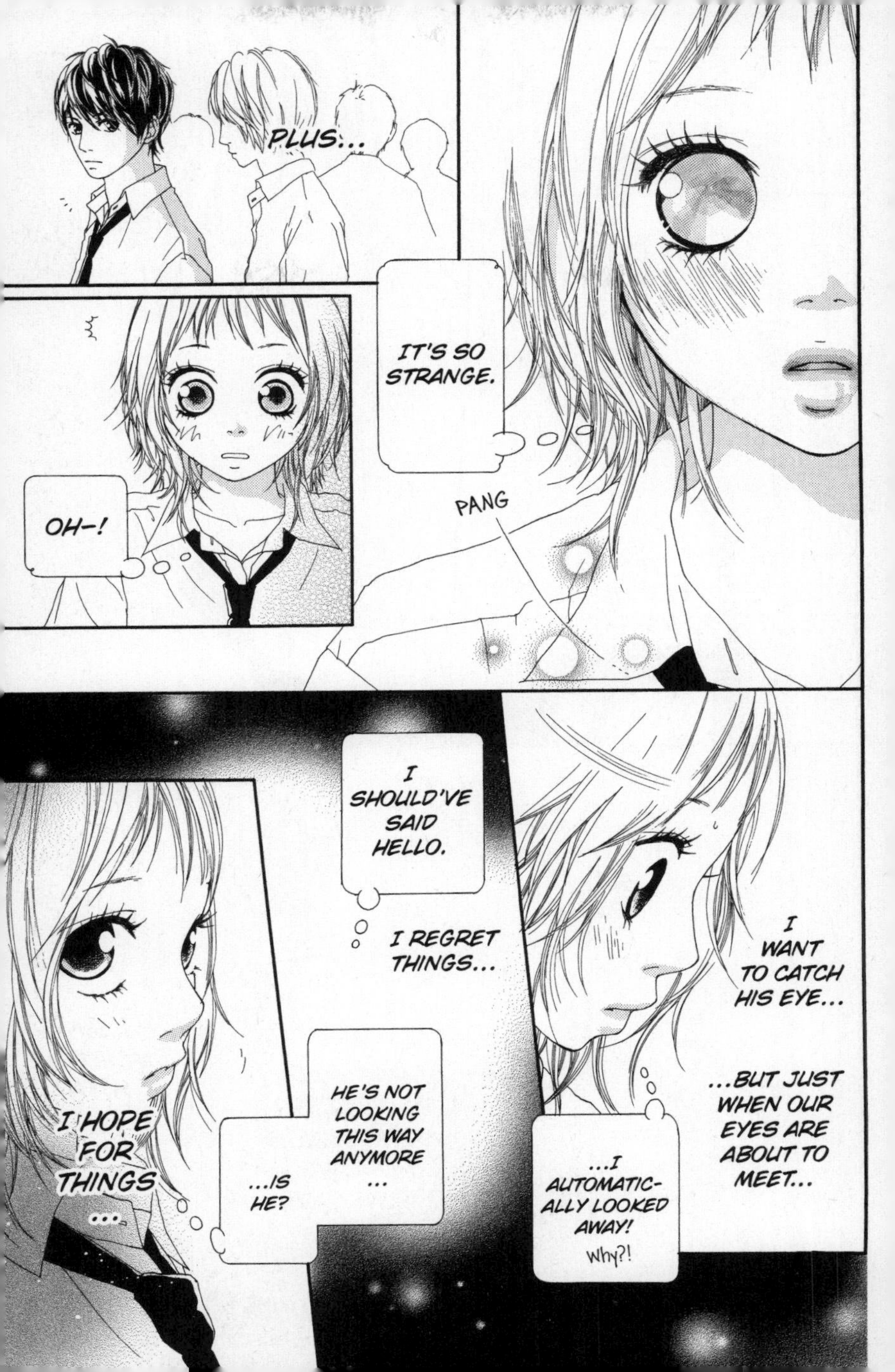
IT'S SO STRANGE.
PANG
PLUS...
OH-!
I WANT TO CATCH HIS EYE...
...BUT JUST WHEN OUR EYES ARE ABOUT TO MEET...
...I AUTOMATIC-ALLY LOOKED AWAY! Why?!
I SHOULD'VE SAID HELLO.
I REGRET THINGS...
HE'S NOT LOOKING THIS WAY ANYMORE...
...IS HE?
I HOPE FOR THINGS...

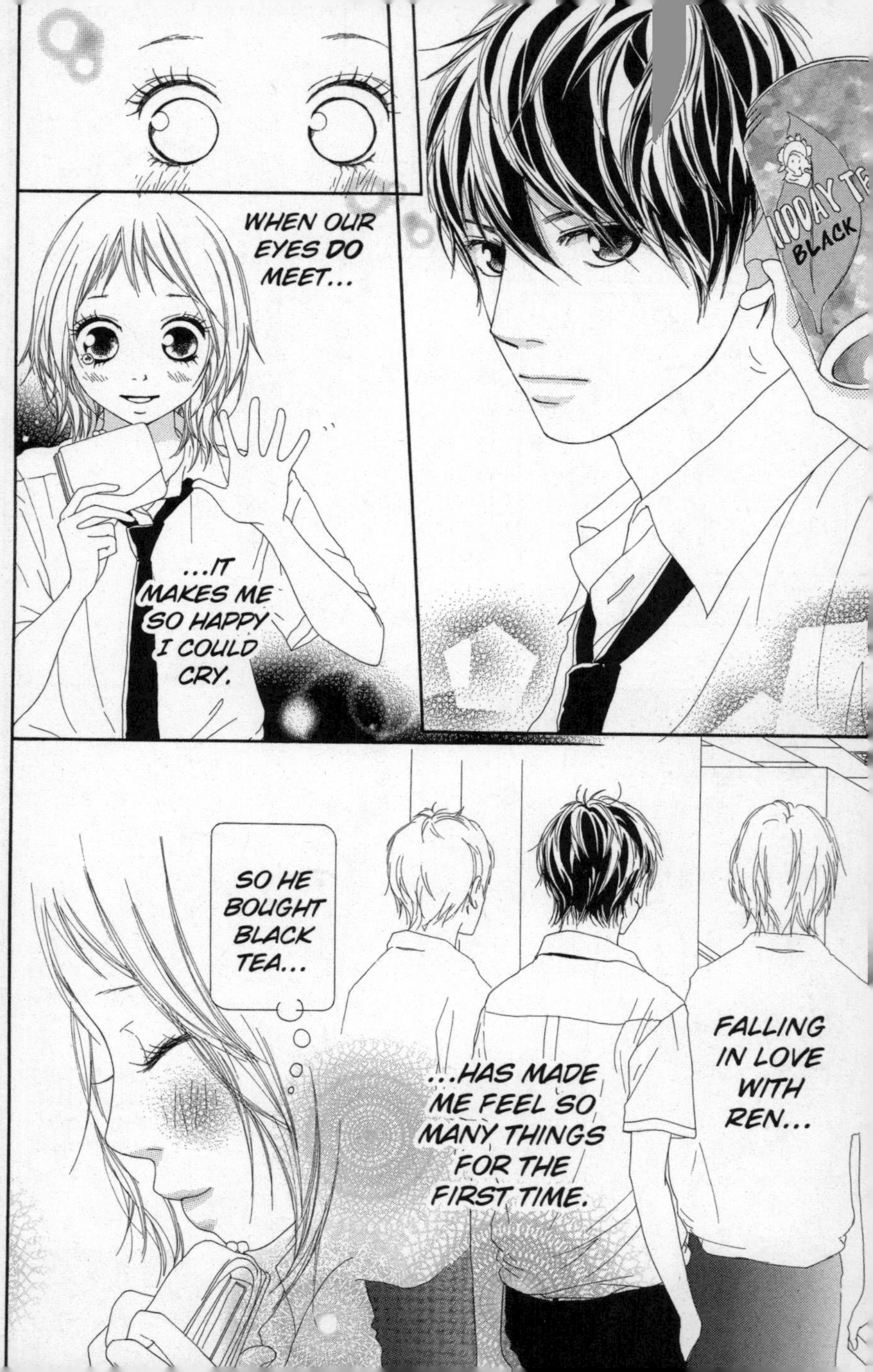
BLACK
WHEN OUR EYES DO MEET...
...IT MAKES ME SO HAPPY I COULD CRY.
FALLING IN LOVE WITH REN...
...HAS MADE ME FEEL SO MANY THINGS FOR THE FIRST TIME.
SO HE BOUGHT BLACK TEA...

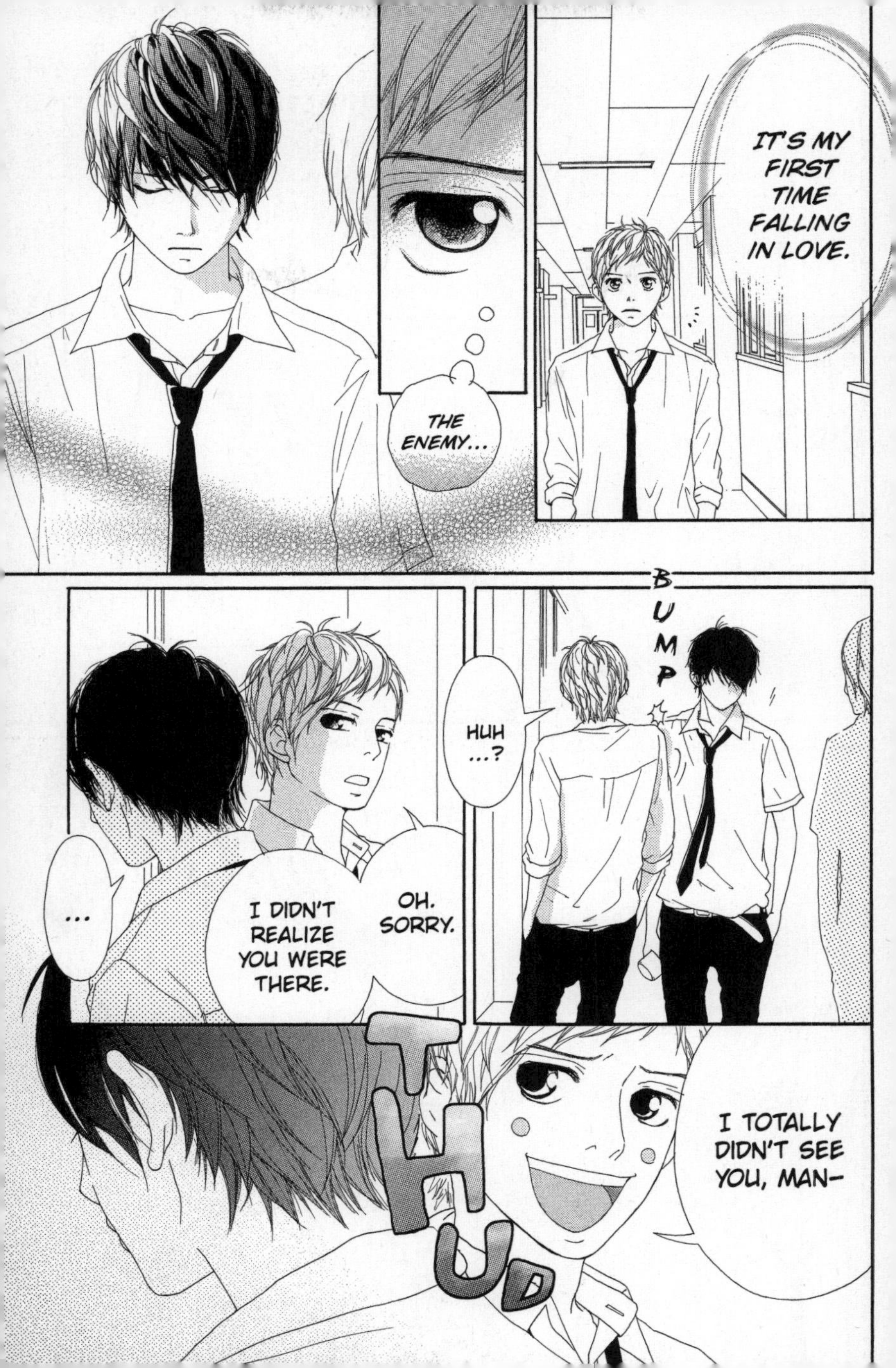
IT'S MY FIRST TIME FALLING IN LOVE.
THE ENEMY...
BUMP
HUH ...?
OH. SORRY.
I DIDN'T REALIZE YOU WERE THERE.
...
THUD
I TOTALLY DIDN'T SEE YOU, MAN–

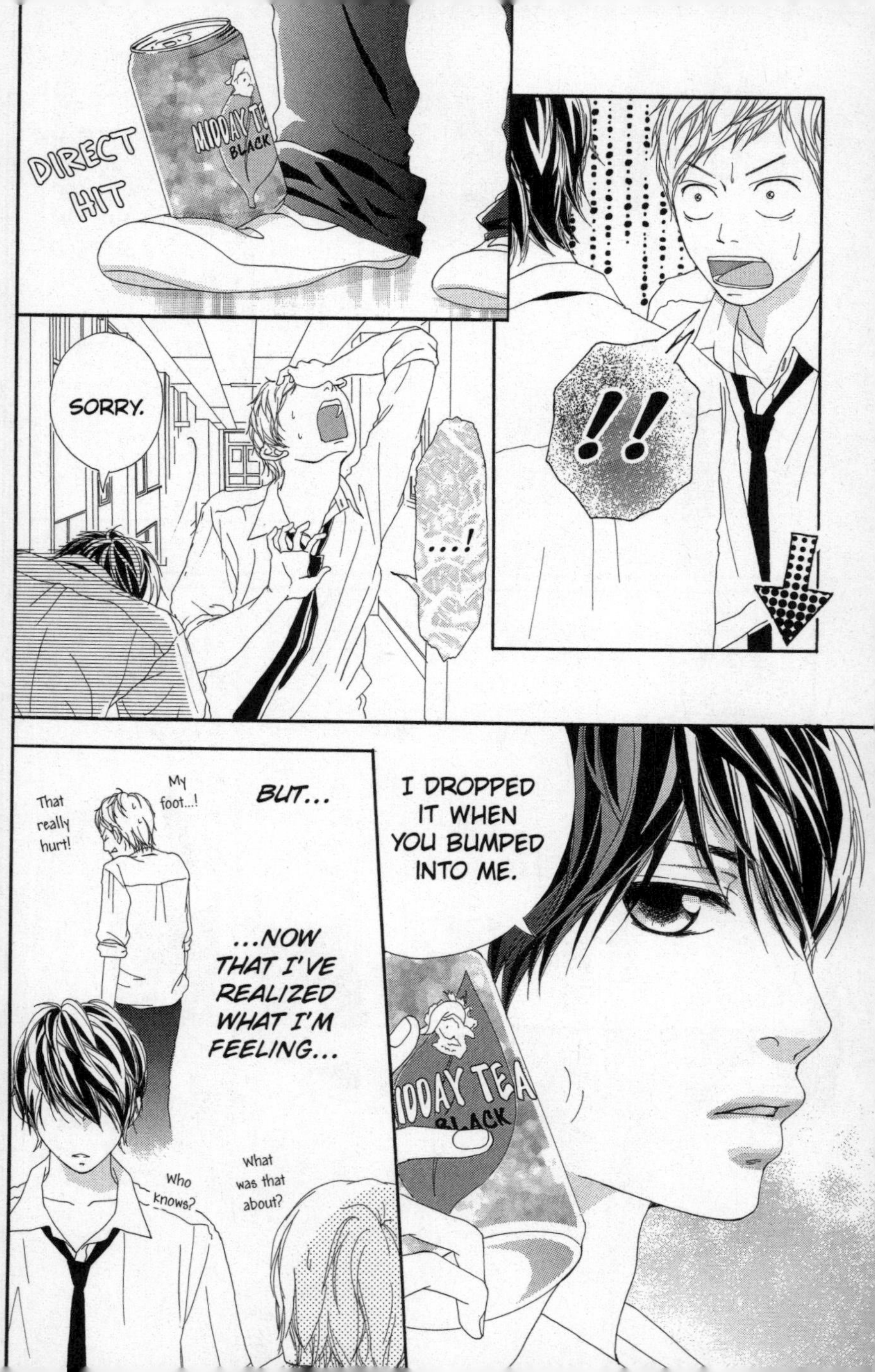
DIRECT HIT
MIDDAY TEA BLACK
!!
SORRY.
...!
I DROPPED IT WHEN YOU BUMPED INTO ME.
MIDDAY TEA BLACK
BUT...
...NOW THAT I'VE REALIZED WHAT I'M FEELING...
My foot...!
That really hurt!
What was that about?
Who knows?

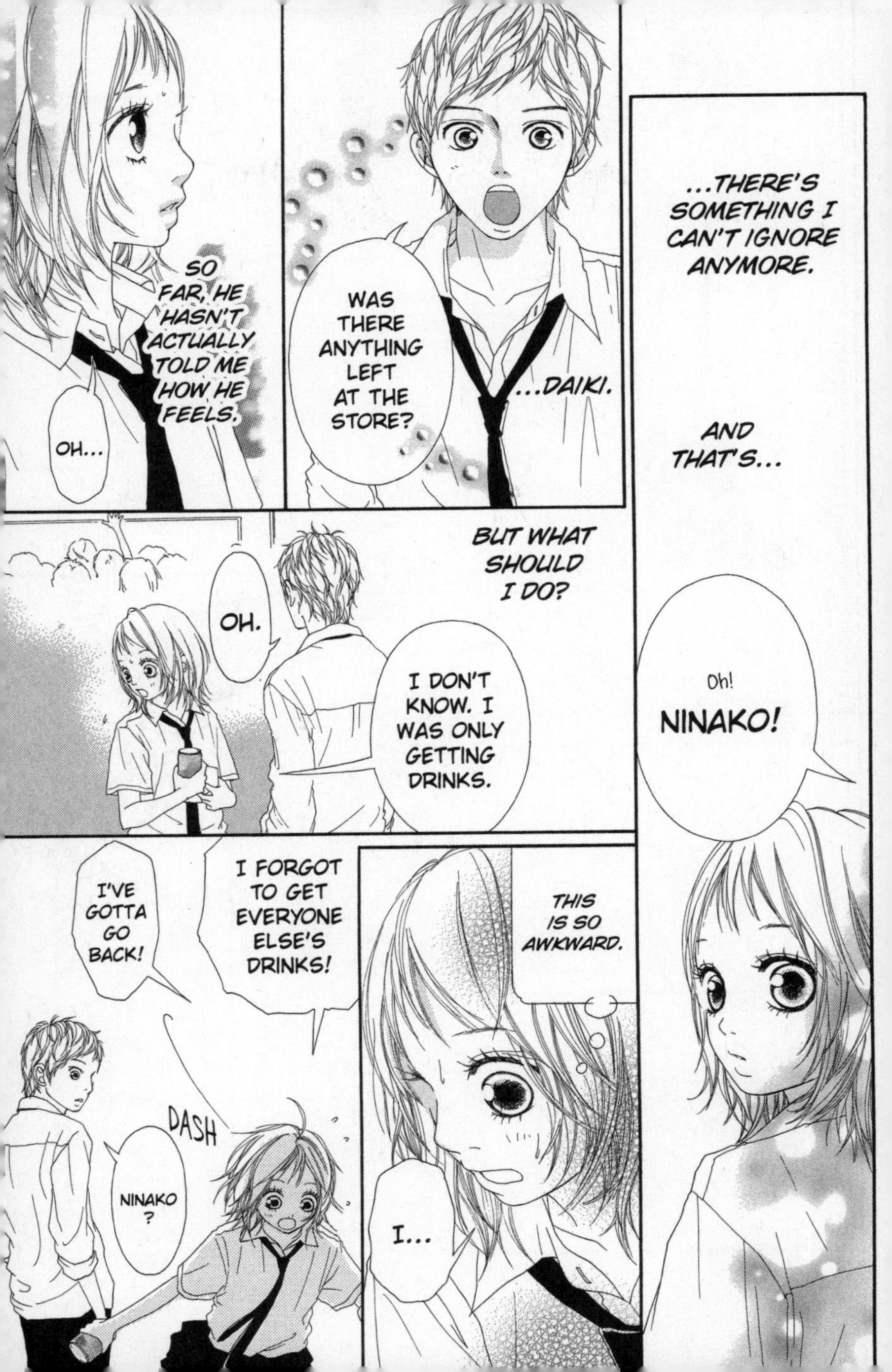

...THERE'S SOMETHING I CAN'T IGNORE ANYMORE.
AND THAT'S...
Oh!
NINAKO!
...DAIKI.
WAS THERE ANYTHING LEFT AT THE STORE?
SO FAR, HE HASN'T ACTUALLY TOLD ME HOW HE FEELS.
OH...
BUT WHAT SHOULD I DO?
I DON'T KNOW. I WAS ONLY GETTING DRINKS.
OH.
THIS IS SO AWKWARD.
I...
I FORGOT TO GET EVERYONE ELSE'S DRINKS!
I'VE GOTTA GO BACK!
DASH
NINAKO?

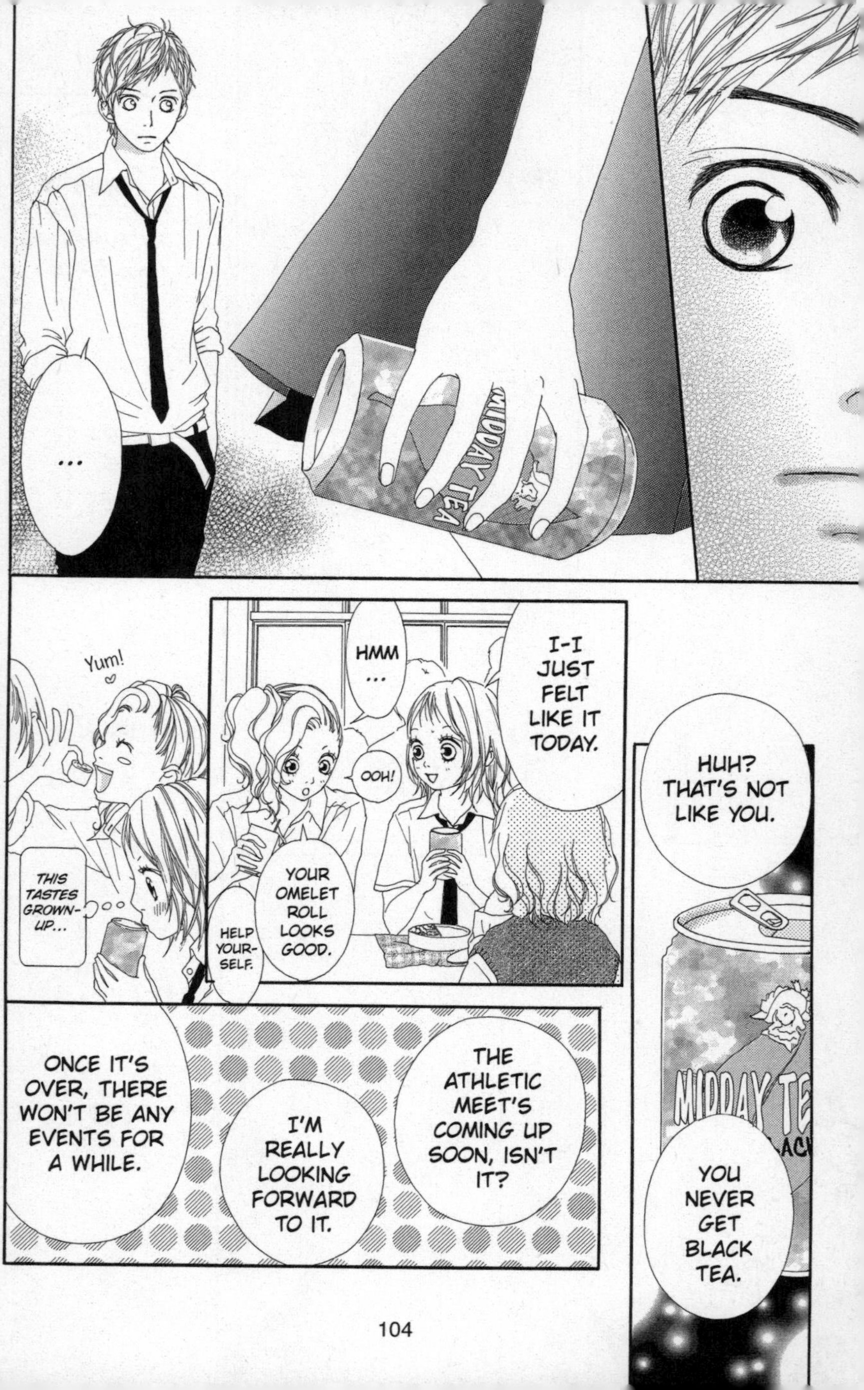
MIDDAY TEA
...
HUH? THAT'S NOT LIKE YOU.
MIDDAY TE
YOU NEVER GET BLACK TEA.
I-I JUST FELT LIKE IT TODAY.
HMM ...
OOH!
YOUR OMELET ROLL LOOKS GOOD.
HELP YOURSELF.
Yum!
THIS TASTES GROWN-UP...
THE ATHLETIC MEET'S COMING UP SOON, ISN'T IT?
I'M REALLY LOOKING FORWARD TO IT.
ONCE IT'S OVER, THERE WON'T BE ANY EVENTS FOR A WHILE.

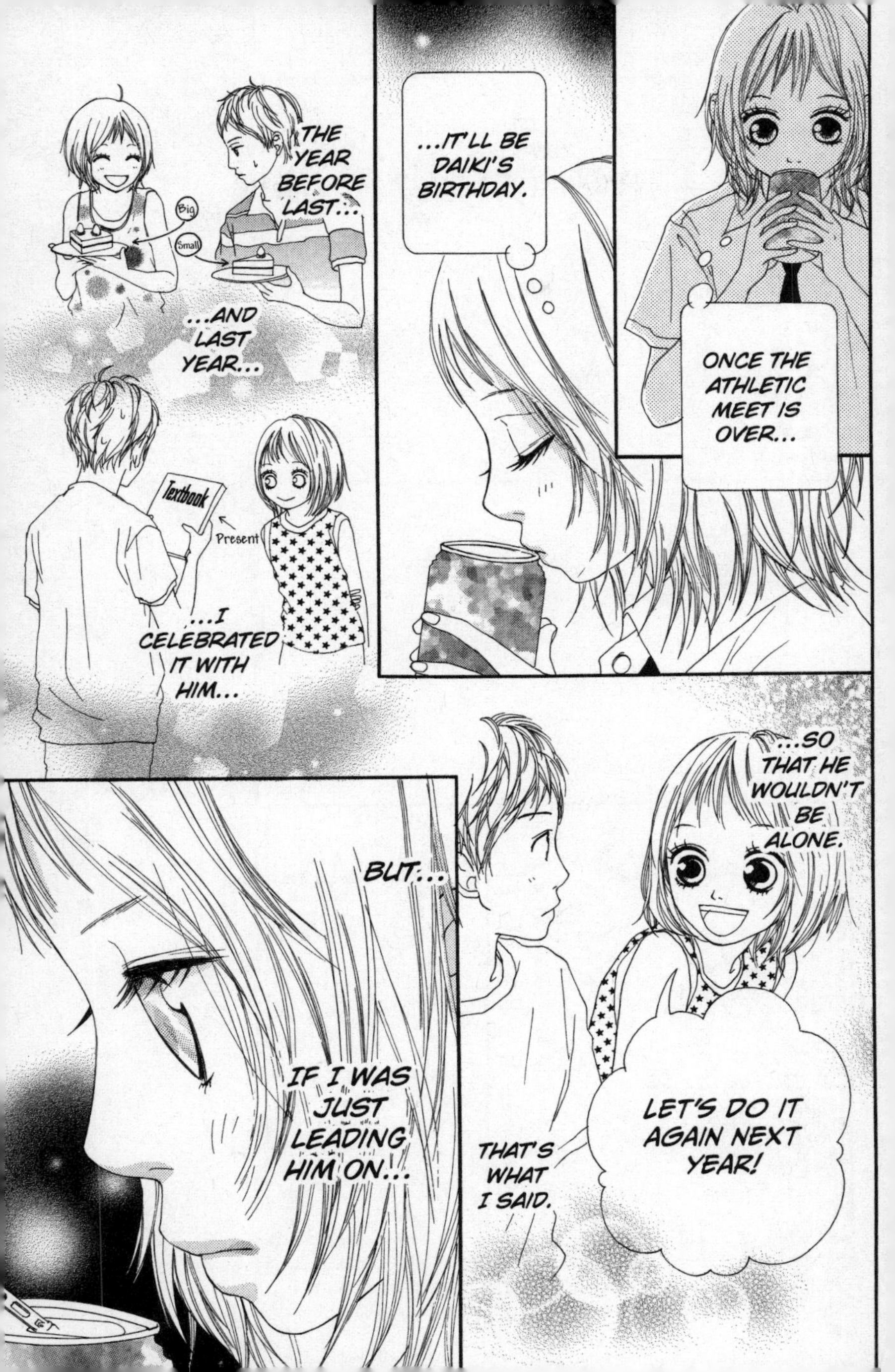

ONCE THE ATHLETIC MEET IS OVER...
...IT'LL BE DAIKI'S BIRTHDAY.
THE YEAR BEFORE LAST...
Big
Small
...AND LAST YEAR...
Textbook
Present
...I CELEBRATED IT WITH HIM...
...SO THAT HE WOULDN'T BE ALONE.
LET'S DO IT AGAIN NEXT YEAR!
THAT'S WHAT I SAID.
BUT...
IF I WAS JUST LEADING HIM ON...

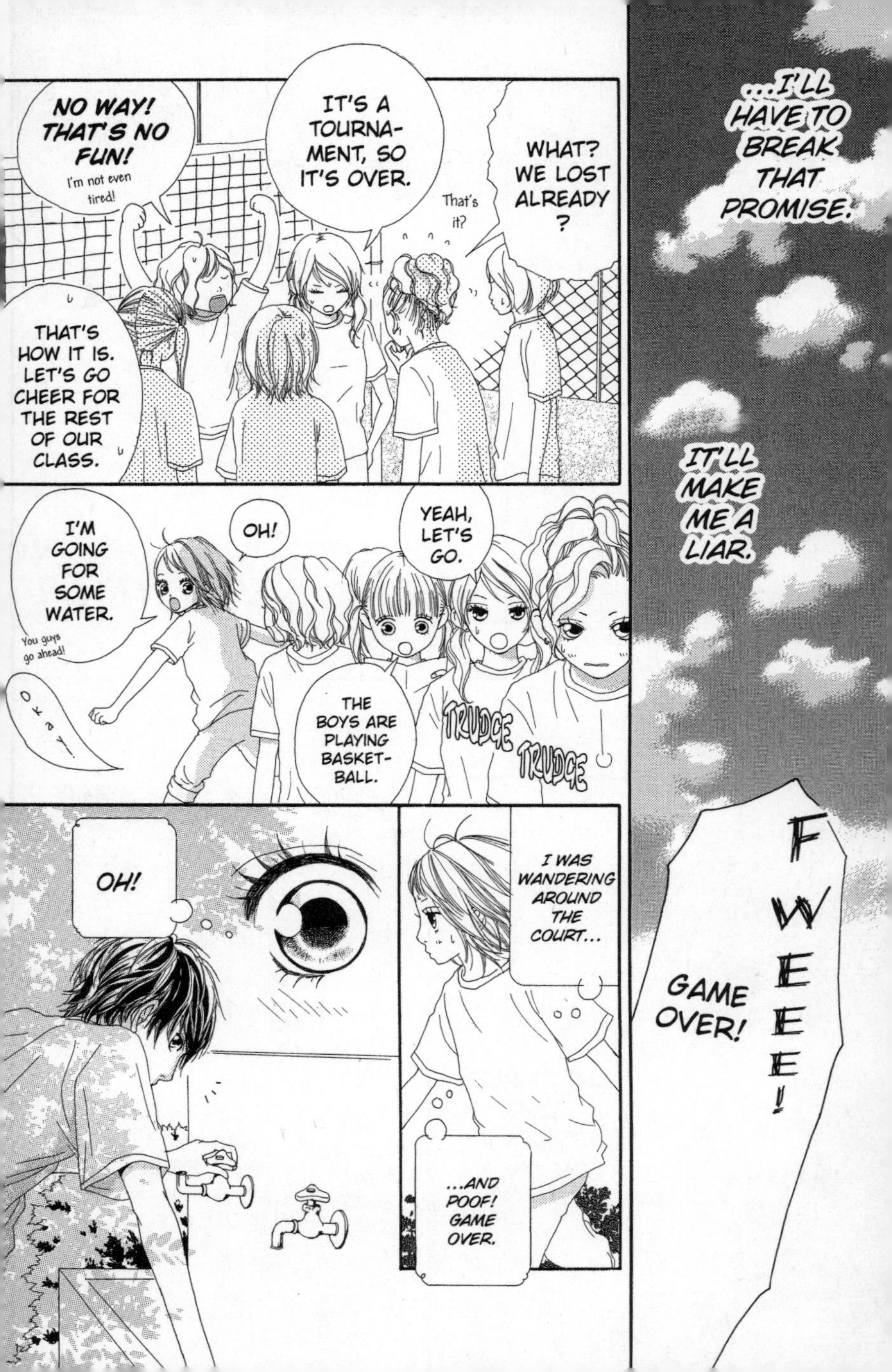
...I'LL HAVE TO BREAK THAT PROMISE.
IT'LL MAKE ME A LIAR.
FWEEE!
GAME OVER!
WHAT? WE LOST ALREADY?
That's it?
IT'S A TOURNAMENT, SO IT'S OVER.
NO WAY! THAT'S NO FUN!
I'm not even tired!
THAT'S HOW IT IS. LET'S GO CHEER FOR THE REST OF OUR CLASS.
YEAH, LET'S GO.
TRUDGE
TRUDGE
THE BOYS ARE PLAYING BASKETBALL.
OH!
I'M GOING FOR SOME WATER.
You guys go ahead!
Okay!
I WAS WANDERING AROUND THE COURT...
...AND POOF! GAME OVER.
OH!

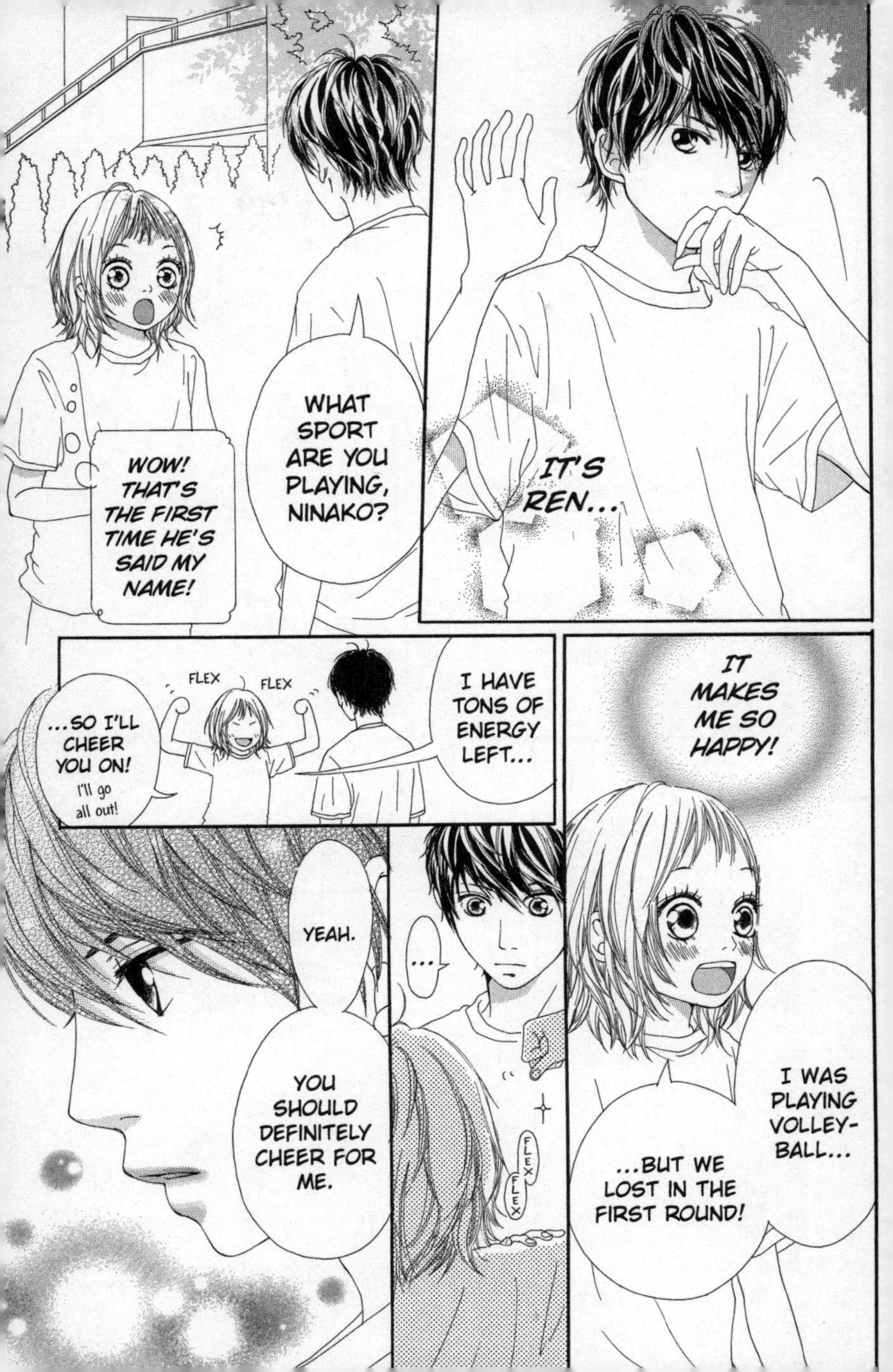
IT'S REN...
WHAT SPORT ARE YOU PLAYING, NINAKO?
WOW! THAT'S THE FIRST TIME HE'S SAID MY NAME!
IT MAKES ME SO HAPPY!
I WAS PLAYING VOLLEY-BALL...
...BUT WE LOST IN THE FIRST ROUND!
I HAVE TONS OF ENERGY LEFT...
FLEX FLEX
...SO I'LL CHEER YOU ON!
I'll go all out!
....
FLEX FLEX
YEAH.
YOU SHOULD DEFINITELY CHEER FOR ME.

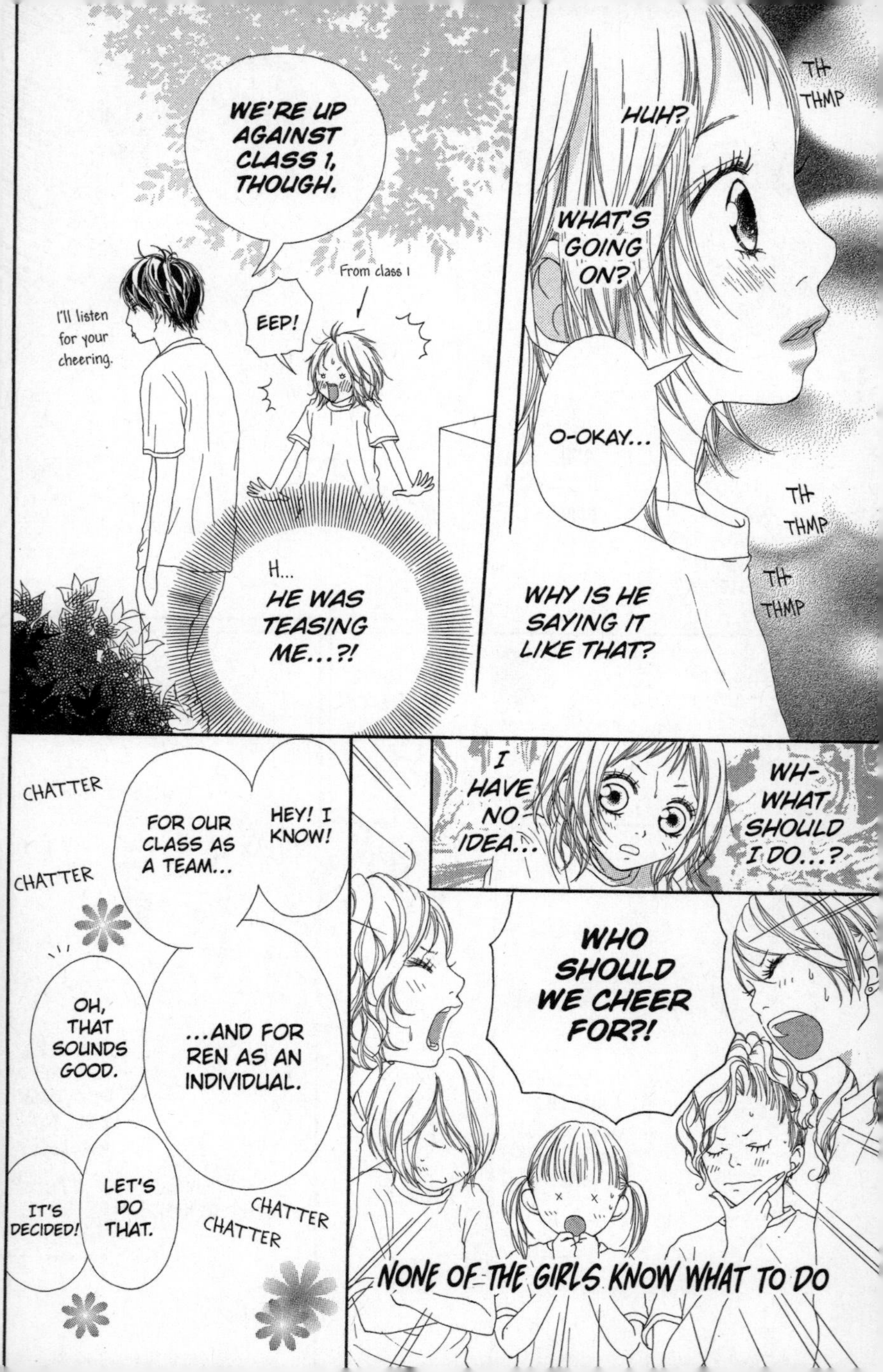
TH THMP
HUH?
WHAT'S GOING ON?
O-OKAY...
TH THMP
TH THMP
WHY IS HE SAYING IT LIKE THAT?
WE'RE UP AGAINST CLASS 1, THOUGH.
I'll listen for your cheering.
From class 1
EEP!
H... HE WAS TEASING ME...?!
WH-WHAT SHOULD I DO...?
I HAVE NO IDEA...
WHO SHOULD WE CHEER FOR?!
NONE OF THE GIRLS KNOW WHAT TO DO
HEY! I KNOW!
FOR OUR CLASS AS A TEAM...
...AND FOR REN AS AN INDIVIDUAL.
CHATTER
CHATTER
OH, THAT SOUNDS GOOD.
CHATTER
CHATTER
LET'S DO THAT.
IT'S DECIDED!

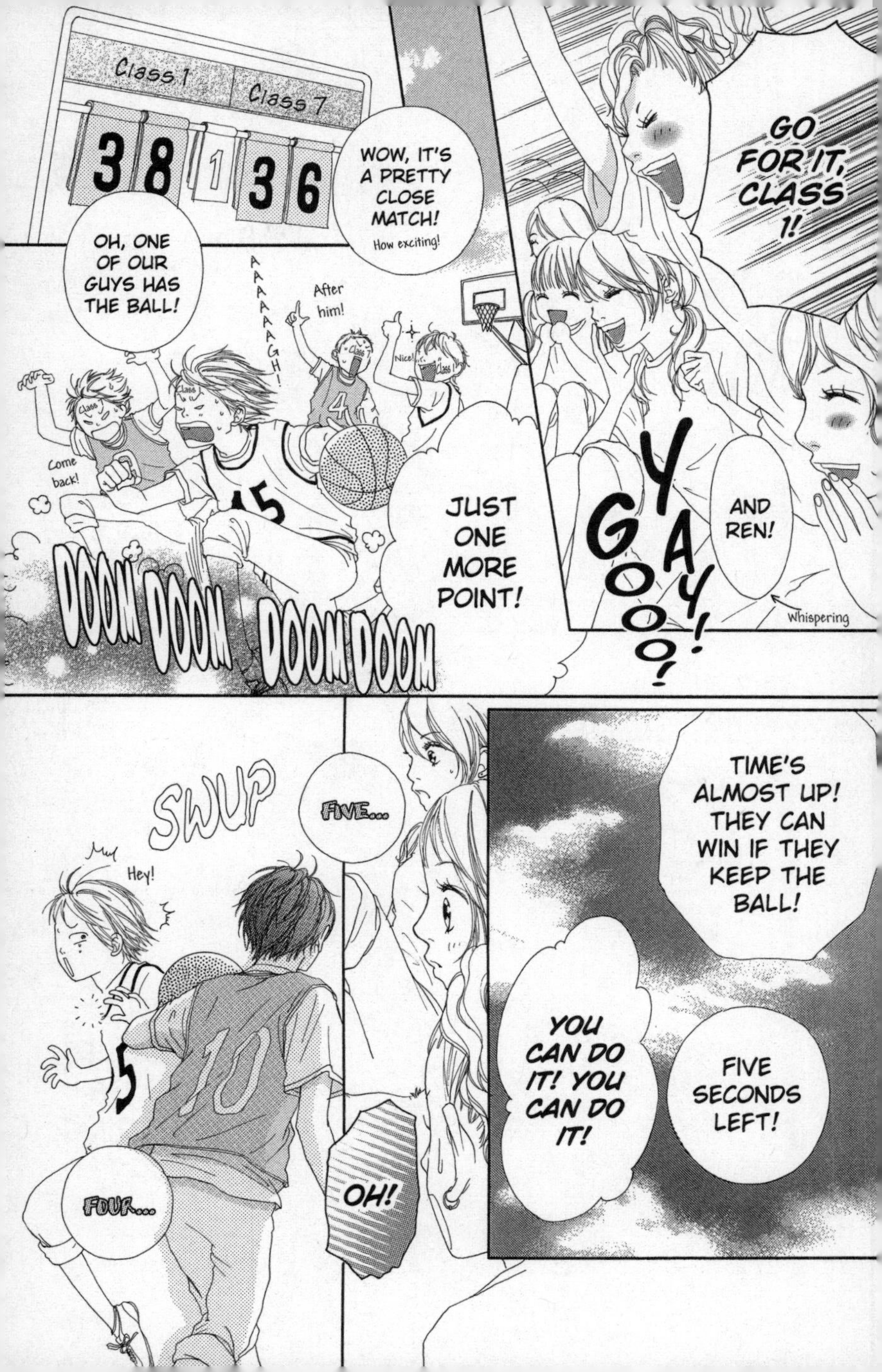
GO FOR IT, CLASS 1!
GOOOO! YAY!
AND REN!
Whispering
Class 1
Class 7
38
1
36
WOW, IT'S A PRETTY CLOSE MATCH!
How exciting!
OH, ONE OF OUR GUYS HAS THE BALL!
AAAAAAAGH!
After him!
Nice!
Come back!
JUST ONE MORE POINT!
DOOM DOOM
DOOM DOOM
TIME'S ALMOST UP! THEY CAN WIN IF THEY KEEP THE BALL!
FIVE SECONDS LEFT!
YOU CAN DO IT! YOU CAN DO IT!
FIVE...
OH!
SWUP
Hey!
FOUR...

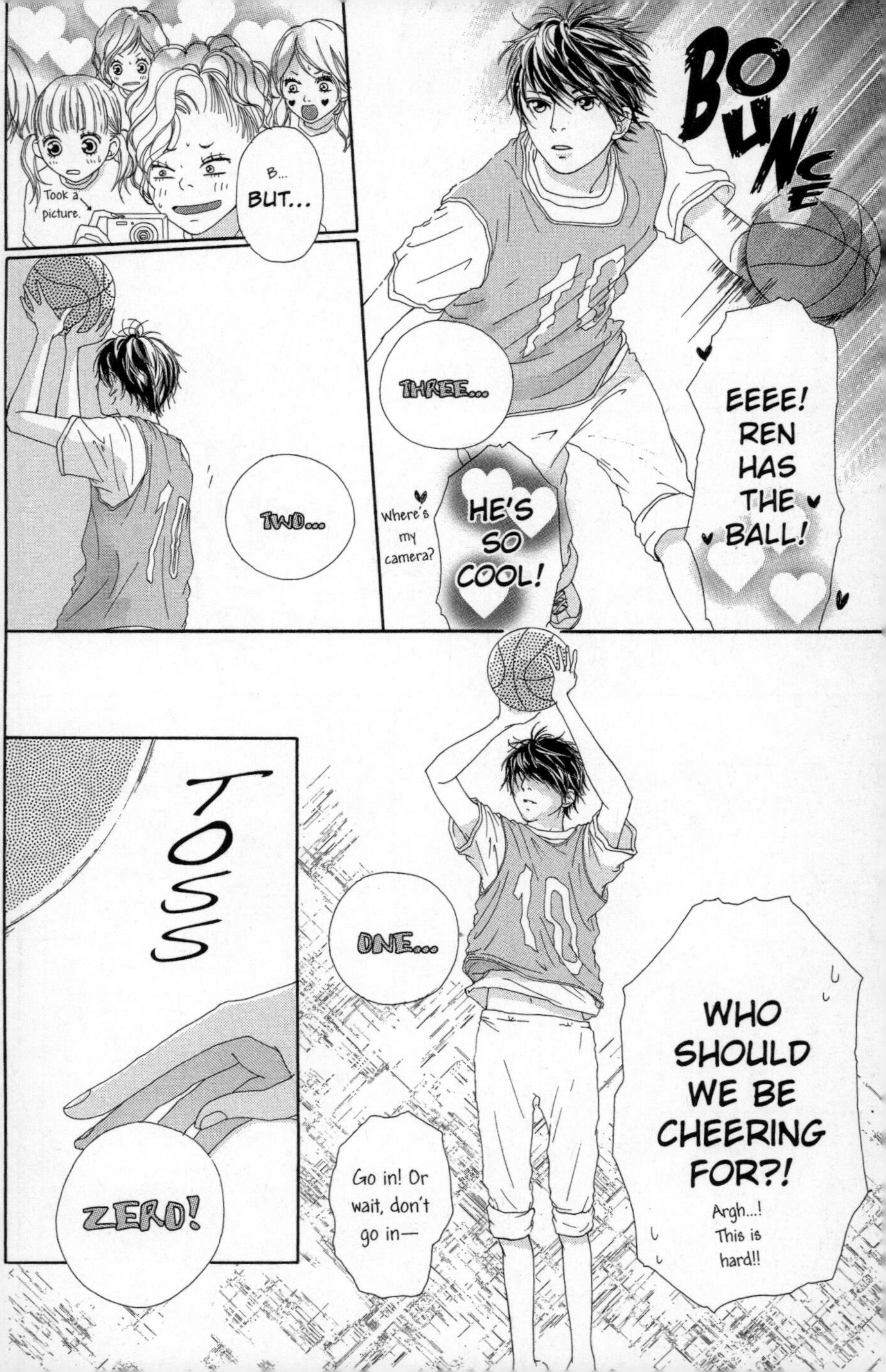
BOUNCE
THREE...
EEEE! REN HAS THE BALL!
HE'S SO COOL!
Where's my camera?
Took a picture.
B... BUT...
TWO...
WHO SHOULD WE BE CHEERING FOR?!
Argh...! This is hard!!
ONE...
Go in! Or wait, don't go in—
TOSS
ZERO!

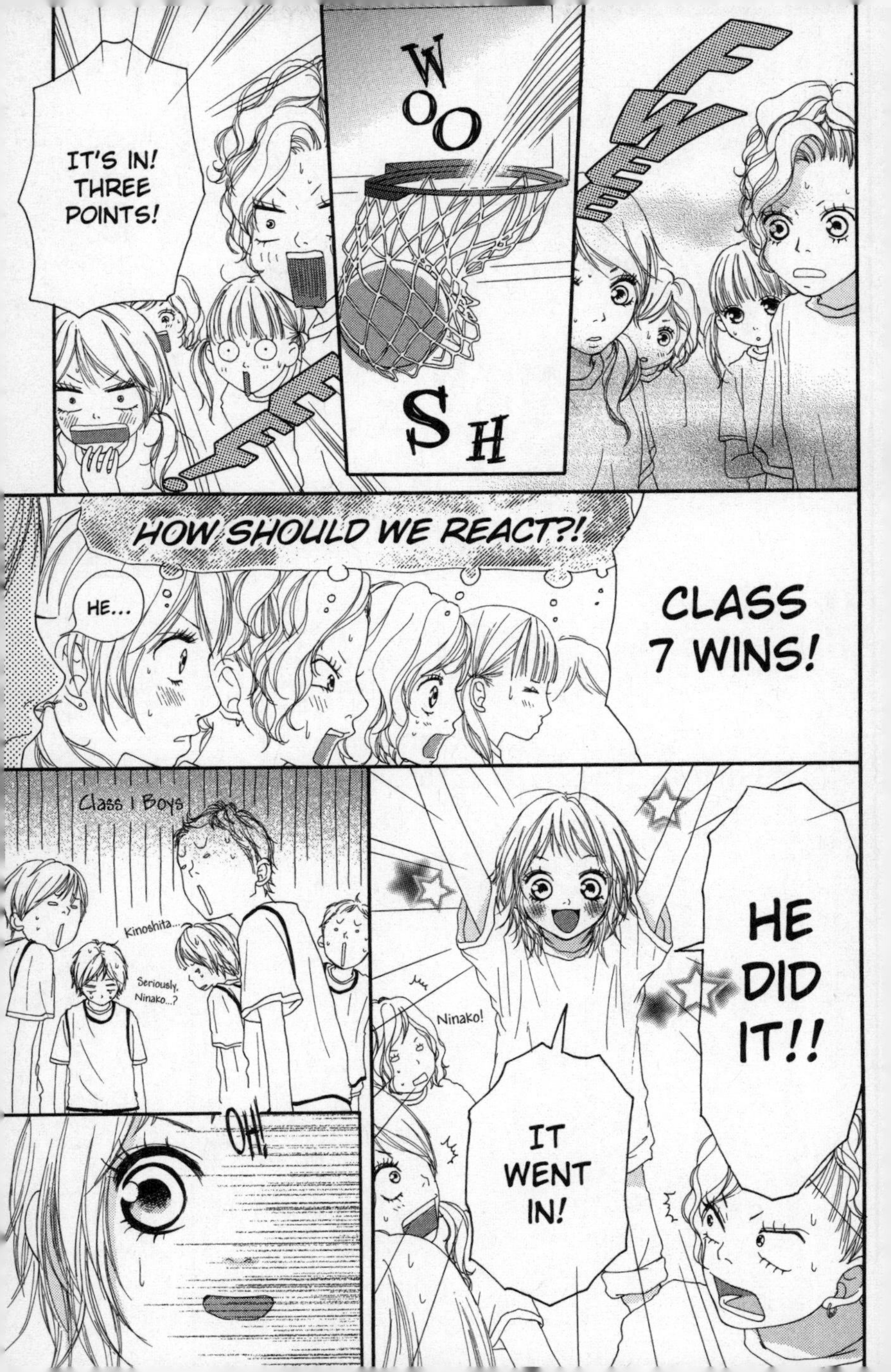
WOOSH
IT'S IN! THREE POINTS!
CLASS 7 WINS!
HOW SHOULD WE REACT?!
HE...
HE DID IT!!
IT WENT IN!
Ninako!
Class 1 Boys
Kinoshita...
Seriously, Ninako...?
OH!

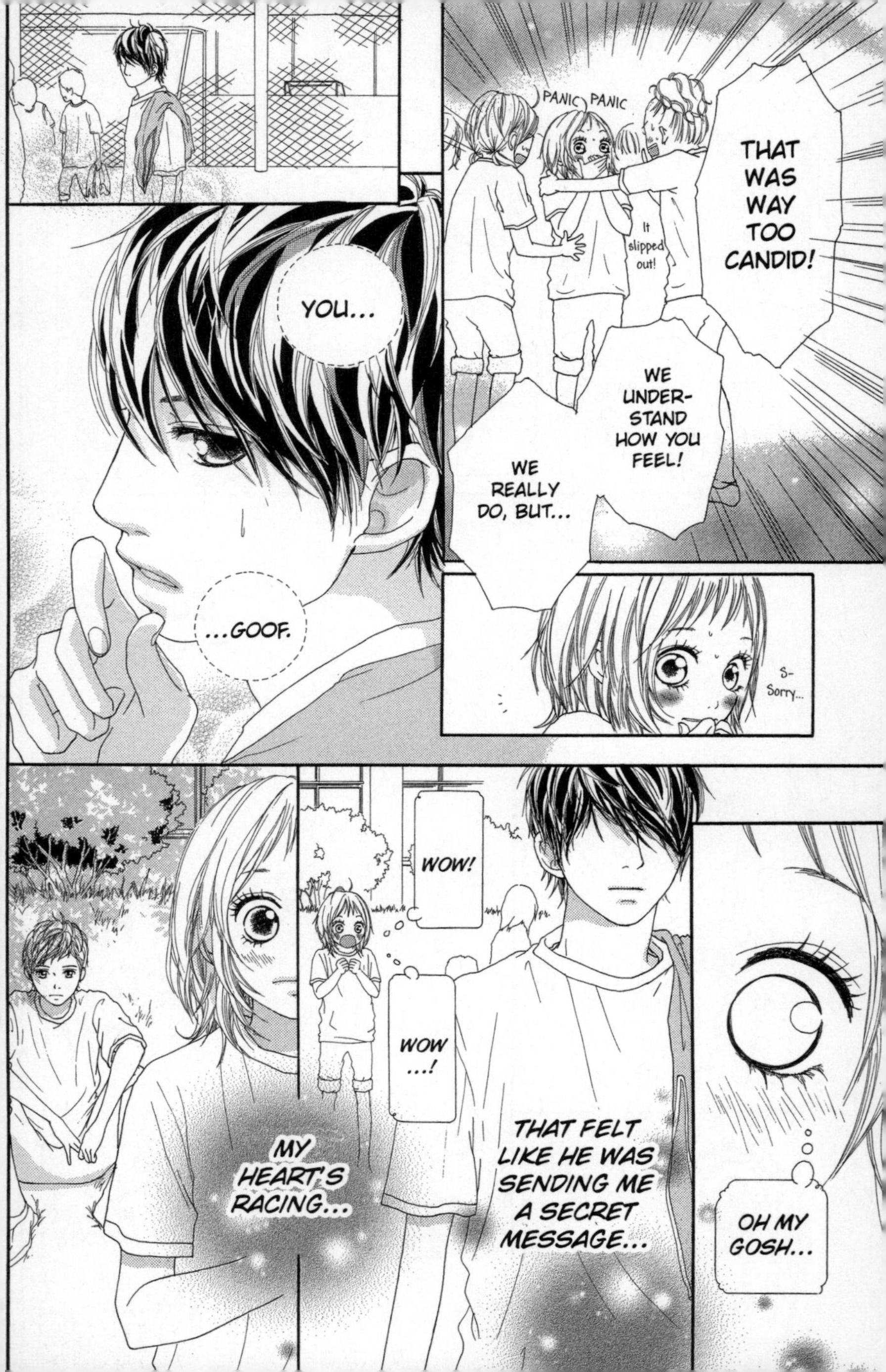
PANIC PANIC
THAT WAS WAY TOO CANDID!
It slipped out!
WE UNDER-STAND HOW YOU FEEL!
WE REALLY DO, BUT...
S- Sorry...
YOU...
...GOOF.
OH MY GOSH...
WOW!
WOW ...!
THAT FELT LIKE HE WAS SENDING ME A SECRET MESSAGE...
MY HEART'S RACING...

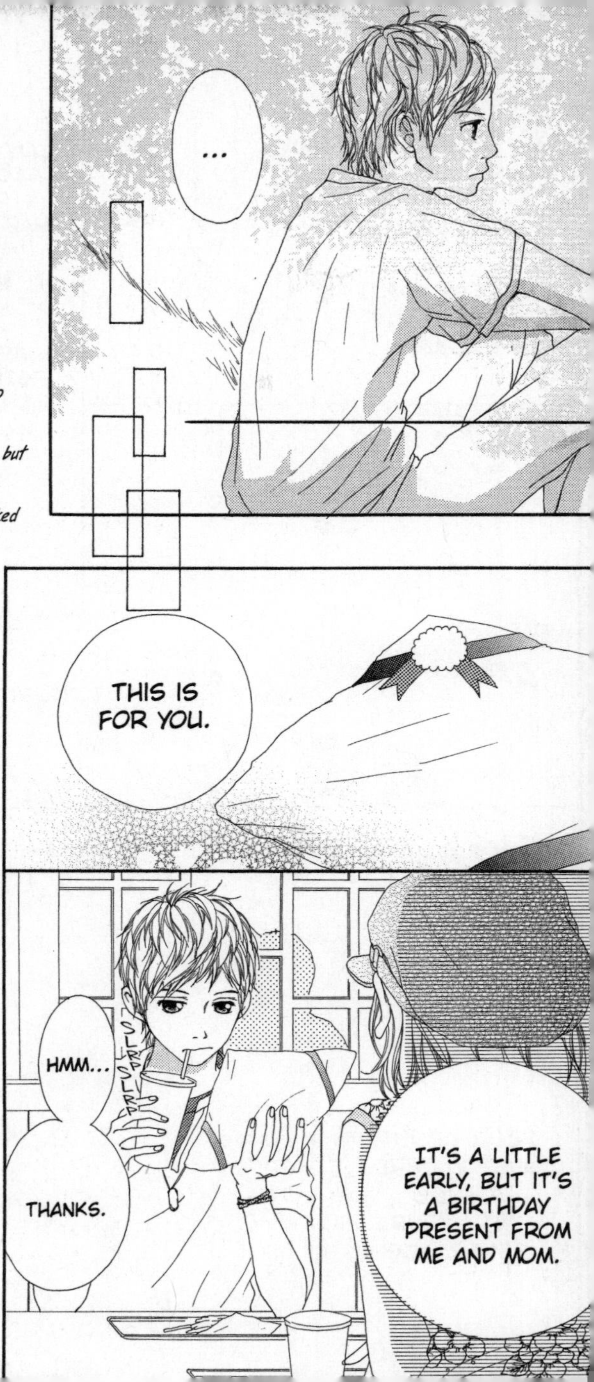
...
THIS IS FOR YOU.
IT'S A LITTLE EARLY, BUT IT'S A BIRTHDAY PRESENT FROM ME AND MOM.
HMM...
SLRP SLRP
THANKS.

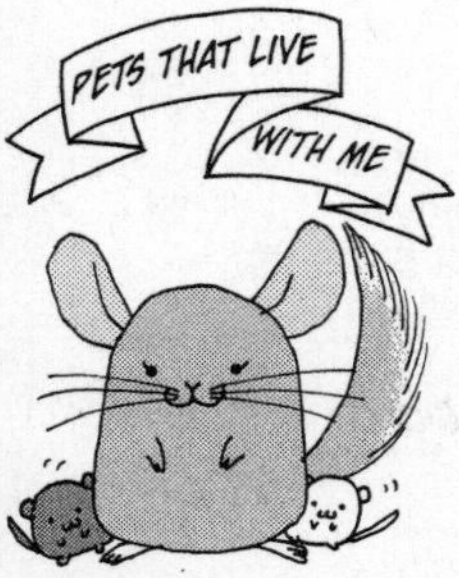
PETS THAT LIVE WITH ME

Komugi just had babies recently. (Chinchillas give birth one or two times a year.)

She's given birth several times, but I'd never actually seen it happen.

One morning, I woke up and looked in her cage...

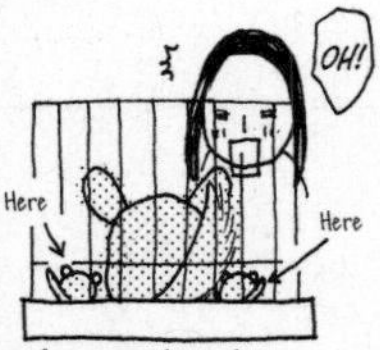
OH!
Here
Here

I figured that they secretly give birth in the middle of the night.

But one evening, when I came home...

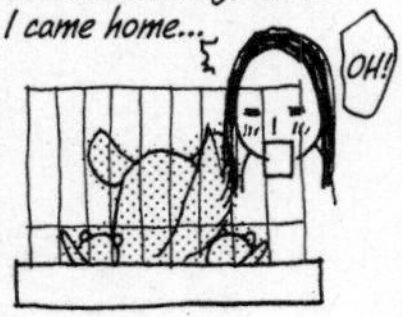
OH!

It happened.

And one afternoon, when I was passing by her cage...

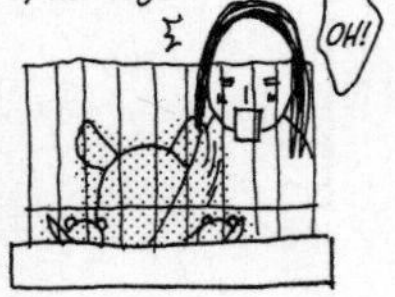
OH!

It happened.

When does she do it?

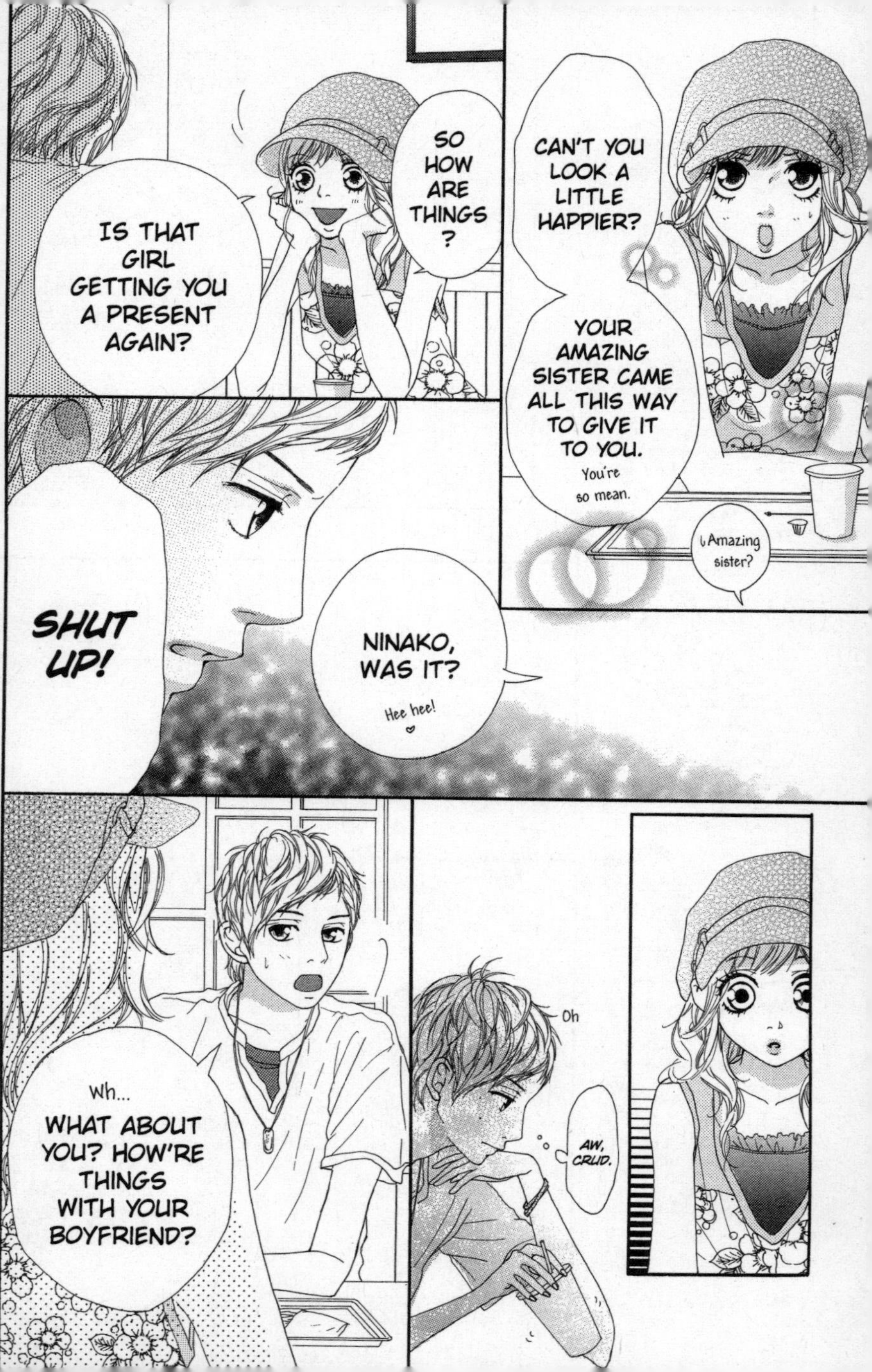
CAN'T YOU LOOK A LITTLE HAPPIER?
YOUR AMAZING SISTER CAME ALL THIS WAY TO GIVE IT TO YOU.
You're so mean.
¿Amazing sister?
SO HOW ARE THINGS?
IS THAT GIRL GETTING YOU A PRESENT AGAIN?
NINAKO, WAS IT?
Hee hee!
SHUT UP!
Oh
AW, CRUD.
Wh...
WHAT ABOUT YOU? HOW'RE THINGS WITH YOUR BOYFRIEND?

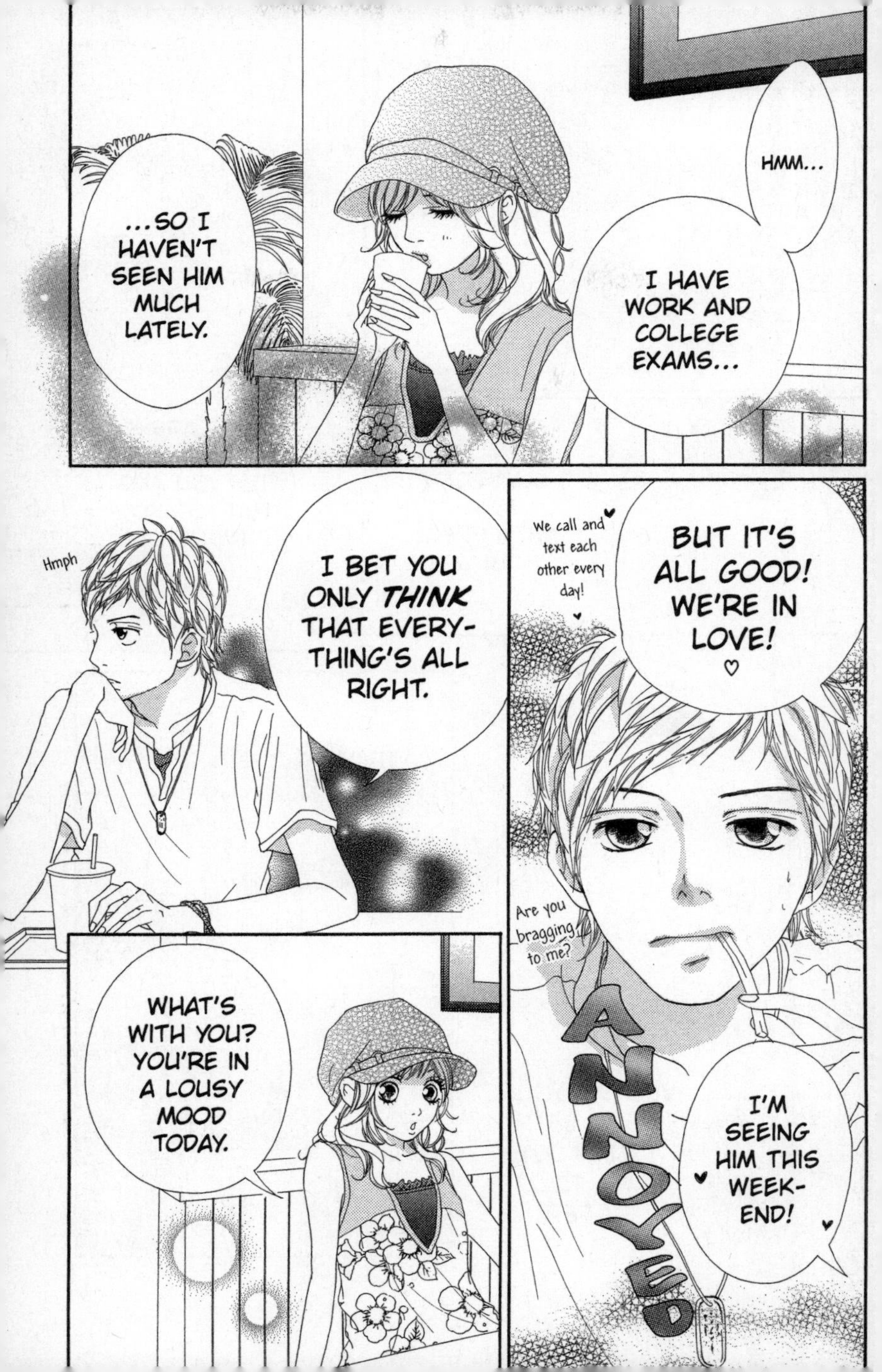
HMM...
I HAVE WORK AND COLLEGE EXAMS...
...SO I HAVEN'T SEEN HIM MUCH LATELY.
BUT IT'S ALL GOOD! WE'RE IN LOVE! ♡
We call and text each other every day!
Are you bragging to me?
ANNOYED
I'M SEEING HIM THIS WEEK-END!
Hmph
I BET YOU ONLY *THINK* THAT EVERY-THING'S ALL RIGHT.
WHAT'S WITH YOU? YOU'RE IN A LOUSY MOOD TODAY.

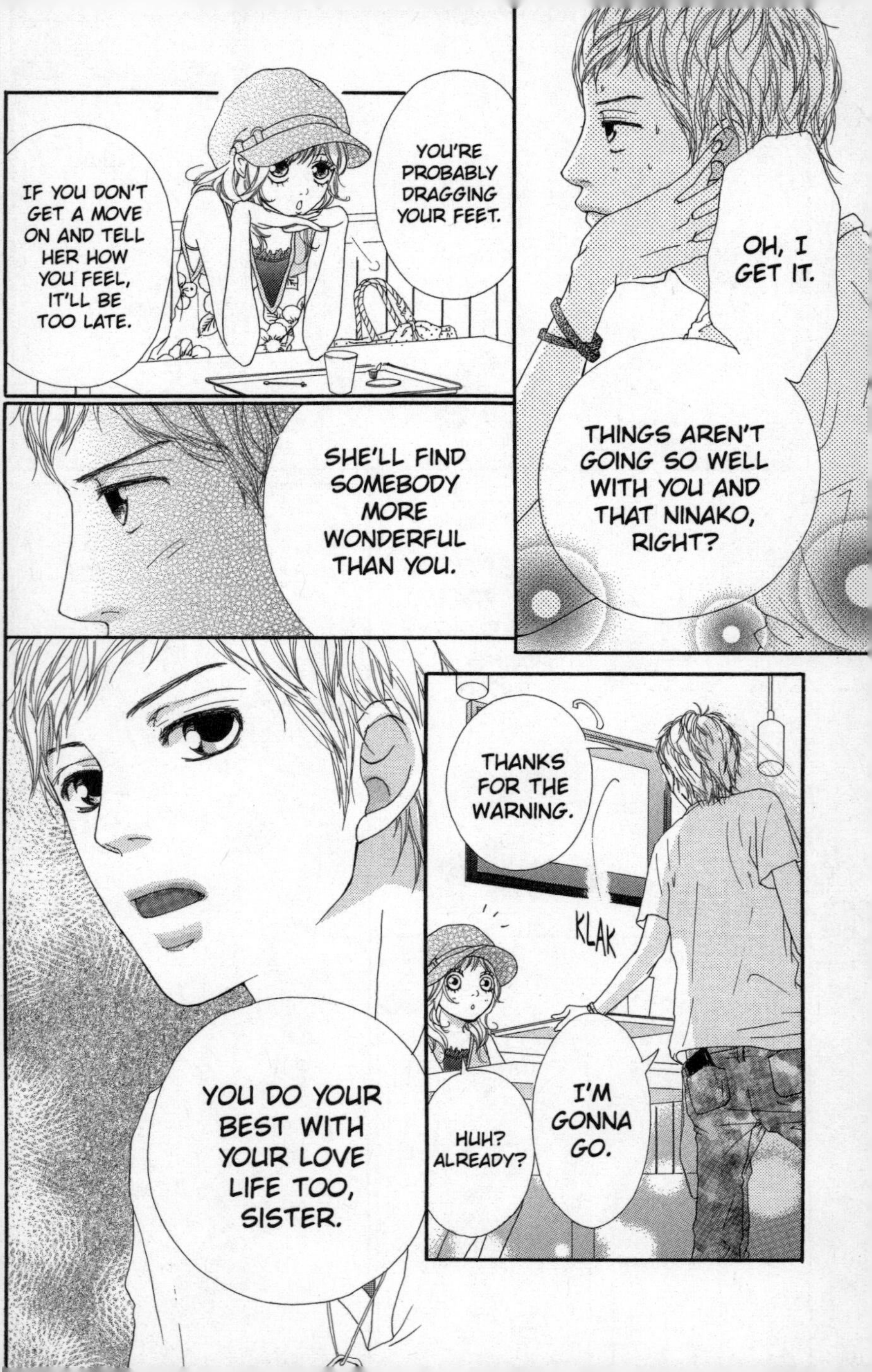
OH, I GET IT.
THINGS AREN'T GOING SO WELL WITH YOU AND THAT NINAKO, RIGHT?
YOU'RE PROBABLY DRAGGING YOUR FEET.
IF YOU DON'T GET A MOVE ON AND TELL HER HOW YOU FEEL, IT'LL BE TOO LATE.
SHE'LL FIND SOMEBODY MORE WONDERFUL THAN YOU.
THANKS FOR THE WARNING.
KLAK
I'M GONNA GO.
HUH? ALREADY?
YOU DO YOUR BEST WITH YOUR LOVE LIFE TOO, SISTER.

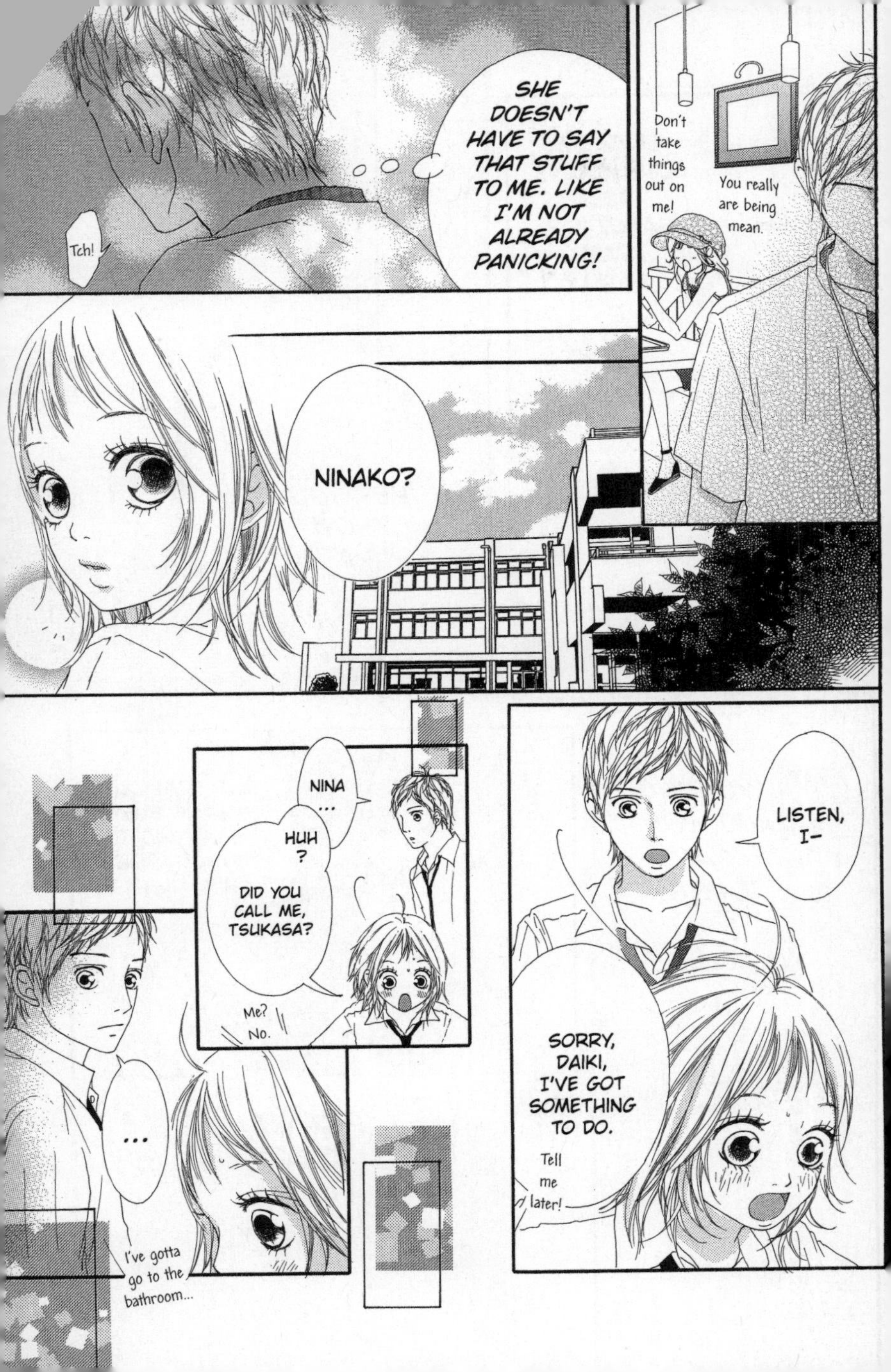
You really are being mean.
Don't take things out on me!
SHE DOESN'T HAVE TO SAY THAT STUFF TO ME. LIKE I'M NOT ALREADY PANICKING!
Tch!
NINAKO?
LISTEN, I—
SORRY, DAIKI, I'VE GOT SOMETHING TO DO.
Tell me later!
NINA...
HUH?
DID YOU CALL ME, TSUKASA?
Me? No.
...
I've gotta go to the bathroom...

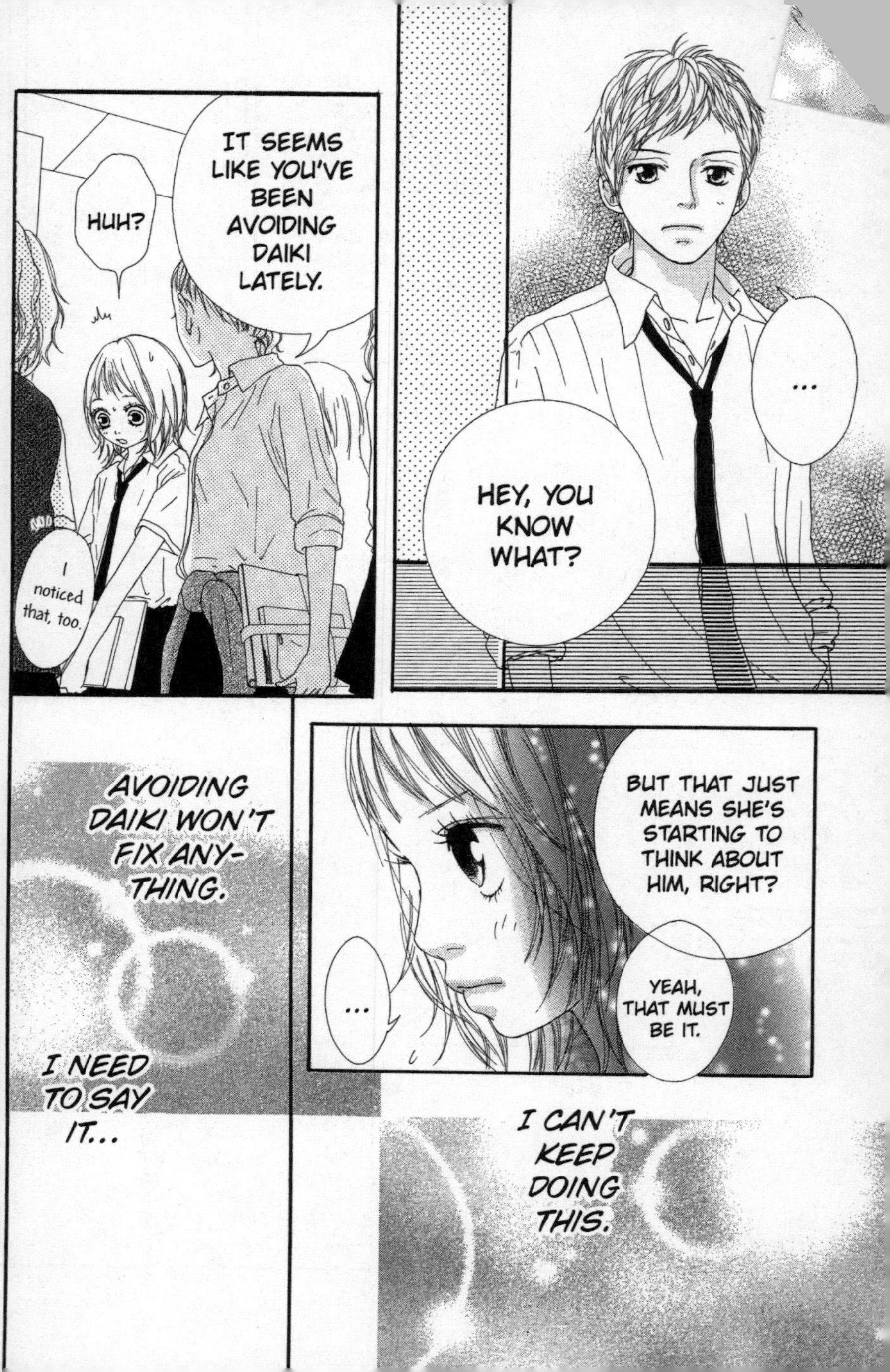
...
HEY, YOU KNOW WHAT?
IT SEEMS LIKE YOU'VE BEEN AVOIDING DAIKI LATELY.
HUH?
I noticed that, too.
BUT THAT JUST MEANS SHE'S STARTING TO THINK ABOUT HIM, RIGHT?
YEAH, THAT MUST BE IT.
...
I CAN'T KEEP DOING THIS.
AVOIDING DAIKI WON'T FIX ANY-THING.
I NEED TO SAY IT...

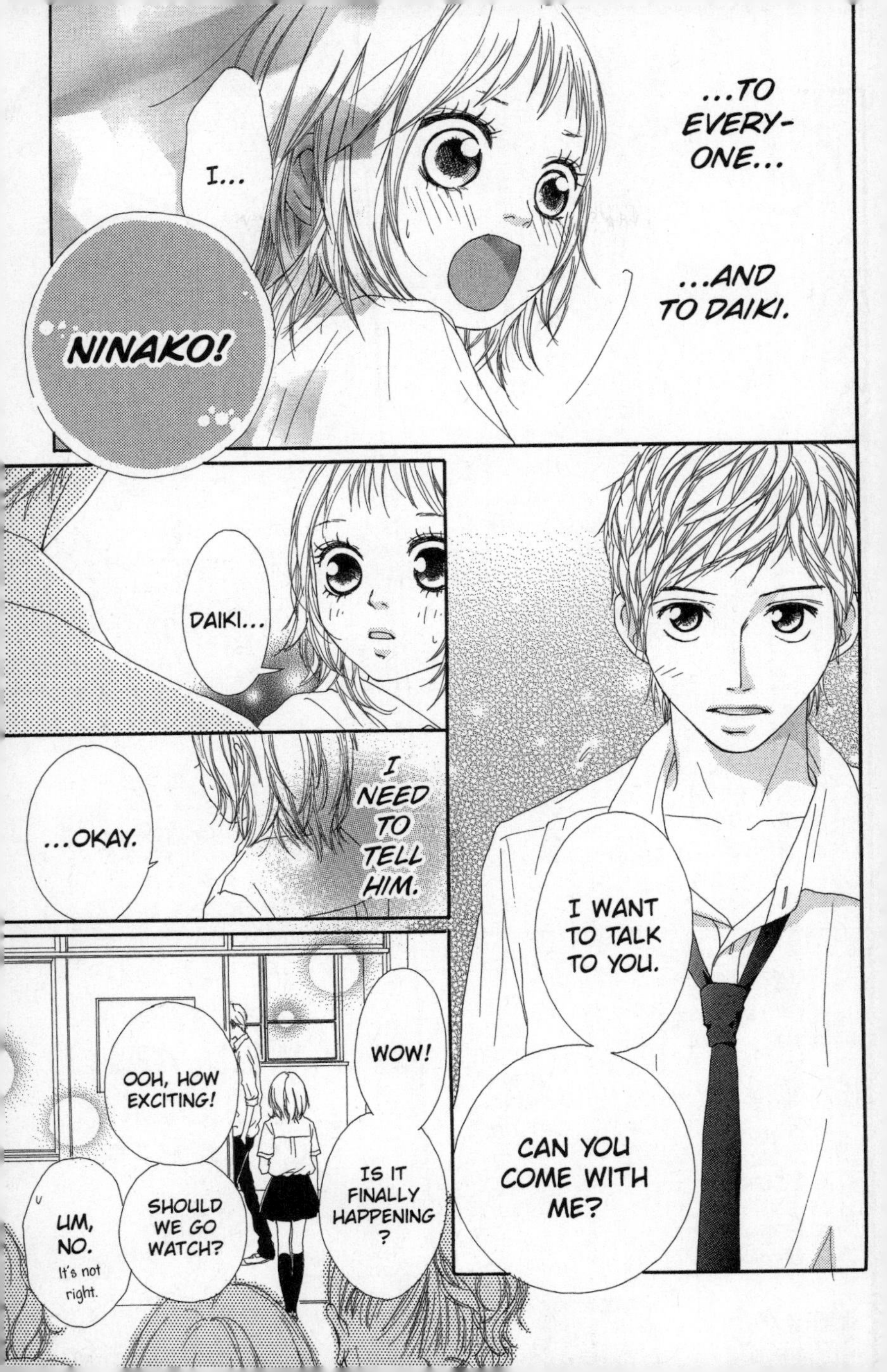
...TO EVERY-ONE...
...AND TO DAIKI.
I...
NINAKO!
I WANT TO TALK TO YOU.
CAN YOU COME WITH ME?
DAIKI...
I NEED TO TELL HIM.
...OKAY.
WOW!
IS IT FINALLY HAPPENING?
OOH, HOW EXCITING!
SHOULD WE GO WATCH?
UM, NO.
It's not right.

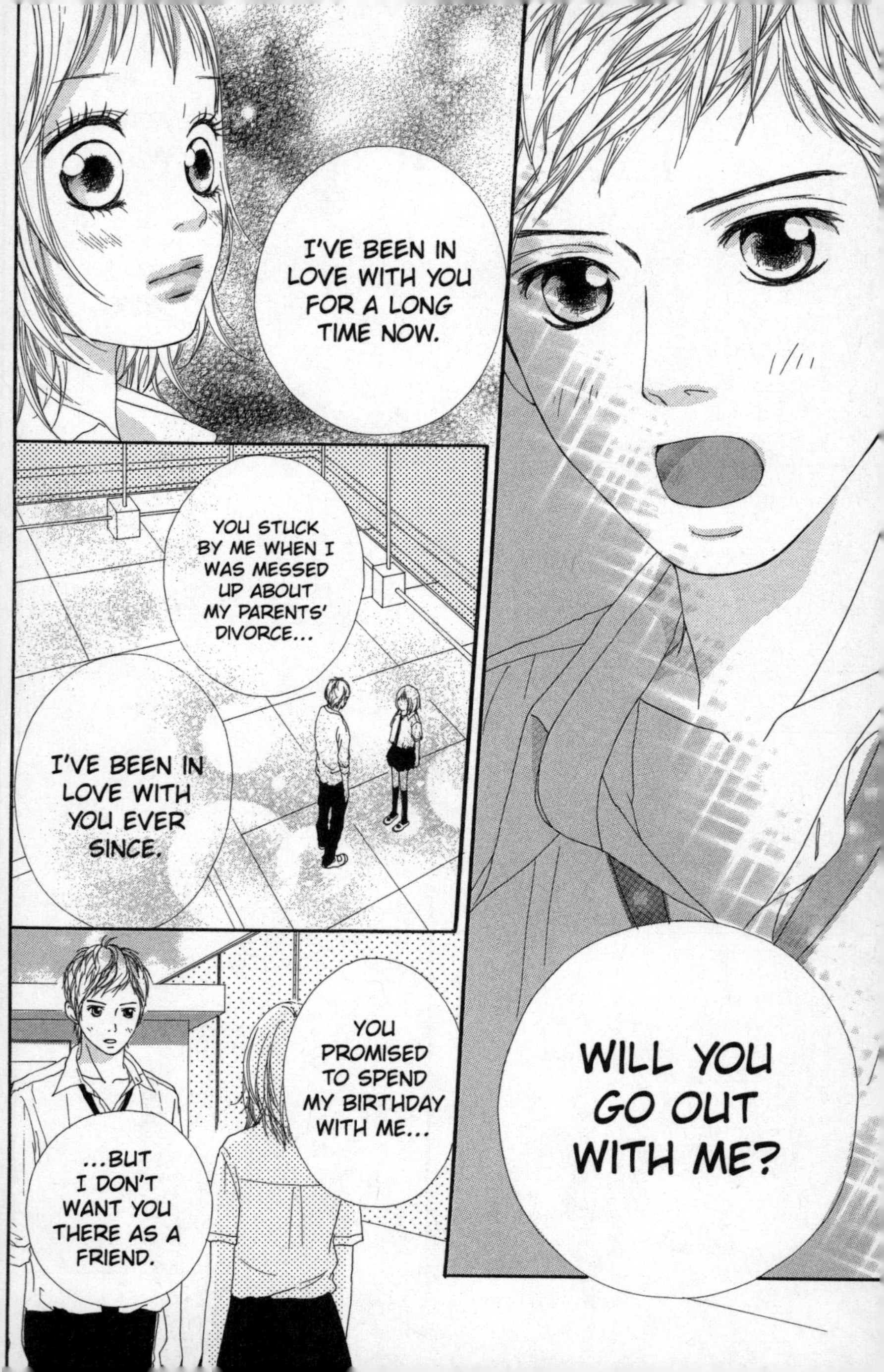
WILL YOU GO OUT WITH ME?
I'VE BEEN IN LOVE WITH YOU FOR A LONG TIME NOW.
YOU STUCK BY ME WHEN I WAS MESSED UP ABOUT MY PARENTS' DIVORCE...
I'VE BEEN IN LOVE WITH YOU EVER SINCE.
YOU PROMISED TO SPEND MY BIRTHDAY WITH ME...
...BUT I DON'T WANT YOU THERE AS A FRIEND.

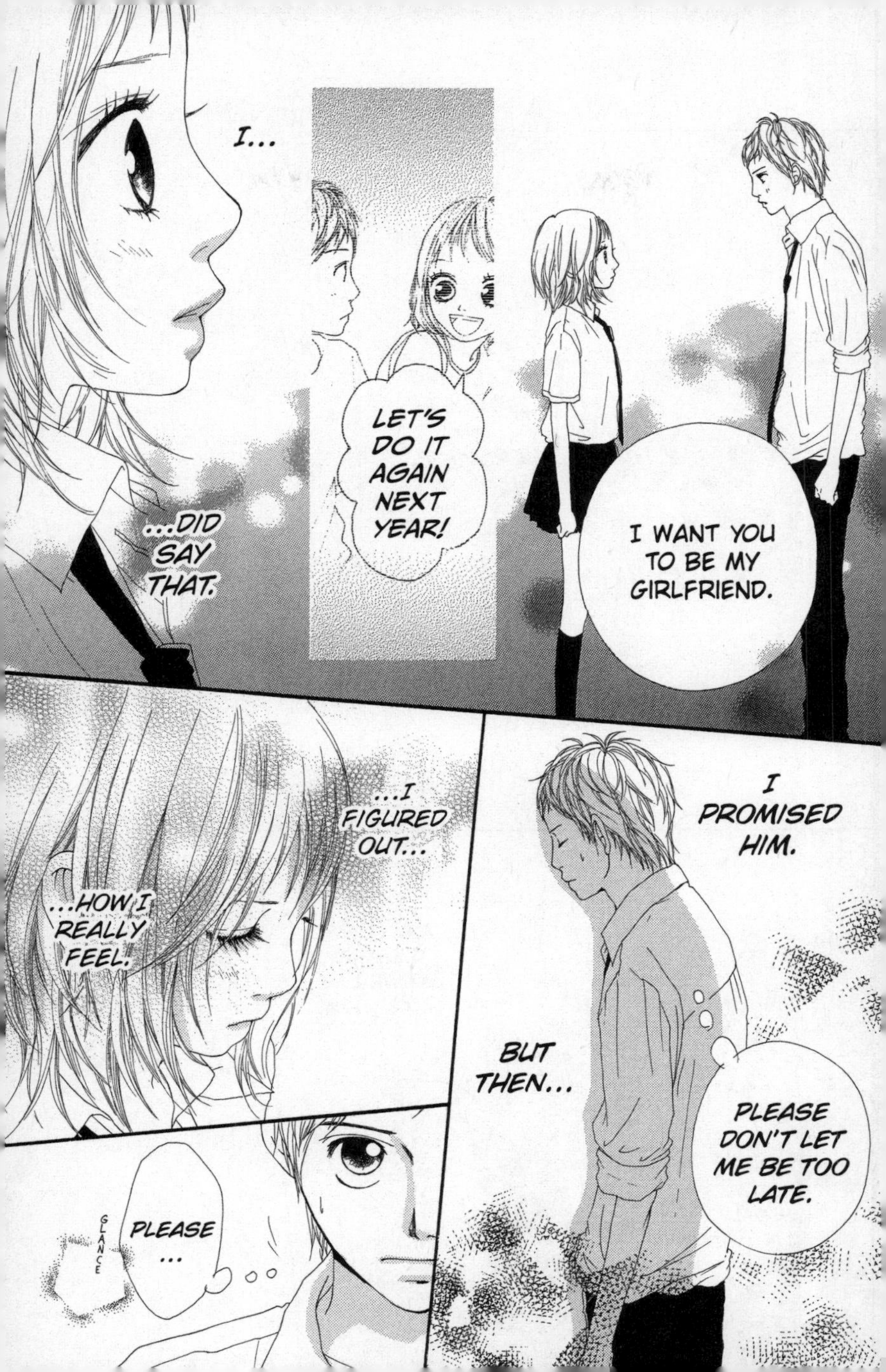
I WANT YOU TO BE MY GIRLFRIEND.
LET'S DO IT AGAIN NEXT YEAR!
I...
...DID SAY THAT.
I PROMISED HIM.
BUT THEN...
PLEASE DON'T LET ME BE TOO LATE.
...I FIGURED OUT...
...HOW I REALLY FEEL.
PLEASE ...
GLANCE

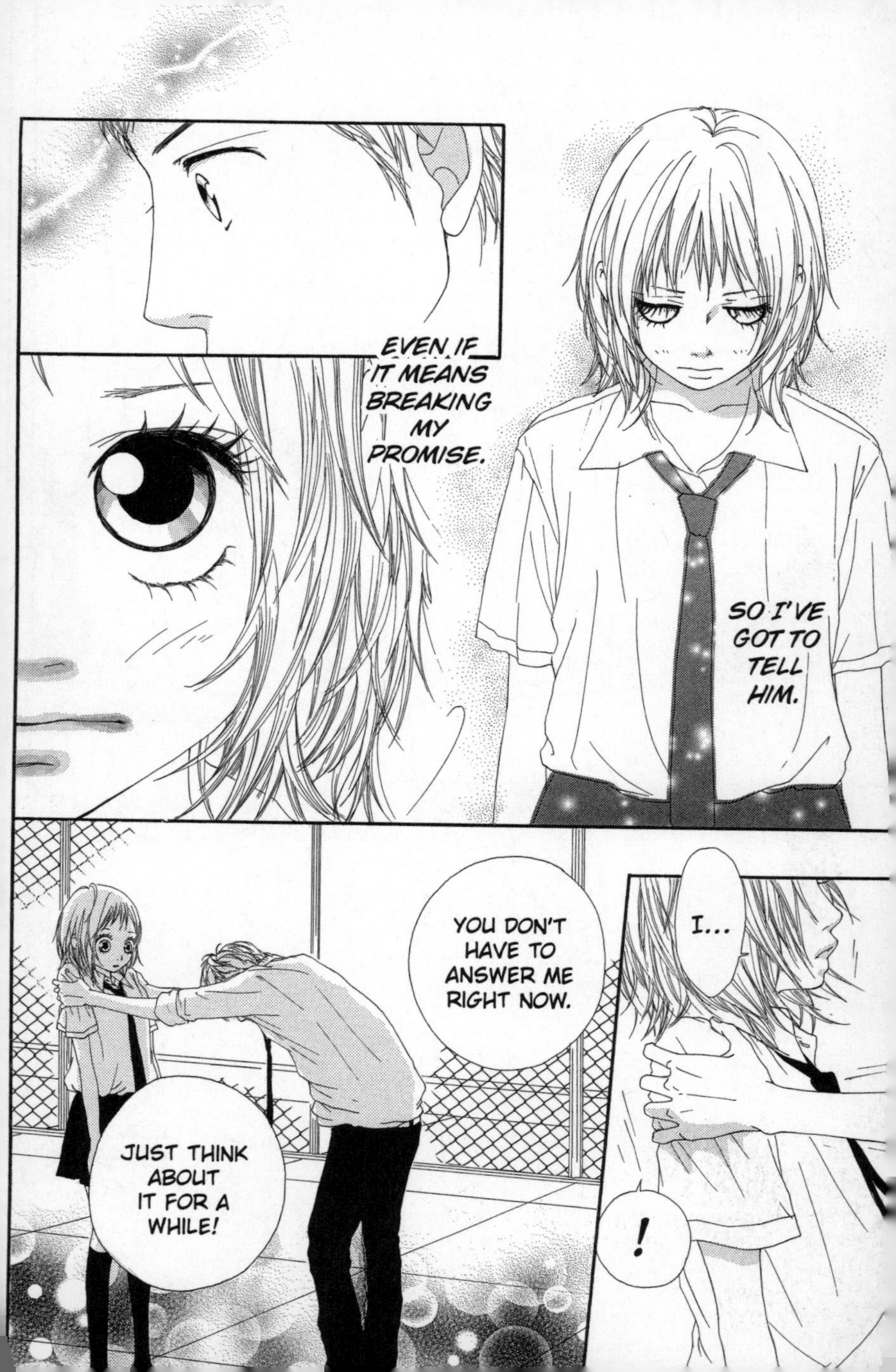
SO I'VE GOT TO TELL HIM.
EVEN IF IT MEANS BREAKING MY PROMISE.
I...
!
YOU DON'T HAVE TO ANSWER ME RIGHT NOW.
JUST THINK ABOUT IT FOR A WHILE!

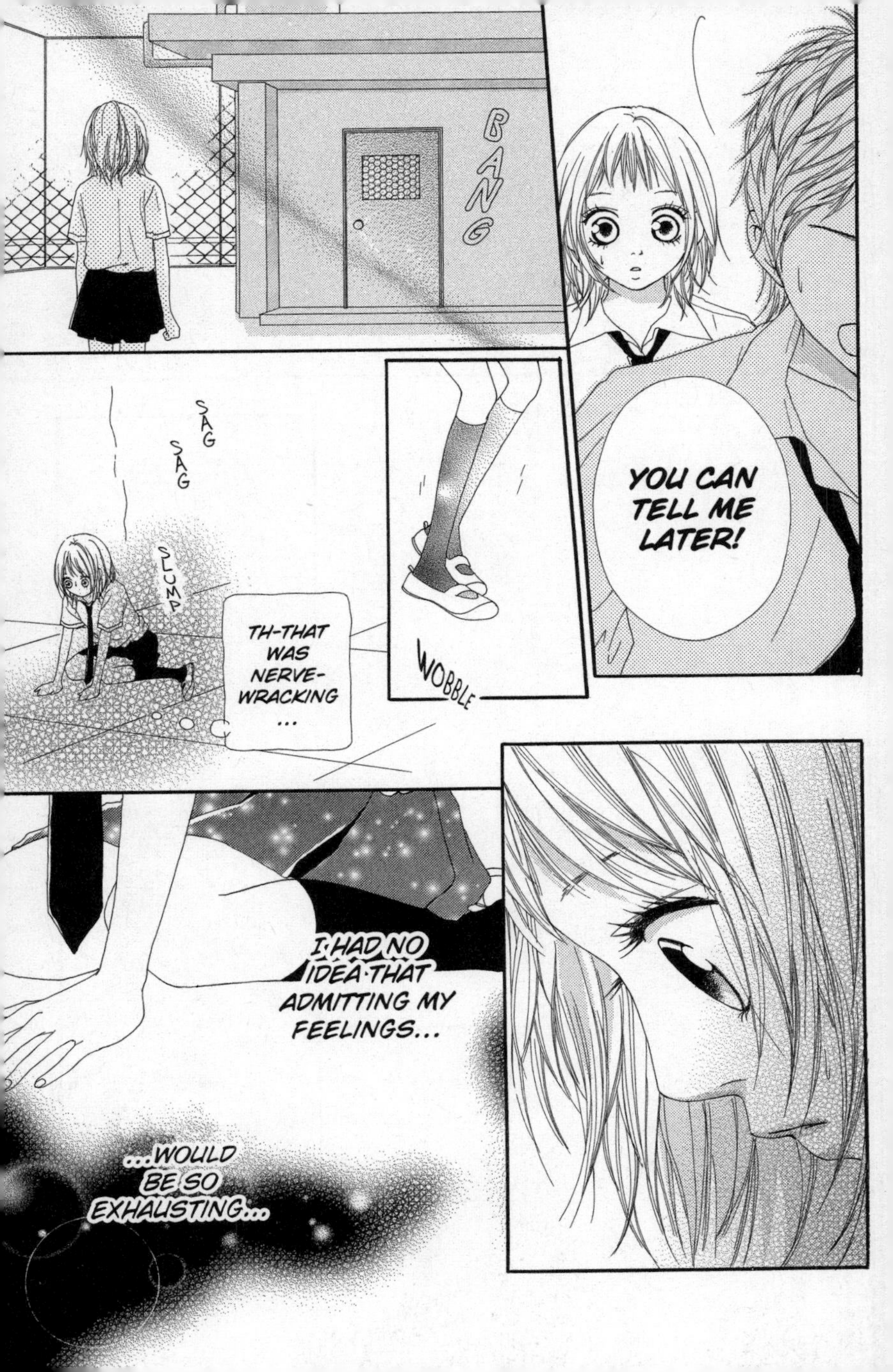

YOU CAN TELL ME LATER!
BANG
WOBBLE
SAG
SAG
SLUMP
TH-THAT WAS NERVE-WRACKING ...
I HAD NO IDEA THAT ADMITTING MY FEELINGS...
...WOULD BE SO EXHAUSTING...

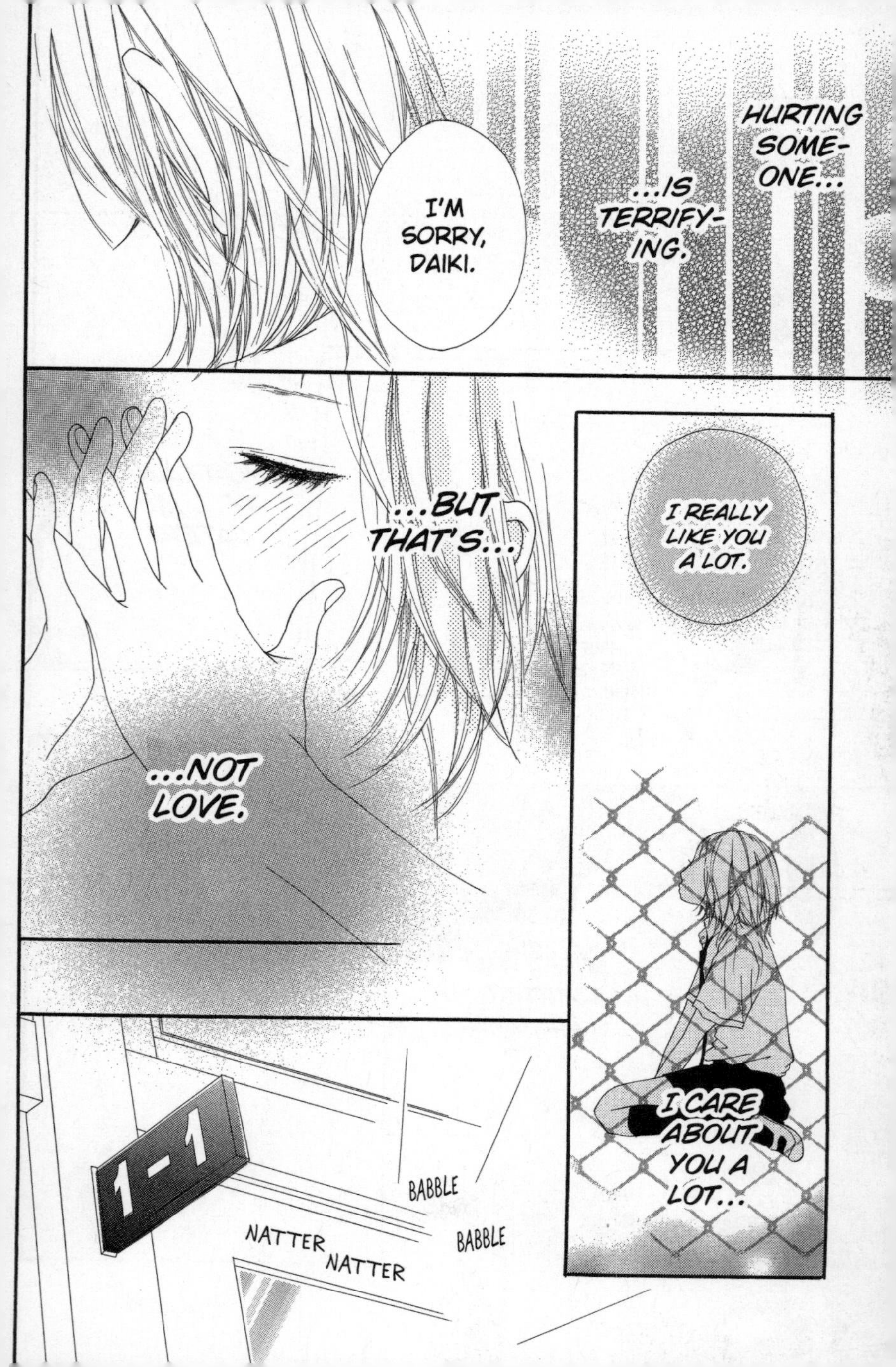
HURTING SOME-ONE...
...IS TERRIFY-ING.
I'M SORRY, DAIKI.
I REALLY LIKE YOU A LOT.
I CARE ABOUT YOU A LOT...
...BUT THAT'S...
...NOT LOVE.
BABBLE
BABBLE
NATTER NATTER
1-1

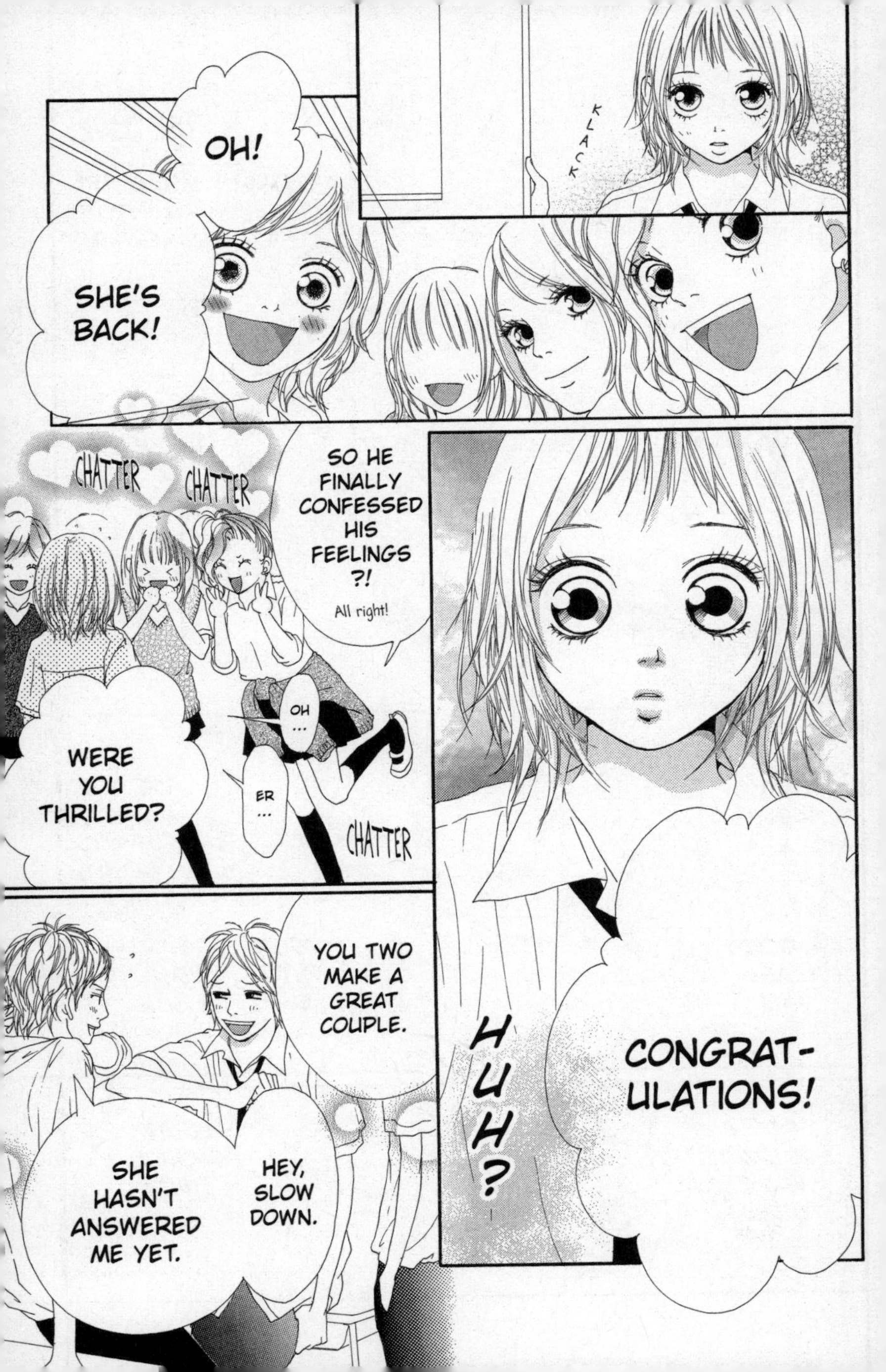
KLACK
OH!
SHE'S BACK!
CONGRAT-ULATIONS!
HUH?
SO HE FINALLY CONFESSED HIS FEELINGS?!
All right!
CHATTER CHATTER
OH...
ER...
WERE YOU THRILLED?
CHATTER
YOU TWO MAKE A GREAT COUPLE.
HEY, SLOW DOWN.
SHE HASN'T ANSWERED ME YET.

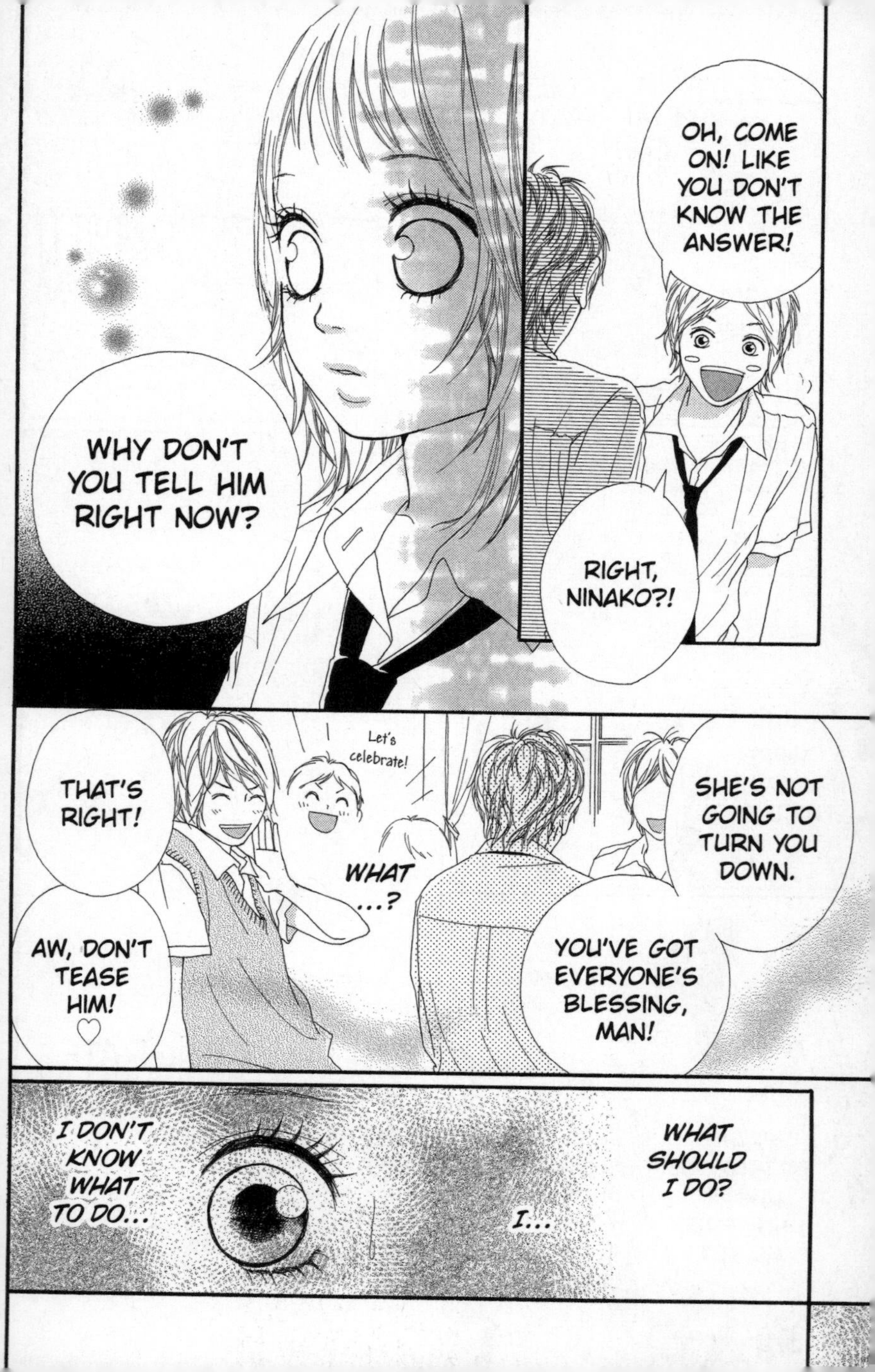
OH, COME ON! LIKE YOU DON'T KNOW THE ANSWER!
RIGHT, NINAKO?!
WHY DON'T YOU TELL HIM RIGHT NOW?
SHE'S NOT GOING TO TURN YOU DOWN.
YOU'VE GOT EVERYONE'S BLESSING, MAN!
Let's celebrate!
WHAT ...?
THAT'S RIGHT!
AW, DON'T TEASE HIM! ♡
WHAT SHOULD I DO?
I...
I DON'T KNOW WHAT TO DO...

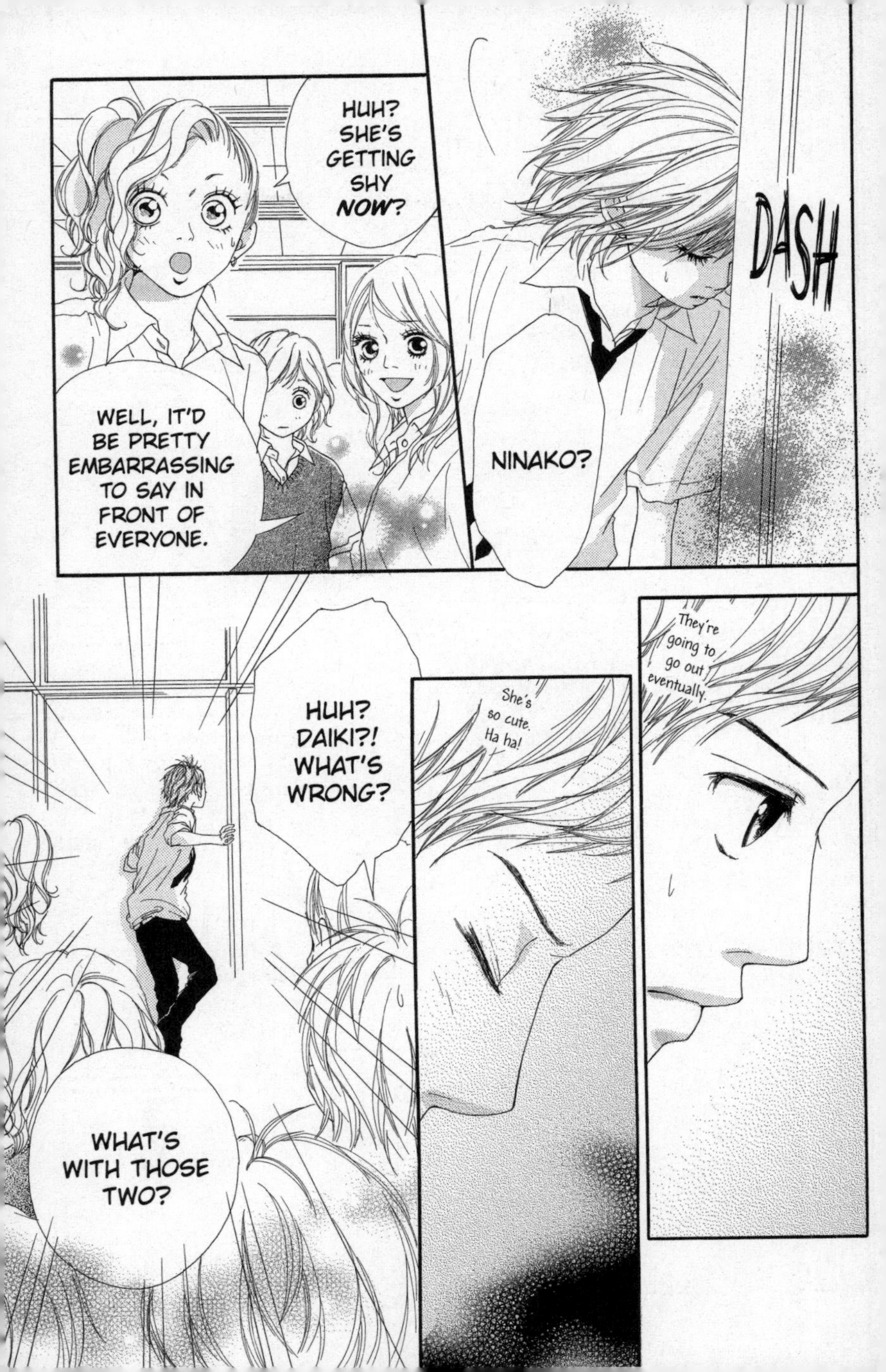
DASH
NINAKO?
HUH? SHE'S GETTING SHY *NOW*?
WELL, IT'D BE PRETTY EMBARRASSING TO SAY IN FRONT OF EVERYONE.
They're going to go out eventually.
She's so cute. Ha ha!
HUH? DAIKI?! WHAT'S WRONG?
WHAT'S WITH THOSE TWO?

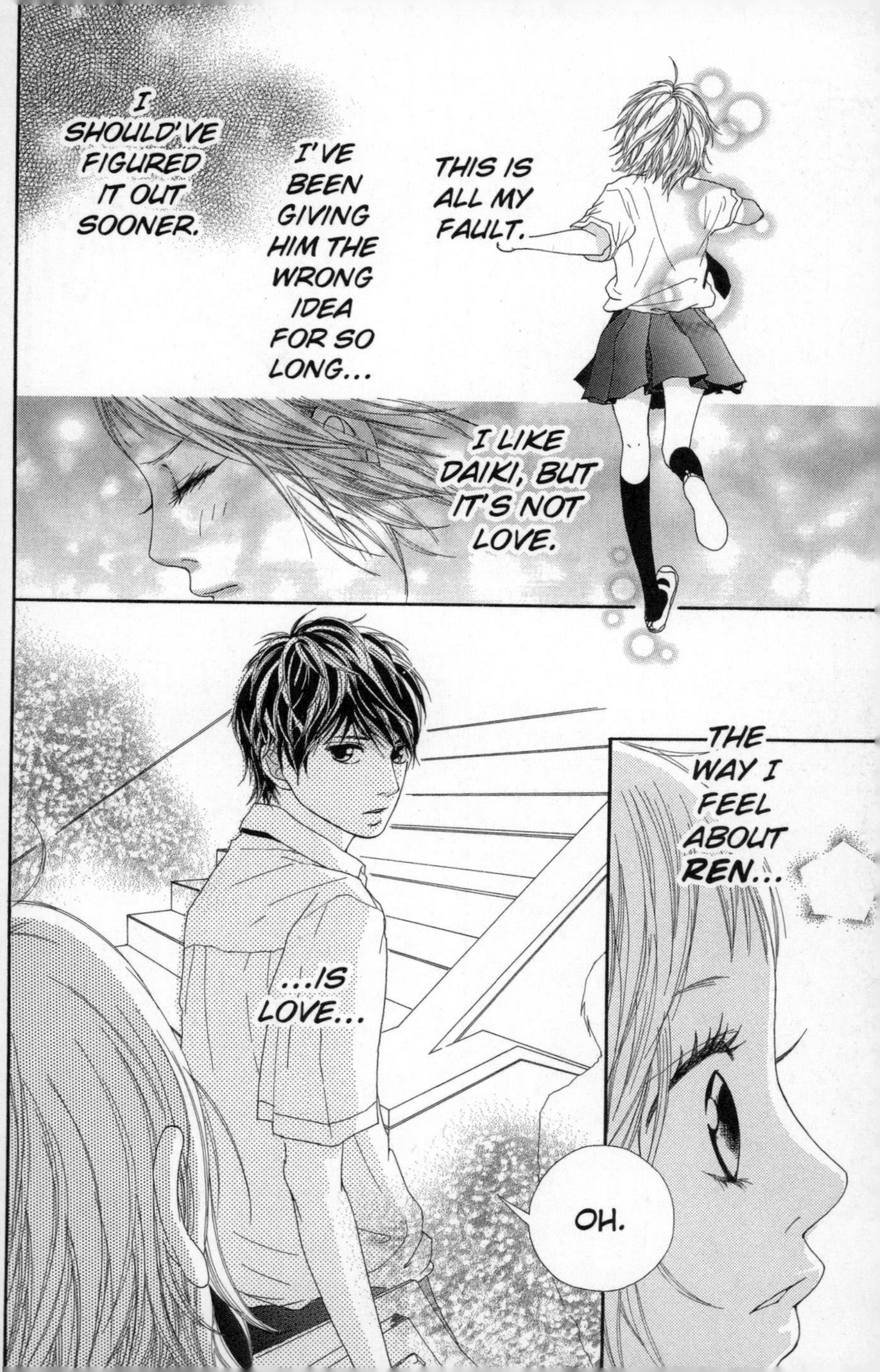
THIS IS ALL MY FAULT.
I'VE BEEN GIVING HIM THE WRONG IDEA FOR SO LONG...
I SHOULD'VE FIGURED IT OUT SOONER.
I LIKE DAIKI, BUT IT'S NOT LOVE.
THE WAY I FEEL ABOUT REN...
...IS LOVE...
OH.

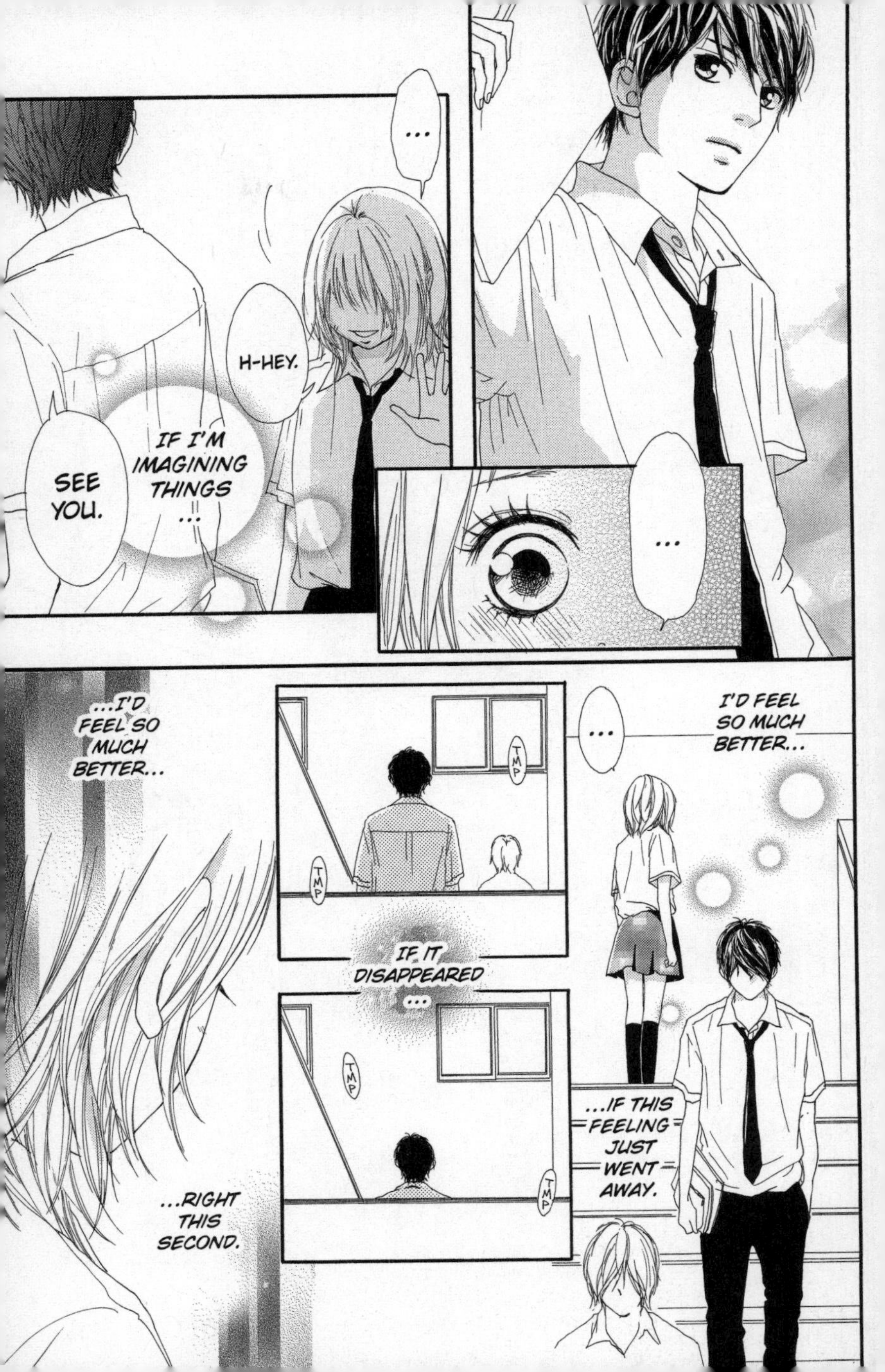
...
...
H-HEY.
IF I'M IMAGINING THINGS ...
SEE YOU.
...
I'D FEEL SO MUCH BETTER...
...IF THIS FEELING JUST WENT AWAY.
TMP
TMP
IF IT DISAPPEARED ...
TMP
TMP
...I'D FEEL SO MUCH BETTER...
...RIGHT THIS SECOND.

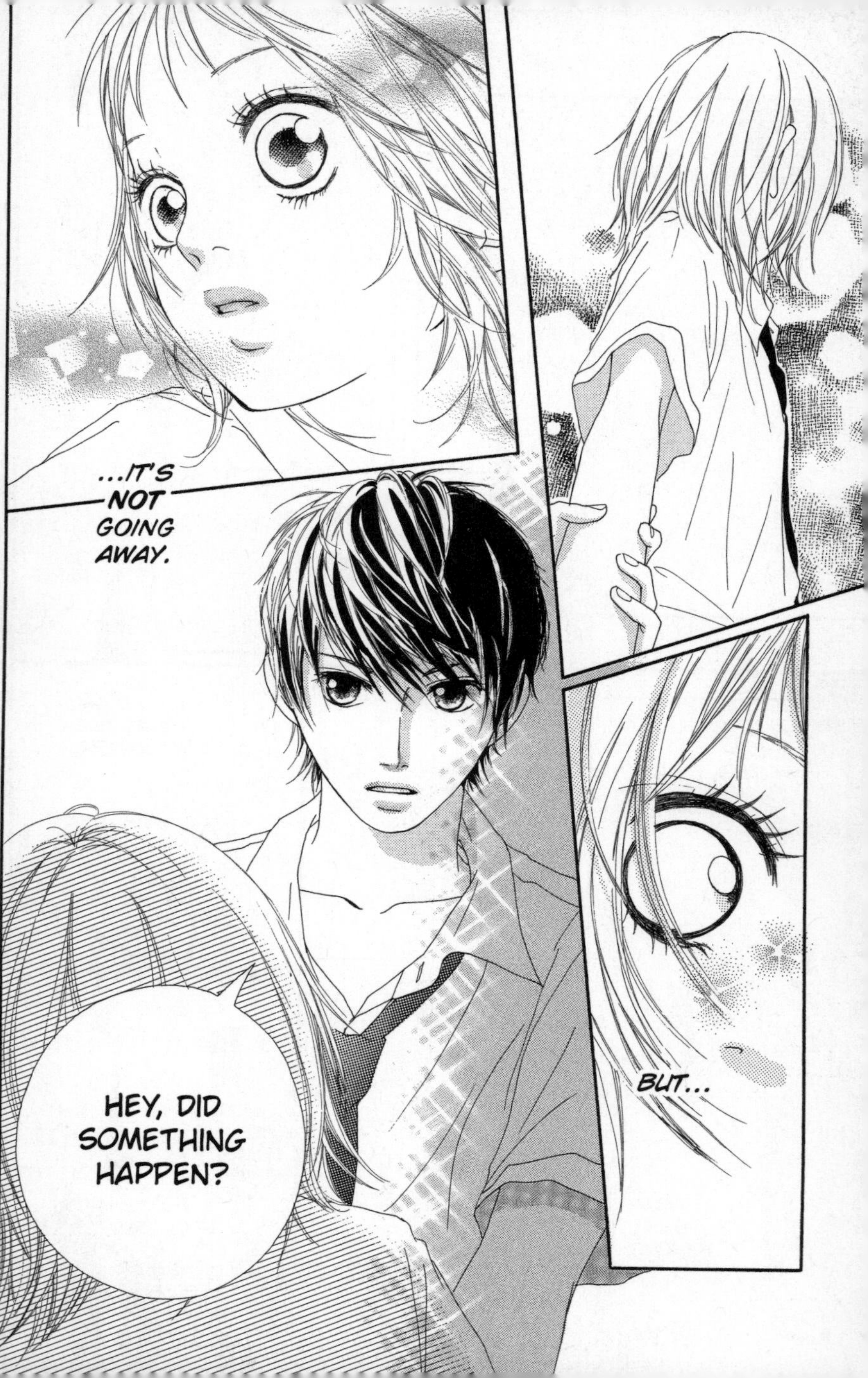
...IT'S NOT GOING AWAY.
BUT...
HEY, DID SOMETHING HAPPEN?

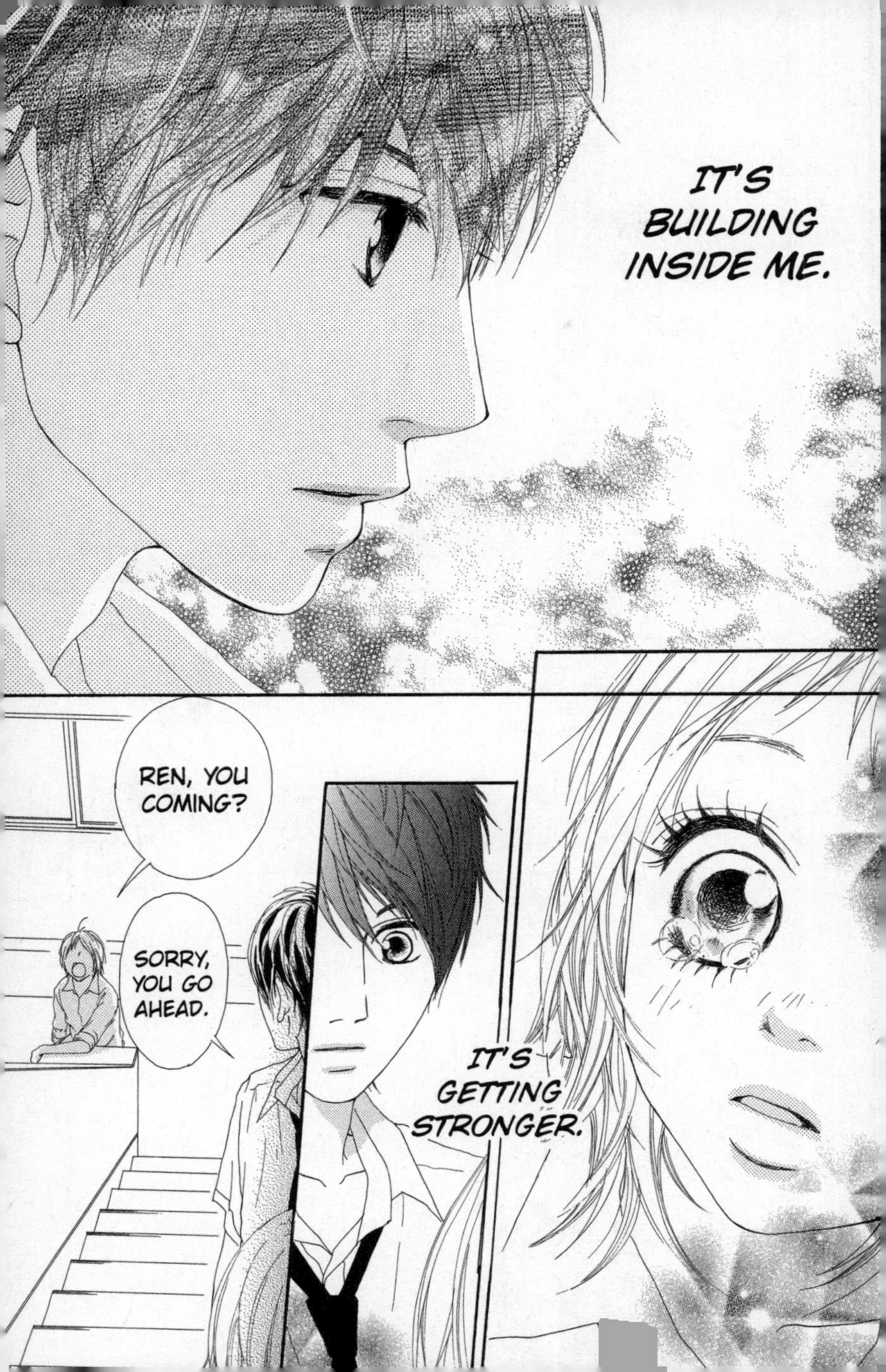
IT'S BUILDING INSIDE ME.
IT'S GETTING STRONGER.
REN, YOU COMING?
SORRY, YOU GO AHEAD.

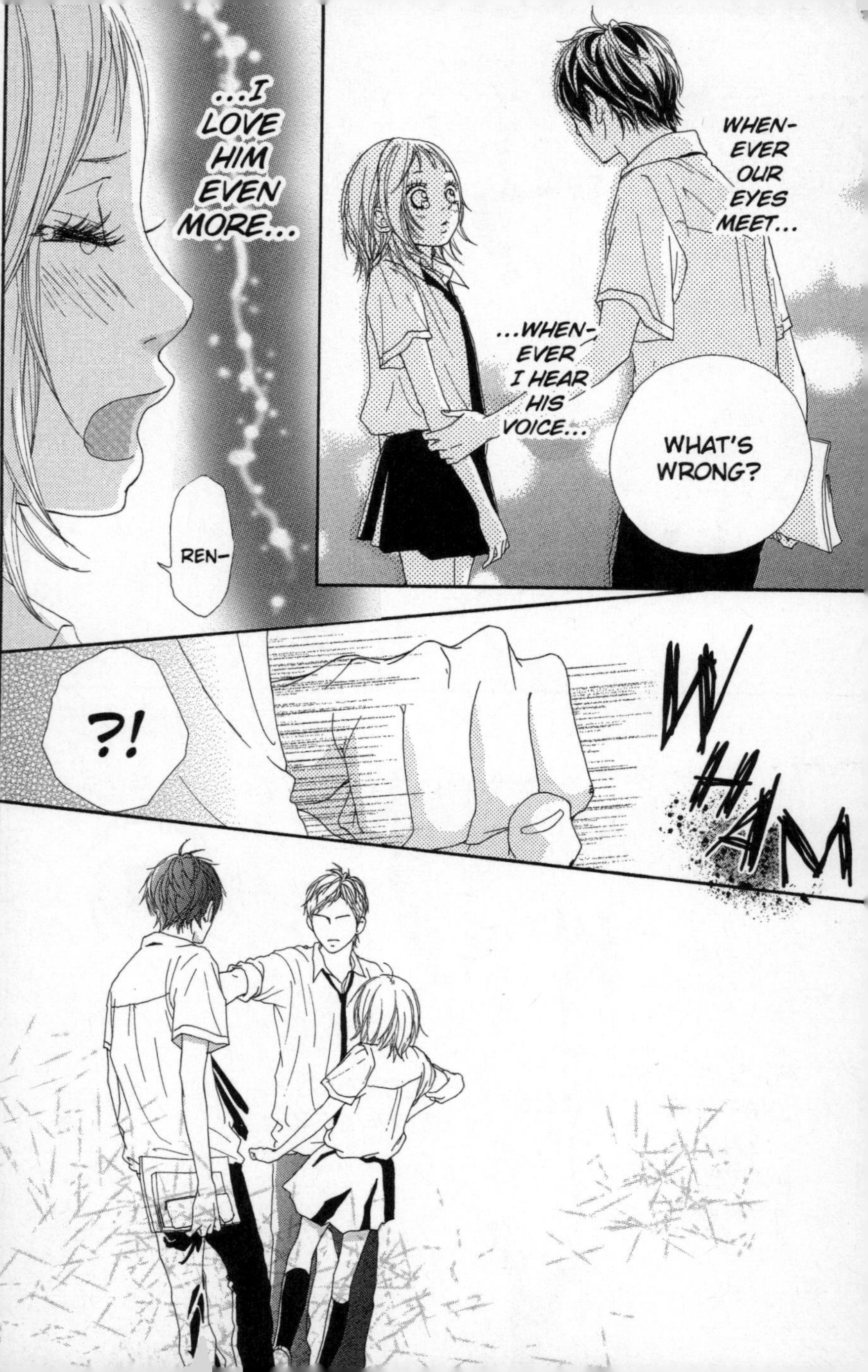
WHEN-EVER OUR EYES MEET...
...WHEN-EVER I HEAR HIS VOICE...
WHAT'S WRONG?
...I LOVE HIM EVEN MORE...
REN-
WHAM
?!

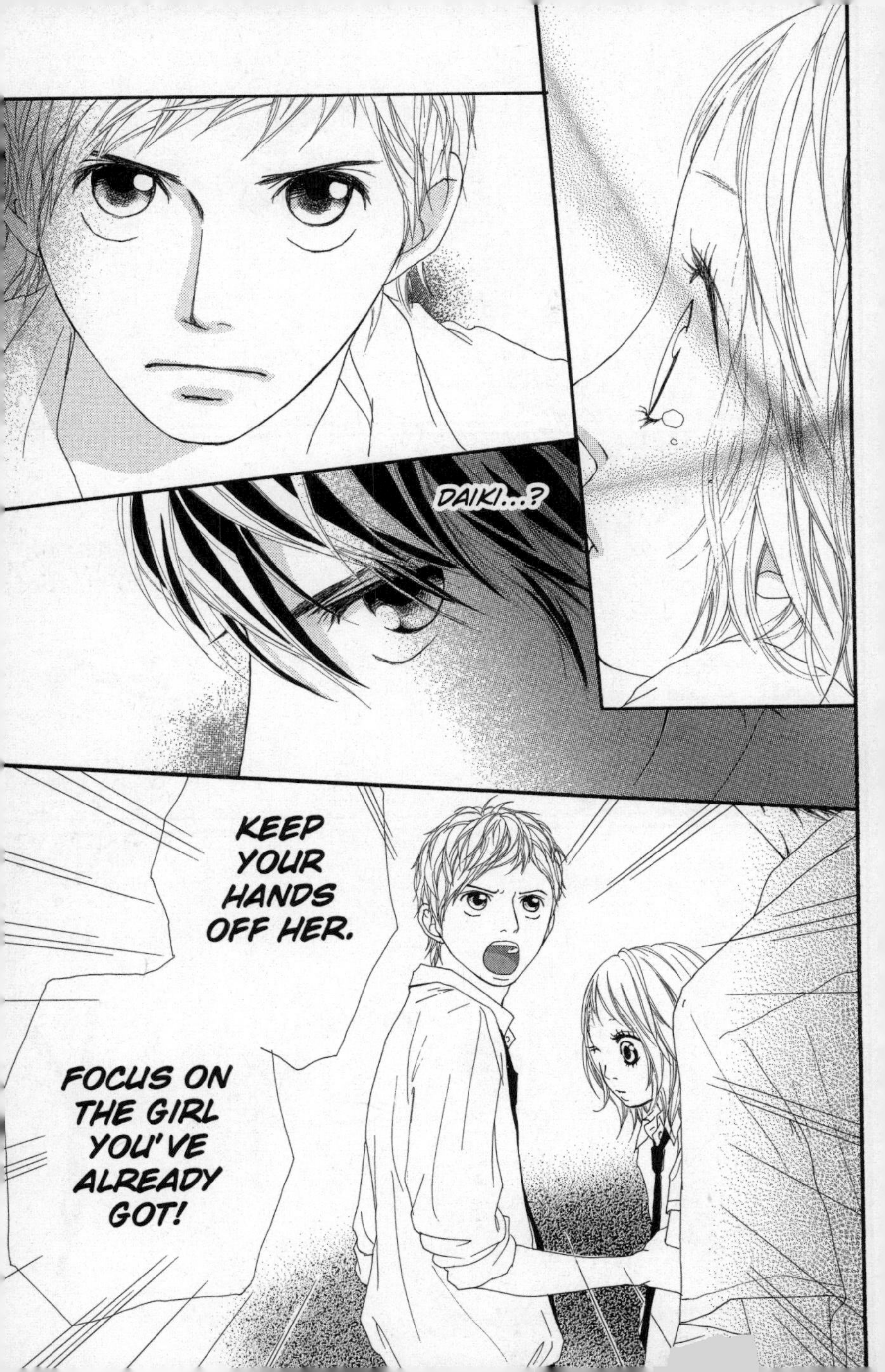
DAIKI...?
KEEP YOUR HANDS OFF HER.
FOCUS ON THE GIRL YOU'VE ALREADY GOT!

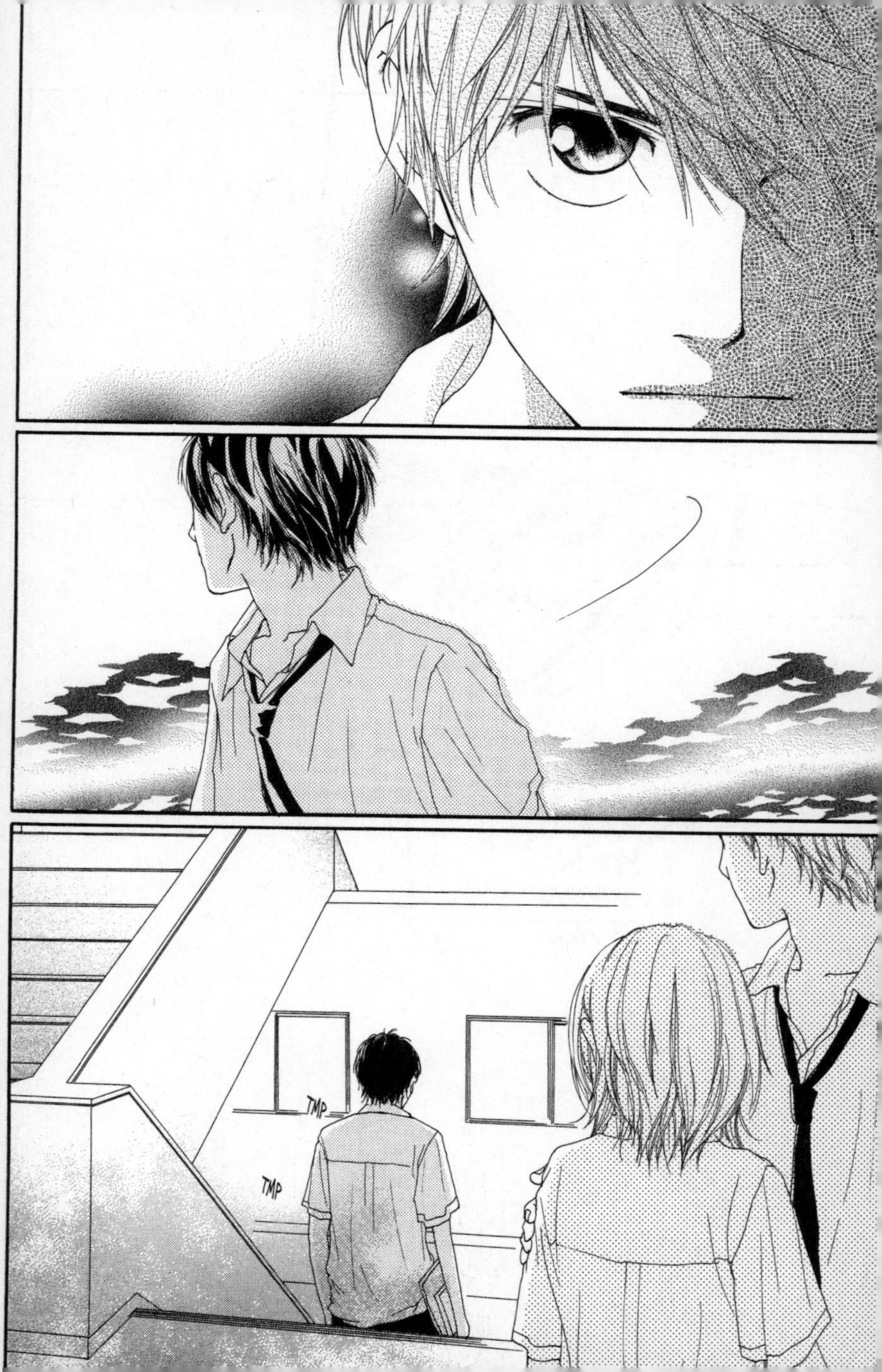
TMP
TMP

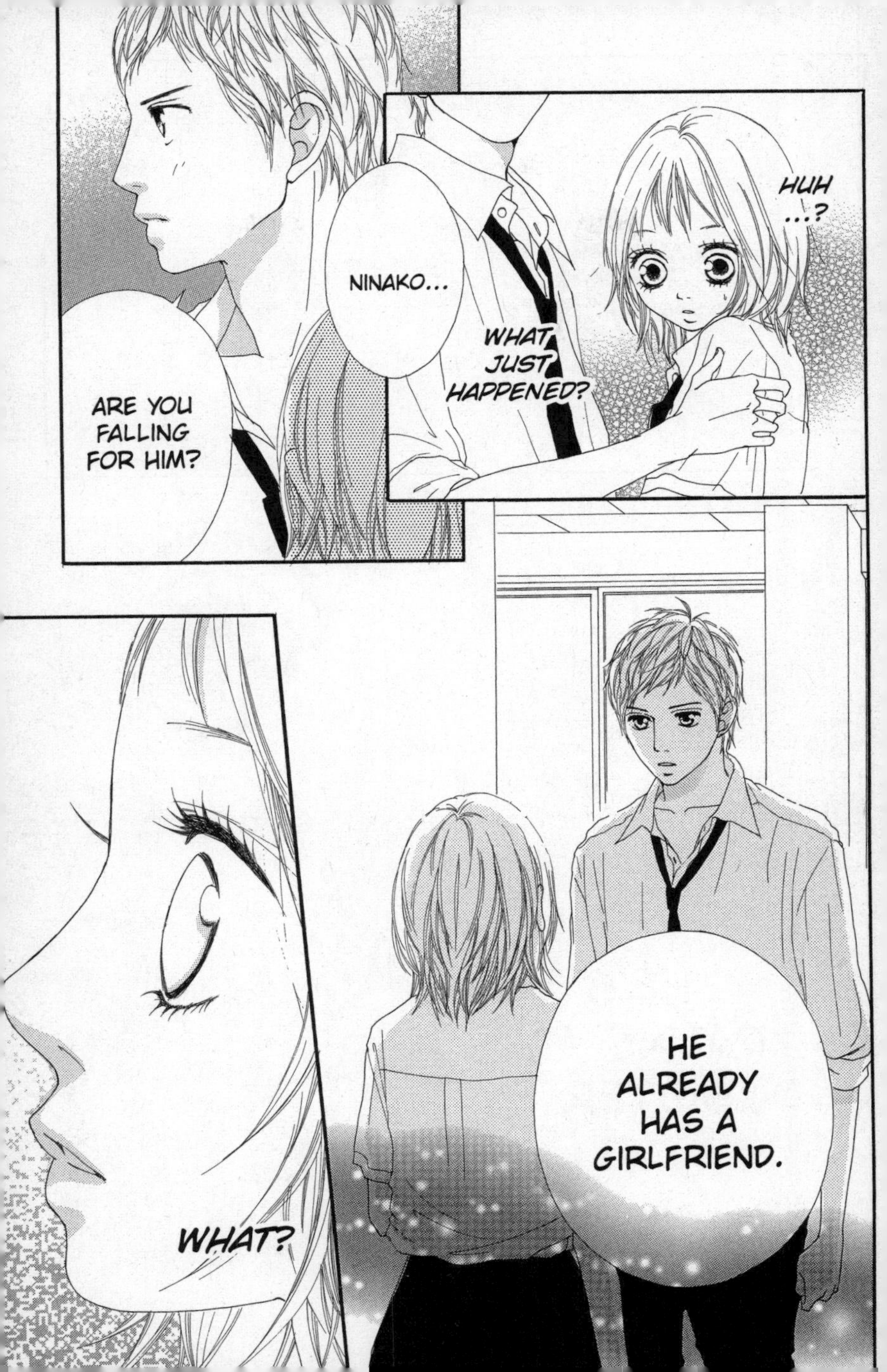
HUH ...?
NINAKO...
WHAT JUST HAPPENED?
ARE YOU FALLING FOR HIM?
HE ALREADY HAS A GIRLFRIEND.
WHAT?

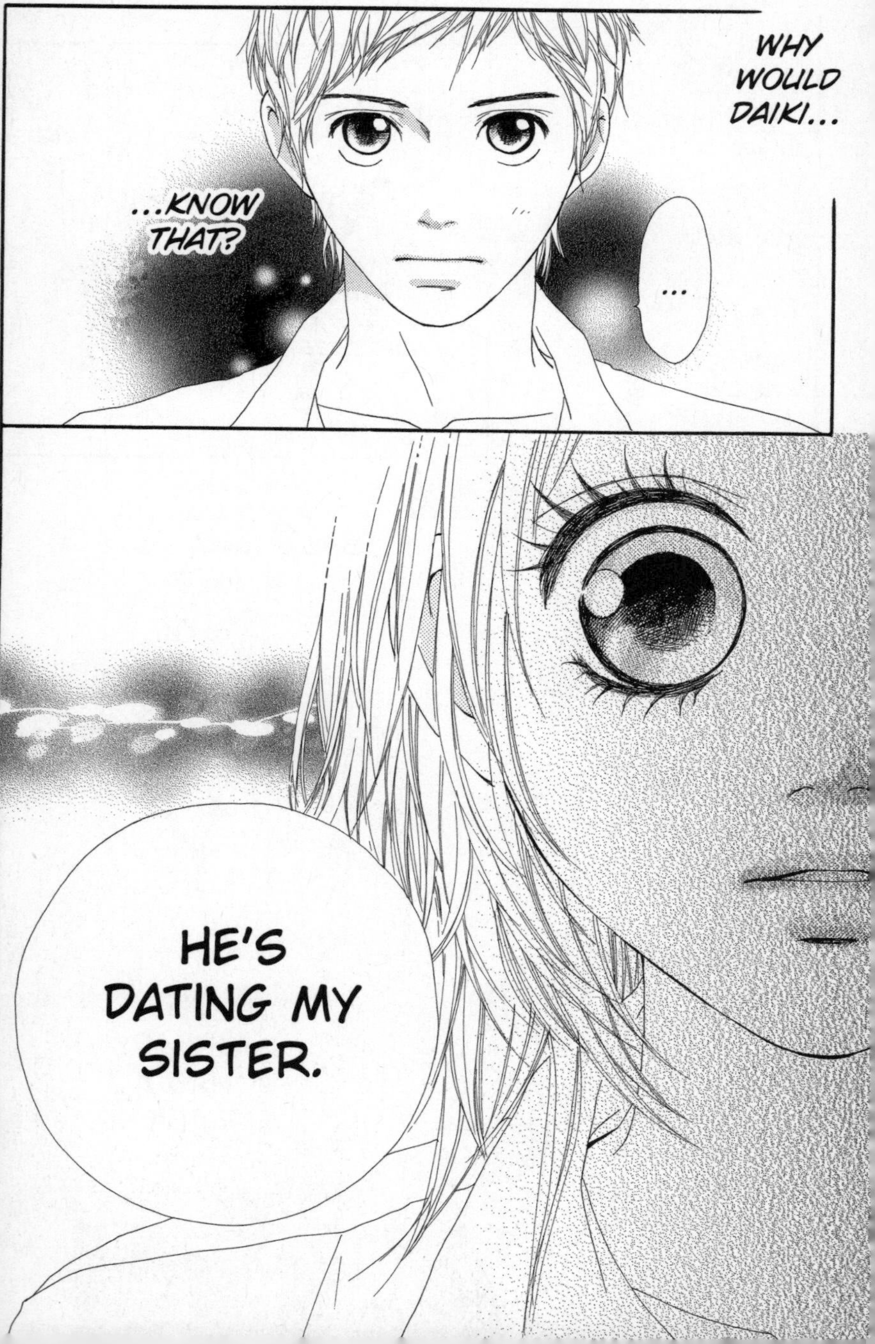
WHY WOULD DAIKI...
...KNOW THAT?
...
HE'S DATING MY SISTER.

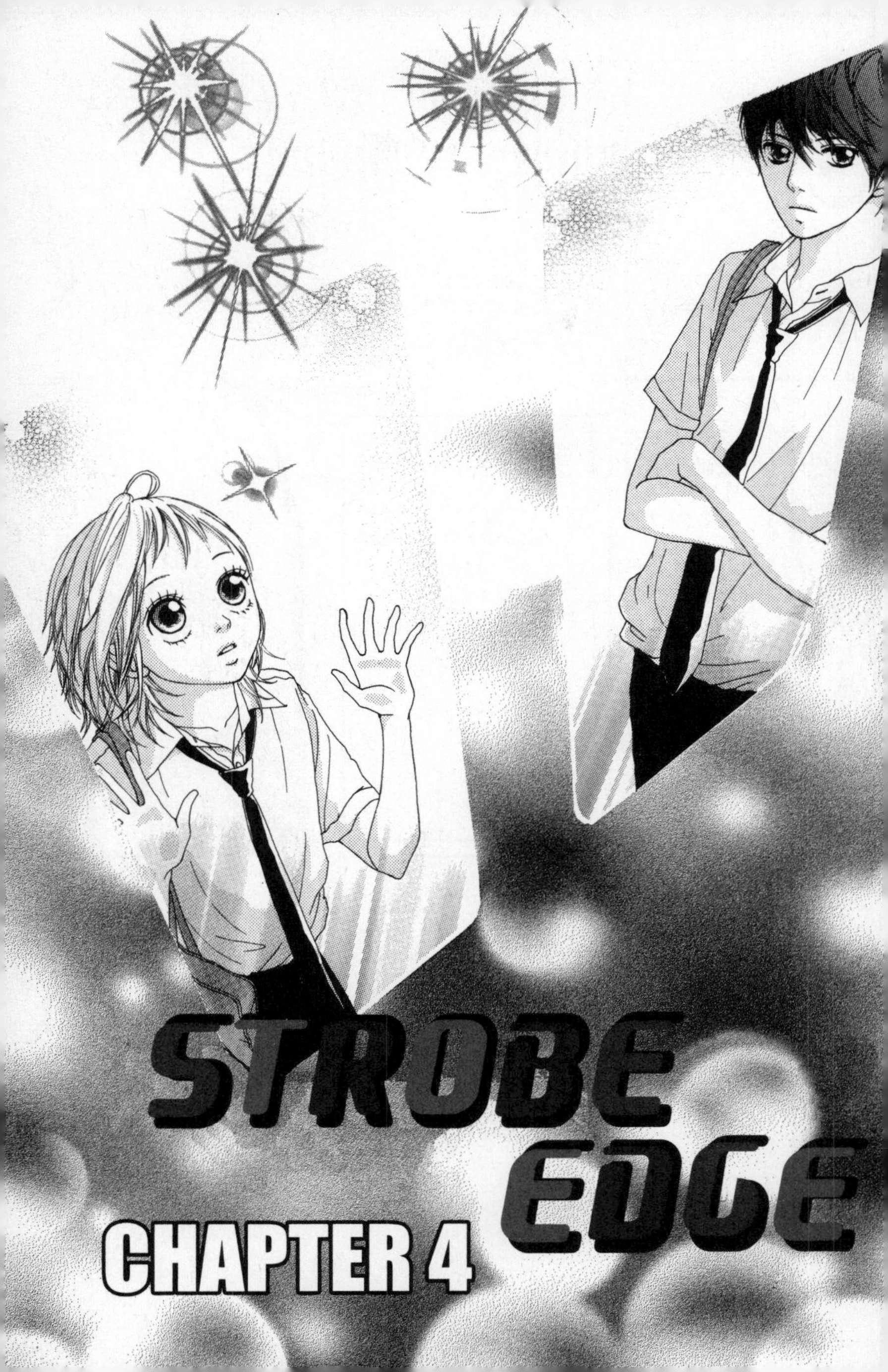
STROBE EDGE
CHAPTER 4

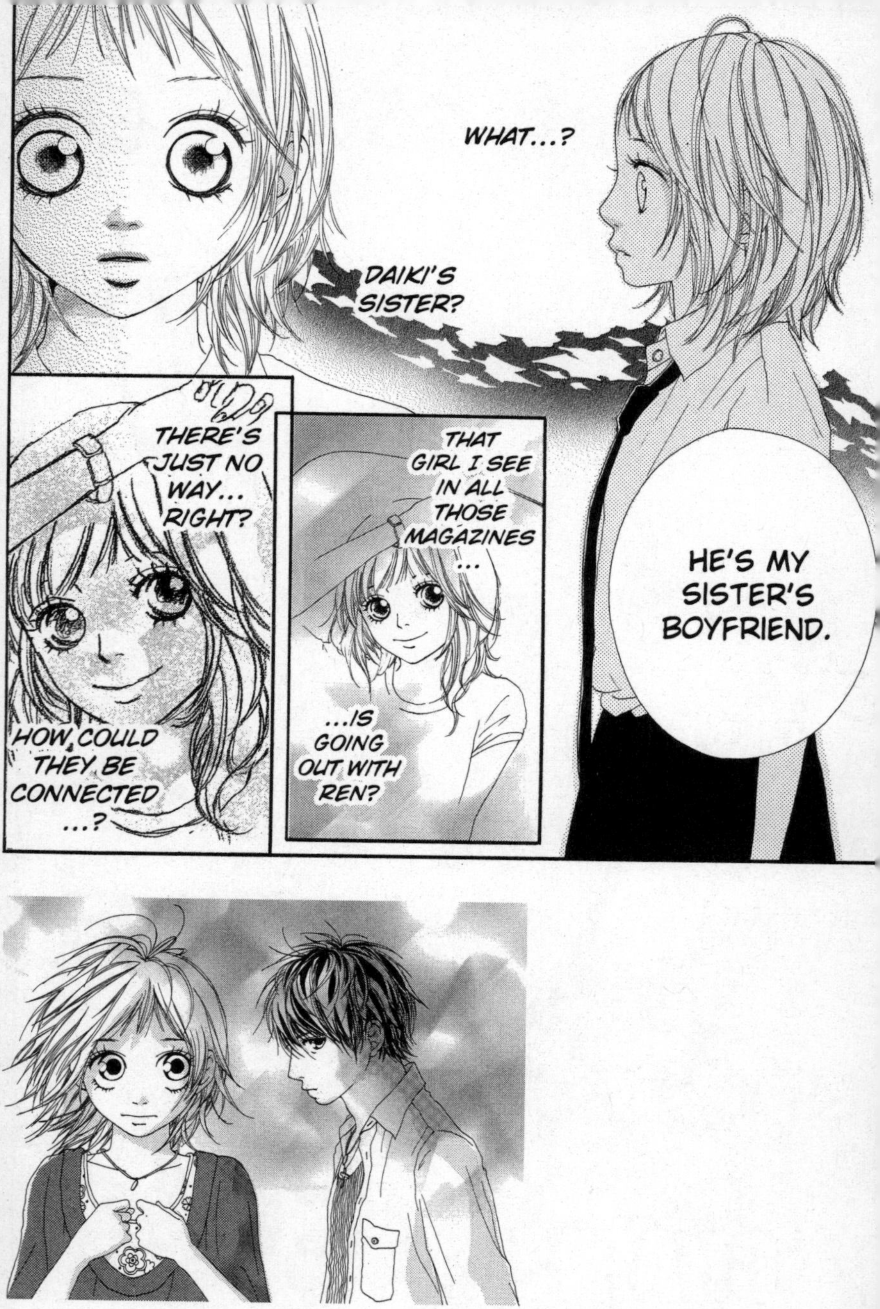
HE'S MY SISTER'S BOYFRIEND.
WHAT...?
DAIKI'S SISTER?
THAT GIRL I SEE IN ALL THOSE MAGAZINES...
...IS GOING OUT WITH REN?
THERE'S JUST NO WAY... RIGHT?
HOW COULD THEY BE CONNECTED...?

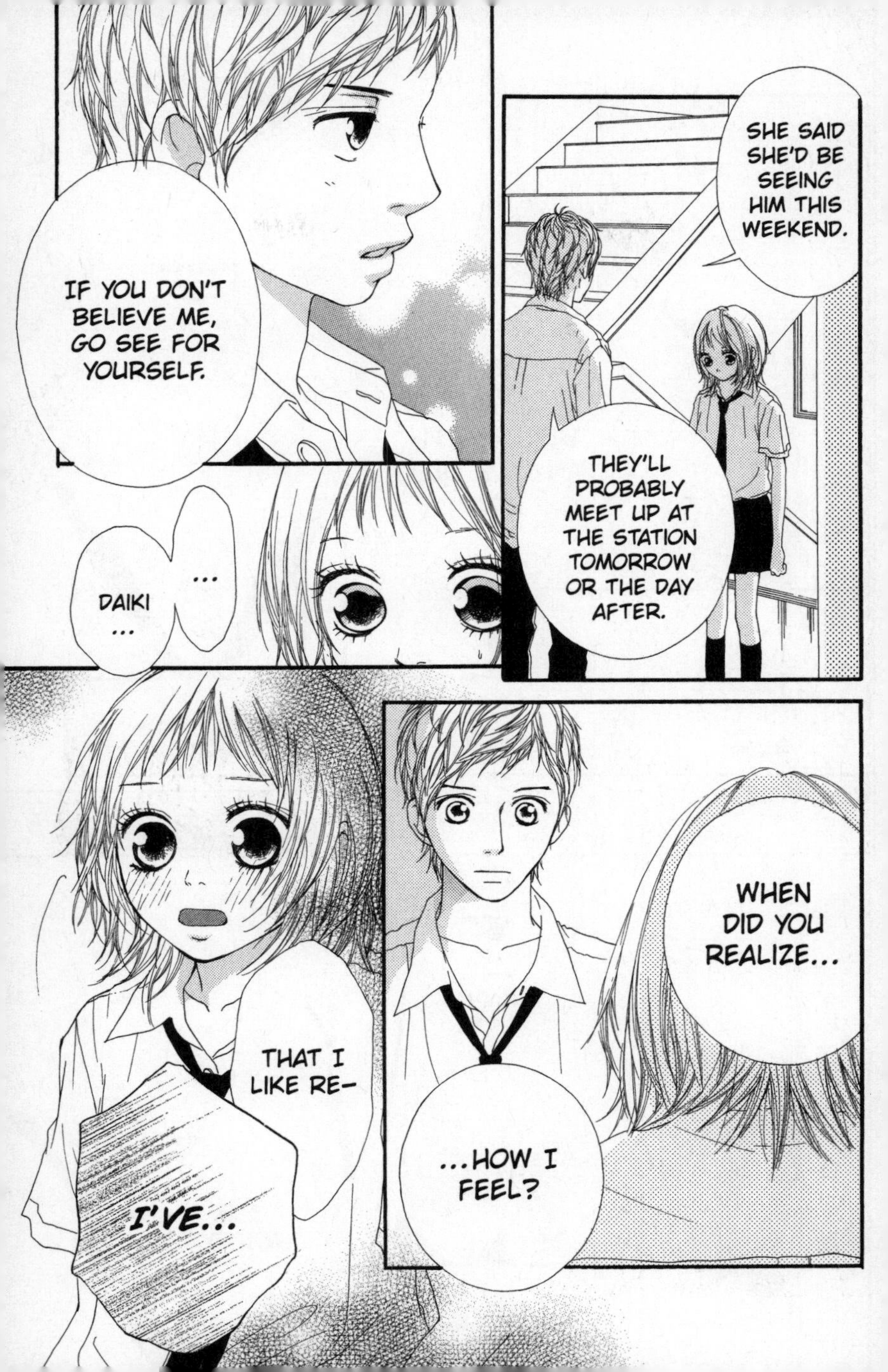
SHE SAID SHE'D BE SEEING HIM THIS WEEKEND.
THEY'LL PROBABLY MEET UP AT THE STATION TOMORROW OR THE DAY AFTER.
IF YOU DON'T BELIEVE ME, GO SEE FOR YOURSELF.
...
DAIKI ...
WHEN DID YOU REALIZE...
...HOW I FEEL?
THAT I LIKE RE-
I'VE...

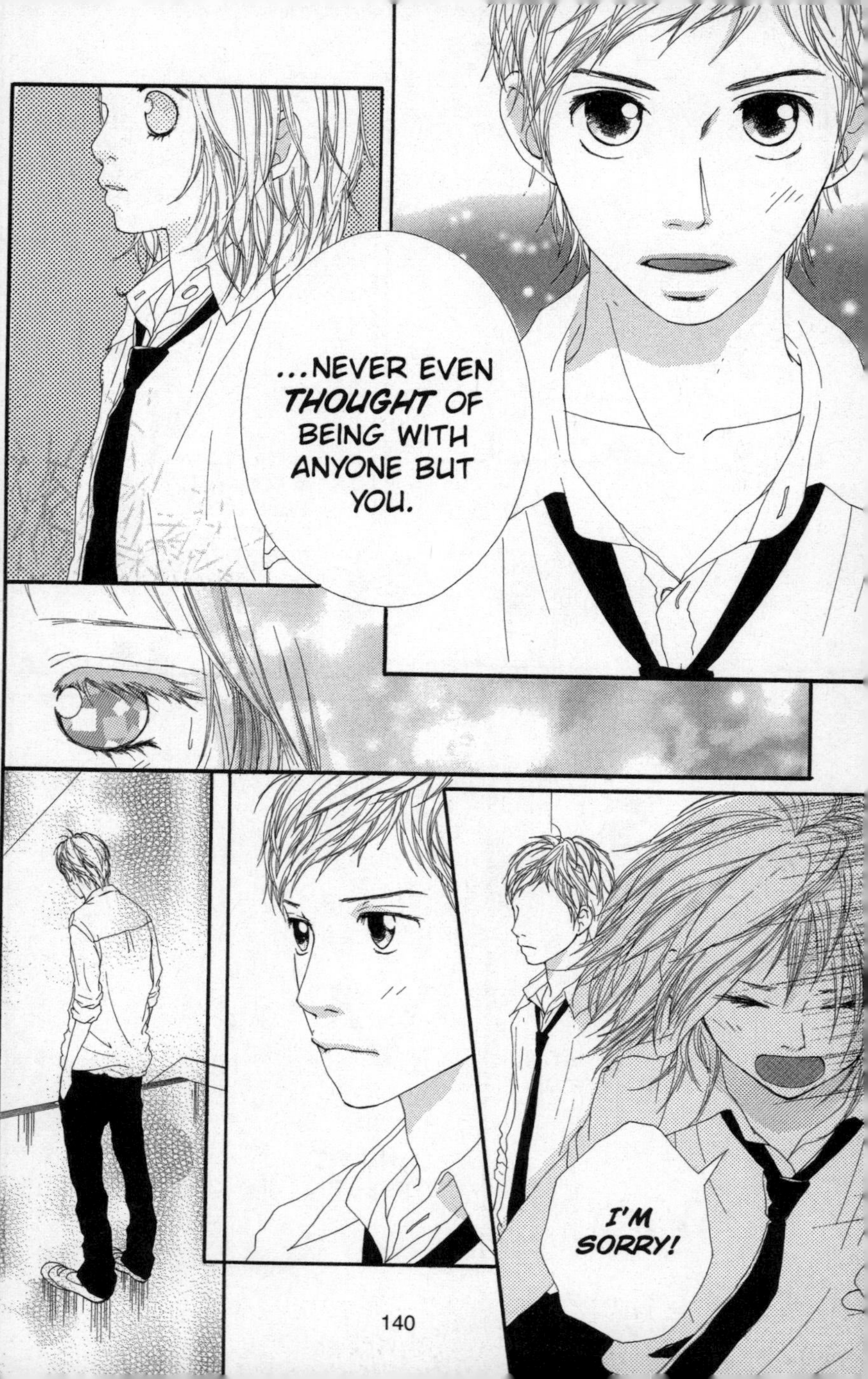
...NEVER EVEN *THOUGHT* OF BEING WITH ANYONE BUT YOU.
I'M SORRY!

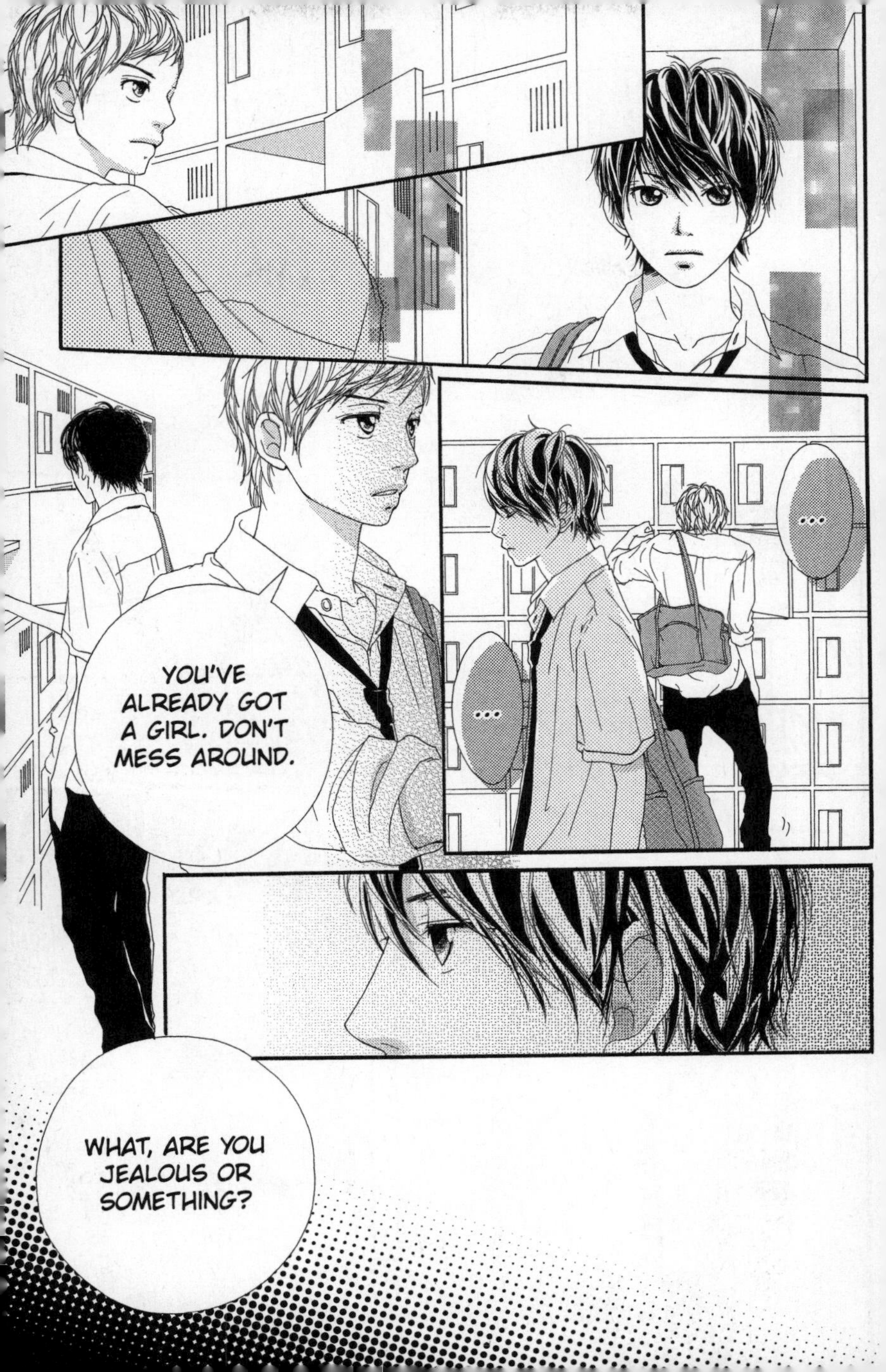
...
...
YOU'VE ALREADY GOT A GIRL. DON'T MESS AROUND.
WHAT, ARE YOU JEALOUS OR SOMETHING?

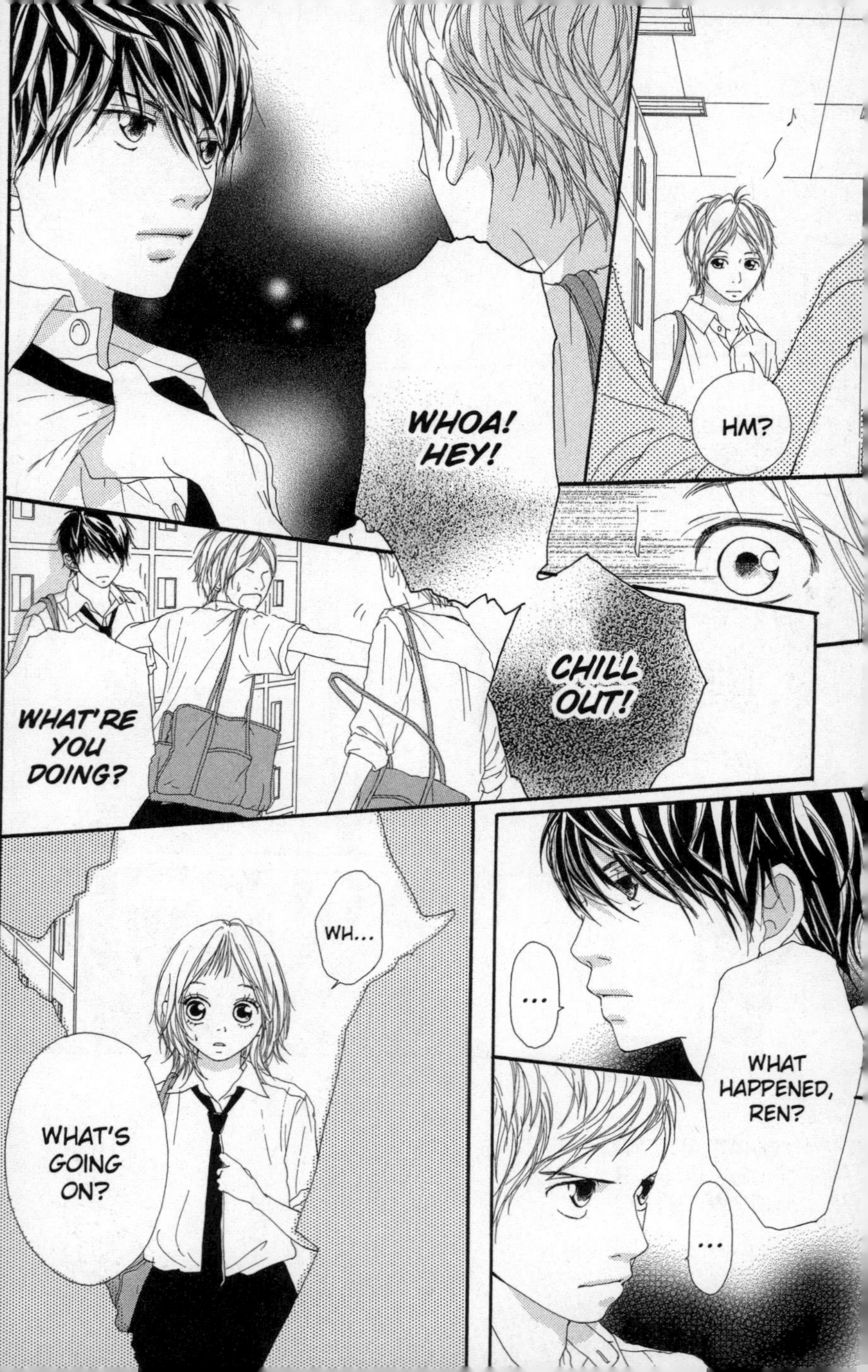
HM?
WHOA! HEY!
CHILL OUT!
WHAT'RE YOU DOING?
...
WHAT HAPPENED, REN?
...
WH...
WHAT'S GOING ON?

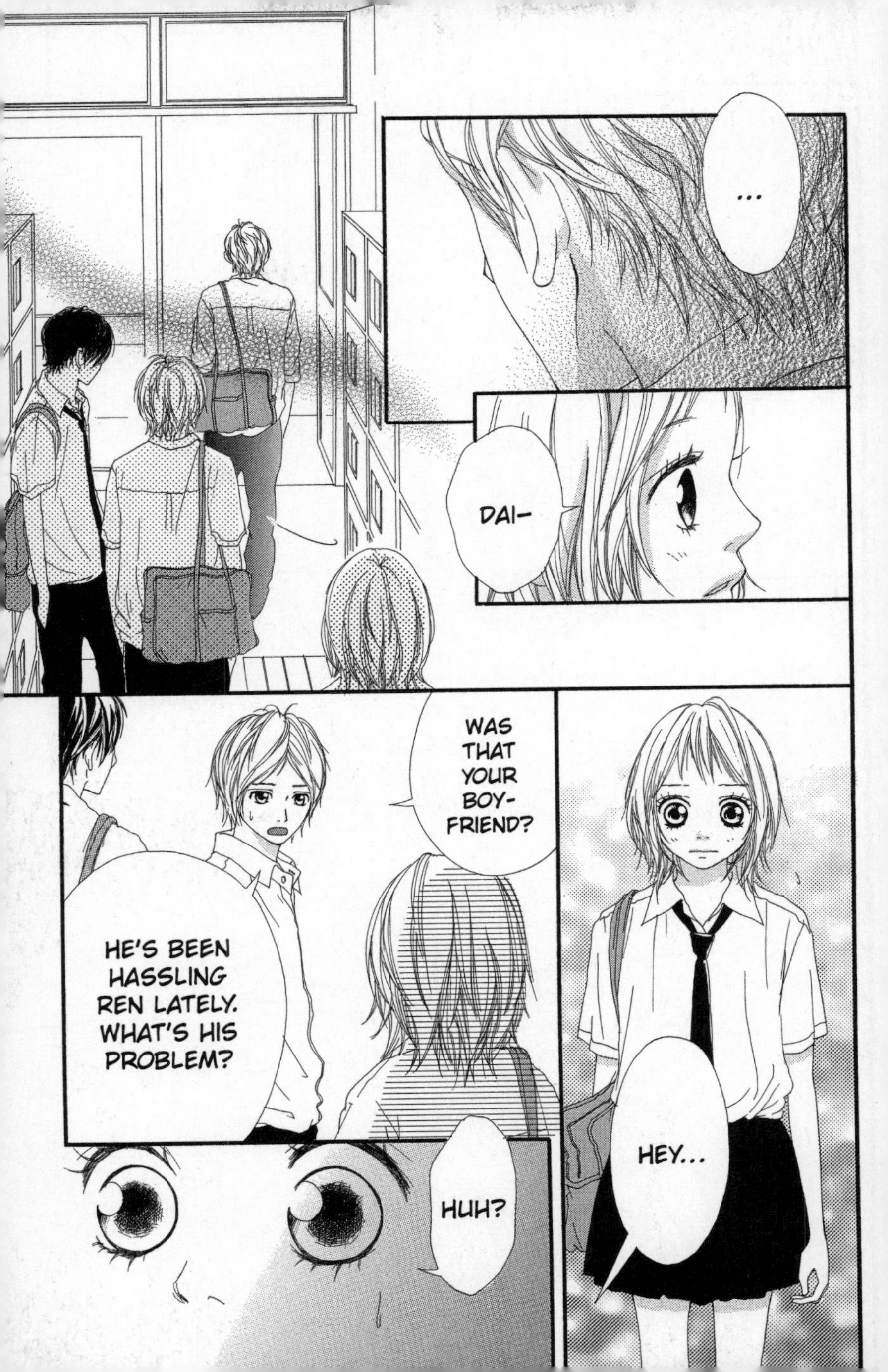
...
DAI-
HEY...
WAS THAT YOUR BOY-FRIEND?
HE'S BEEN HASSLING REN LATELY. WHAT'S HIS PROBLEM?
HUH?

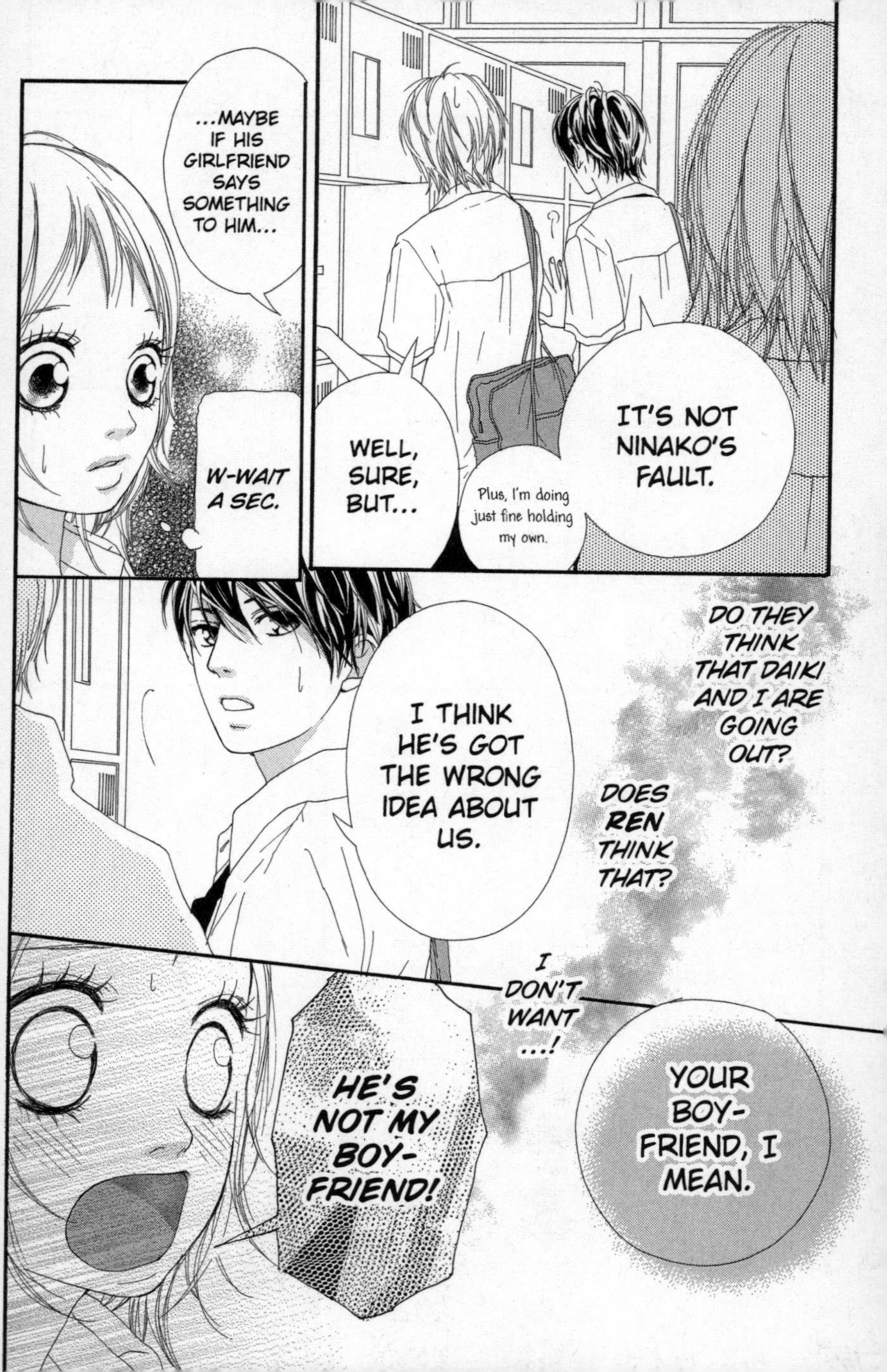
IT'S NOT NINAKO'S FAULT.
Plus, I'm doing just fine holding my own.
WELL, SURE, BUT...
...MAYBE IF HIS GIRLFRIEND SAYS SOMETHING TO HIM...
W-WAIT A SEC.
DO THEY THINK THAT DAIKI AND I ARE GOING OUT?
DOES REN THINK THAT?
I THINK HE'S GOT THE WRONG IDEA ABOUT US.
YOUR BOY-FRIEND, I MEAN.
I DON'T WANT ...!
HE'S NOT MY BOY-FRIEND!

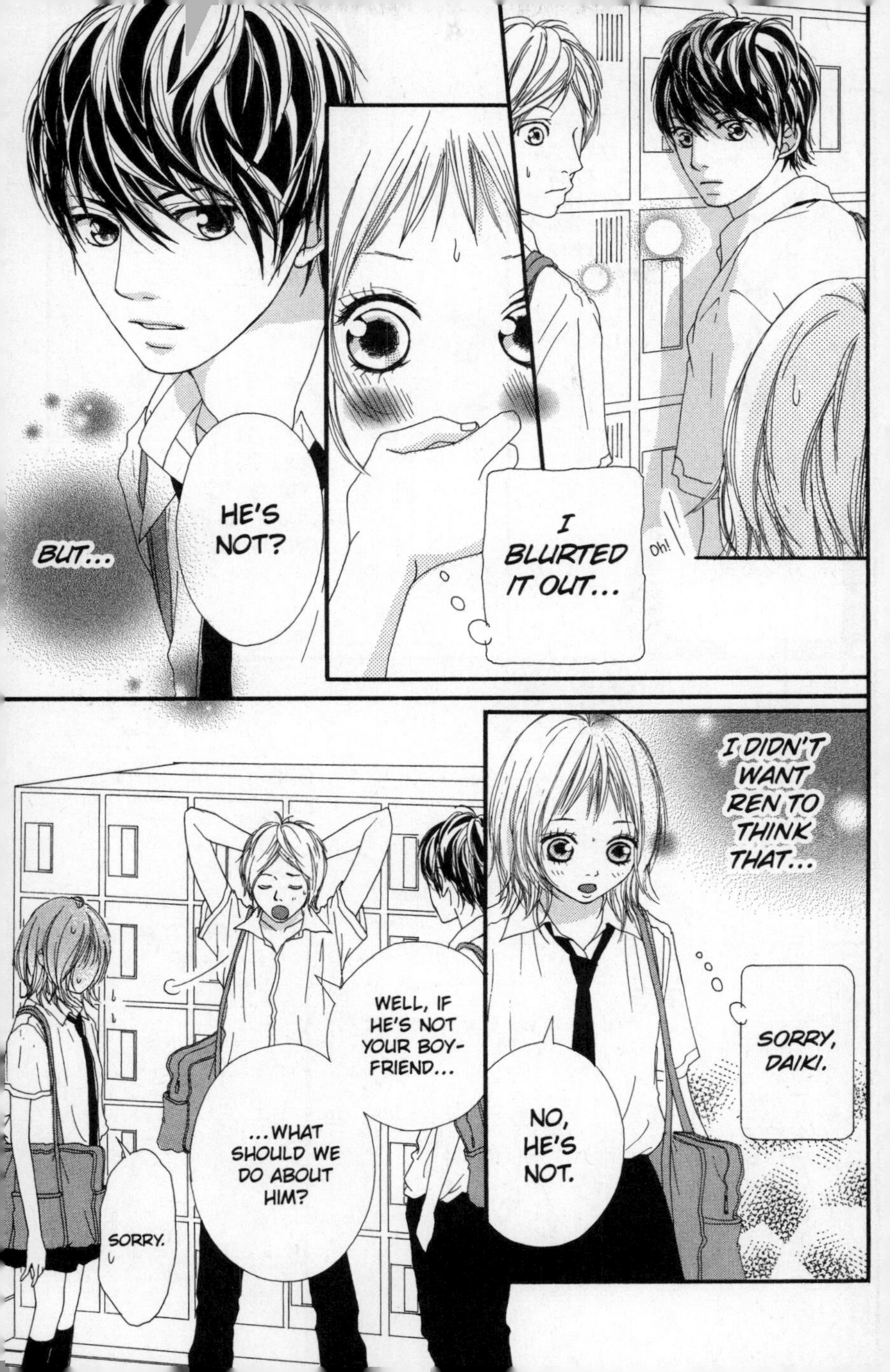
Oh!
I BLURTED IT OUT...
HE'S NOT?
BUT...
I DIDN'T WANT REN TO THINK THAT...
SORRY, DAIKI.
NO, HE'S NOT.
WELL, IF HE'S NOT YOUR BOY-FRIEND...
...WHAT SHOULD WE DO ABOUT HIM?
SORRY.

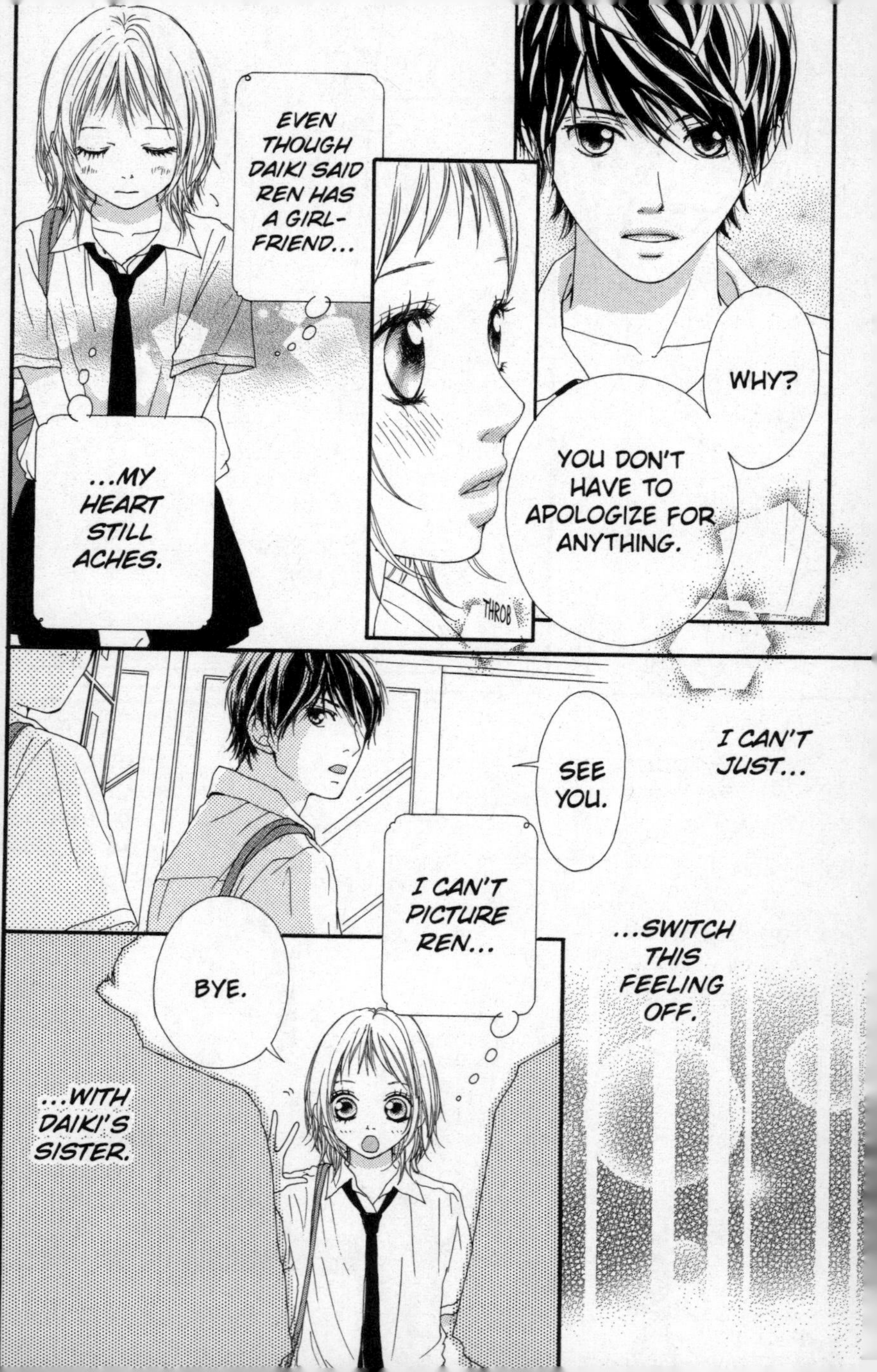
WHY?
YOU DON'T HAVE TO APOLOGIZE FOR ANYTHING.
THROB
EVEN THOUGH DAIKI SAID REN HAS A GIRL-FRIEND...
...MY HEART STILL ACHES.
I CAN'T JUST...
...SWITCH THIS FEELING OFF.
SEE YOU.
BYE.
I CAN'T PICTURE REN...
...WITH DAIKI'S SISTER.

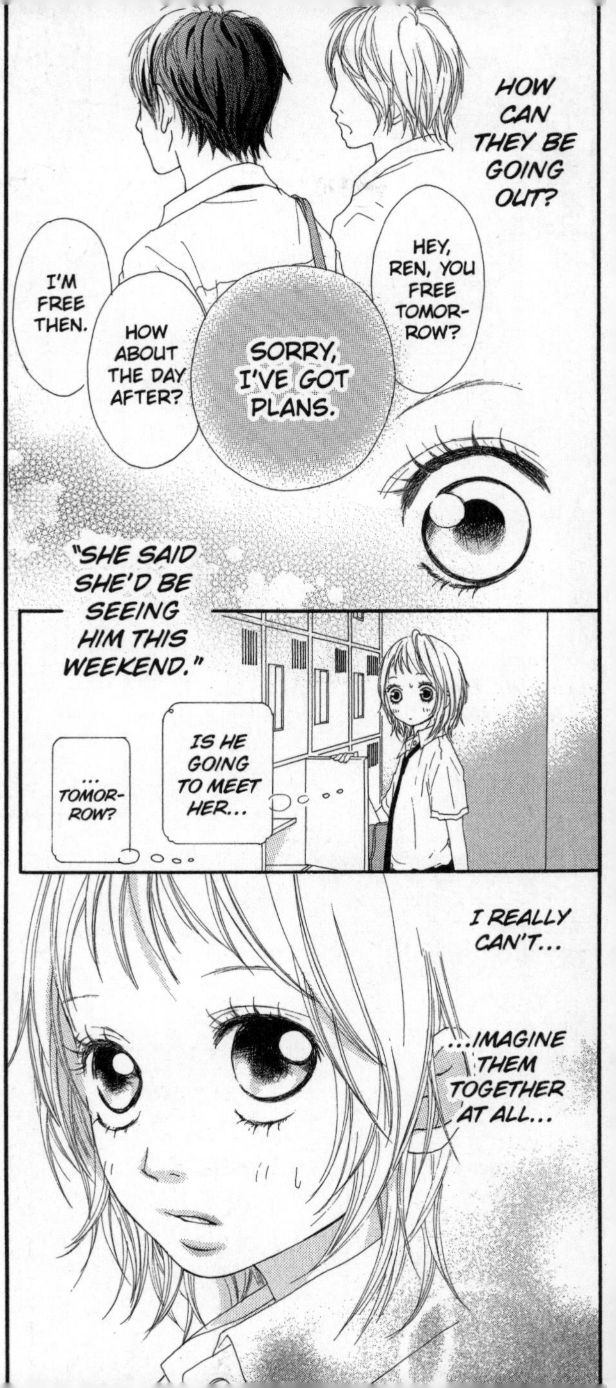
HOW CAN THEY BE GOING OUT?
HEY, REN, YOU FREE TOMORROW?
SORRY, I'VE GOT PLANS.
HOW ABOUT THE DAY AFTER?
I'M FREE THEN.
"SHE SAID SHE'D BE SEEING HIM THIS WEEKEND."
IS HE GOING TO MEET HER...
...TOMORROW?
I REALLY CAN'T...
...IMAGINE THEM TOGETHER AT ALL...

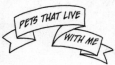

PETS THAT LIVE WITH ME

Baby chinchillas are born with fur, and before you know it, they're scampering around. Or at least they're already running all over the place by the time I know they're there.

They're so cute!

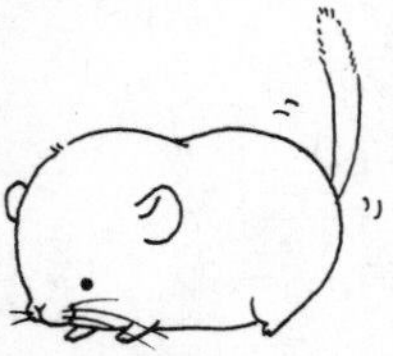

↑ Like this

They're about two heads in length. It's hilarious! Their ears are still small. Their tails aren't so much fuzzy as kinda shabby.

Ta-da!

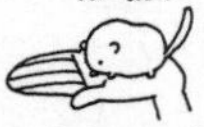

They can fit in the palm of your hand.

Their mother (Komugi) doesn't care at all when I touch the babies.

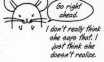

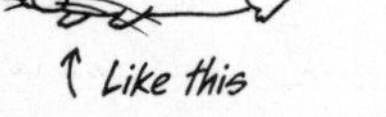
Go right ahead.

I don't really think she says that. I just think she doesn't realize.

I really need them to grow up quickly. I can't get any work done like this!

They're so cute that I spend all my time playing with them...

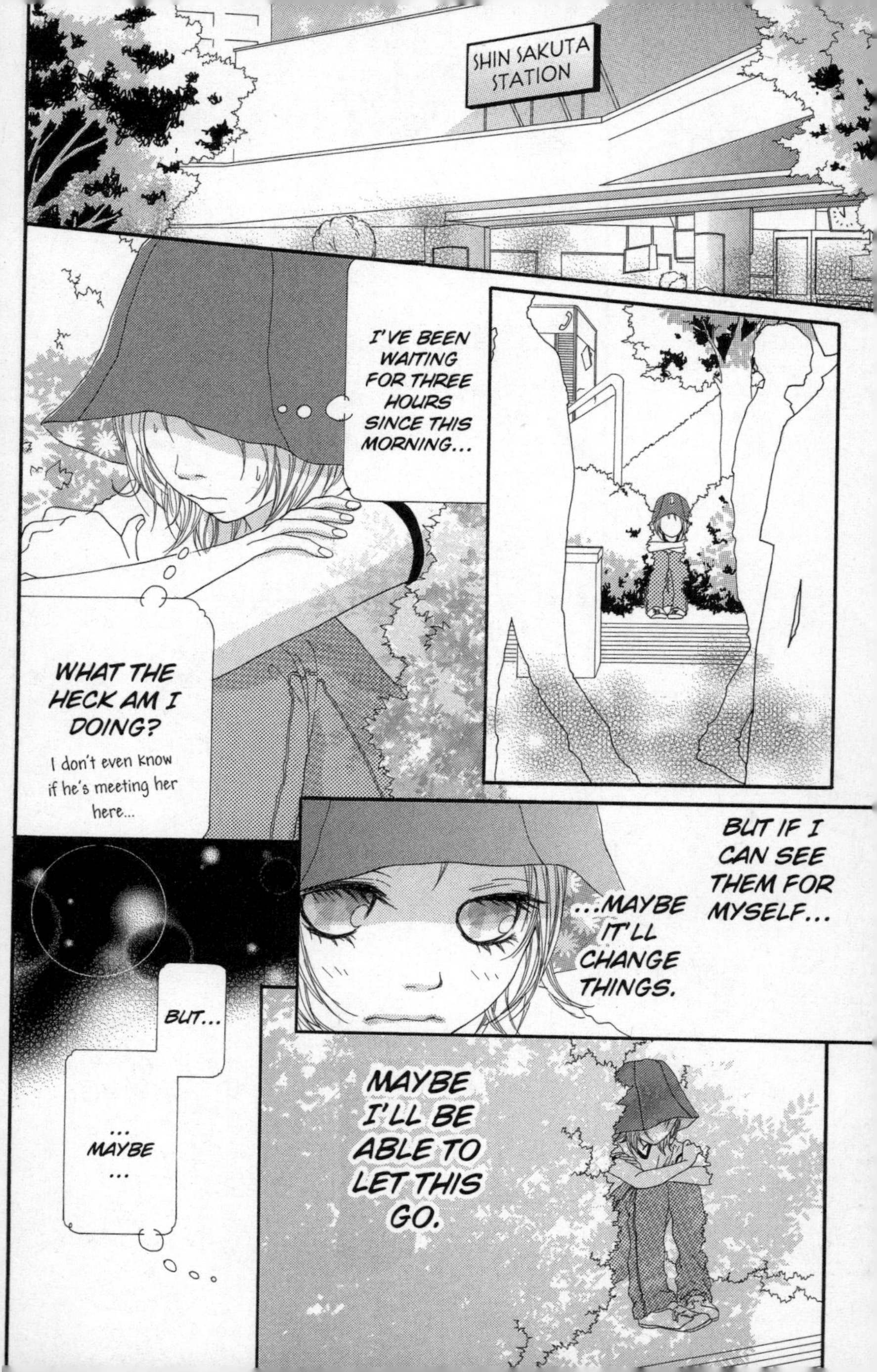
SHIN SAKUTA STATION
I'VE BEEN WAITING FOR THREE HOURS SINCE THIS MORNING...
WHAT THE HECK AM I DOING?
I don't even know if he's meeting her here...
BUT IF I CAN SEE THEM FOR MYSELF...
...MAYBE IT'LL CHANGE THINGS.
BUT...
...MAYBE...
MAYBE I'LL BE ABLE TO LET THIS GO.

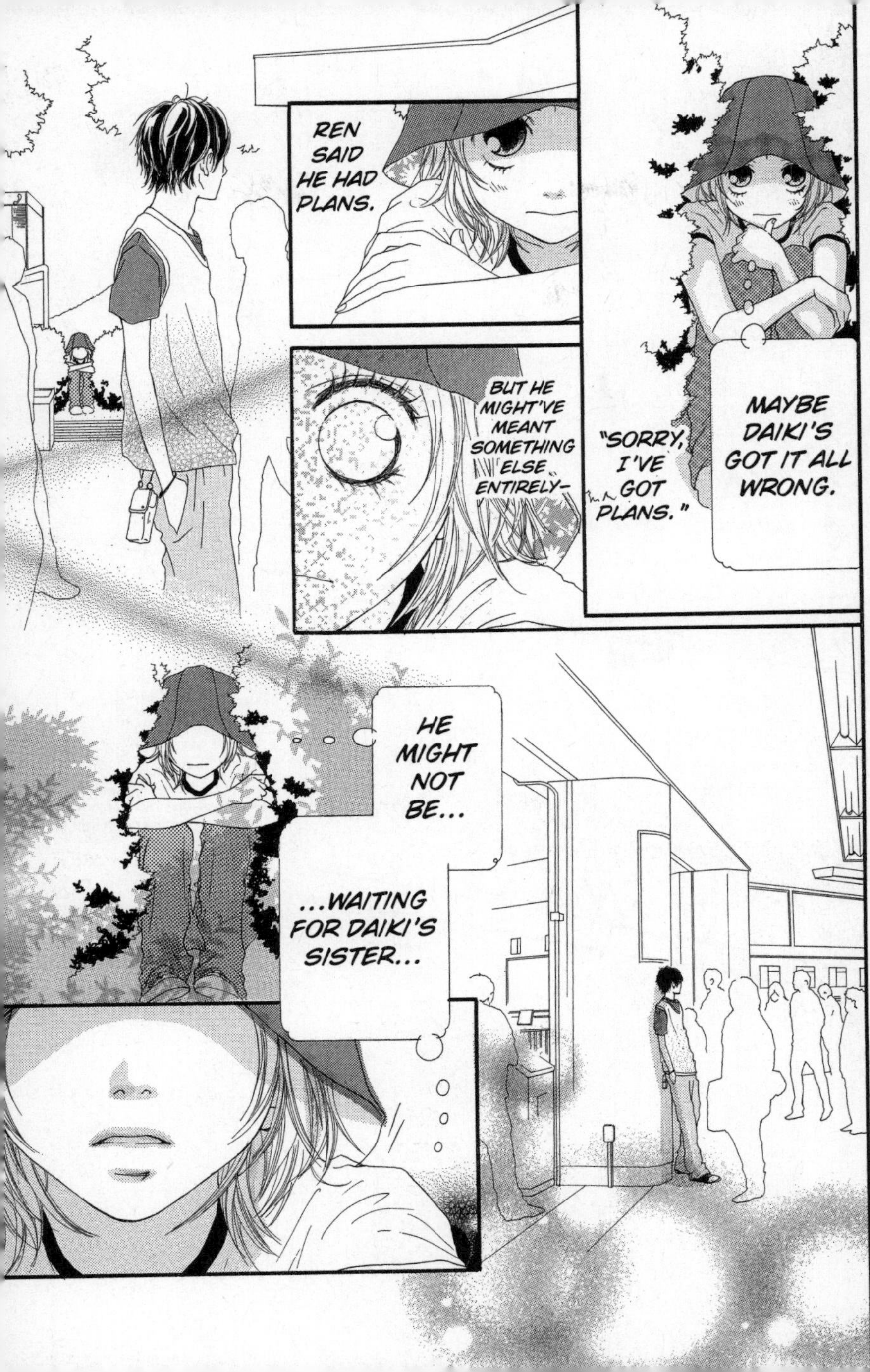
MAYBE DAIKI'S GOT IT ALL WRONG.
"SORRY, I'VE GOT PLANS."
REN SAID HE HAD PLANS.
BUT HE MIGHT'VE MEANT SOMETHING ELSE ENTIRELY–
HE MIGHT NOT BE...
...WAITING FOR DAIKI'S SISTER...

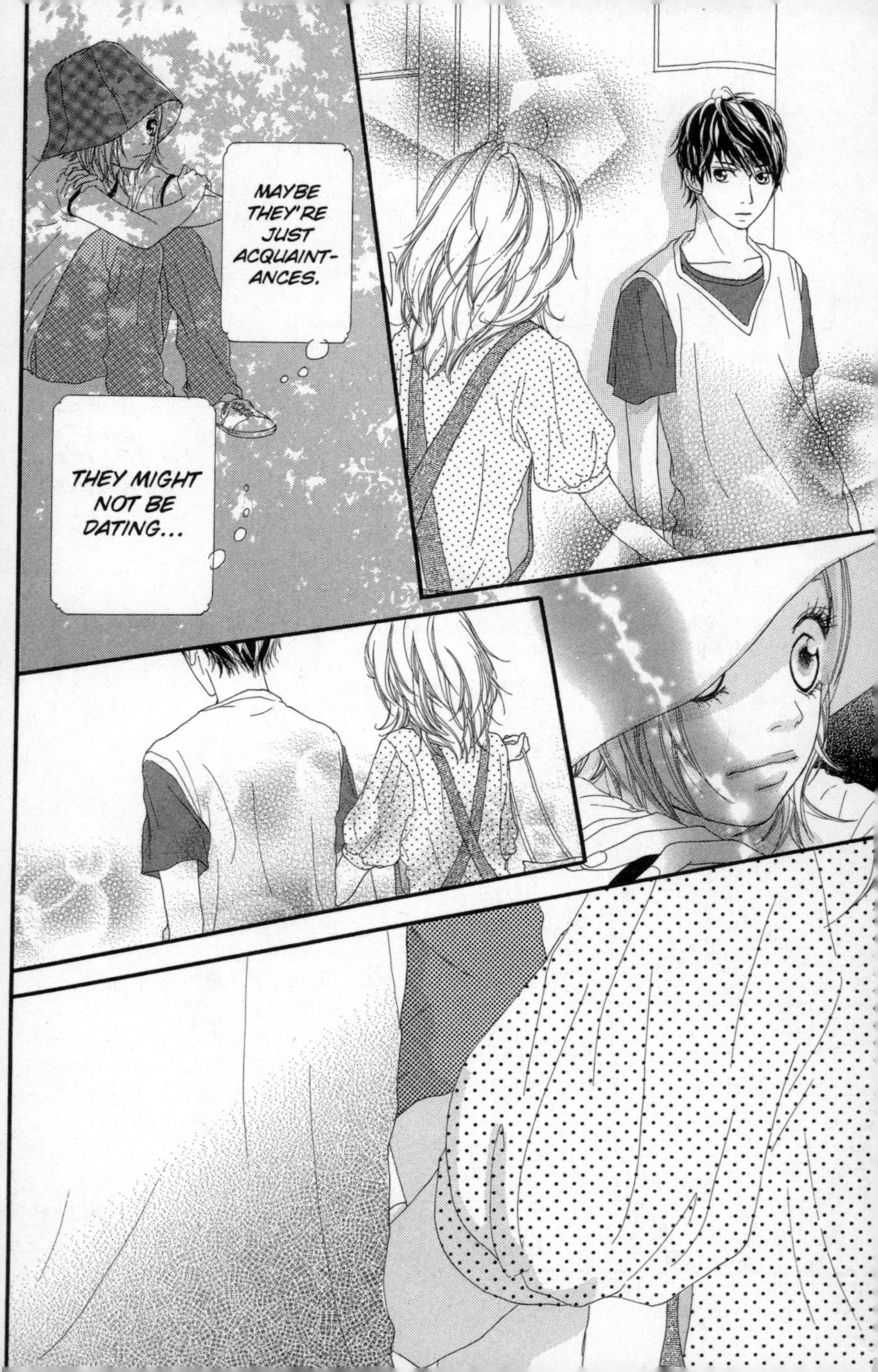
MAYBE THEY'RE JUST ACQUAINT-ANCES.
THEY MIGHT NOT BE DATING...

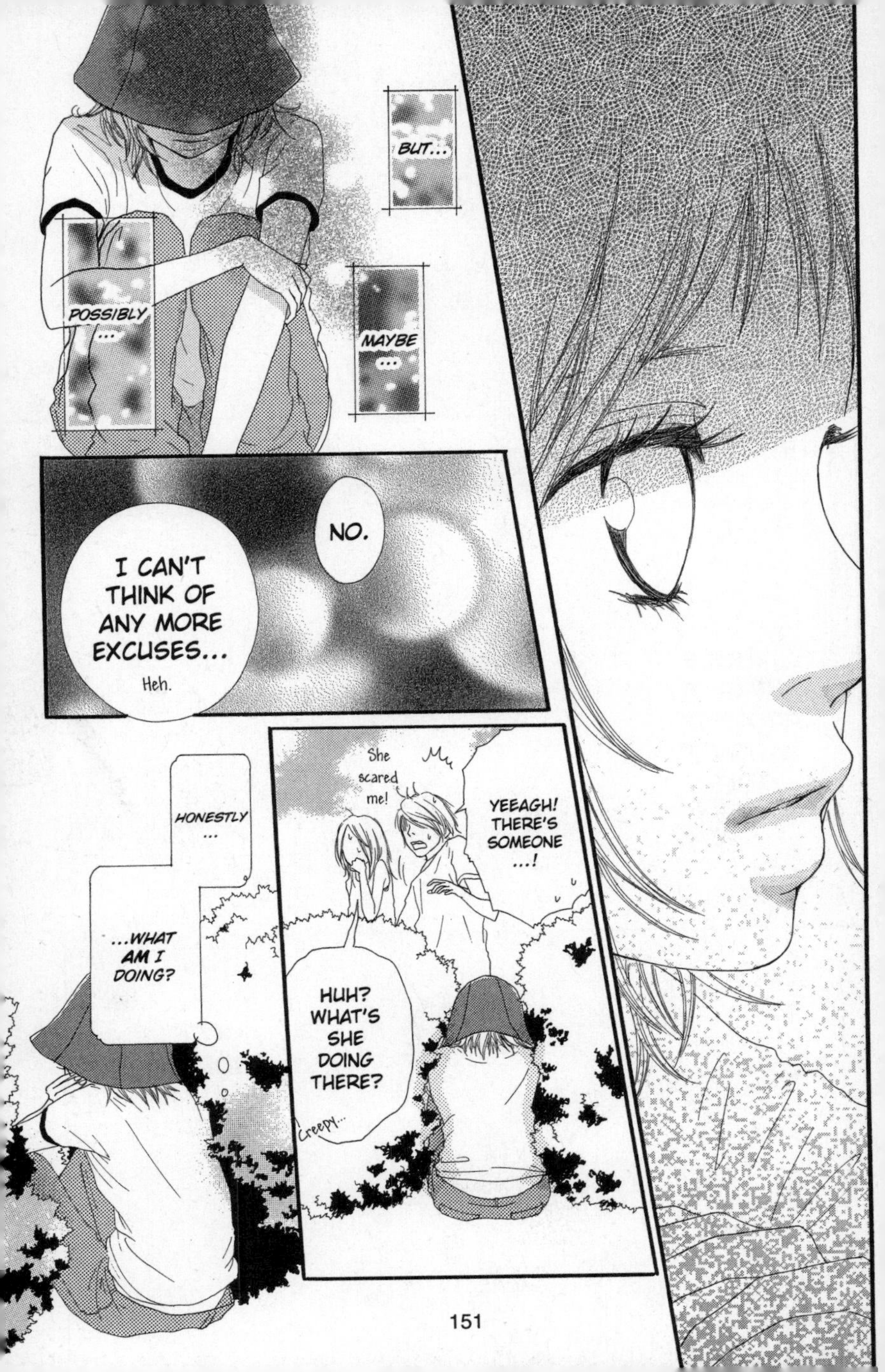
BUT...
MAYBE...
POSSIBLY...
NO.
I CAN'T THINK OF ANY MORE EXCUSES...
Heh.
She scared me!
YEEAGH! THERE'S SOMEONE...!
HUH? WHAT'S SHE DOING THERE?
Creepy...
HONESTLY...
...WHAT AM I DOING?

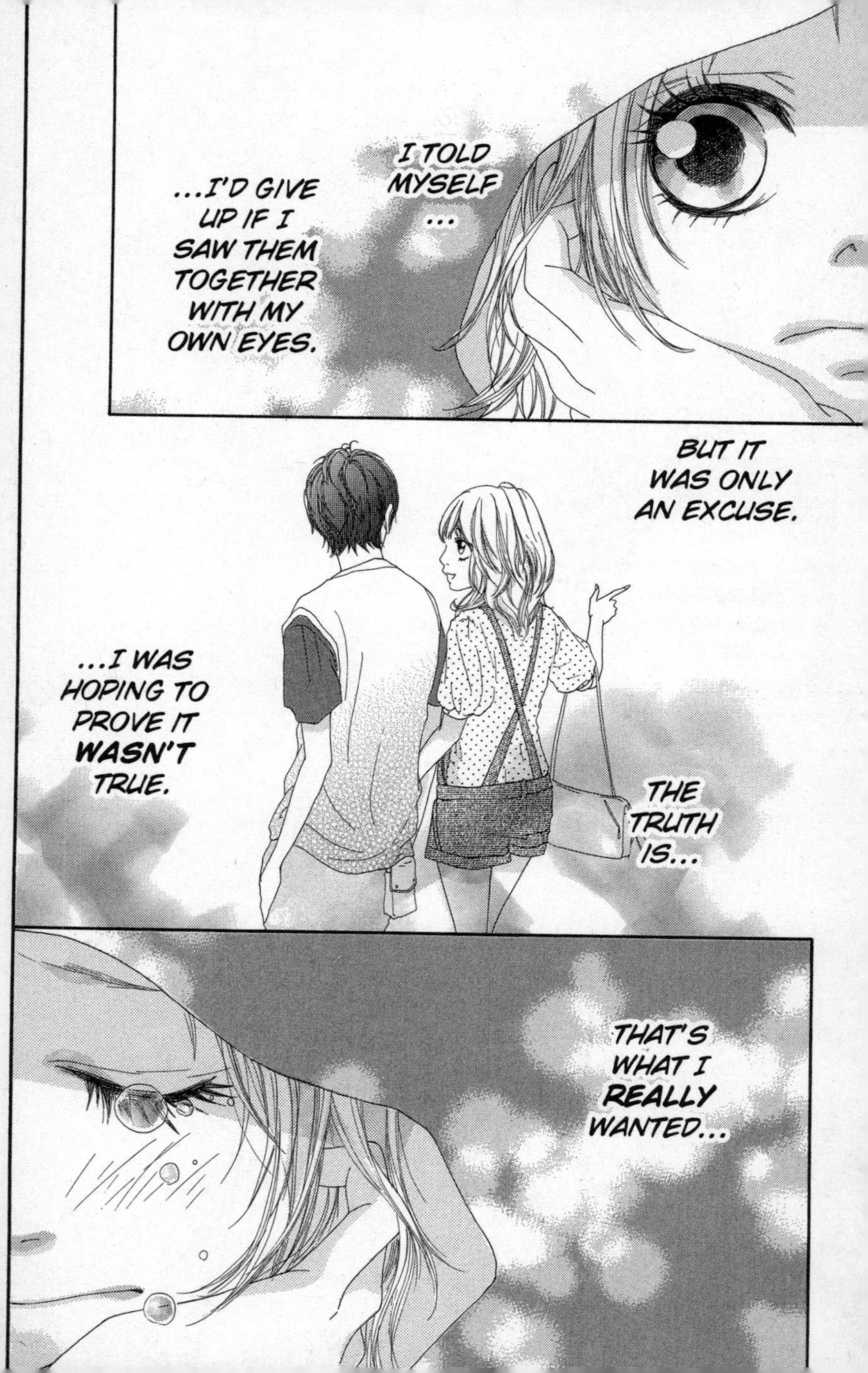
I TOLD MYSELF...
...I'D GIVE UP IF I SAW THEM TOGETHER WITH MY OWN EYES.
BUT IT WAS ONLY AN EXCUSE.
THE TRUTH IS...
...I WAS HOPING TO PROVE IT **WASN'T** TRUE.
THAT'S WHAT I **REALLY** WANTED...

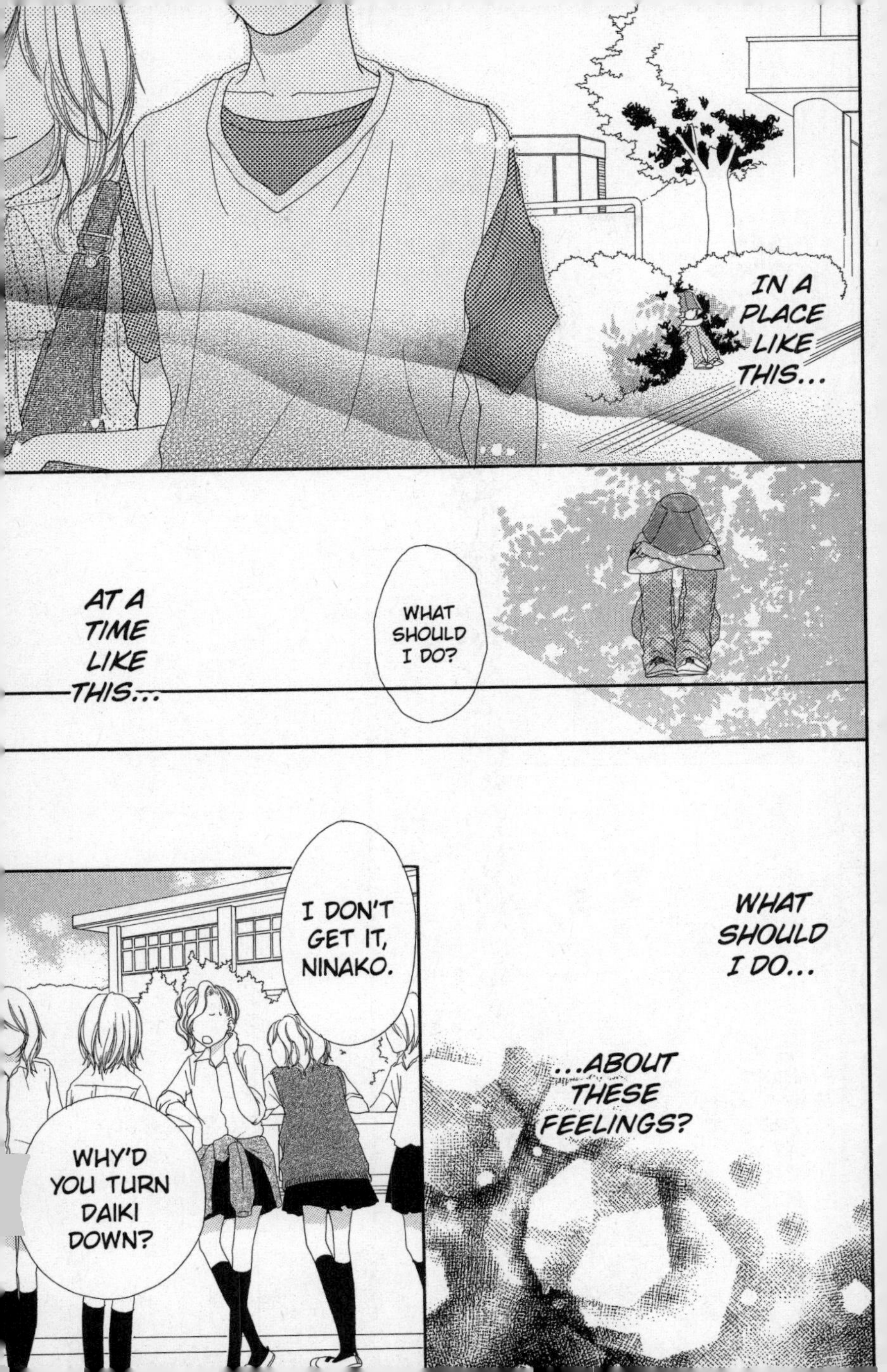
IN A PLACE LIKE THIS...
WHAT SHOULD I DO?
AT A TIME LIKE THIS...
WHAT SHOULD I DO...
...ABOUT THESE FEELINGS?
I DON'T GET IT, NINAKO.
WHY'D YOU TURN DAIKI DOWN?

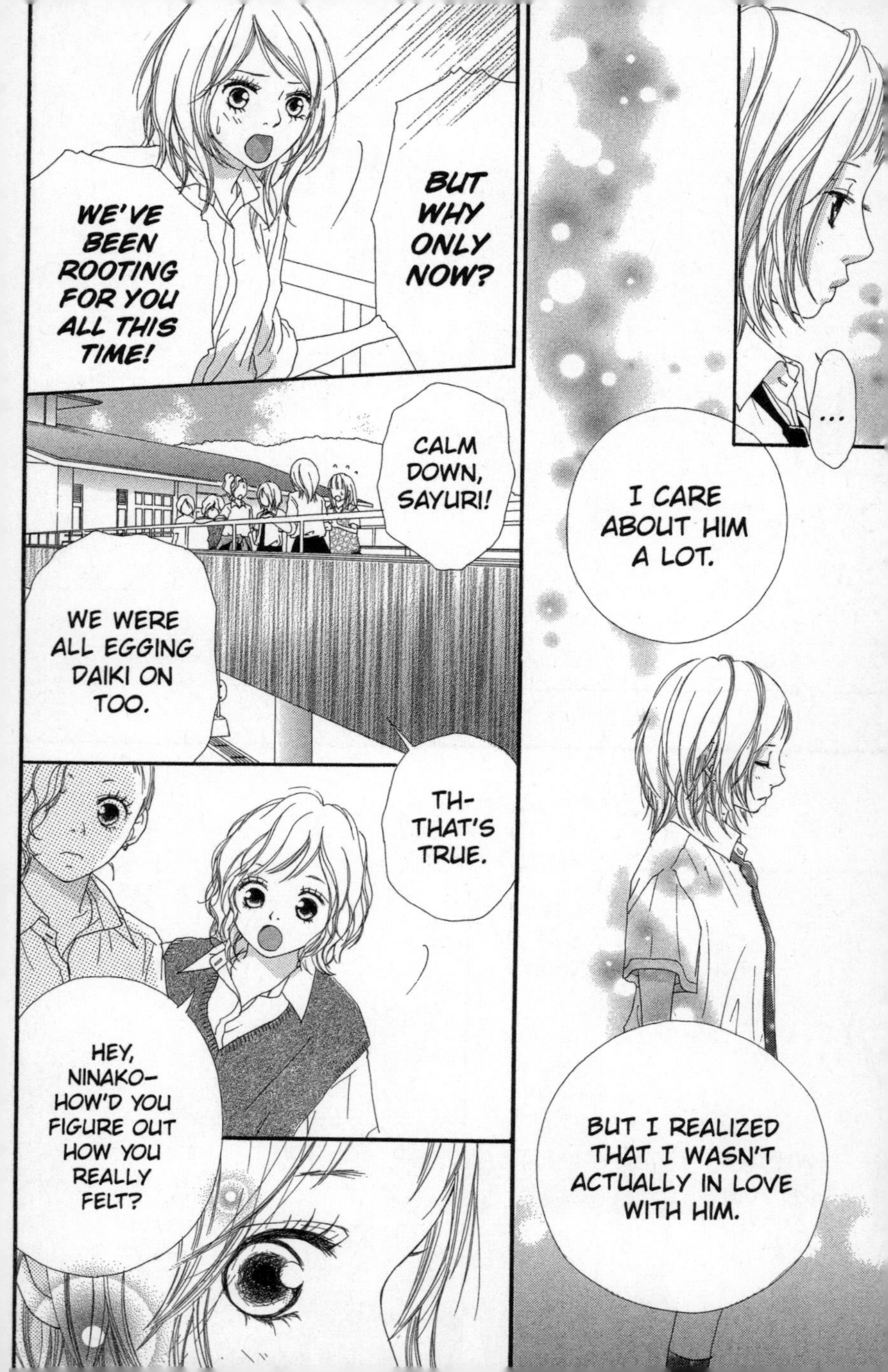
...
I CARE ABOUT HIM A LOT.
BUT I REALIZED THAT I WASN'T ACTUALLY IN LOVE WITH HIM.
BUT WHY ONLY NOW?
WE'VE BEEN ROOTING FOR YOU ALL THIS TIME!
CALM DOWN, SAYURI!
WE WERE ALL EGGING DAIKI ON TOO.
TH-THAT'S TRUE.
HEY, NINAKO-HOW'D YOU FIGURE OUT HOW YOU REALLY FELT?

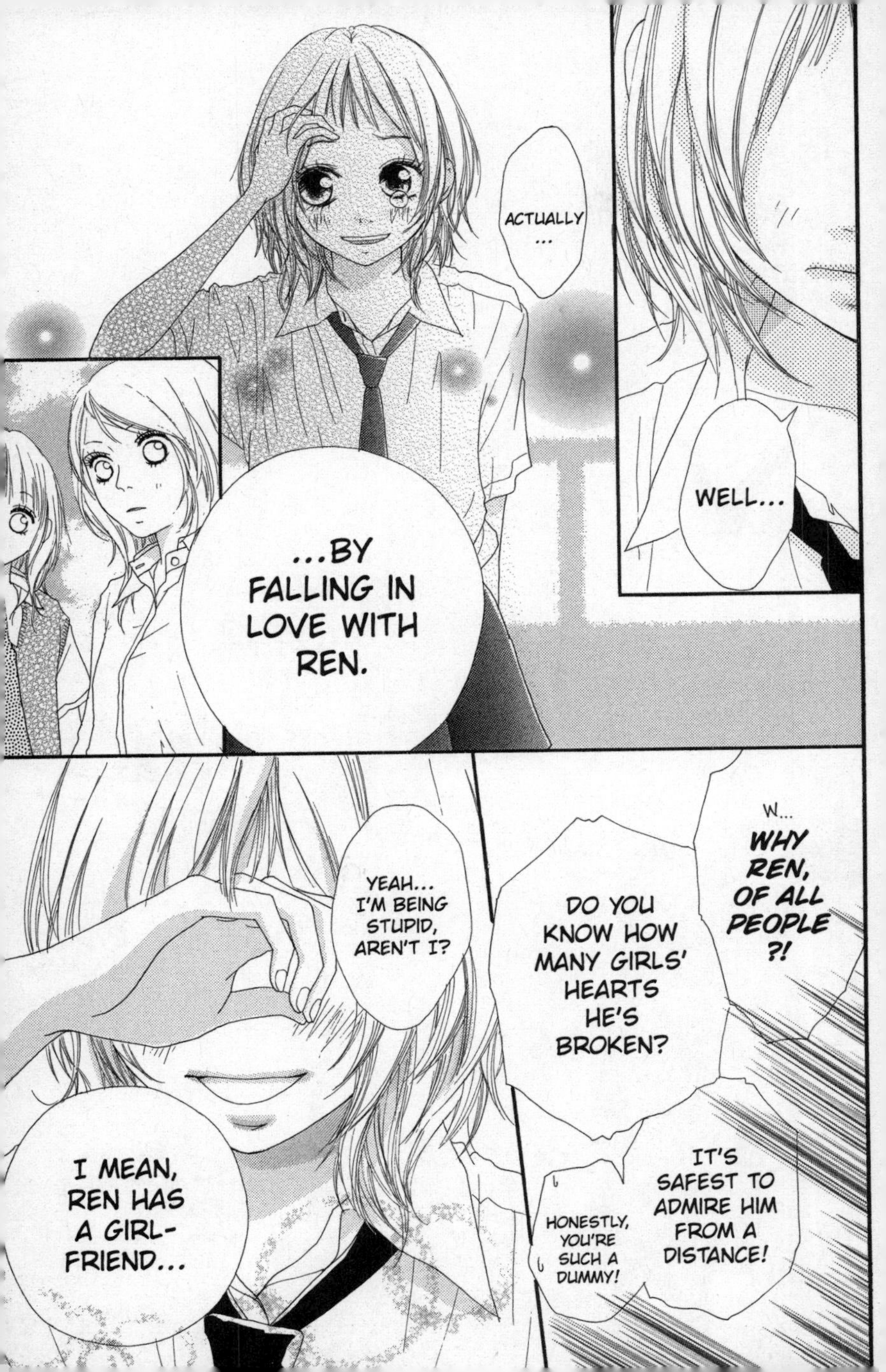
WELL...
ACTUALLY ...
...BY FALLING IN LOVE WITH REN.
W... WHY REN, OF ALL PEOPLE?!
DO YOU KNOW HOW MANY GIRLS' HEARTS HE'S BROKEN?
IT'S SAFEST TO ADMIRE HIM FROM A DISTANCE!
HONESTLY, YOU'RE SUCH A DUMMY!
YEAH... I'M BEING STUPID, AREN'T I?
I MEAN, REN HAS A GIRL-FRIEND...

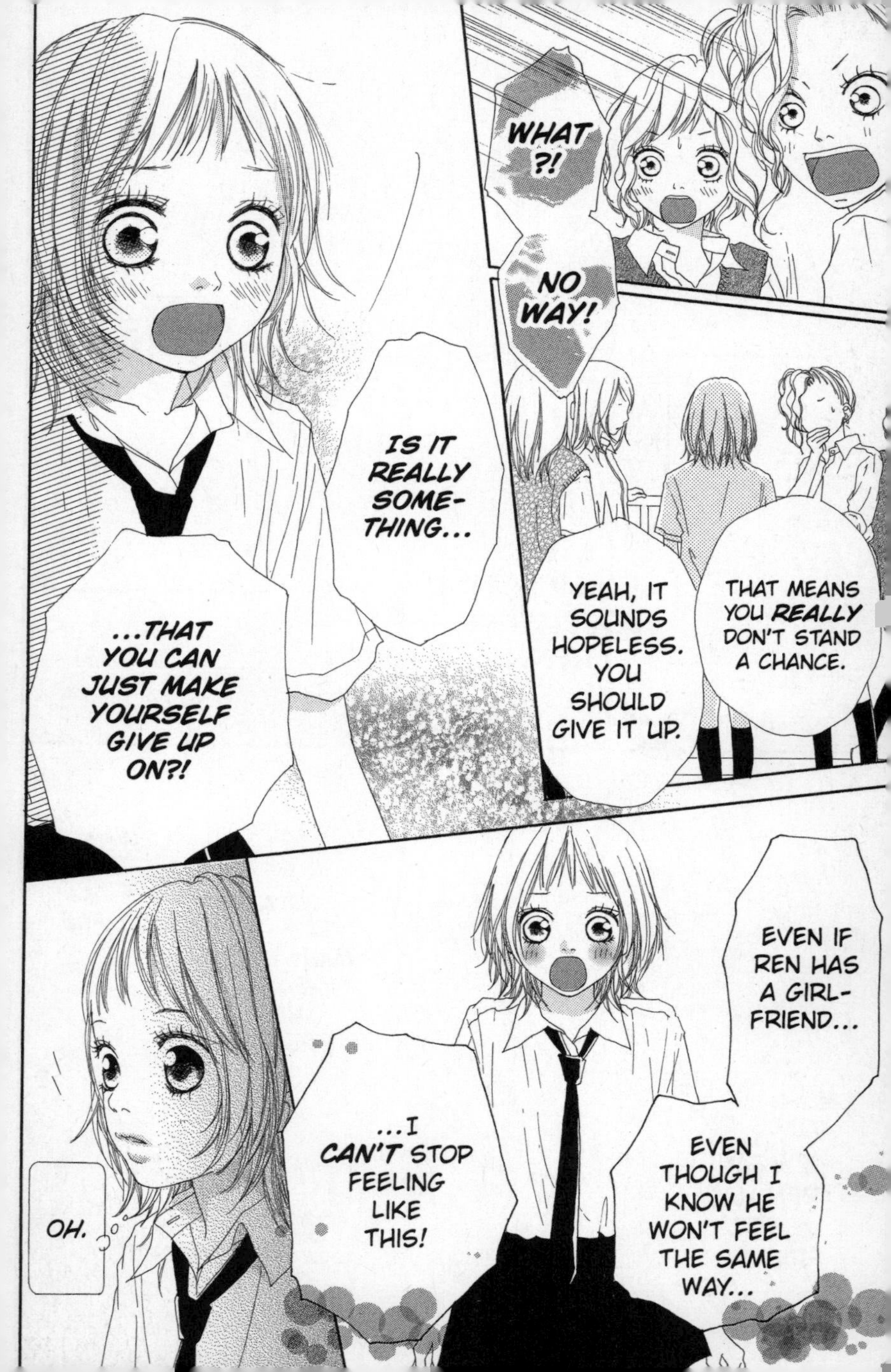
WHAT?!
NO WAY!
THAT MEANS YOU REALLY DON'T STAND A CHANCE.
YEAH, IT SOUNDS HOPELESS. YOU SHOULD GIVE IT UP.
IS IT REALLY SOME-THING...
...THAT YOU CAN JUST MAKE YOURSELF GIVE UP ON?!
EVEN IF REN HAS A GIRL-FRIEND...
EVEN THOUGH I KNOW HE WON'T FEEL THE SAME WAY...
...I CAN'T STOP FEELING LIKE THIS!
OH.

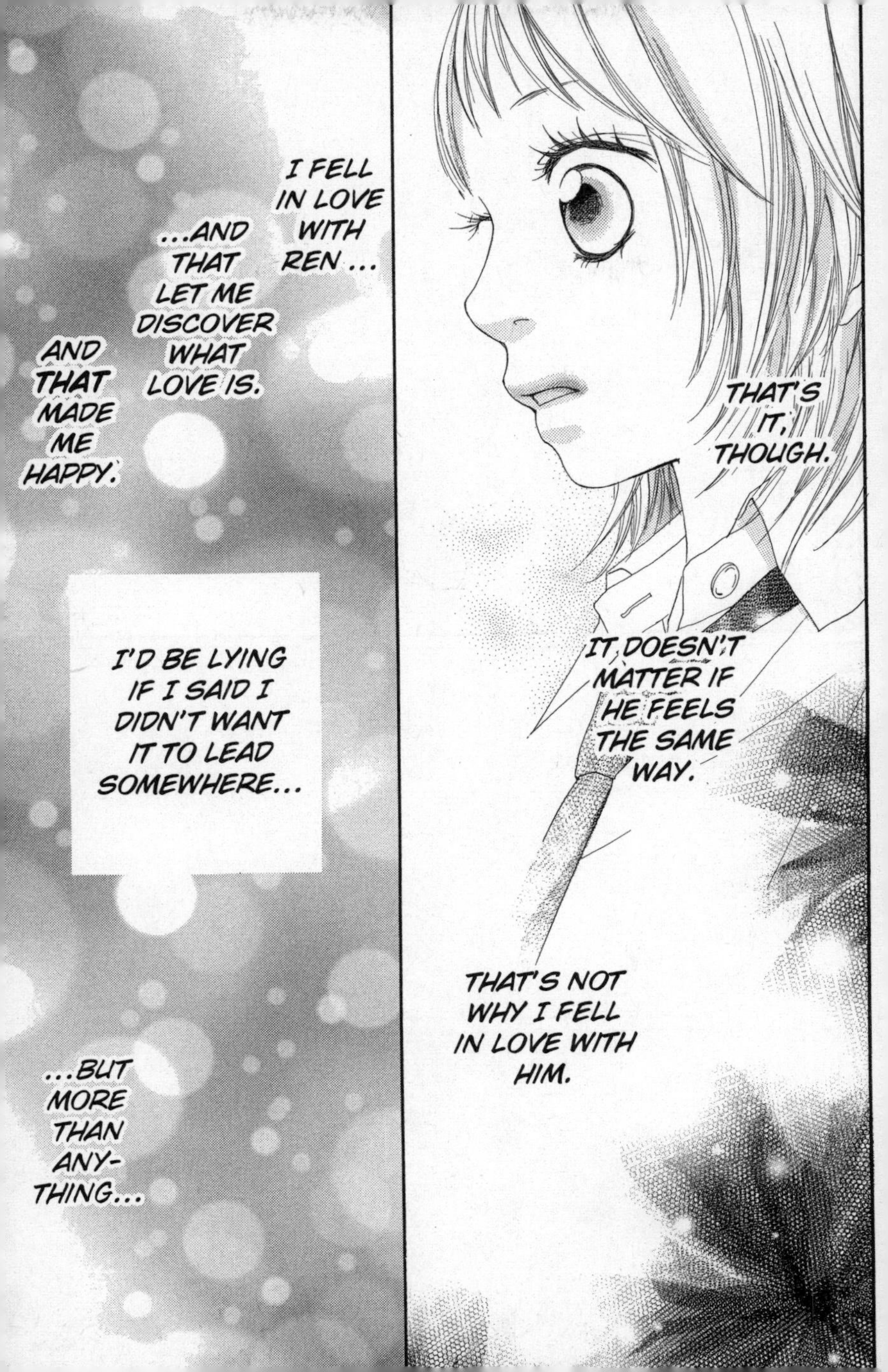
THAT'S IT, THOUGH.
IT DOESN'T MATTER IF HE FEELS THE SAME WAY.
THAT'S NOT WHY I FELL IN LOVE WITH HIM.
I FELL IN LOVE WITH REN...
...AND THAT LET ME DISCOVER WHAT LOVE IS.
AND THAT MADE ME HAPPY.
I'D BE LYING IF I SAID I DIDN'T WANT IT TO LEAD SOMEWHERE...
...BUT MORE THAN ANYTHING...

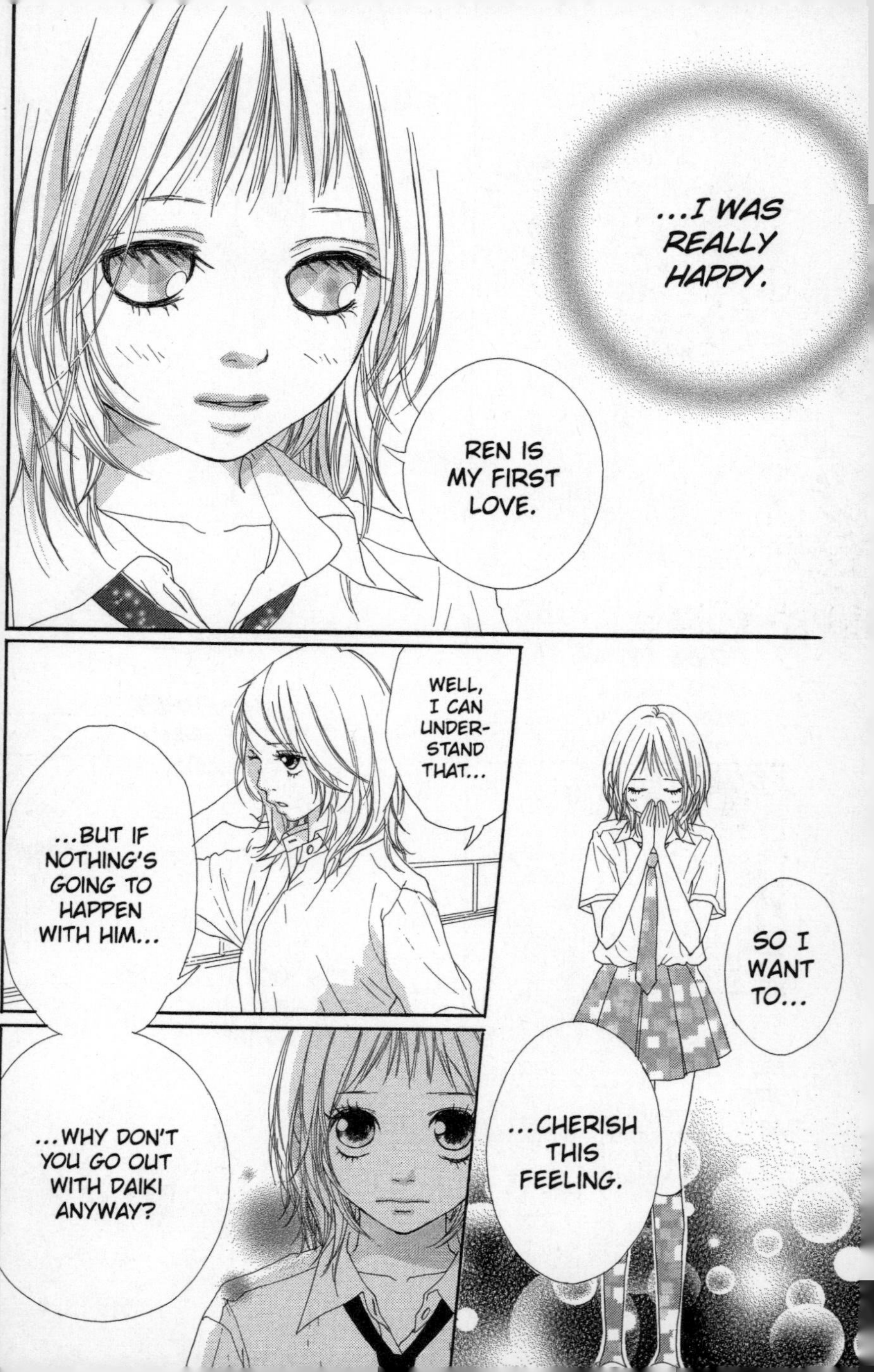
...I WAS REALLY HAPPY.
REN IS MY FIRST LOVE.
SO I WANT TO...
...CHERISH THIS FEELING.
WELL, I CAN UNDERSTAND THAT...
...BUT IF NOTHING'S GOING TO HAPPEN WITH HIM...
...WHY DON'T YOU GO OUT WITH DAIKI ANYWAY?

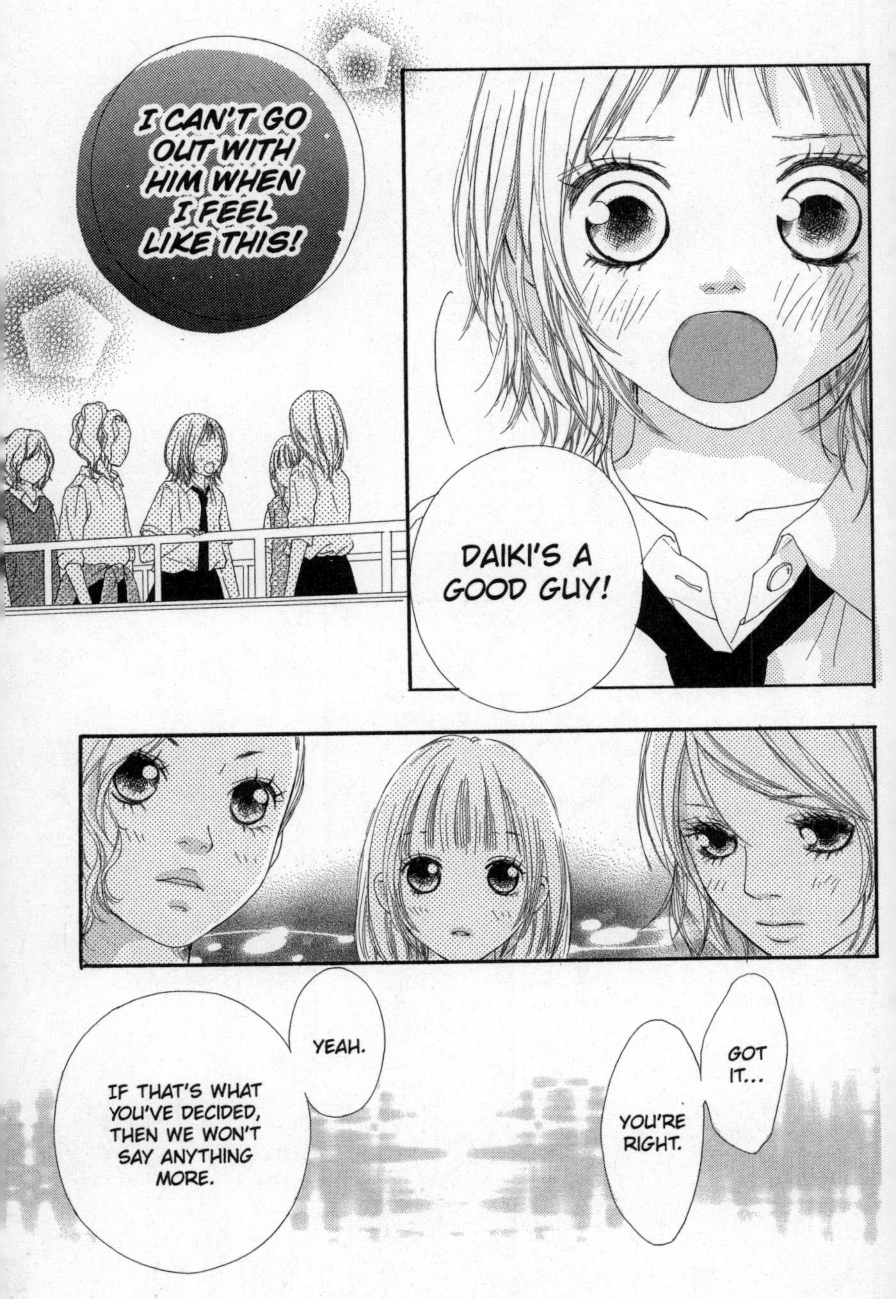
DAIKI'S A GOOD GUY!
I CAN'T GO OUT WITH HIM WHEN I FEEL LIKE THIS!
GOT IT...
YOU'RE RIGHT.
YEAH.
IF THAT'S WHAT YOU'VE DECIDED, THEN WE WON'T SAY ANYTHING MORE.

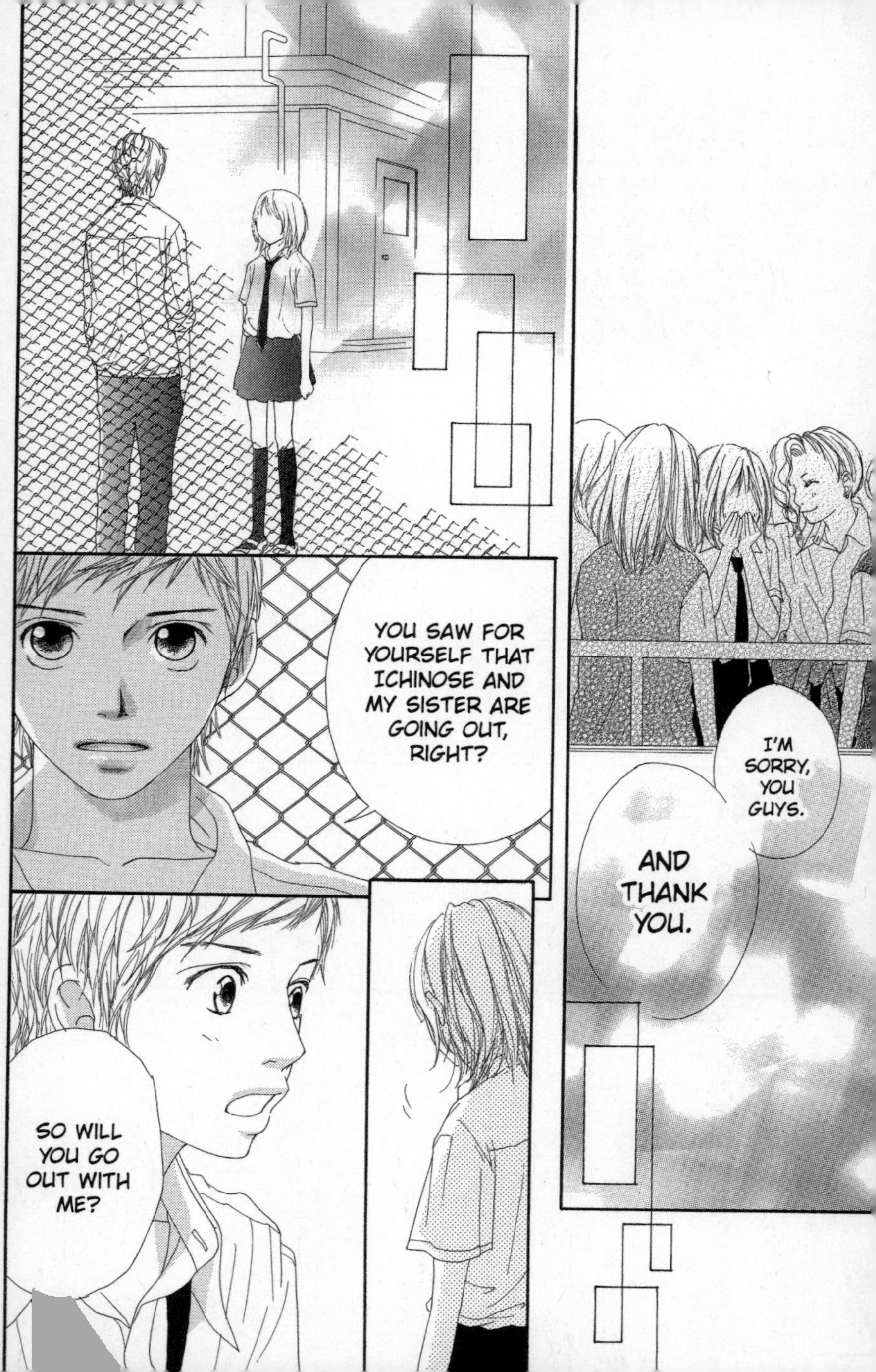
I'M SORRY, YOU GUYS.
AND THANK YOU.
YOU SAW FOR YOURSELF THAT ICHINOSE AND MY SISTER ARE GOING OUT, RIGHT?
SO WILL YOU GO OUT WITH ME?

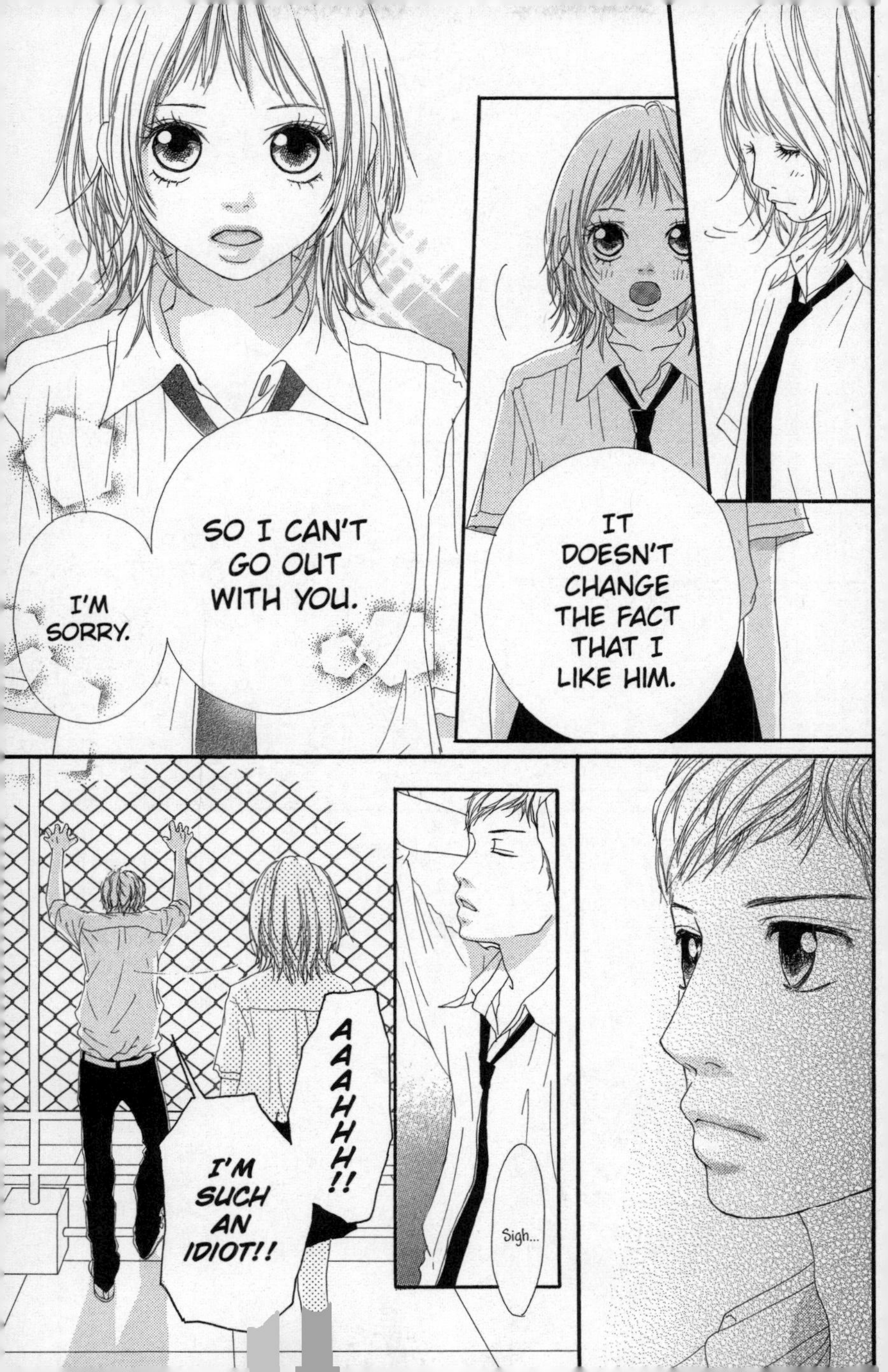
IT DOESN'T CHANGE THE FACT THAT I LIKE HIM.
SO I CAN'T GO OUT WITH YOU.
I'M SORRY.
Sigh...
AAAAHHHH!!
I'M SUCH AN IDIOT!!

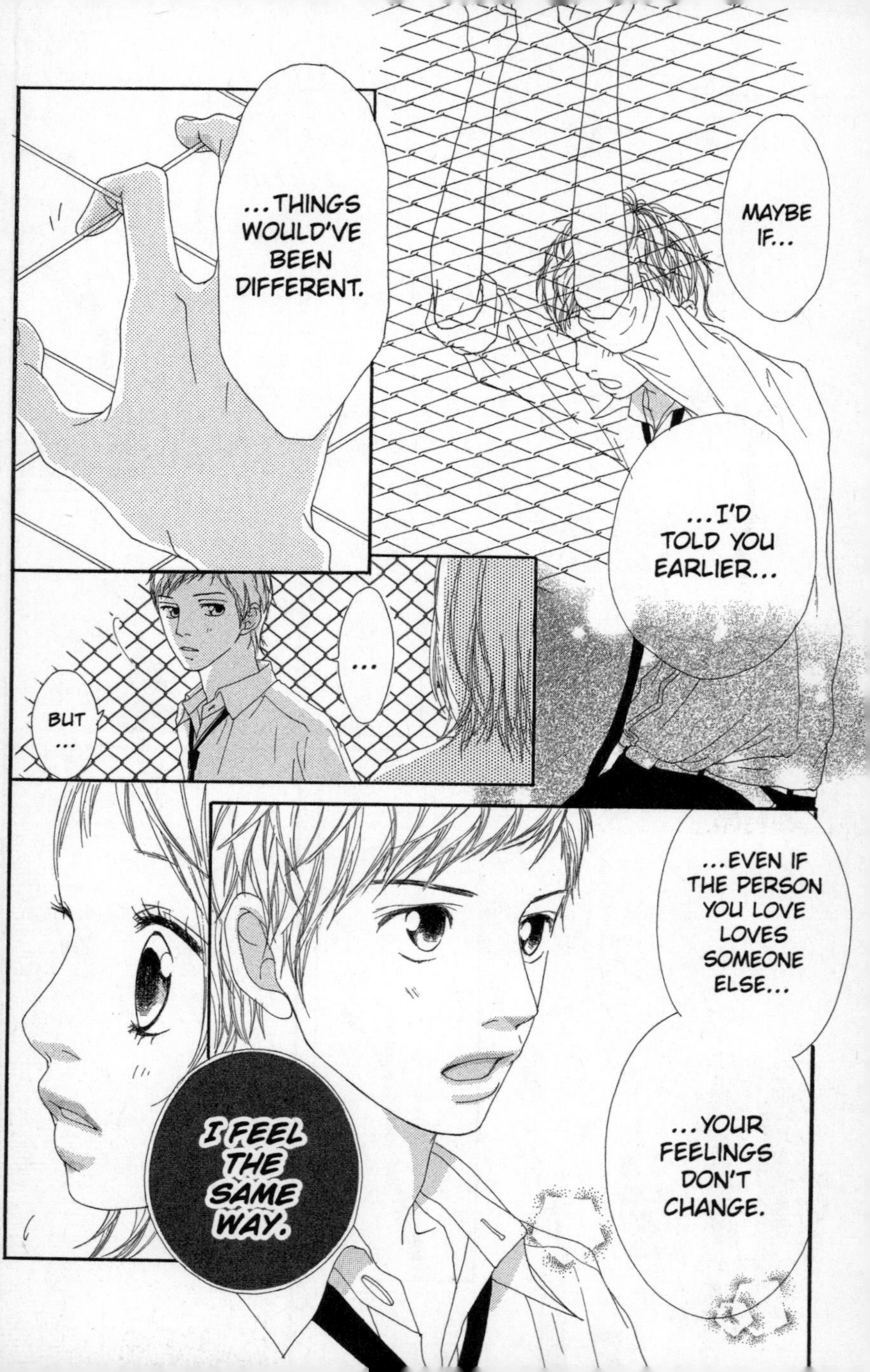
MAYBE IF...
...I'D TOLD YOU EARLIER...
...THINGS WOULD'VE BEEN DIFFERENT.
...
BUT ...
...EVEN IF THE PERSON YOU LOVE LOVES SOMEONE ELSE...
...YOUR FEELINGS DON'T CHANGE.
I FEEL THE SAME WAY.

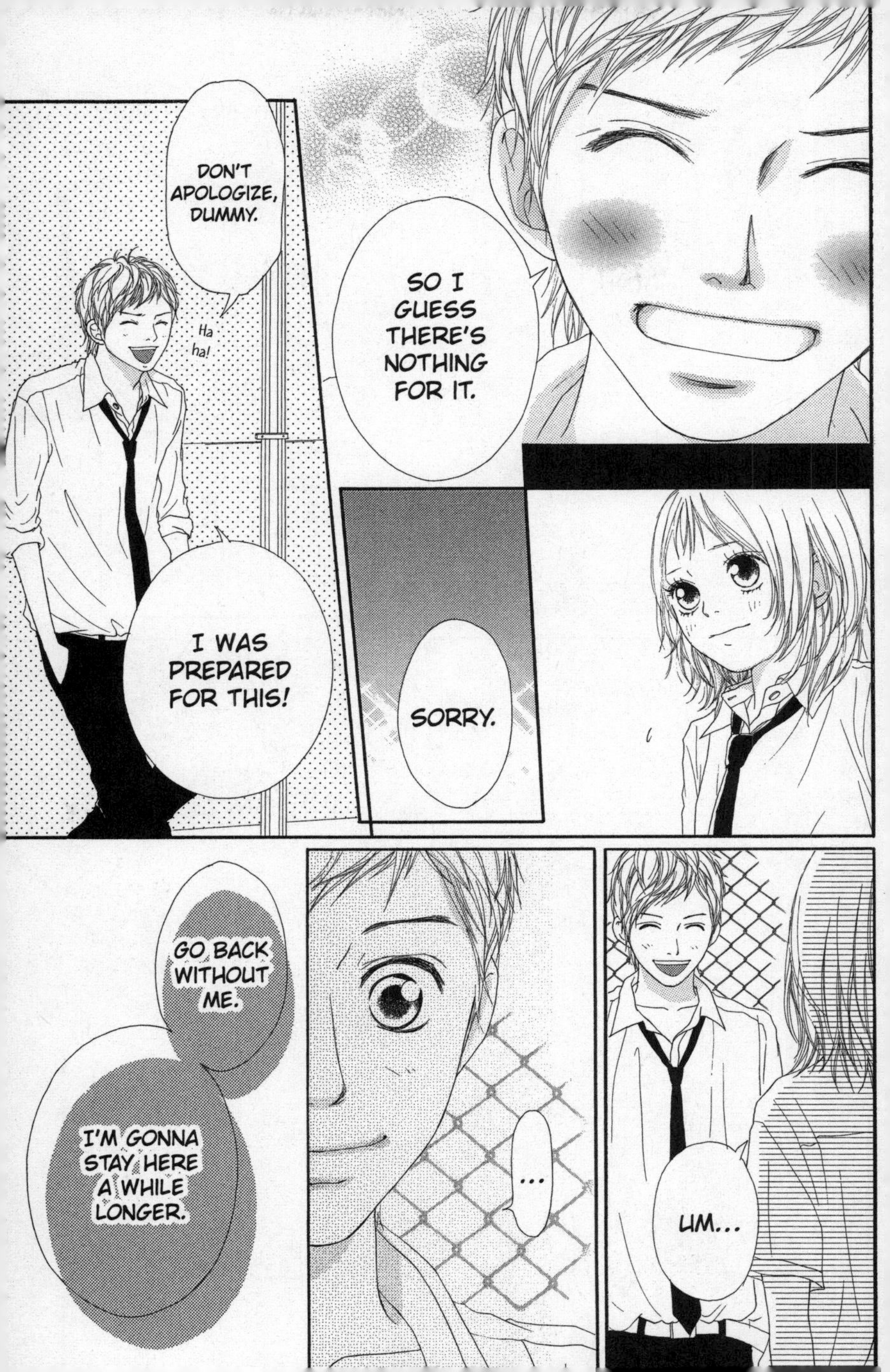
SO I GUESS THERE'S NOTHING FOR IT.
SORRY.
DON'T APOLOGIZE, DUMMY.
Ha ha!
I WAS PREPARED FOR THIS!
UM...
...
GO BACK WITHOUT ME.
I'M GONNA STAY HERE A WHILE LONGER.

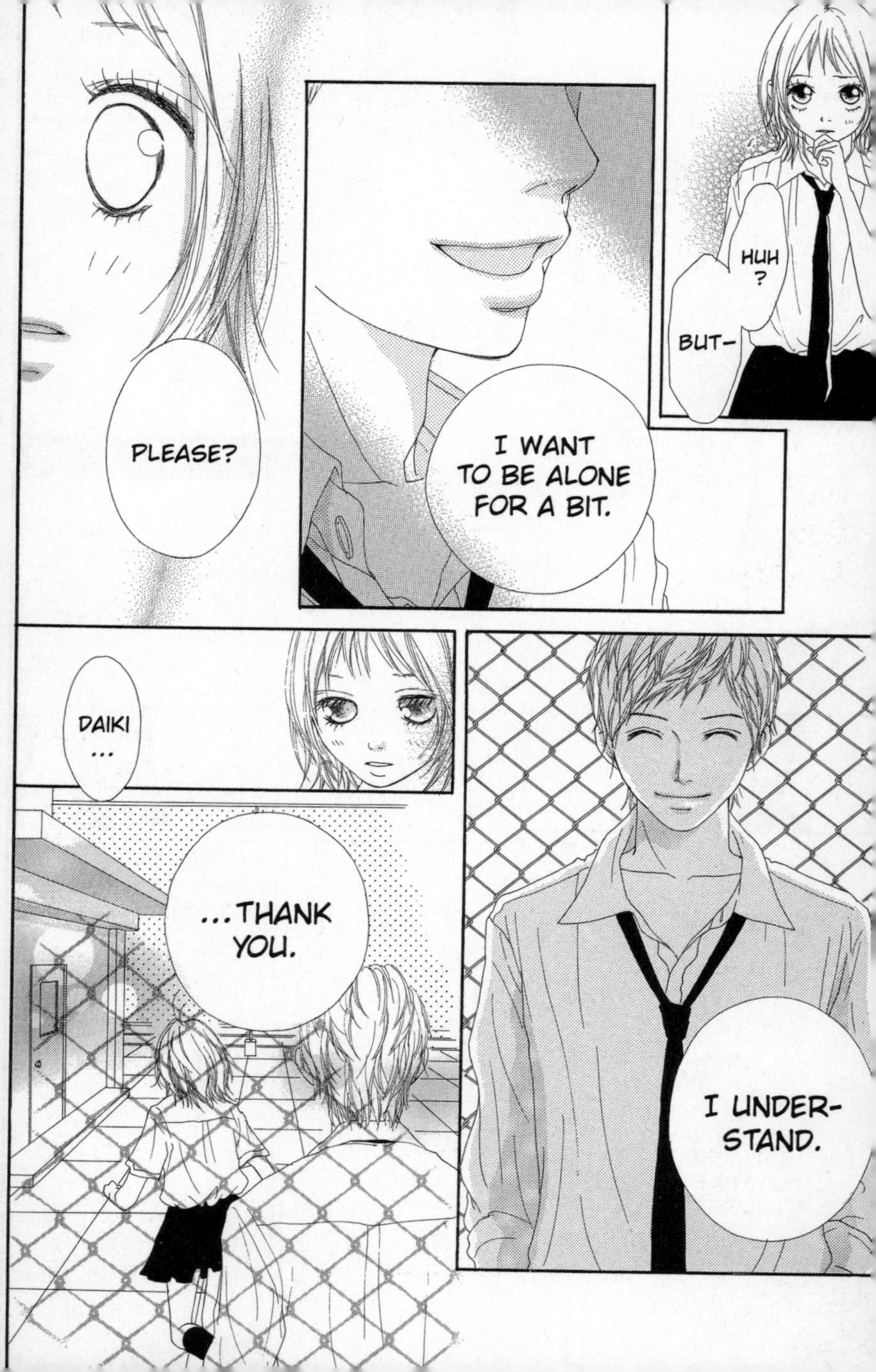
HUH?
BUT–
I WANT TO BE ALONE FOR A BIT.
PLEASE?
I UNDER-STAND.
DAIKI...
...THANK YOU.

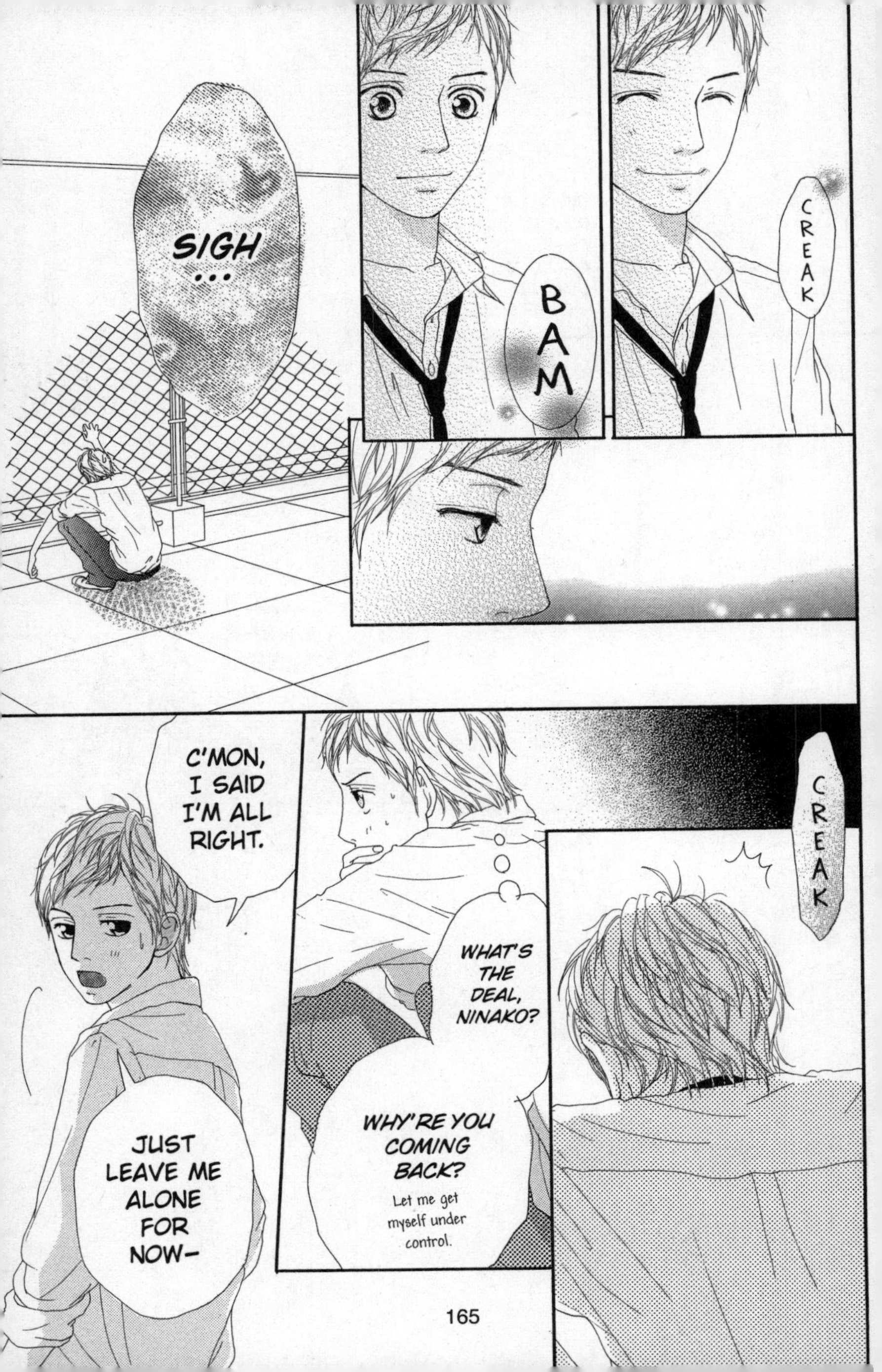
CREAK
BAM
SIGH...
CREAK
WHAT'S THE DEAL, NINAKO?
WHY'RE YOU COMING BACK?
Let me get myself under control.
C'MON, I SAID I'M ALL RIGHT.
JUST LEAVE ME ALONE FOR NOW-

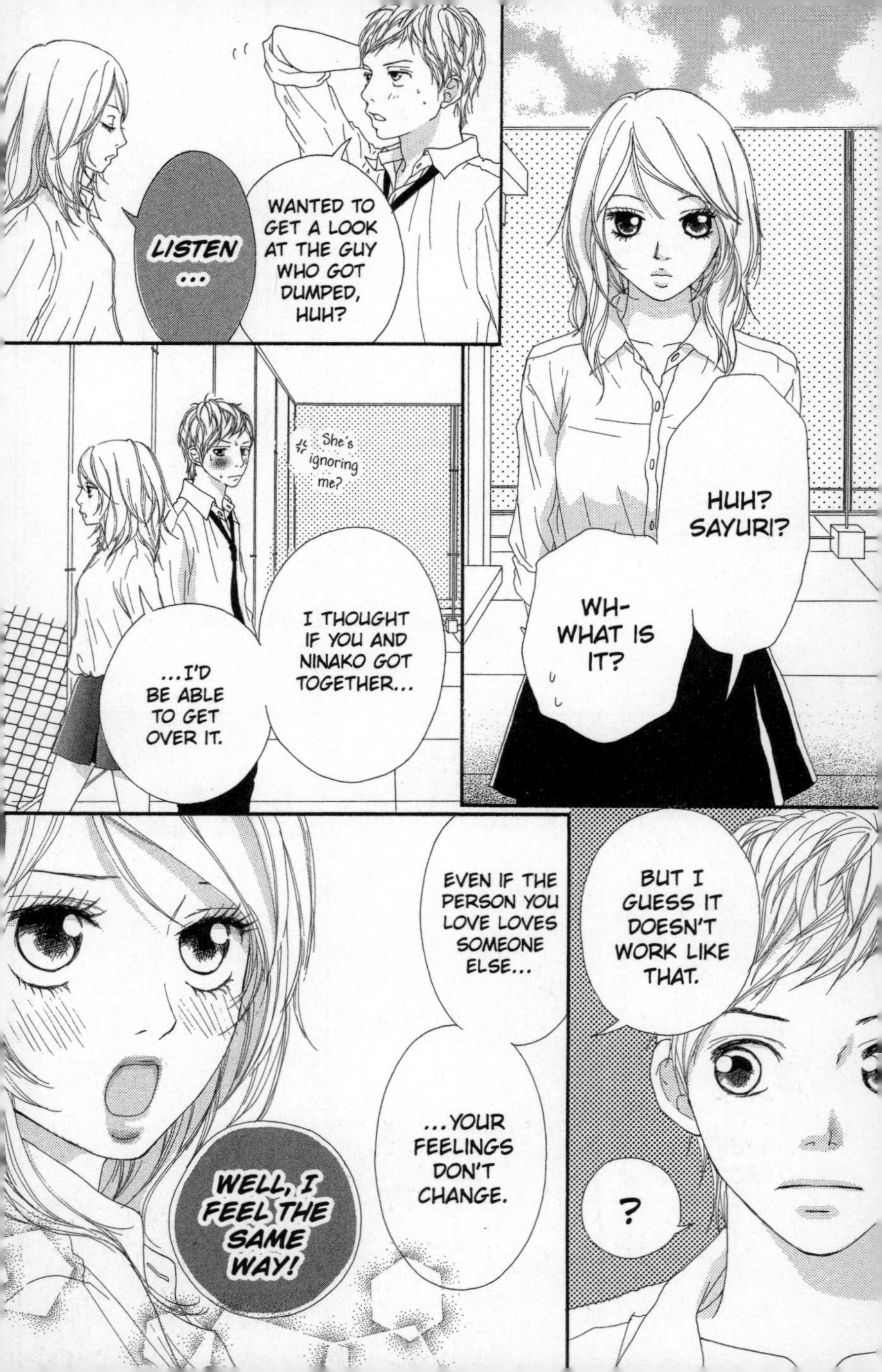
HUH? SAYURI?
WH- WHAT IS IT?
WANTED TO GET A LOOK AT THE GUY WHO GOT DUMPED, HUH?
LISTEN...
She's ignoring me?
I THOUGHT IF YOU AND NINAKO GOT TOGETHER...
...I'D BE ABLE TO GET OVER IT.
BUT I GUESS IT DOESN'T WORK LIKE THAT.
?
EVEN IF THE PERSON YOU LOVE LOVES SOMEONE ELSE...
...YOUR FEELINGS DON'T CHANGE.
WELL, I FEEL THE SAME WAY!

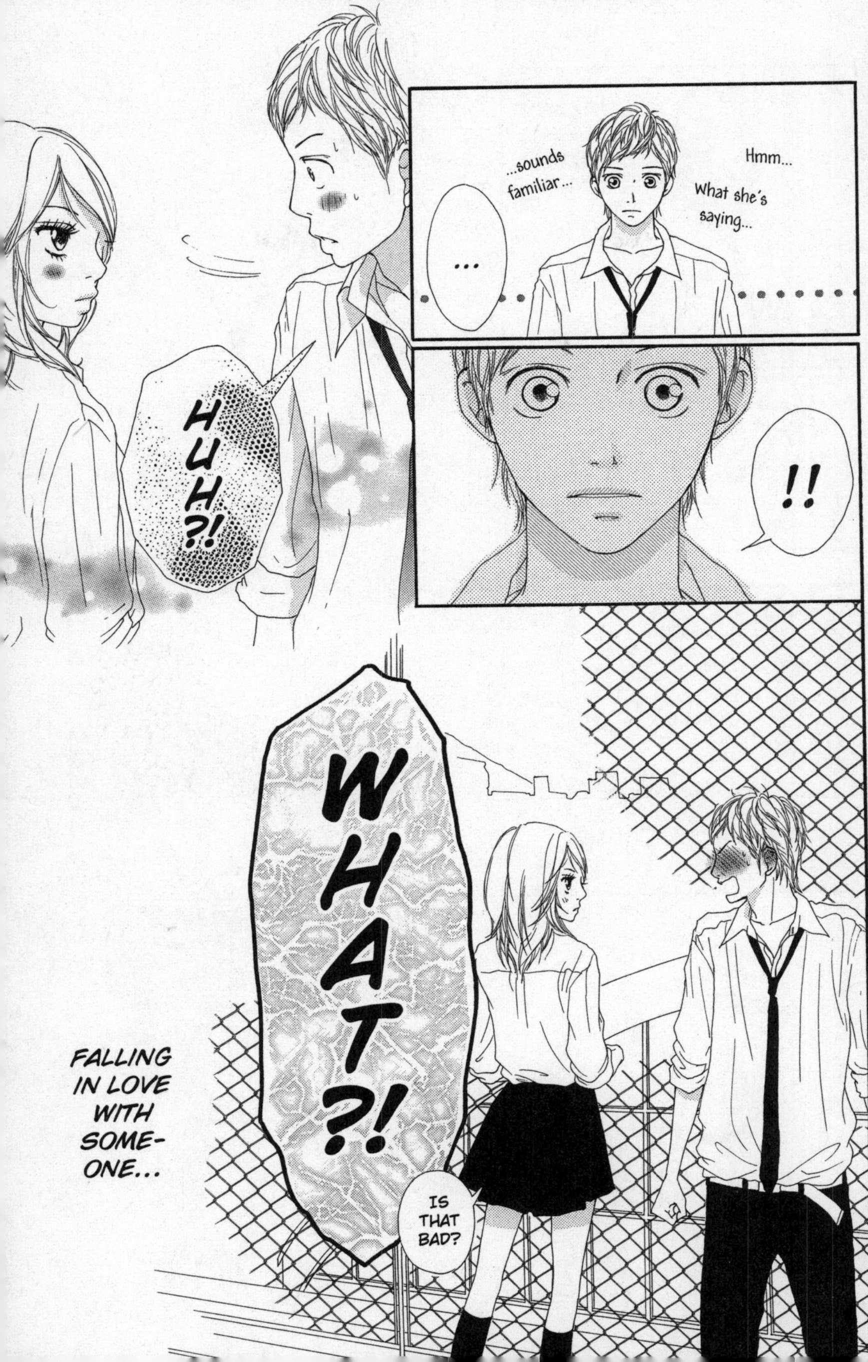
Hmm...
What she's saying...
...sounds familiar...
...
!!
HUH?!
WHAT?!
IS THAT BAD?
FALLING IN LOVE WITH SOME-ONE...

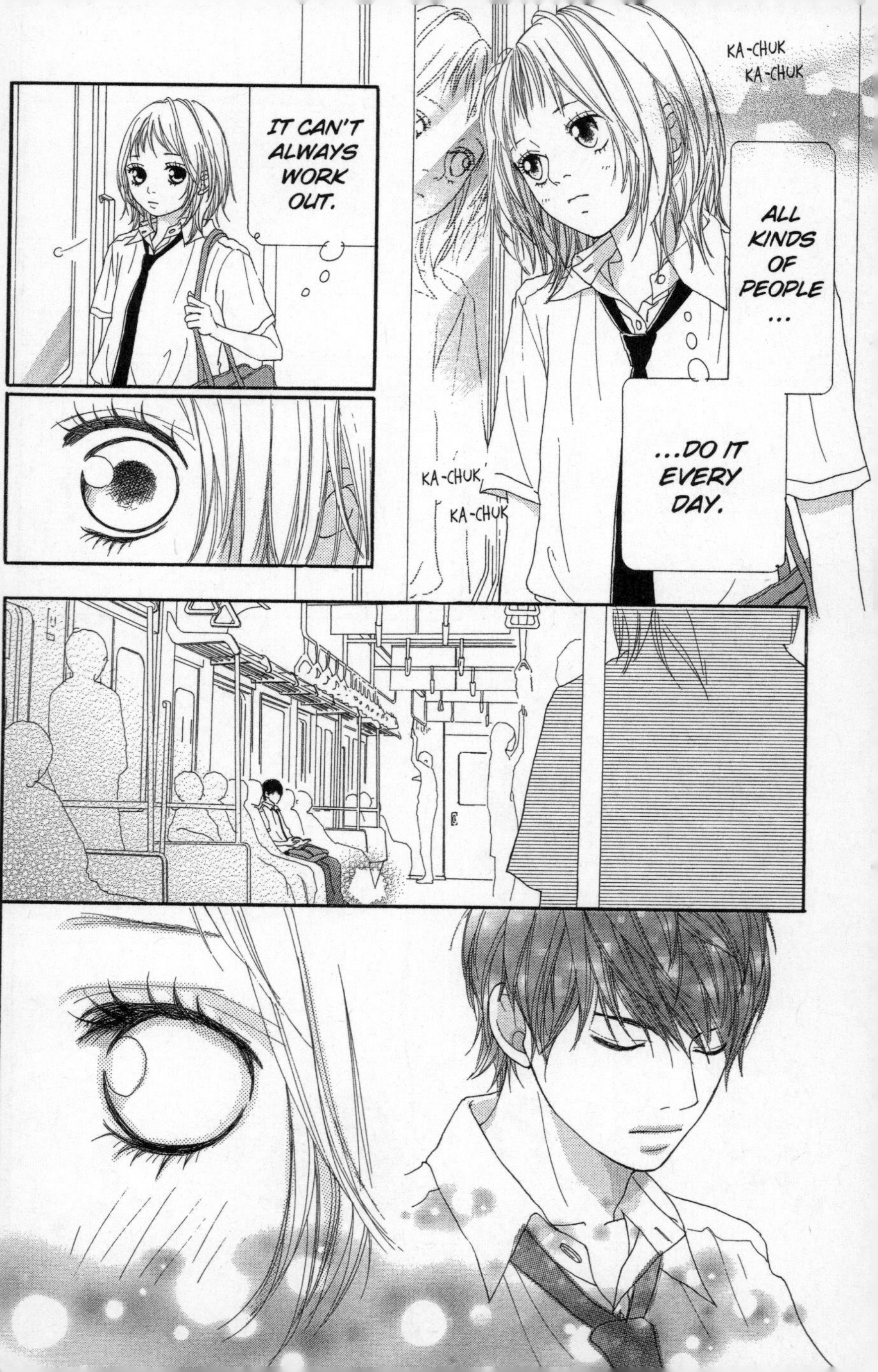
KA-CHUK
KA-CHUK
ALL KINDS OF PEOPLE ...
...DO IT EVERY DAY.
KA-CHUK
KA-CHUK
IT CAN'T ALWAYS WORK OUT.

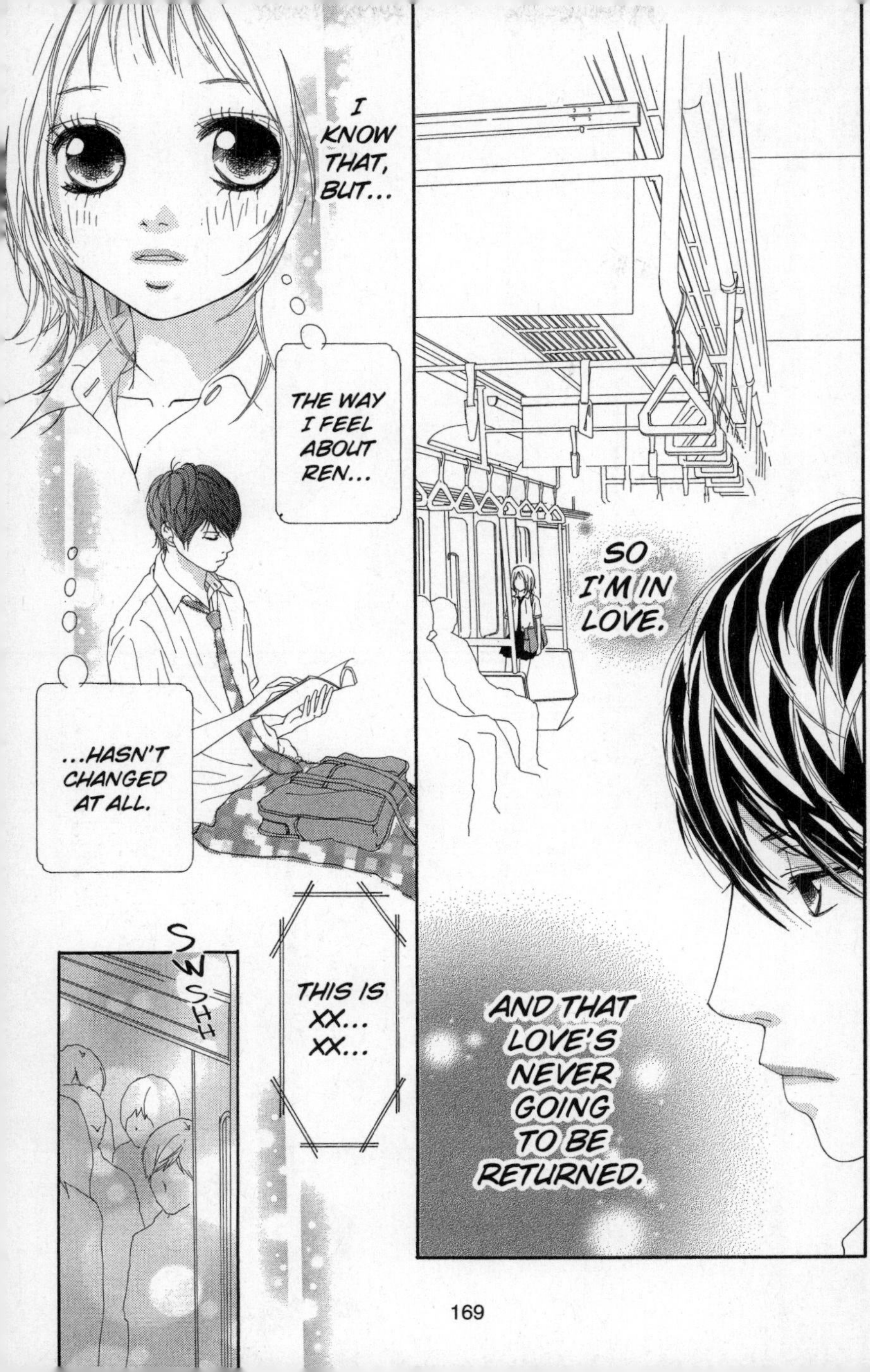
SO I'M IN LOVE.
AND THAT LOVE'S NEVER GOING TO BE RETURNED.
I KNOW THAT, BUT...
THE WAY I FEEL ABOUT REN...
...HASN'T CHANGED AT ALL.
SWSHH
THIS IS XX... XX...

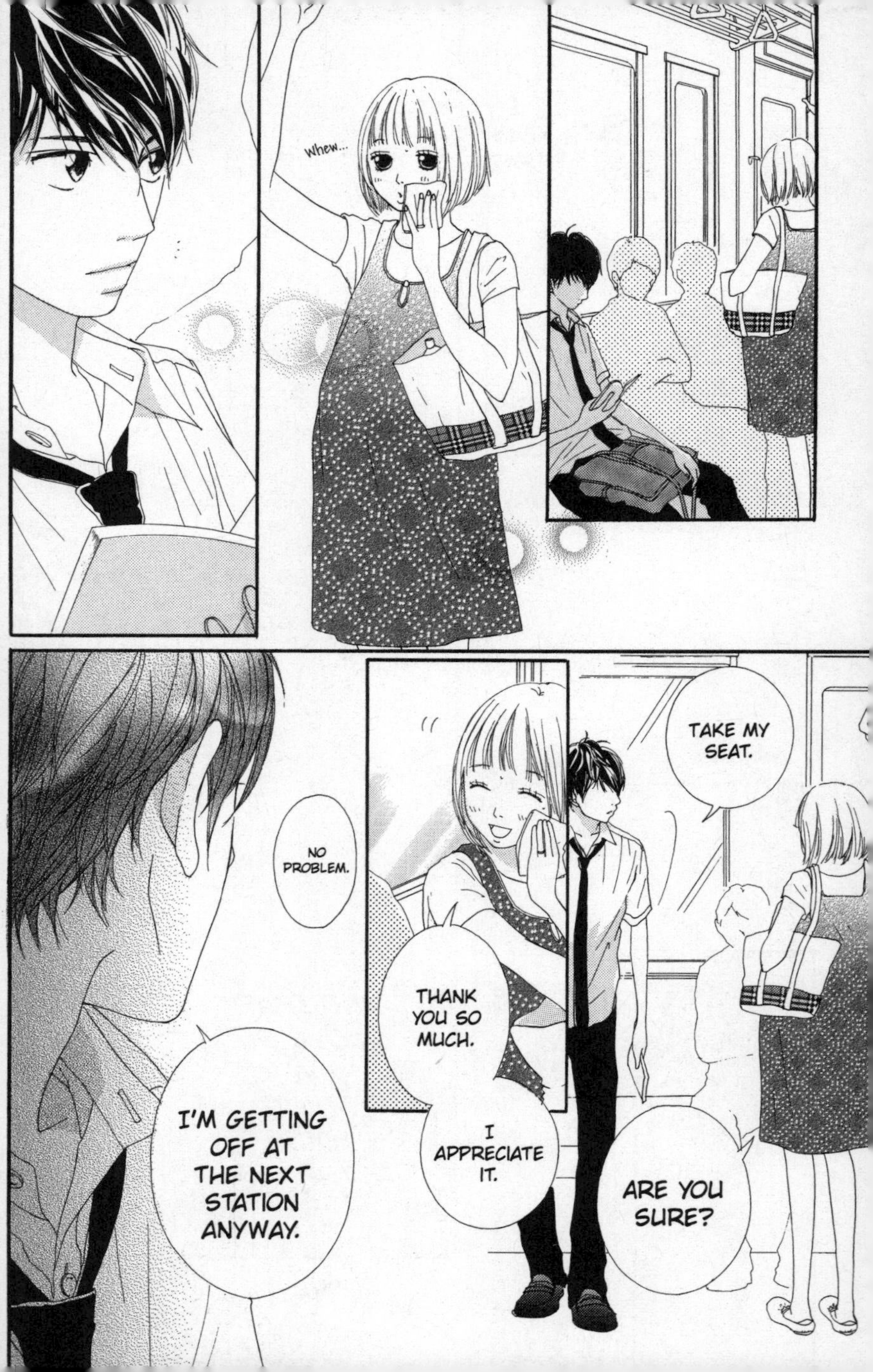
Whew...
TAKE MY SEAT.
ARE YOU SURE?
I'M GETTING OFF AT THE NEXT STATION ANYWAY.
THANK YOU SO MUCH.
I APPRECIATE IT.
NO PROBLEM.

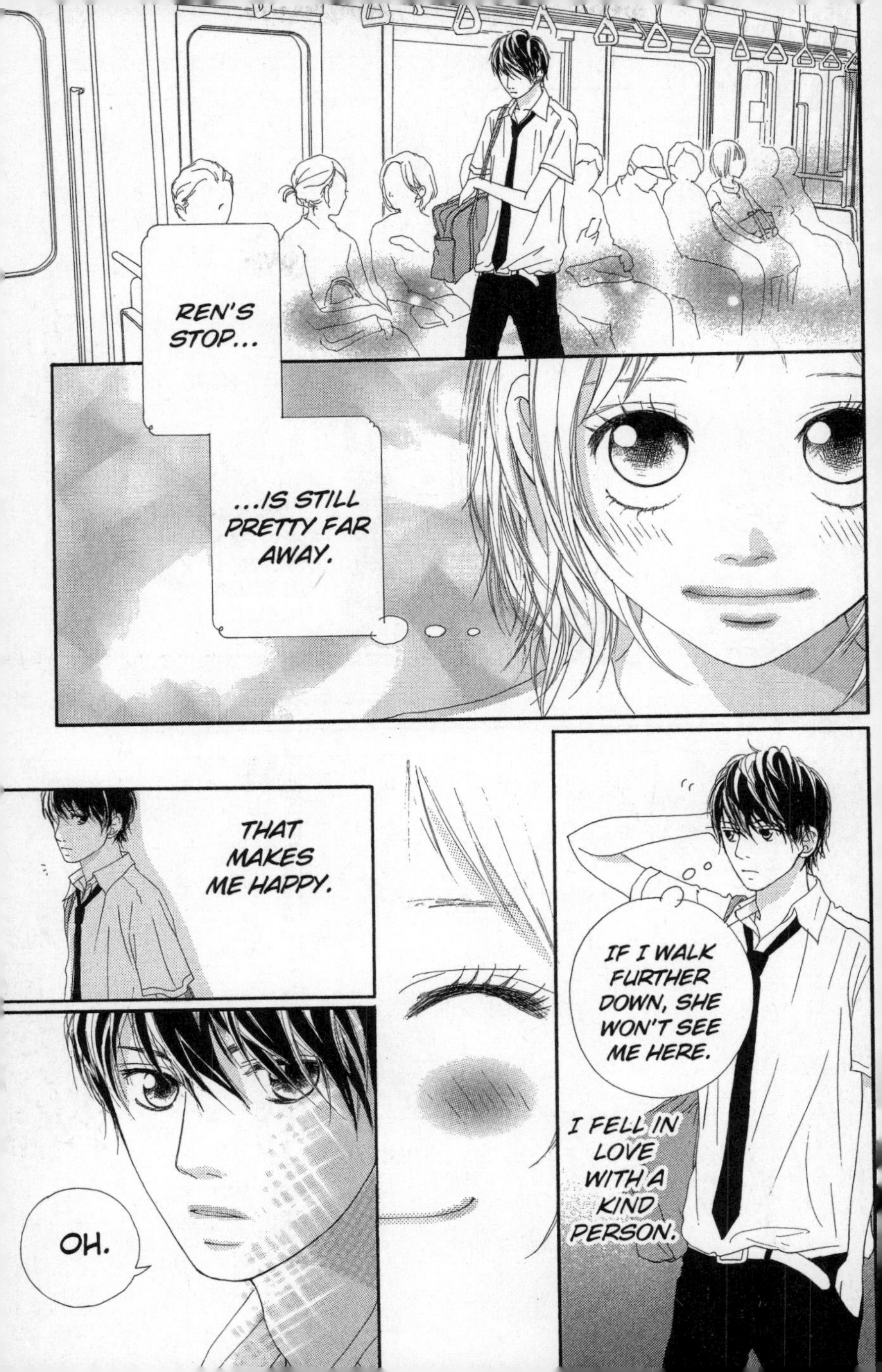
REN'S STOP...
...IS STILL PRETTY FAR AWAY.
IF I WALK FURTHER DOWN, SHE WON'T SEE ME HERE.
I FELL IN LOVE WITH A KIND PERSON.
THAT MAKES ME HAPPY.
OH.

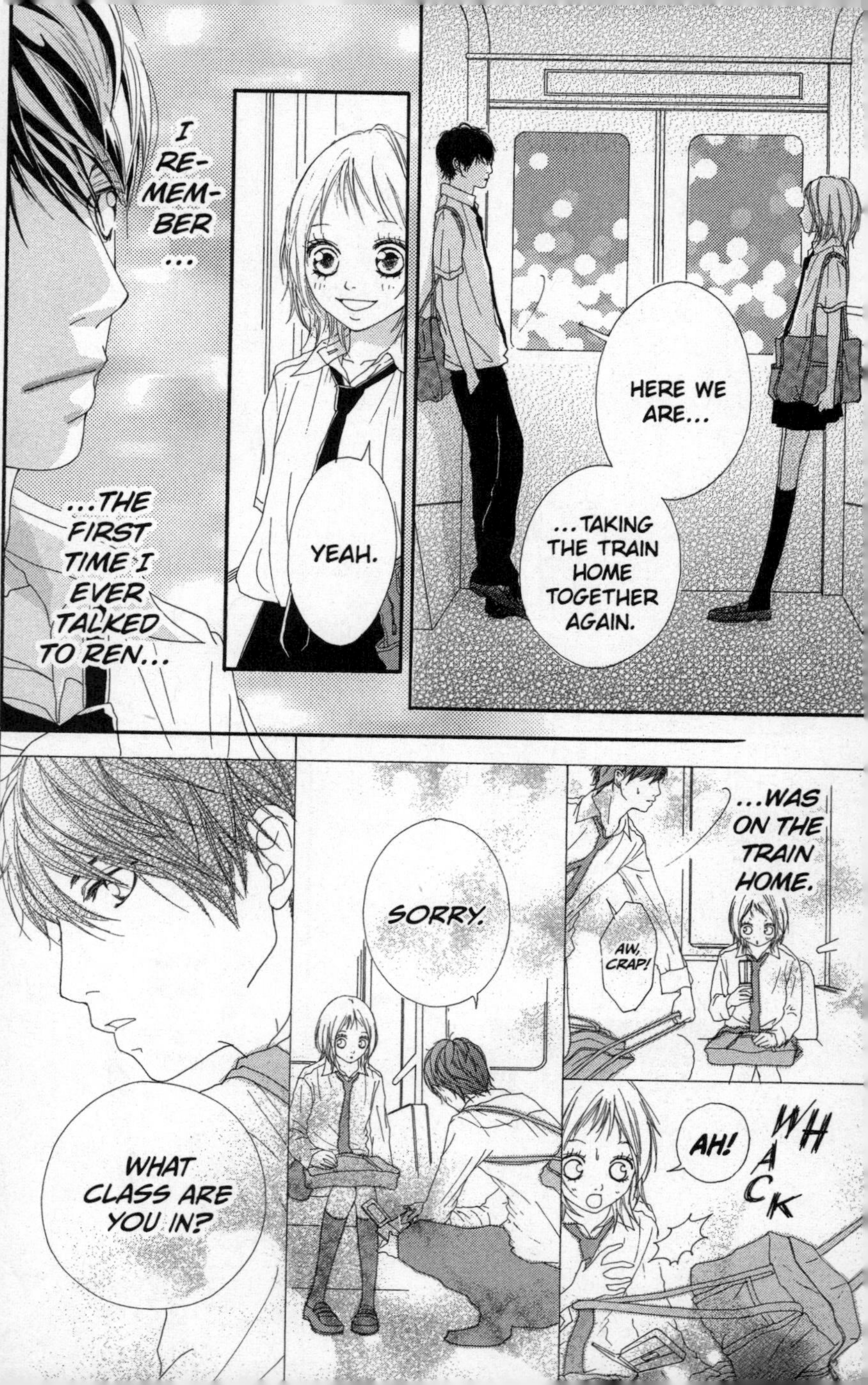
HERE WE ARE...
...TAKING THE TRAIN HOME TOGETHER AGAIN.
YEAH.
I RE-MEM-BER...
...THE FIRST TIME I EVER TALKED TO REN...
...WAS ON THE TRAIN HOME.
AW, CRAP!
WHACK
AH!
SORRY.
WHAT CLASS ARE YOU IN?

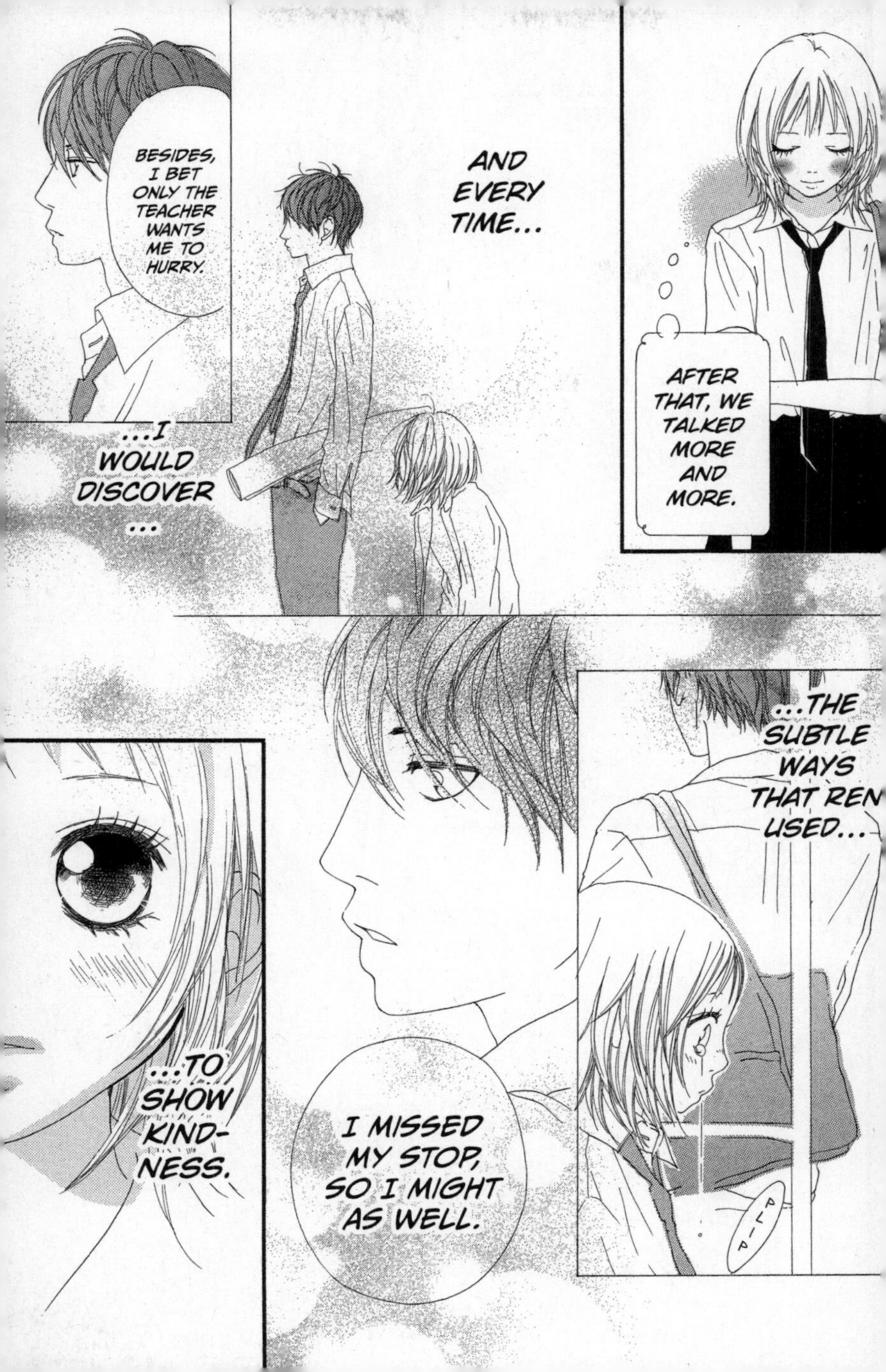
AFTER THAT, WE TALKED MORE AND MORE.
AND EVERY TIME...
BESIDES, I BET ONLY THE TEACHER WANTS ME TO HURRY.
...I WOULD DISCOVER...
...THE SUBTLE WAYS THAT REN USED...
PLIP
I MISSED MY STOP, SO I MIGHT AS WELL.
...TO SHOW KINDNESS.

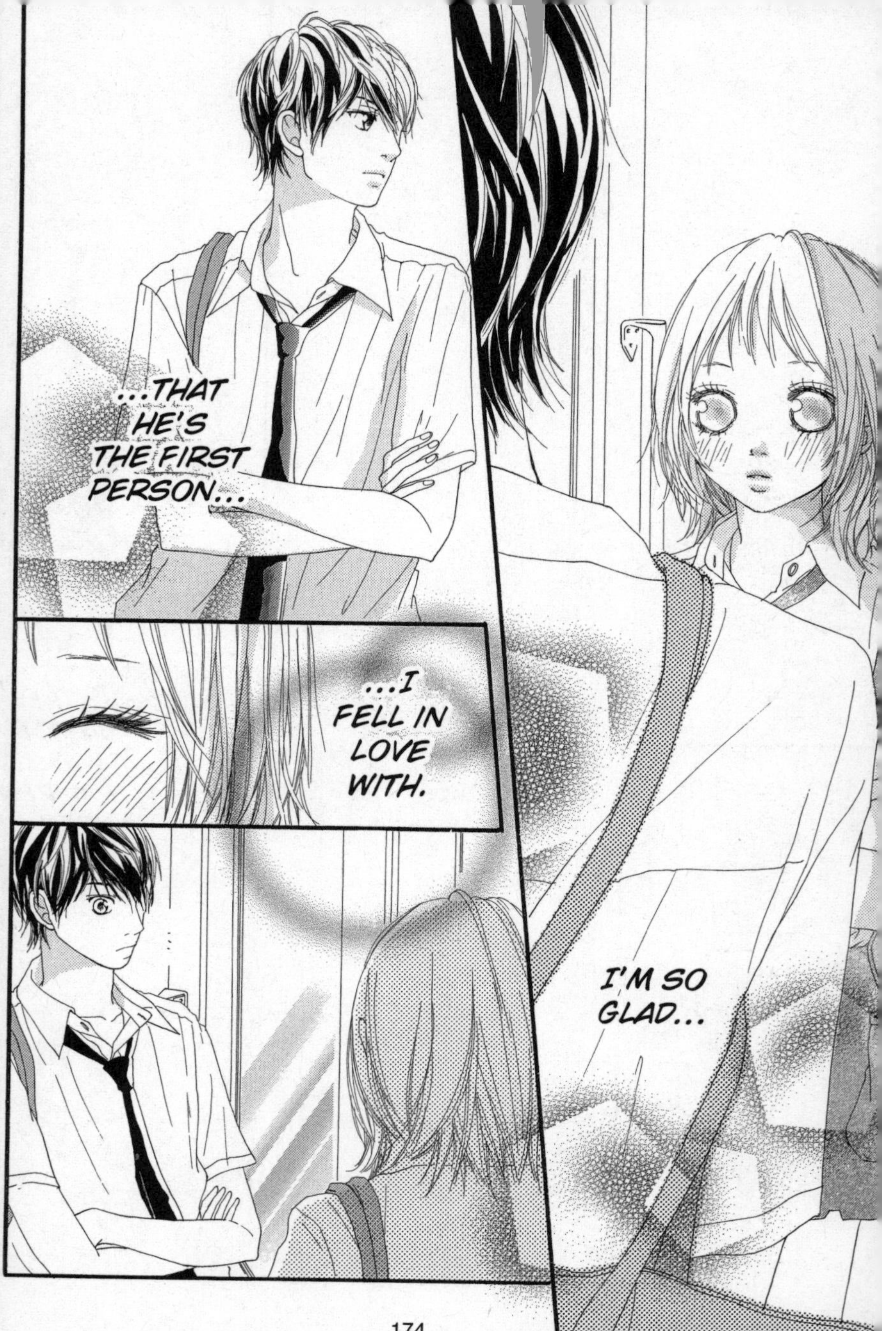
I'M SO GLAD...
...THAT HE'S THE FIRST PERSON...
...I FELL IN LOVE WITH.

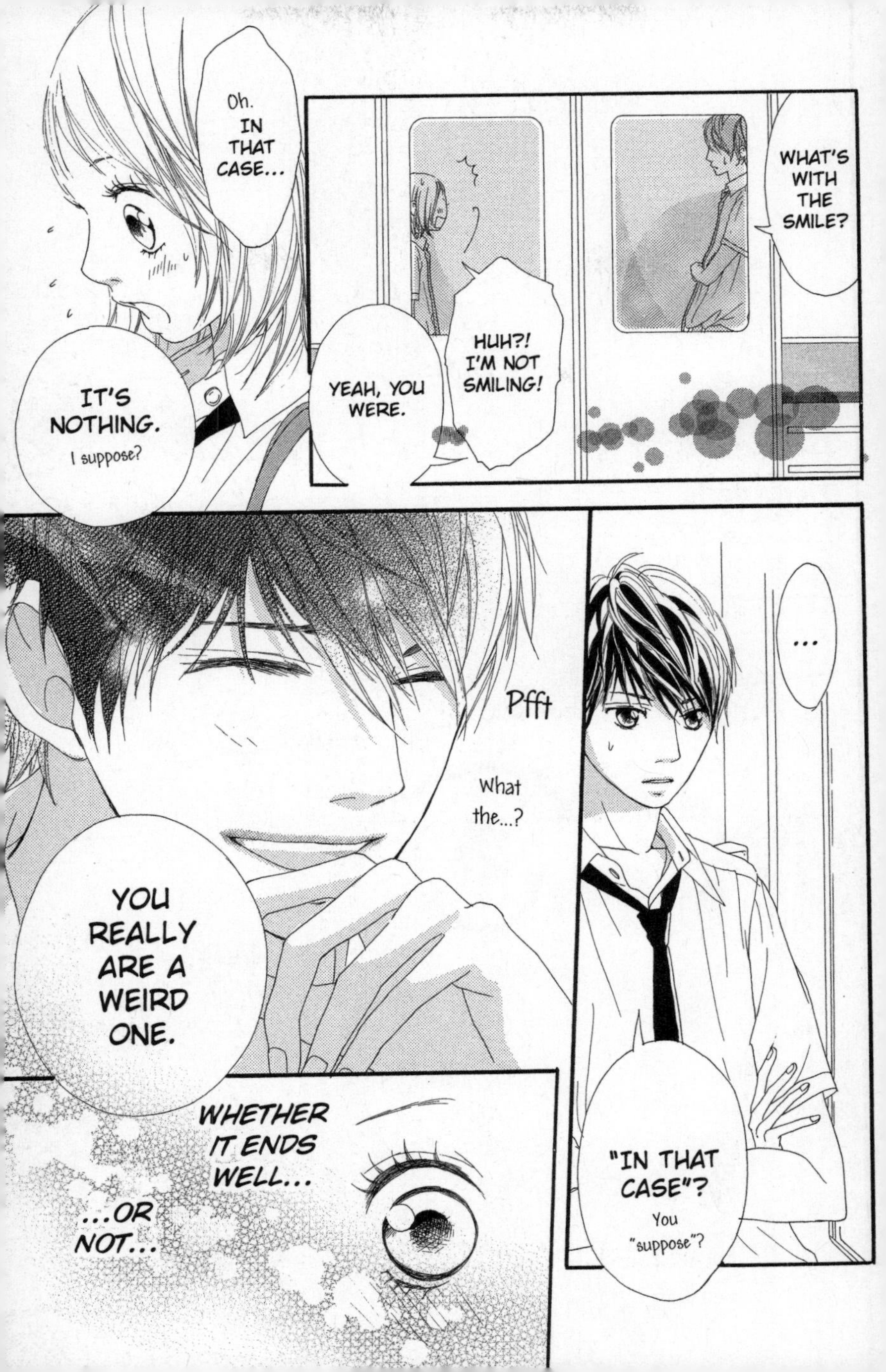
WHAT'S WITH THE SMILE?
HUH?! I'M NOT SMILING!
YEAH, YOU WERE.
Oh. IN THAT CASE...
IT'S NOTHING. I suppose?
...
What the...?
"IN THAT CASE"? You "suppose"?
Pfft
YOU REALLY ARE A WEIRD ONE.
WHETHER IT ENDS WELL...
...OR NOT...

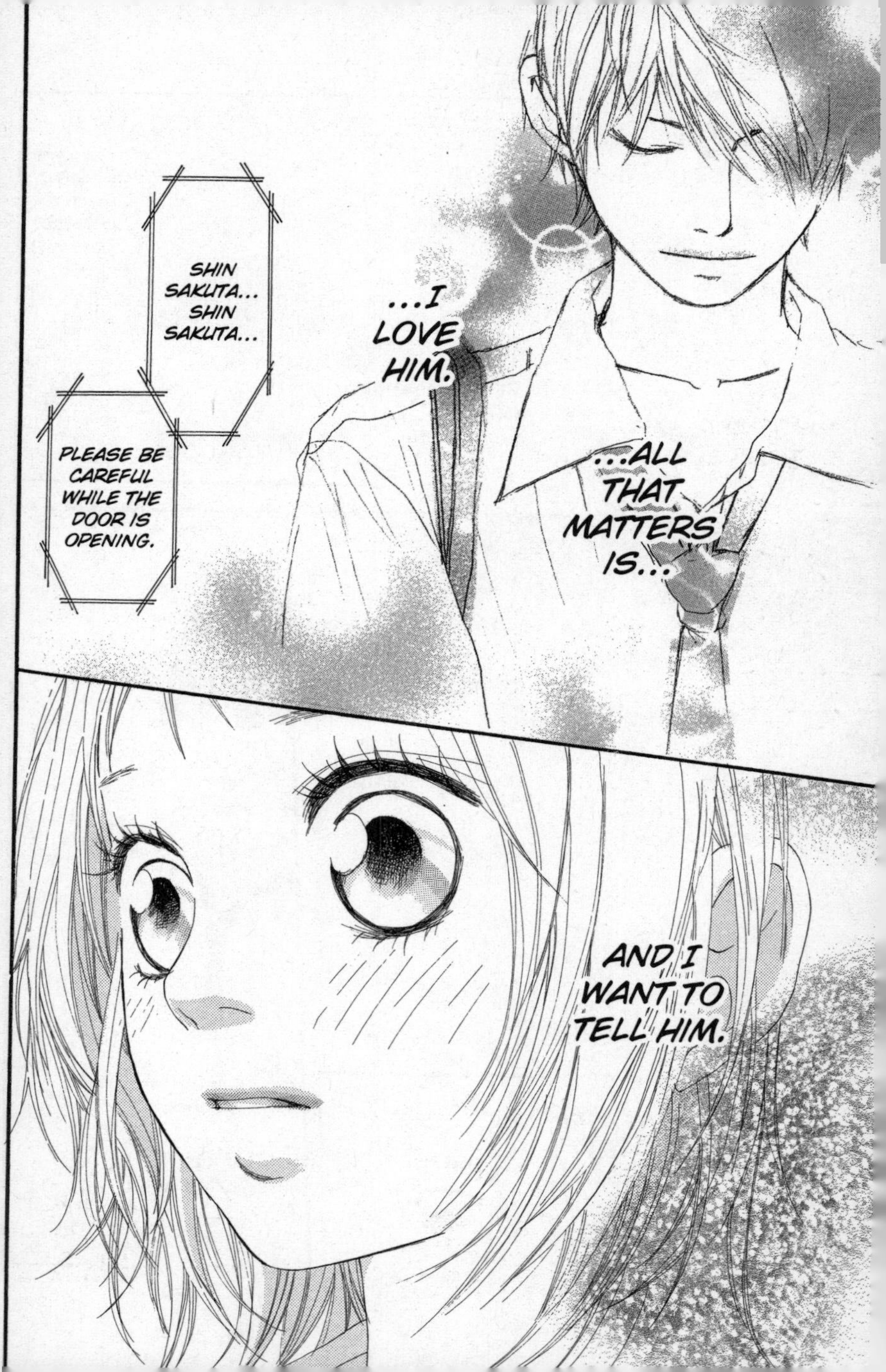
...ALL THAT MATTERS IS...
...I LOVE HIM.
SHIN SAKUTA... SHIN SAKUTA...
PLEASE BE CAREFUL WHILE THE DOOR IS OPENING.
AND I WANT TO TELL HIM.

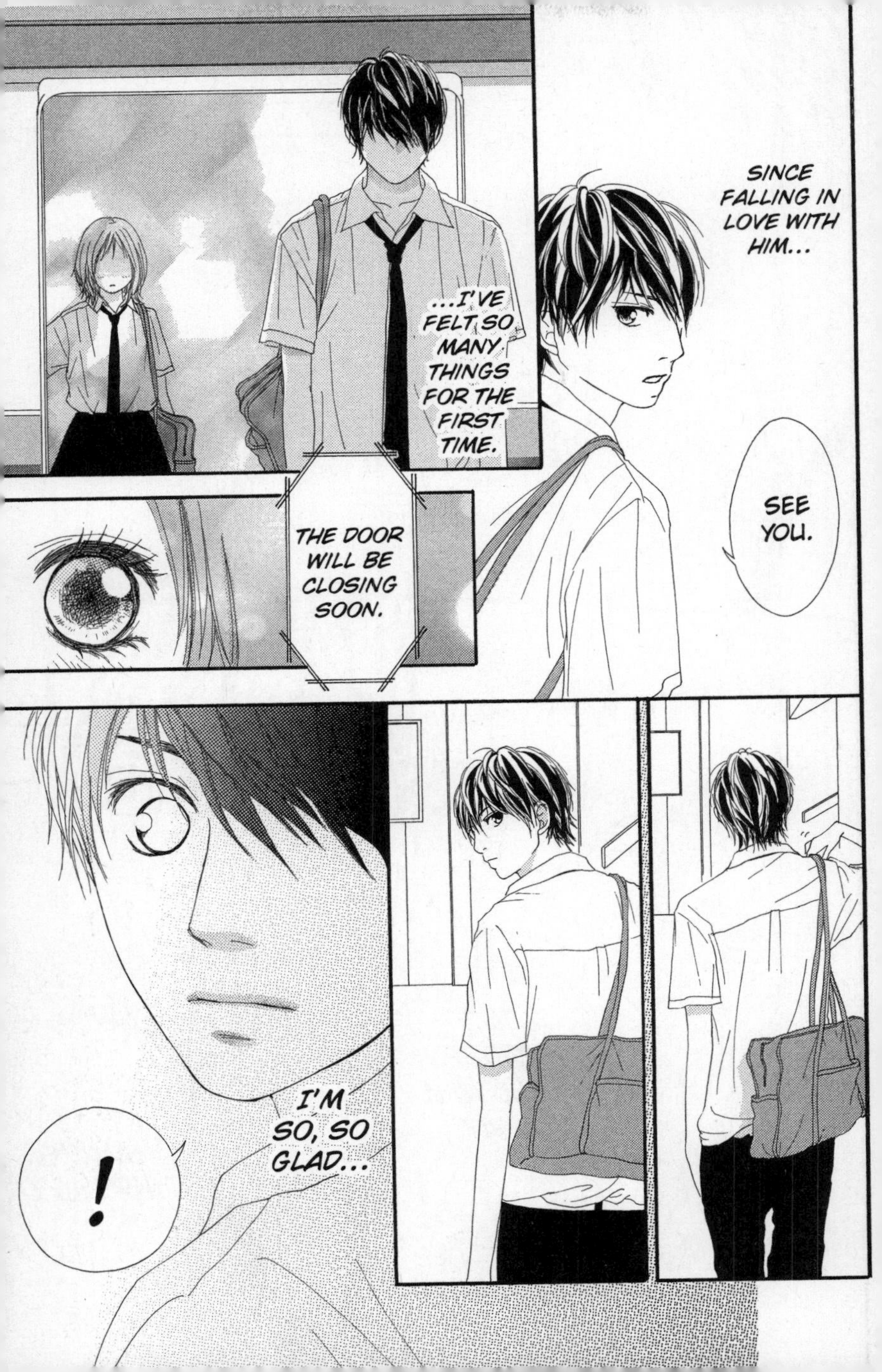
SINCE FALLING IN LOVE WITH HIM...
SEE YOU.
...I'VE FELT SO MANY THINGS FOR THE FIRST TIME.
THE DOOR WILL BE CLOSING SOON.
I'M SO, SO GLAD...
!

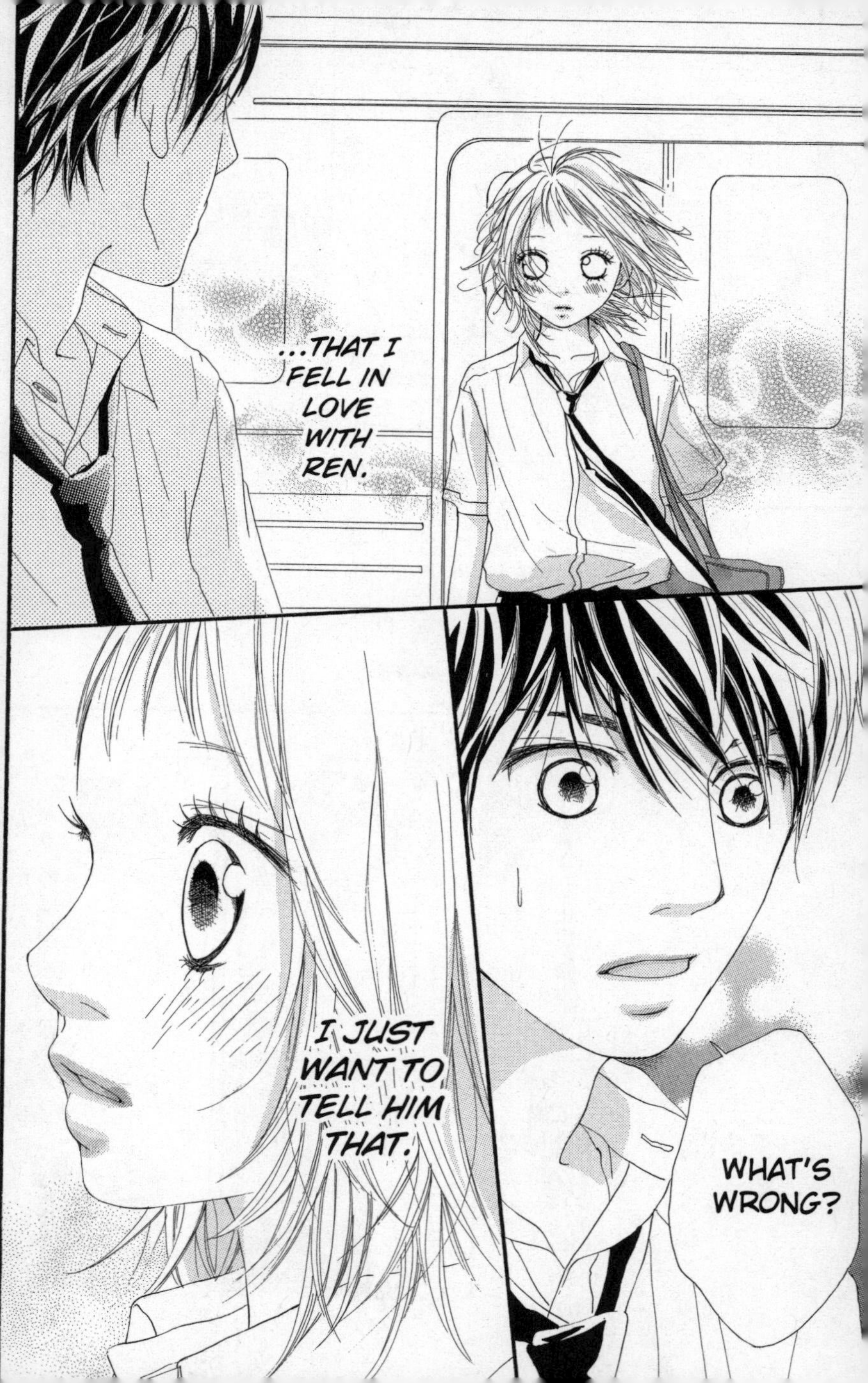
...THAT I FELL IN LOVE WITH REN.
WHAT'S WRONG?
I JUST WANT TO TELL HIM THAT.

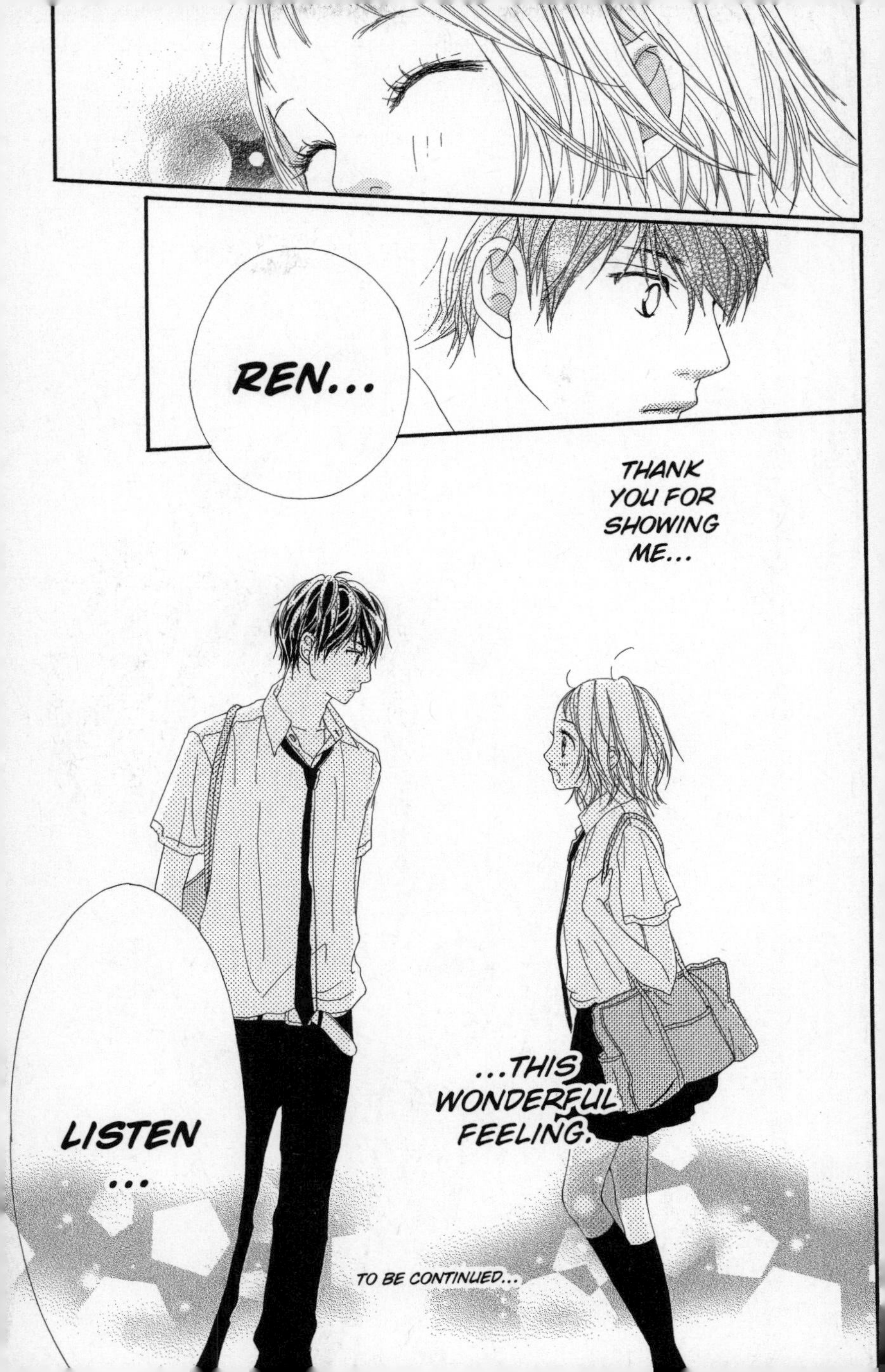
REN...
THANK YOU FOR SHOWING ME...
...THIS WONDERFUL FEELING.
LISTEN...
TO BE CONTINUED...

# THANK YOU VERY MUCH!

Thank you for reading all the way to the end! And thank you to those of you who just browsed through, too. (I hope someday you'll read the whole thing.)

And thank you so much to everyone who took the time to write to me! I can't reply to all of your letters, but I do read all of them. I read them over and over! ♥ ♥ ♥ ♥ ♥ ♥ ♥

I'm so grateful that you take time to read my manga and write to me about it. I'm working hard and pouring my heart into it. I'm trying to make it as interesting as possible so that you don't feel like I've wasted your time. At the very least, I hope you'll want to buy my manga to kill time or something.

I'll keep working really hard, and I hope you'll keep reading this series!

★Saki★

...in volume 2.

To be continued...

The mechanical pencil that I always use hasn't been working well lately. Sometimes the lead doesn't come out when I click it. I think it's because I dropped it a lot. I've been using it for work all this time, so it just doesn't feel right to use a different one. I hope it doesn't break. I'm kinda worried...

—Io Sakisaka

Born on June 8, Io Sakisaka made her debut as a manga creator with *Sakura, Chiru*. Her works include *Call My Name*, *Gate of Planet*, and *Blue*. Her current series, *Ao Haru Ride*, is currently running in *Bessatsu Margaret* magazine. In her spare time, Sakisaka likes to paint things and sleep.

# STROBE EDGE
## Vol. 1
### Shojo Beat Edition

STORY AND ART BY
## IO SAKISAKA

English Adaptation/Ysabet MacFarlane
Translation/JN Productions
Touch-up Art & Lettering/John Hunt
Design/ Yukiko Whitley
Editor/Amy Yu

STROBE EDGE © 2007 by Io Sakisaka
All rights reserved.
First published in Japan in 2007 by SHUEISHA Inc., Tokyo.
English translation rights arranged by SHUEISHA Inc.

Printed in the U.S.A.

Published by VIZ Media, LLC
P.O. Box 77010
San Francisco, CA 94107

10 9 8 7 6 5 4 3 2
First printing, November 2012
Second printing, May 2014

www.viz.com     www.shojobeat.com

# Surpr...

## You may...

It's true: In keeping with the original Japanese comic format, this book reads from right to left—so action, sound effects, and word balloons are completely reversed. This preserves the orientation of the original artwork—plus, it's fun! Check out the diagram shown here to get the hang of things, and then turn to the other side of the book to get started!

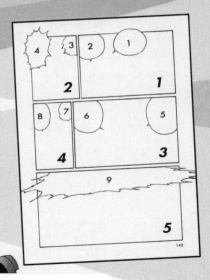